MACMILLAN AND CO., Limited
LONDON · BOMBAY · CALCUTTA
MELBOURNE

THE MACMILLAN COMPANY
NEW YORK · BOSTON · CHICAGO
DALLAS · SAN FRANCISCO

THE MACMILLAN CO. OF CANADA, Ltd.
TORONTO

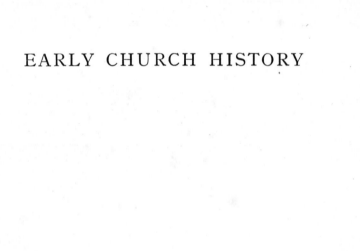

EARLY CHURCH HISTORY

EARLY
CHURCH HISTORY

TO A.D. 313

BY

HENRY MELVILL GWATKIN

DIXIE PROFESSOR OF ECCLESIASTICAL HISTORY, CAMBRIDGE ; LATE GIFFORD LECTURER, EDINBURGH
AUTHOR OF 'SELECTIONS FROM EARLY WRITERS ILLUSTRATIVE OF
CHURCH HISTORY TO THE TIME OF CONSTANTINE'

IN TWO VOLUMES

VOL. II

MACMILLAN AND CO., LIMITED
ST. MARTIN'S STREET, LONDON

1912

CONTENTS

CHAPTER XIV

PAGE

JEWISH INFLUENCES 1

CHAPTER XV

GNOSTICISM 19

CHAPTER XVI

MONTANISM 73

CHAPTER XVII

IRENAEUS 97

CHAPTER XVIII

THE EASTERN EMPERORS 114

CHAPTER XIX

THE SCHOOL OF ALEXANDRIA 154

CHAPTER XX

ORIGEN 180

CHAPTER XXI

PAGE

THE ROMAN CHURCH 213

CHAPTER XXII

AFRICA—TERTULLIAN 232

CHAPTER XXIII

DECIUS AND VALERIAN 251

CHAPTER XXIV

THE DISCIPLINE QUESTIONS 274

CHAPTER XXV

THE LONG PEACE 306

CHAPTER XXVI

THE GREAT PERSECUTION 326

TABLE OF EMPERORS 368

INDEX 371

MAP

MAP OF ROMAN EMPIRE IN ITS GREATEST EXTENT. *End of Volume*

CHAPTER XIV

JEWISH INFLUENCES

THE revelation of the Christ is not a law of outward conduct which can be laid down once for all, but a historical fact of inexhaustible significance. For the very reason that its essence is universal, its conception and expression by men must be partial, according to diversities of race and character. Hence the vast variety of Christianity. While other systems are hampered by fundamental laws and particular institutions, the Gospel has but two rites ordained of Christ, and those are of the simplest. Given the love of God and man quickened and enlightened by the love of Christ, we cannot go far wrong.

But this variety has another side. Christianity did not win the throne of the world without a struggle; and if each of its rivals was defeated in its turn, they all contrived to retain a good deal of their power in Christian forms. If each of them yielded to the inward might of Christianity, each of them deeply modified its outward historical expression. It is idle to complain for instance of the historical necessity under which Christian doctrine was expressed in the language of Greek philosophy, and afterwards of Roman law. But language and thought influence each other, and jointly modify the doctrine. So along with the outward warfare of conversions resulting in the transfer of individuals, there was a subtler internal discord which issued in the splitting off of sects and the formation of schools of thought. Thus in the apostolic age the Jewish converts brought into the churches many a scruple of Jewish legalism, the Gentiles many a scandal of Gentile lawlessness.

The three great rivals of the Gospel were Judaism, and what we may call Orientalism [1] and Hellenism. We are not in this connexion giving the terms any local reference, or regarding them as definite religions. They are rather convenient expressions for modes of thought and groups of tendencies pervading many worships and philosophies according to differences of race and personal character. Buddhism in the Far East cannot well be added as a fourth rival. It was already a great and ancient faith, and can boast of older and larger councils than the Christian : but it scarcely came in contact with the West, and such influence as it had on Christian thought was chiefly through Manichaeism ; [2] whereas Judaism, Orientalism and Hellenism are never absent from the history of the Christian church. The three tendencies are generally distinct and easily separable in the mixed systems which grew up after the Greek and Roman conquests in Asia. Greece and Rome themselves, greatly as they differ from each other, are generically

[1] Though there are serious objections to the use of *Orientalism* in this meaning, it is hard to find a better word. It has the advantage of indicating the rough general contrast of Europe and Asia, and it is not made unsuitable by the fact that the working of dualism in Persia had an exceptional character.

[2] Thus the attempt of J. Kennedy (*Journ. Royal Asiatic Society* Apr. 1902) to trace Buddhism in the system of Basilides seems more interesting than convincing.

alike when the comparison is with Israel or Persia. Even in the disputed case of Essenism, the doubt is not about the existence of such an element as is here called Oriental; only whether it might not have been of native Jewish growth. So too the Oriental element is plain enough in Gnosticism; but it is an open question whether or not it always came in by way of Eastern thought.

It will be convenient to begin with a broad general account of the three tendencies, so as to shew the nature of their several influences on Christianity before endeavouring to trace them historically.

Judaism then was (so to say) a form of Deism. God had revealed himself in his unity and holiness and separation from sin; but the nature of the revelation pointed forward as much as any special prophecy to something better. If God is holy, a confessedly imperfect revelation cannot be his last word in history. This thought was a great qualification of the Deism, and it was clearly seen by the prophets, especially Jeremiah;[1] but the Jew of a later age refused to see it. Knowing that sin is the root of evil, and mistaking the Law which was meant to reveal sin[2] for the means of overcoming sin, he clung timidly to the letter, and thought only of "making a hedge round it." The Law of the Lord is a dangerous pit forsooth, and needs to be fenced. So an age of growing formalism shrank more and more from the glorious and awful Name, while men of more sober piety retraced the ancient records in quest of mediating angels or a mystic Word. In short, the Jew refused to see the local and temporary purpose implied in every special adaptation of the Law to his own special circum-

[1] Jer. xxxi. 31 sq.   [2] Rom. vii. 13.

stances, and overlooked even the plain fact that it
was physically impossible for the Jews of the Dispersion to observe it. So he proclaimed its eternity
just when it was ready to vanish away. But a
God conceived in terms of law is not a God who
delighteth in mercy, but a hard taskmaster whose
holiness can only be satisfied with works of law.
So human pride found its outlet in a *gnosis* of
revelation—in the knowledge of the learned, how
to do those works.

Thus the Jewish converts tended to bring in the
Pharisaic conception of the Law as eternal. The
Gospel was no new covenant, but a mere cleansing of
the old; and salvation was still by works of law.
So there was no need of a mediator and lawgiver
higher than Moses. Jesus of Nazareth might be a
prophet, he might be the Messiah and the king of
Israel, but he could not be more. He was still the
servant of the Law, not its master. He could not
be the end of the Law, the everlasting Priest, or in
any full sense the Son of God.

What is here called Orientalism is not a local
religion but a permanent tendency of human nature
which is well developed in the East, but may shew
itself anywhere. In early Christian times it was a
resultant of complex forces. In addition to widespread superstitions like demon-worship, it had a
Chaldean element of star-worship, theogonies, charms
and soothsaying; a Syrian element of stern asceticism and gross licentiousness by turns; an Egyptian
element of mystery, of ceremonial, and of looking
for judgment to come. All these are plain in sundry
of the Gnostic sects, and most of them take a colour
from the Greek world around them; but the deepest

influence of all was a Persian element of Dualism, and
this is what we shall chiefly have to keep in view.

Orientalism then begins with the question,
Whence is evil? This is a false start, for clearly
the first question should have been, What is evil?
Now physical evil is that part of the order of things
which is or may be unpleasant to ourselves, whereas
moral evil is disorder of our own creation. Closely
as the two are connected in experience, and largely
as physical evil is caused by moral evil, the two are
utterly different in character, and any endeavour to
lump them together under the common name of
" evil " is pure confusion of thought. So the
ancients generally came to a dilemma. Either evil
is somehow unreal, or the good God is not the author
of all things. The only escape is to deny that God
is good : and this was rightly refused, for it is worse
than a confusion of thought. Accepting then the
dilemma, the Greeks generally leaned to Pantheism,
which maintains the goodness of God by explaining
away the reality of evil, making it a necessary factor
or a necessary stage in the process of growth.
Oriental thought turned the other way, to dualism. If God is good and " evil " real, the simplest
plan is to confront the good God with an independent though perhaps inferior evil power of some
sort.

Only now is the question asked, What is evil?
Which part of creation is good, and which is bad?
The Oriental felt that the spiritual nature is the
higher, mistook the contrast of higher and lower for
one of good and bad, and came to the conclusion
that matter is evil. Christianity declares that the
world is good, except so far as sin has disordered it :

Orientalism pronounces it essentially bad. If then evil resides in matter, the good God is not only separate as in Judaism from the world of matter, but positively opposed to it.

The inference is clear. If the world is essentially evil, the good God cannot be its maker, and we must have some demiurge or other for the work of creation. That demiurge may be an evil being or at best a bungler, but cannot be truly good. Again, if there be a redemption as the Gospel tells us, it is a redemption not from sin but from evil, that is, from matter. Hence the redeemer cannot have come in flesh, for flesh is matter, and therefore evil; nor can it be any part of his work to redeem the body. Yet again, if matter is evil, it is our duty to escape from it. As we cannot well go out of the world, the next best thing is to shew our contempt of the body by wallowing in vice as a thing indifferent. Some of the Cynics tried that plan, and were well hissed for it. Greek moderation and Roman gravity could overlook a good deal, but they drew the line at a Bacchanalia held more than occasionally. In Syria public feeling might be different; but most of the Gnostics took the one method left—to combat the body with ascetic practice. Thus human pride found its outlet in a *gnosis* of asceticism which divided mankind very sharply into saints and sinners. The double standard was an evident necessity, if the world was not to come to an end of itself.

Hellenism deified the world which Orientalism pronounced so evil. The guiding power was placed inside it instead of outside, so that the unity of creation was secured by making the world operate itself. This guiding power might be distributed

through the parts of the world, or it might pervade
the world as a whole.   In one case we have the many
gods of the polytheists, in the other the mundane soul
of pantheism.   The one was the vulgar, the other the
philosophical form of Hellenism.   They agreed however in recognizing no true God outside the world.
The gods of the polytheists were only demigods of
this world's order, and the mundane soul was not
a personal being at all.   So also the problem of evil
was kept inside the limits of the world.   In the
cruder polytheisms evil did but represent among men
the anarchy of Olympus ; and when this became too
grotesque, the philosophers found it a place as a
necessary stage or a necessary factor of the world's
development.   In either case, the question was
physical rather than moral.   Thus while the gods
required nothing more than the customary sacrifices
accurately performed, pantheism demanded only
knowledge, so that human pride found its outlet in
a *gnosis* of education and philosophy.

So heathen converts brought in with them a
tendency to look on Christ as a demigod of the
Hellenic type, as a hero and a benefactor, but not
as the Son of God.   The Gospel would be regarded,
not as a spiritual revelation of life in him, but as a
mystery dispensed by priests, and chiefly demanding
right belief and accurate performance of the ritual.
In this way Hellenism came near to some aspects of
Orientalism.

The direct contest with Judaism belongs chiefly to
the apostolic age, that with Orientalism to the Gnostic
period, and that with Hellenism to the third and
fourth centuries.   But it must be remembered that
all three are permanent elements in history, so that

their influence on Christian thought has never ceased
—Judaism for instance is visible enough in the
Puritans, Orientalism in the monks, Hellenism in
the church revolution of the Nicene age : and all
three enter largely into catholicism, inside and outside the church of Rome.

We can deal at once with Judaism and Gnosticism ;
but the influence of Hellenism cannot be fully
discussed before the Nicene age.

Of the contest with Judaism we have already traced
the part which lies within the apostolic age. It
began with Stephen, and became acute when first
Barnabas and then Peter sanctioned the active preaching of the Gospel to the Gentiles. Its first great
landmark is the apostolic conference in 50, which
freed the Gentile converts from the obligation of the
Law. Henceforth St. Paul's work was pertinaciously
opposed by the Judaizers, whether they leaned to
Pharisaism as in Galatia, or to Essenism as at Colossae.
The next great epoch of the contest is the retreat to
Pella in 66, followed by the destruction of Jerusalem.
Henceforth the Judaizers could not even properly
keep the Law themselves, much less force it on others.
The separation was no longer only from Pharisees and
Sadducees, but from " the Jews " generally—of the
Israel of God from the synagogue of Satan. So the
breach went on widening till the revolt of Bar-Cochab
in 132 brought on a third great crisis. The Christians
stood aside again, and were bitterly persecuted for
refusing to join the war. When the contest was over,
a new Jerusalem rose on the ruins of the old : but it
was a Gentile and a heathen city—the Roman colony
of Aelia Capitolina—and the Jews were not allowed

even to set foot in it, so that when the Christians
returned they returned as Gentiles.

The destruction of the temple must have forced
the Jewish Christians to reconsider their position.
To the unbelieving Jews the synagogues and the
traditions had long been the practical centre of religion, so that the cessation of the temple services
made little difference. Sacrifices were discontinued,
a few adjustments were made, and then things settled
down comfortably into a sort of stereotyped Pharisaism which has continued ever since. But the Christian Jews in their retreat at Pella could not evade the
question, whether he who had " destroyed this place "
had not also "changed the customs which Moses
had delivered." [1] Had not St. Paul's warnings come
true ? If the Law could no longer be kept without
further Pharasaic evasions, was not this an intimation
from heaven that it need no longer be kept at all ?
Many of them must have joined the increasing
majority of Gentile Christians, and thenceforth lived
as Gentiles. The dwindling remnant rapidly sank
into trans-Jordanic sects of small importance to the
church at large. Greek thought instead of Jewish
was becoming the atmosphere in which the churches
lived. Hellenistic thought gave place to purely
Hellenic, and Jewish Proselytism was rapidly sup-
planted by the Christian missions which more fully
satisfied the spiritual needs of the Gentiles. "The
religion of fulfilment destroyed the religion of
promise." [2]

Some of the numerous Judaizing sects were so far
moderate that men like Justin were willing to receive
them as brethren, though others refused. Their

---

[1] Acts vi. 14.   [2] Möller (v. Schubert) *K.G.* 78.

positions seem to have been nearly that held by
James the Lord's brother, but with the important
difference that they maintained it after the fall of
Jerusalem.   They endeavoured to keep the Law
(circumcision and the sabbath in particular, but
not the traditions) as a national custom still binding
on Jews, or at least on themselves, though not to
be imposed on Gentile Christians.   Their doctrine
of the Lord's Person is disputed.   They seem to
have accepted his birth from a virgin; but it is
not clear how far they took this to imply a higher
nature than that of men.   Upon the whole, the
position of these Nazarenes, as Epiphanius calls them,
was an illogical and unsuccessful attempt to be Jews
and Christians at once.   The Jews cursed them with
the rest of the *Minim* or heretics, and the Christians
more than doubted of them.   It is no small sign of
the vitality of Jewish ideas, that the Nazarenes were
not extinct in Peraea near the end of the fourth
century.

The Judaizing spirit is stronger in Ebionism,[1]
which indeed is rather a Jewish than a Christian
heresy.   The Ebionites fall into two divisions, corresponding to Pharisees and Essenes among the Jews.
The Pharisaic form of Ebionism was the earlier.   In
this the Law was held to be universal and eternal,
so that salvation was by works.   This implied the
rejection of St. Paul, whom they denounced as an
apostate, and the chief corrupter of the word of

---

[1] From אֶבְיוֹן the needy. But it must remain an open question whether
they so called themselves as the "poor in spirit" whom the Lord pronounced
blessed : or whether it was an abusive name given them by the Jews, and
afterwards accepted by themselves, like the Χριστιανοί generally, or the
Gueux of Holland. Ebion is not found before Ps.-Tert. (not in Irenaeus or
Origen) as a personal founder of the sect, and seems mythical.

God. Their slanders against him were many. Gentile
Christians of course they did not acknowledge. Jesus
of Nazareth was the son of Joseph and Mary, so that
the miraculous birth was rejected, and with it his
pre-existence and divine worship. At his Baptism
the Spirit of Jehovah lighted on him, so that it is
roughly equivalent to the Jewish legend that Messiah
shall not know his office till Elijah comes to anoint
him. To the canonical narrative the Gospel *according to the Hebrews* added the fire kindled on Jordan,
and the words from heaven, Thou art my son, this
day have I begotten thee. But the man Jesus was
never more than a man like other men; so that
when the Spirit forsook him, only a common man
suffered on the cross, and shall come again hereafter
to reign a thousand years on earth.

In this we must notice the contact of Ebionism
with Gnosticism. The stumbling-block of that age
was not so much the Lord's divinity as his crucifixion. Because he suffered, said the Jew, he was
not divine. Because he was divine, replied the
Gnostic, he did not suffer. Thus the Judaizers and
the Gnostics had a common interest in explaining
away his sufferings, for they were agreed that
divinity and suffering are inconsistent with each
other. So they introduced a higher power as the
real Christ. The Ebionites made the Spirit of the
Lord (in the Jewish sense) light on a common man,
so that the sufferings of the cross were only those of
a common man. The Gnostics clothed a heavenly
power with the appearance of manhood, so that
those sufferings were only in appearance. In either
case, it is denied that the Redeemer suffered at all.

But Gnosticism was the growing power in that

age, while Judaism was declining. Ebionism gradually passed from the Pharisaic to an Essene form,
in which Gnostic elements are stronger. How far
Pharisaic Ebionites grew "broader" as they grew
older, or how far the Essene Ebionite schools were
new, is more than we can say : but at all events they
hold at the end of the second century something like
the place the others had held at its beginning.

Essene Ebionism, like Essenism itself, is a complicated and obscure question. Pharisaism is a
definite system fairly well known to us, so that we
can see what sort of ideas converted Pharisees were
likely to bring into the church ; but Essenism stands
for an obscure complex of Jewish and Oriental
thought. We cannot even say for certain whether
the Essenes were Orientalizing Jews or Judaizing
Orientals.

Our knowledge of the Essene Ebionites comes
mostly from the fragments of the Book of Elchasai,
the Clementine Homilies and Recognitions, and the
accounts of Hippolytus, Origen and Epiphanius. The
Book of Elchasai (hidden power) was brought to Rome
in the time of Callistus by Alcibiades of Apamea, who
obtained it from the Seres (Chinese) "who belonged
to Parthia," and delivered it to Sobiai (his sworn
followers) by the direction of an angel 96 miles high
who had appeared to Elchasai in the third year of
Trajan (A.D. 100). That angel was the Son of God,
and a female of the same size was the Holy Spirit.[1]
He prescribed circumcision and the sabbath, but lustrations instead of sacrifice. Callistus was then re-
laxing the rule of penance ; but Alcibiades "thinking

[1] The Aramaic colouring is plain in the words Elchasai and Sobiai, and
in the feminine gender given to the Holy Spirit.

himself the better cheat," quite outdid him.   He said
that a new baptism for the remission of sins had been
proclaimed.   The very worst of sinners had only " to
be immersed (and that in his clothes) a second time
in the name of the great and most high God, and in
the name of his Son, the great king, and to call upon
the seven witnesses written in this book—the heaven
and the water and the holy spirits and the angels of
prayer and the oil and the salt and the earth."   The
same baptism was also good for the bite of a mad dog.

Alcibiades was a quack pure and simple : the
Clementines are only romances of a similar school.
The plot is quite in the modern style, which indeed
is the style of the Greek novels generally.   Clement
tells the story himself to James the Lord's brother, and
about the end of the fourth century it was translated
into Latin by Ruffinus, on his usual plan of leaving
out offensive passages.   Clement then was a noble
Roman related to the emperor, converted by Barnabas
at Rome.   Following him to Caesarea he meets Peter ;
and then the adventures begin.   They turn largely on
the evil doings of Simon Magus (an evident caricature
of St. Paul) who withstands Peter at Caesarea, and
afterwards pursues him with all the arts of slander
and magic.   But the human interest lies chiefly in
the restoration to Clement of his lost relations.   First
his mother Mattidia is discovered by Peter in a
beggar-woman on the steps of a temple at Antaradus ;
then she recognizes her other two sons in Nicetas and
Aquila, two disciples of Simon who had gone over to
Peter.   After this Peter meets on the sea-shore an
old man who maintains that all things are governed
by the influence of the stars ; but when he tells the
story of his own life in proof of it, he turns out to be

Faustinianus the father of Clement. So Clement's relatives are all happily restored to him, and all duly baptized one after another by Peter. This is the main story, though there are some subordinate legends, like that of the ordination of Zacchaeus.

But the romance is the vehicle of a theory of religion, somewhat toned down from that indicated by the fragments of the Book of Elchasai, but in outline the same. It is a vast scheme of reconciliation for Jews and Christians and Gnostics. It starts from " Christianity as old as the Creation," though the particular version of Christianity recognized as the one original and true revelation is not that patronized by Matthew Tindal. Yet the two have points of likeness, for they both claim to be a return to primitive simplicity. If the Clementines agree with the Pharisaic Ebionites in making the Law an essential part of Christianity, they do not mean the Law as the Jews had it, but the Law criticized on Essene principles, by cutting out sacrifice as a moral difficulty, and stories like the Fall as libels on the patriarchs. Tindal might have approved so far : but then they part company with him, keeping rigidly to circumcision (though not for heathens) and the sabbath, devising atoning lustrations of their own, making much of ascetic observances, and commanding abstinence from wine and animal food. Again, the identity of true religion in all ages is made to depend on a series of incarnations of the Word or Wisdom of God, of whom Adam was the first and Jesus the last. Thus the uniqueness of the Incarnation was denied, and with it that of the Lord's Person, so that the Gospel is not a new revelation, but simply a republication of the one primaeval religion. Hence the

Essene Ebionites rivalled the Pharisaic in hatred of
St. Paul.

We need not trace them further. The special
interest of the Clementines is that we see in a system
opposed to Gnosticism the working, not so much of
Gnosticism itself as of a spirit allied to Gnosticism,
or rather perhaps of a way of thinking wider than
Gnosticism, though well expressed in Gnosticism. It
is however worth notice that while the Clementines
make Peter the Apostle of the Gentiles, James the
Lord's brother is represented as the true vicar of
Christ in supreme command of the churches. They
contribute only indirectly to the later legend of Peter
by bringing him to Rome and making his activity
so conspicuous that his shadowy superior was easily
forgotten.

If the Judaizing sects were less important than the
Gnostic, the reason is partly that Judaizing doubts of
our Lord's deity were neither so deep nor so specious
as Gnostic doubts of his manhood, partly also that
Jewish influences were checked by the bitter hatred
which grew up between Jews and Christians. The
Jews hated worse than heathens these heretics and
renegades who had not only forsaken Moses and the
fathers, but gone and worshipped a vile wretch of a
crucified impostor. Better go into a heathen temple
to pray, said a proverb of later times, than into a
house of the *Minim*. Nor were the *Minim* behind in
hate. It is the oppression of the poor which stirs the
wrath of James; but his climax is, Ye condemned, ye
slew the Just: doth he not resist you?[1] St. John has
shaken off the dust of Judaism, and with him "the
Jews" are always the enemy. Barnabas taunts them

[1] James v. 6.

with having mistaken their own Law from first to
last, the *Teaching* calls them "the hypocrites," and
even Aristides lays a malicious emphasis on "pierced
by the Jews."

Yet every now and then they met in friendly
controversy. Justin's *Dialogue with Trypho* seems
to report an actual discussion. But Trypho[1] is no
common Jew. He accosts Justin in the colonnade at
Ephesus, telling him how he had learned from a
philosopher to be courteous to all who wore the
philosopher's cloak. Justin is surprised that a Jew
should study the philosophers when he has the law
and the prophets. "But are not the philosophers
also seekers after God?" Presently Justin tells the
story of his own life—how he too had sought long
for God in vain. Of his teachers, the Stoic knew
nothing, the Peripatetic only wanted his money, and
the Pythagorean required an absurd amount of
learning, and a long initiation. Then came a
Platonist, who gave him at any rate a worthier
conception of God. While he was thinking over
these things, he fell in with an old man by the sea-
shore, who shewed him that philosophy gives no clear
knowledge of God, and referred him to the writings of
the prophets, "for these things cannot be understood,
unless God and his Christ give us understanding."
The old man went his way, and Justin saw him no
more: but the fire was kindled in his soul, and it
was not long before he became a Christian.

Trypho replies courteously. It was good to study
philosophy, but it is not good now to trust in a man.
So he advises him in all friendship to be circumcised

---

[1] Some see in Trypho the great R. Tarphon, who may have fled like Trypho
from the wars of Hadrian's time. But what is known of R. Tarphon is very
unlike the tolerant philosophical Judaism of Trypho.

and keep the Law.   We must not run after Christs,
for we do not know who the Christ is, and he does
not know himself till Elijah comes and anoints him.
Trypho admires the Gospels, for he had taken care to
read them, and only doubts whether any one is able
to keep such lofty precepts.   But he really cannot
understand how men who make profession of piety
can neglect a Law which they do not deny to be
divine, or how they can put their trust in one who is
not only nothing more than a man, but actually a
crucified man.   This leads to a two days' discussion
ranging over the whole of the Old Testament, and
bringing out most of the stock passages of prophecy.
Of particular interpretations we have had samples
in the *Demonstration* of Irenaeus;[1] but the main
line of Justin's argument is fairly clear.   He has first
to shew that though the Law is divine, it is not
eternal.   Next he has to prove that Jesus of Nazareth
was more than a man—that he is truly divine, and
that his incarnation, crucifixion, resurrection and
ascension were all foretold.   This brings him upon
delicate ground, and once or twice his charges against
the Jews are almost too much for Trypho's courtesy.
It remains for him to set forth the conversion of the
Gentiles, the true Israel, and the rejection of the
Jews if they will not accept the new covenant of
Christ.   In the end Trypho declares himself greatly
edified by the discussion, politely wishes him a
prosperous voyage, and asks to be remembered as a
friend.

But Trypho was an exceptional Jew.   As a rule,
there were no more malicious enemies of the Gospel
than the Jews.   They were the very "workshop of

---

[1] See Ch. xi.

persecution," always ready to perpetrate or instigate
or help in murder and outrage.   It was a holy work
—in Polycarp's case it was even better than keeping
the sabbath.   It was as the Lord had said, Every
one that killeth you will think he is offering service
to God.

JEWISH INFLUENCES

Commentaries on N.T., esp. Lightfoot's *Excursus on St. Paul and the
Three* in *Ep. Gal.*   Hort *Judaistic Christianity*, Arts in *D.C.B.* on Justin etc.

CHAPTER XV

GNOSTICISM

VAST as is the subject of Gnosticism, it forms no more than a chapter from the long history of Oriental influences on the civilization of the European nations. Those influences need to be traced historically, for the questions raised by Orientalism are problems of all ages, and its answers to them are due to permanent leanings of human nature found in men of all nations. Latent they may be or obscured by other tendencies, but never absent. If then we seem to find traces of Orientalism in say the observances of the Pythagoreans, in Plato's theory of creation, or in the worship of the Essenes, we must not hastily conclude that there is no accounting for them without direct influence from Eastern peoples. Though the earlier thought of Greece and Israel was strongly opposed to Orientalism, the moral questions it raises were not ignored—witness the Greek Nemesis and the book of Job—but upon the whole they were answered in another way. The direct influence of the East hardly becomes important before its conquest by Alexander; and even in later times we cannot set down all Oriental thinking as an importation from the East. In the political sphere for instance the Empire at Ravenna and the mediaeval

Papacy are strongly marked with Orientalism which must have been chiefly of Western growth. In fact, Orientalism may come to the surface in any age or country where society or a part of it is infected with the weary hopelessness of Asia.

Three main stages of the history lie before us. The first is the influence of Orientalism on Greek thought in Stoicism, and even in the later phases of the Neoplatonic reaction, which as Plotinus left it was chiefly Greek. A second stage of influence on Judaism appears in Essenism, whatever be its historical origin. Then in the false teachers at Colossae we see it passing into a third stage of influence on Christianity, represented by Gnosticism, and even in the reaction of the Clementines. Further stages of influence in Mahometanism, and again on Western Europe through the Crusades, are beyond our limits. Thus the movement as a whole is older than the Gospel, and has no necessary connexion with Christianity. It is the sort of eclecticism which grows up in every age of religious ferment. Something of the sort is very common, for instance, in Japan, where men take as much or as little as they please of Christianity, and fill it out with Buddhism or anything else that may be convenient. Ancient Eclecticism was at first heathen or Jewish, and only takes the particular form of Gnosticism at the point where it begins to be influenced by the Christian belief that the redemption is through Christ.[1] Gnosticism may therefore be provisionally described as a number of schools of philosophy, Oriental in general character, but taking in the idea of a redemption through Christ, and further modified

1 Well put by Harnack *What is Christianity?* E.Tr. 205-7.

in different sects by a third element which may
be Judaism, Hellenism or Christianity. In this way
we at least start from something strongly marked in
the Gnostic systems, though even this is nearly
wanting in the Basilides of Hippolytus, whereas the
mere etymology (γνῶσις, and esoteric teaching) not
only gives us something by no means peculiar to
Gnosticism, but would compel us to exclude Marcion
and to include Clement of Alexandria, and perhaps
the church itself when the *disciplina arcani* became
prevalent. If we exclude Buddhism ourselves, we
do so on the ground that it is not more directly
connected with Christianity than it is with Druidism,
though distant influences on both sides are not
unlikely, so that in this way it may touch the fringe
of Gnosticism.

Here it is to be noted that the Gnostics took over
only the idea of a redemption through Christ, not
the full Christian doctrine, for they made it rather
a redemption of the philosophers from matter than a
redemption of mankind from sin. In fact, Gnosticism
was rather a philosophy than a religion, as being
commonly more interested in systems of the universe
than in relations of worship. If it was not without
moral earnestness of a common-sense middle-class
kind, especially in its more Christian schools, its
chief efforts were directed to philosophical questions
like that of the origin of evil. It was much more
at home in cosmogonies than in a world of sinners.
It was the first of the long series of heterodox
philosophies inside and outside the church which
could not refuse to see the centre of the world's
history in "that Jesus whom they crucified." Yet
it sprang chiefly from the intellectual pride of the

ancient world, and its patronage of the Gospel sometimes carried a touch of the old heathen contempt. In fact, most of the Gnostic schools attacked the Gospel on three sides at once, denying its historical basis, its claim to authority, and its doctrine of the spiritual freedom and equality of men. There was some reason for a reaction against the timid, over practical, traditional and somewhat Judaizing Christianity of the subapostolic age ; but the main attack was on the Gospel itself. The Gnostics mostly kept to the ancient ideals of specula- tion and of an intellectual aristocracy, so that they were as much opposed as any heathens to the " inwardness " of Christianity, with its ultra- democratic appeal to the image of God in all men. The very name of Gnostics denoted the men of knowledge, the wise men, the philosophers, the superior persons who knew the world of reality, not merely the appearances which were as much as the *profanum vulgus* could understand. Esoteric teaching was common in ancient times ; and when it was applied to a revelation, it became the teaching of a secret meaning beyond the reach of common people. The contrast of true and false knowledge is implied in our Saviour's claim to reveal the truth, and is expressly drawn by St. Paul and St. John ; [1] but the Ophites and Carpocrates appear to have been the first who called themselves Gnostics, and from them the name spread to others, of whom some deserved it less than they did. Marcion, for instance, rejected the theory of esoteric teaching. Thus the spiritual equality of Christianity was overthrown by a *gnosis* of speculation, the open tradition of the

[1] *e.g.* 1 Cor. ii. iii. 1 Ti. v. 20.

churches by a secret tradition of the Gnostics.   This
they often supported with books of their own which
they called apocryphal or esoteric, though their enemies
took up the word in a bad sense.   Some of these may
not have been of Gnostic origin, like the docetic
Gospels of Peter and Philip, and the Acts of Paul
and Thecla.   The latter was composed in the second
century by a presbyter in Asia, who was deposed for
writing it, and it at any rate commended itself to the
Gnostics by its depreciation of marriage.   Others
were distinctively Gnostic, like the ascetic Gospel of
Matthias used by the Valentinians, and the Cainite
Gospel of Judas Iscariot, which made the Betrayal a
meritorious deed : and they seem to have had other
"Gospels" which were rather theological treatises
than Gospels in any proper sense.

But their general resource was in strange theories
of accommodation—that while our Lord spoke the
language of common Christianity to the common
people, he was privately teaching something higher,
Valentinianism for example, to some select disciples.
Philosophy was the solid reality, the facts of revelation no more than a mass of parables and symbols
which pointed to it.   In truth, the principles of
interpretation were in so unsettled a state that the
Gnostics could always find what they wanted in
Scripture, just as some of the heathens found everything in Homer.   Their exegesis was utterly arbitrary.
The parables in particular lent themselves readily to
allegorizing methods of interpretation which could
make anything mean anything.[1]

[1] Our chief orthodox authorities are passages of Justin, the great works of
Irenaeus, Hippolytus and Epiphanius, sundry treatises of Tertullian, and the
summaries of Ps.-Tert. (= Victorinus of Pettau, *cir*. 300) at the end of the *de
Praescr.*, and of Philaster of Brescia, late in the fourth century.

Let us begin with a general survey of Gnosticism, rather striking a rough average of opinions common to most of the sects than endeavouring to describe the doctrines of any one sect. There will be some advantages in first viewing the movement as a whole without regard to details and exceptions.

The problem then of the Gnostics was rather philosophical than religious. Given the fact of Christ and the new creation coming from him, it is required to find its place in the logical development of the universe. It is Hegel's problem, and the answer, like Hegel's, is a philosophy in the garb of religion.

The first step is to explain—what the Gospel leaves a mystery—the origin of a spiritual and therefore on Gnostic principles a pure world. As the Gnostics started from the usual abstract conception of God as a being above all attributes, the transition from the infinite to the finite was usually explained by a necessary process of self-limitation of the Supreme.

Lipsius in 1865 held that Ps.-Tert., Epiph. Phil. all used (A), a book of 32 heresies from Dositheus to Noetus, written by Hippolytus 190-195 at the suggestion (as Photius says) of Irenaeus. He also maintained that Ir. and Hipp. used the lost *Syntagma* of Justin, which he mentions *Apol.* i. 26. Harnack in 1873 corrected the date of (A) to 199-217 (or 200-210 *A.C.L.* i. 223) in the time of Zephyrinus putting his larger *Refutatio* (*Philosophumena*) *cir.* 230 (or rather earlier *A.C.L.*), and held that the use of the Σύνταγμα was not proved. Salmon in 1885 raised the question whether the Gnostic works quoted by Hipp. were not all by one hand, and therefore forgeries. Kuntze came to the conclusion that it is impossible to restore the Σύνταγμα, so that we cannot go behind the statements of Ir., which moreover he makes on personal knowledge. Epiph. depends entirely on Ir., while Ps.-Tert. and Phil. used (A), which however must have been a meagre and insignificant production.

Putting together all our sources of information, the right conclusions would seem to be (1) that (A) was a work of some size, used by Epiph. as well as by Ps.-Tert. and Phil. ; (2) that both Ir. and Hipp. used genuine Gnostic works and used them honestly, but did not always rightly understand them, or properly distinguish between a founder's teaching and developments (often radical changes) made by his followers. We all know the controversialist's habit of ascribing the eccentricities of a section to the whole party.

Occasionally they assigned it a motive, forgetting
that every motive implies an attribute of some sort.
Generally then we have a series of necessary emana-
tions, each giving rise to others further from the
source and therefore supposed to be weaker, till at
last we reach the possibility of contact with matter.

The next thing to be explained is the possibility of
a material and therefore on Gnostic principles an evil
world. This again the Gospel leaves a mystery.
Our doctrine of "creation out of nothing" means
only that matter has no existence independent of the
will of God, or more precisely points to such a
development from the unseen according to his will
that while by faith we apprehend the fact, we can by
reason form no conception of the process as a natural
evolution. Science has nothing to say about origins.
But on the Gnostic principle that God is the active
cause of everything he permits, we cannot trace evil
(physical and moral evil are lumped together) to any
human or other freewill; and therefore matter must
be allowed more or less of a real independence beyond
God's control. At this point however we get a
moderate and an extreme doctrine, very roughly
corresponding to Gieseler's division of the Gnostics
into Egyptian and Syrian sects. In general, the
Alexandrian Gnostics were influenced by Greek
thought, and specifically by the Platonic conception
of matter as something dead and unsubstantial. In
this case it could offer no more than a passive resistance, and the pure finite emanation spark was rather
imprisoned in it than corrupted by it. The Syrian
Gnostics were influenced by the more advanced dualistic thought of the East, which commonly looked on
matter as an active power of evil encroaching on the

kingdom of light, and infecting it with an abominable mixture.

Corresponding logically, though perhaps not always actually, to these two views of the nature of matter were two forms of asceticism, a moderate and an extreme. The moderate asceticism, which prevailed chiefly among the Gnostics who were less hostile to Judaism, did not necessarily or always go very far beyond what may be required by true Christian unselfishness: but in principle it differed entirely. Instead of the loving spirit which thankfully receives the pleasures of life as no less God's teaching than its sorrows, and refuses them only on definite grounds of danger to self or offence to others, it is animated by the selfish and ungrateful cowardice whose first impulse is to think vaguely that every creature of God is bad, and to be refused, that he may not tempt us with it, for we know that he is a hard man. When the body is taken for the sinful element, the gravest dangers of immorality are close at hand as a natural reaction from unnatural and therefore ungodly austerity. They were very real even among the more moderate sects, and the scandals were often of the grossest when asceticism took its extreme form. This indeed is a case where extremes meet. The Gnostics who leaned to Christianity had a stern moral purpose, and pushed austerity to an extreme. Marcion made marriage a bar to Baptism, and Tatian roundly denounced it as seduction and fornication. The more pagan sects and some of the quacks preferred to shew their independence of the body by following all its passions as things of no moral significance whatever. It was no great thing, said some of them, to restrain desire; the real victory was to indulge it to the uttermost, and yet keep the spirit pure. All these forms of hostility to matter have one doctrine in common—that the evil of it is original, and beyond the power of redemption to remove. Though Gnosticism might strive, and sometimes did strive with no little earnestness and purity to rescue a people from the world, it could never cherish any such glorious hope as St. Paul's, of the restoration of the whole creation.

The Gnostics were generally agreed in distinguishing the demiurge or creator from the Supreme, and in identifying him with the God of the Old Testament. So here again there were two views—a moderate and an extreme. In some sects the demiurge is the clumsy instrument of the Supreme, in others an unconscious one, and the world is gone wrong because he mismanaged his work. He may be one of a group of angels, perhaps the highest of angels; but the redeemer who comes to mend his bungled work ought to be higher still. To a certain distance the theory is only an extension of Judaism, for the later Jews in their anxiety to keep God from contact with the world had introduced a ministry of angels for the creation and the giving of the Law,[1] though they never allowed it to obscure the fundamental doctrine that God is the true Creator. Now if we lift these angels a step higher, so as to make them more or less independent, we have passed from Judaism to Gnosticism, and are not far removed from the Neoplatonic hierarchy of gods and demons, for there is now no reason why we should not develop the angels indefinitely. From another point of view the

---

[1] Acts vii. 53, Gal. iii. 19 (see Lightfoot) resting on Deut. xxxii. 8, Ps. lxviii. 17 (שִׁנְאָן אַלְפֵי, lit. thousands of repetition).

theory is opposed to Judaism, for though the Old Testament is recognized as the highest revelation of its own time, it is only accepted with the important reserve that the God of the Jews was not the Supreme as they supposed. In fact, they place it lower than Islam does. In the extreme view the opposition to Judaism is sharper still. The demiurge is positively evil, jealous and revengeful, so that some of the most advanced sects read the Old Testament backward, with Pharaoh and Ahab for saints, Moses and Elijah for sinners, and the God of the Jews very fairly answering to our ideas of the devil.

Corresponding again were two views of the Person of Christ—a moderate and an extreme. In the one, his manhood was allowed to be real, but nothing more than the instrument of the higher power which dwelt in him, with no significance or value of its own. Sometimes the higher Christ was supposed to come upon the lower at his baptism and to leave him before the crucifixion—a theory which differs from Ebionism only on the nature of the higher Christ. On the more advanced and consistent view, the Incarnation was visionary from first to last. If he seemed to have a body, it was not real; and if he seemed to eat and drink and suffer pain, it was no more than seeming. The one thing evident was that the redeemer who came to deliver us from matter could not come in a material body.

Before we come to the classification of the Gnostic sects, we shall have to speak of Simon Magus, "the hero of the romance of heresy," whom Irenaeus considers the author of all the heresies. We find him in the Acts regarded by the people of Samaria as "the Power of God which is called Great," and playing the

impostor with great success. Justin tells us that he
was a Samaritan of Gitta, that he came to Rome in
the days of Claudius Caesar, worked miracles and was
honoured as a god, so that the Senate and people set
up a statue to him inscribed SIMONI DEO SANCTO on the
island of the Tiber,[1] and most of the Samaritans still
worshipped him. Irenaeus also tells us that Simon
gave himself out to be the Highest Power, who
appeared to the Jews as the Son, came down to the
Samaritans as the Father, and dwelt among the
Gentiles as the Holy Spirit. One Helena, whom he
found living as a harlot at Tyre, was the "first
conception" of his mind, the mother of all, the Ennoia.
This Highest Power conceived the idea of by her means
creating angels and archangels : so she went down
and brought them forth, and they in their turn made
the world. But they made it badly, and through
envy and in their ignorance of the Supreme they
suffered not Ennoia to return to heaven, but kept her
here on earth, suffering shame and continual transmigration from one woman's body to another. At
one time she was the Helen of the Trojan war, and at
last she sank into a harlot at Tyre. However, these
angels gave the Law and inspired the prophets for
the purpose of keeping men in slavery. Therefore
the Highest Power came down, passing through the
world of angels and changing his form at every stage
till he appeared in Judaea as a man who seemed to
suffer and did not, and now revealed himself in Simon
for the deliverance of Ennoia (the lost sheep) and of
the men that were his own. So the Simonians
cultivated magic and evil arts, and gave themselves

---

[1] This is a clear mistake, for when the statue was found in 1574, the
inscription proved to be SEMONI SANCO DEO FIDIO—a Sabine god.

up to uncleanness, " for they were saved by grace and
not by just works, so that they were free to do what
they pleased "—just and unjust being distinctions
made by the angels, which they were not bound to
regard. They also worshipped statues of Simon and
Helena in the forms of Zeus and Athena.

Justin is in the main a good witness against his
own countrymen, though he is wrong about the statue,
and may be mistaken in bringing Simon to Rome at
all. Of this however we must not be too sure, for
Rome was the natural resort of such impostors. Be
that as it may, this is the point which the romancers
fastened on, though they shifted his visit from the
reign of Claudius to that of Nero, in order to bring
the Magus into collision with Peter. The germ of
the story tho bare statement that Peter withstood
him at Rome—can be traced back as far as Hippolytus ;
but for the full romance of Simon's miracles and defeat
we must go to the Clementines, and the *Acts* of Peter
and Paul.

Keeping to history, we shall see that the system is
almost as little Gnostic as it is Christian. True, there
is a good deal in it which reminds us of Gnosticism.
It starts by reducing revelation to an affair of
intellect, it has a mythology of demiurgic powers,
it deals with the moral law and with Judaism as
many of the Gnostics did, and its Patripassian Trinity
is significant : but we see very little of the Christian
element which is an essential part of Gnosticism.
The descent of the Highest Power may be suggested
by the Incarnation, and the designation of Ennoia as
the lost sheep is certainly Christian : but the coming
of the Lord is a subordinate event, not the centre of
the whole process as Gnostics and Christians agreed

to make it. Moreover, Simon's own claim to be the Highest Power is enough to stamp the system as a direct rival to the Gospel, not a Gnostic interpretation of it.[1]

This is even more evident in Simon's disciple Menander, who was also a Samaritan. As he taught at Antioch, Irenaeus may be right in making him the personal link joining Simon to Saturninus and the Gnostics proper. His doctrine was much the same as Simon's, except that he made the Supreme unknown, and gave himself out as the Saviour, sent to teach men the magic which would enable them to overcome the demiurgic angels. Baptism was in his own name, and carried the promise, not of resurrection only, but of immortal youth on earth. This last statement may be a misunderstanding of his teaching : but it is not summarily disproved by the fact that the sect survived its founder. Menander's followers may have been as robust in faith as those of Joanna Southcott. With Menander we may also class the shadowy figures of Dositheus and Cleobius, of whom next to nothing is known. All these seem to belong rather to the age of false Messiahs than to that of Gnosticism.

Now that we are coming to the Gnostics proper, it is important to notice that they were rather schools of thought inside the churches than sects outside them. They seldom cared to form churches of their own, and even Marcion seems always to have aimed at peace with the bishops. They were quite content with

---

[1] Simon Magus most fully discussed by A. C. Headlam (Art. in Hastings' *D.B.*), but he does not meet Salmon's difficulty (Art. in *D.C.B.*) that if Justin's Simon is a real Gnostic, as they both suppose, he must be much later than the Simon of the Acts. But I see nothing on Simon's system beyond a generalized Orientalism and an incidental use of Christianity which may well belong to the first century. There is no specific mark of Gnosticism upon it.

common Christianity for common people.   It was all very well so far as it went, and the unlearned could not be expected to get beyond it; but they must themselves deal with it in an enlightened spirit, and restate its doctrines more philosophically.   Common Christians were the natural men; they were the spiritual, who knew the mysteries of the kingdom of God.   The object was to keep the power of the Gospel, and yet to rise above the limitations which common Christianity placed on culture and common life,[1] so there was no need for any secession.   Accordingly, though many individuals may have formed ephemeral schools and coteries of Gnostics, only the Valentinians and the Marcionites appear to have grown into sects of lasting historical importance.   The Valentinians are found at least as late as Julian's time : the Marcionites lasted still longer, and may even have contributed something to the origin of the Paulicians in the seventh century.

We now have before us the difficult question of the classification of the Gnostic "sects."   Clement of Alexandria divided them into ascetic and licentious sects; Theodoret into monistic and dualistic.   Neander classifies them as either not unfriendly to Judaism or entirely hostile to it.   Gieseler contents himself with a geographical arrangement of Alexandrian and Syrian Gnostics, which as we have seen roughly corresponds to a division into moderate and extreme, though it provides no place for Marcion.   Others prefer to group them chronologically ; and this method

[1] This is the point of complaints like those of Agrippa Castor (*ap.* Eus. iv. 7) that Basilides taught that there was no harm in eating εἰδωλόθυτα or in "unguarded" denial of the faith in time of persecution : or those of Anon. *ap.* Eus. v. 28 against reckless criticism and devotion to heathen learning. On the other hand (Eus. v. 16) the Marcionites had many martyrs.

also has great advantages, though it fails to shew the affinities of divergent lines of development. Baur refines on Neander, dividing the sects into those who accepted both Judaism and heathenism as revelations of a lower order, those who so accepted Judaism only, and those who rejected both. The objection to it is that the second class is made for the Clementines, which are better connected with Ebionism, while Marcion stands alone in the third.

In fact, an entirely satisfactory classification is impossible. If Gnosticism were only a complex of definite sects, the difficulty might be overcome; but it is rather a general term like Protestantism, and equally stands for prevalent opinions and a general attitude, not for a definite system of doctrine like Marcionism or Lutheranism. As no single character marks all the Gnostics and no others, so also no single character always brings together allied sects and no others. We must take all characters into account, and do the best we can. Just as Cerinthus and Tatian lie on the outskirts of Gnosticism itself, so other sects will have a doubtful place among our classes, divide them as we may; and if a teacher is rightly placed in one class, his disciples will sometimes pass into another. Perhaps we shall do best if we start from our definition of Gnosticism, and classify the sects according as the third element is Judaism, Hellenism or Christianity. This is Baur's plan, but with a difference. We eliminate the Oriental framework and the idea of redemption through Christ, and look at the general character of what remains. The difficulty will be in deciding whether some feature of a system belongs to the Oriental framework or to the third element. Thus old wives' fables may come in

anywhere : but where shall we place the endless
genealogies ? Upon the whole, they seem rather
Judaic than Oriental. Even if the Jews got the hint
from the East, the Gnostics appear to have received
it from the Jews. Thus we can make a fairly regular
series. We begin with Cerinthus, who stands on the
border line between Ebionism and Gnosticism, and
Saturninus, in whom the mythological element is
more fully developed. The Greek influence is much
stronger in Valentinus and Basilides, though the disciples of the latter reverted more or less to Judaizing
ideas. In the Ophites and Carpocrates the Greek
element is dominant, and almost smothers the
Christian. We close with the decidedly Christian
Gnostics, Marcion and Tatian, though the last is as
much an eccentric churchman as a Gnostic in the
proper sense.

Cerinthus then flourished in Asia near the end of
the first century. We may pass over the traditions
which attach his name to almost every Judaizer in
the New Testament : but the story of St. John fleeing
from the baths because Cerinthus was there is told
by Irenaeus on the authority of Polycarp. He does
not say that he heard it himself, but it is quite
in character with all that we know of St. John.
Cerinthus is on the meeting ground of Ebionites and
Gnostics, and may fairly be classed with either. He
begins with an unknown Supreme, and refers the
work of creation to " powers widely separated from
the Authority that is over all, and ignorant of the
God who is over all." One of these inferior angels he
singles out as the God of the Jews, who gave the
Law. Jesus was the son of Joseph and Mary, and
differed from other men only in greater wisdom and

righteousness. On him came down at his baptism
the Christ in the form of a dove sent down from the
Supreme ; and then he began to preach the unknown
Father and to work miracles. But the Christ departed
from him before the crucifixion, so that it was only
Jesus who suffered and rose again, and shall return
to reign in Jerusalem for a thousand years of sensuous
pleasures before the consummation.[1]

Jerome has a story that the Fourth Gospel was
written against Cerinthus : but St. John evidently
has a much wider purpose, though he may be glancing
at Cerinthus (among others) in his definition of the
deceiver and the antichrist as he that confesseth not
Jesus Christ as come in flesh. On the other hand,
the Apocalypse agreed so well with the Chiliasm of
Cerinthus that some were found who accused him of
having forged the book. The vestige of truth in the
charge is that both the Apocalypse and Cerinthus are
moving in the primitive environment of Jewish ideas
and *naïve* literalism from which Chiliasm arose.

Saturninus (or Satornilus) was a native of Antioch,
and taught in Syria about the time when Basilides
was flourishing in Egypt. His system is nearly that
of Cerinthus, with the mythology more developed,
and apparently no Chiliasm. We have as before an
unknown Father, who made angels, archangels,
powers, authorities. The world was made by seven
angels, and man too. A bright image was let down
for a moment from the supreme power, and they
could not detain it. So they said, Let us make man
after the image and after the likeness.[2] But when

---

[1] Epiphanius outdoes himself in blundering about Cerinthus : but the
above (mainly from Irenaeus) seems the most likely account.

[2] Gen. i. 26 κατ᾽ εἰκόνα καὶ καθ᾽ ὁμοίωσιν, omitting ἡμετέραν.

they had made him, he could not stand upright, but crawled like a worm, till the Power above had mercy on him, because he was made in the divine image, and sent a spark of life which made him live. After death that spark runs back to its kindred, while the rest of him is resolved into its elements. The Saviour was without birth or body or figure, and only in appearance a man, and the God of the Jews was one of the angels : and because it was the Father's will to destroy the God of the Jews and the rest of the archons, therefore the Christ came to save them that had the spark of life. For the angels had formed a bad sort of men as well as a good one, and because the demons helped the bad, therefore came the Saviour. Saturninus further held that marriage and procreation are from Satan, and most of his followers also abstained from animal food. The prophecies were given partly by the demiurgic angels, partly by their enemy Satan.

This is the outline given by Irenaeus ; and from it we see how Saturninus is the link between Simon and Menander on one side, and the Ophites in one direction, Basilides and Valentinus in another. The system itself is weak enough. It would have been more coherent if Saturninus had made the demiurgic angels purely righteous like Marcion's God of the Jews : but he has so fully traced evil to them that Satan is superfluous, and must be regarded as an idle relic of Jewish ideas.

We come now to sects which shew stronger signs of the influence of Greek philosophy—those named after Valentinus and Basilides. Valentinus was the greatest of the Gnostics—an acute thinker with a touch of mysticism, and a philosopher's delight in

contemplating things *sub specie aeternitatis.* Local
tradition in the time of Epiphanius made him a native
of the coast of Egypt; and, if so, his philosophical
training was most likely received at Alexandria.
However, he came to Rome during the episcopate
of Hyginus, and flourished there till that of Pius
—roughly, under the emperor Pius (138 - 161).
Tertullian says that he broke off from the church
because he was disappointed of a bishopric—perhaps
that of Rome in 138—but this is too common a
story about heresiarchs to be accepted without better
evidence.   It is likely enough that he made orthodox
professions, and time was needed to discover his un-
soundness.   Much of his teaching was excellent, and
his peculiarities were often only hinted.[1]   Some of
the fragments quoted by Clement and Hippolytus
are enigmatical.

Valentinus, says Victorinus, "teaches a pleroma
and thirty aeons, and these he arranges in syzygies
or couples.   The first of them are Bythos and Sige,
from whom came forth a seed, and in it Mind and
Truth.   From these burst forth Word and Life, and
from these again came Man and Church.   From
these two came twelve aeons, and ten more from
Word and Life, making thirty aeons, so that the
pleroma consists of eight and ten and twelve.   The
thirtieth aeon desired to see Bythos, and came up
to the higher parts of the pleroma for the purpose,
and was not able to bear the sight of his greatness,
but fainted and would have dissolved away if he
whom they call Horus had not been sent to
strengthen her, which he did by pronouncing the

---

[1] Tert. *adv. Val.* 1 " Nihil magis curant, quam occultare, quod praedicant
. . titulis et argumentis verae religionis . . . per ambiguitates bilingues."

word Iao. This aeon, whom he calls Achamoth,
fell a prey to certain passions of desire, and from
these passions brought forth matter—the offspring
of her terror and fear and grief and tears. This is
the reason why heaven and earth and all things in
them are weak and fragile and transitory and mortal.
For from her terror, says he, came the darkness, from
her fear and ignorance the spirit of wickedness
and malice, and from her grief and tears the springs,
the rivers and the sea. Christ was sent from the
First Father, namely Bythos. He had not the
substance of our body, but brought a spiritual body
from heaven, passing through the virgin Mary like
water through a pipe, receiving nothing from her.
The resurrection of this flesh of ours he denies. Of
the law and the prophets he approves some parts
and rejects others. He has also a Gospel of his
own in addition to ours." [1]

Victorinus does not pretend to give this as more
than an outline which leaves many questions of
importance unanswered ; and he has certainly made
it a dreary outline. Yet even these dry bones are
enough to shew the vastness of the plan. But we
miss the iridescent colours of eloquence and poetry
which made it the most seductive of all the Gnostic
systems. For its own age it had a fascination of
mystic grandeur like that of Pantheism for ours.
One point stands out at once. Love was the source
of the spiritual world, for the First Father, says he,
"was all love, and love is not love, if there be not
that which is loved" : and love—presumptuous love
—is the source of the material and evil world. It is
but another poetic vesture for, Ye shall be as gods,

[1] Ps.-Tert. *Praescr.* 49. The Gospel will be that of Matthias.

knowing good and evil. But with all his Jewish
fables and endless genealogies, Valentinus moves in
a world of Platonic transcendentalism, and draws
from this the inspiration for his bold endeavour to
place the origin of evil in the higher or spiritual
sphere. It is an imposing system: yet its epitaph,
like that of Pantheism, might be written from its
own *Pistis Sophia*:—" I was watching far off, and
I saw a light, and I thought, I will go there, and
reach the light. And I went; and I found myself
in darkness."

The outline given by Victorinus would seem fairly
to represent the original system; but its lacunae
will have to be filled up from the varying accounts of
Irenaeus and Hippolytus, which would seem to stand
rather for the schools of Valentinianism—the Italian
and the Eastern—which arose in the next generation.
We need not attempt to trace their intricate details,
but we cannot pass over the question of the Person
of Christ, on which Victorinus tells us practically
nothing, except that the Incarnation was unreal.
It appears then that the Eight (or Ogdoad) the
Ten, and the Twelve aeons[1] stood in groups at
increasing distances from Bythos, who is known
only to his direct offspring Mind or Monogenes.
But with the distance increased the desire to know,
till in the last aeon Sophia it became a passion.
She brought forth a formless offspring and fell into
great distress; and this was the origin of material
substance. Hereupon Bythos through Monogenes

[1] The Valentinians were not agreed on the computation of the aeons.
Some included Bythos and Sige, and made them the parents of the rest.
Others added Christ and the Holy Spirit, reducing Sige to a nonentity, and
making Bythos alone produce the whole thirty—like the sow in Virgil,
comments Tertullian.

put forth Horus, whom they call Cross[1] and Redeemer, who stopped Sophia and purified her of her desire before admitting her to the Pleroma, while he crucified (*i.e.* fenced off) her desire which remained outside, a spiritual substance without form. After this Monogenes according to the providence of Bythos put forth a last couple of aeons male and female—Christ and the Holy Spirit.[2] Christ taught the aeons that they must be content to know that Bythos is infinite and incomprehensible, and can only be seen or heard or known through Monogenes; while the Holy Spirit completed the harmony of the aeons by making each like each. In their joy at this happy result, all the aeons joined to produce Jesus or Soter, the perfect beauty and constellation of the Pleroma, and with him a guard of angels. As it is written, In him dwelleth all the Pleroma of the deity.[3]

Then the higher Christ had mercy on the desire of Sophia, which they call Achamoth, and stretched beyond the Cross (fence) to give her form, though not knowledge.[4] So she too endeavoured to follow Christ back into the Pleroma, and she too was stopped by Horus with the magic name Iao, and fell a prey to passions from which the elements arose, and Satan or Cosmocrator[5] with his evil angels; and when she turned to Christ who had given her life, there arose the Demiurge—an animal nature like herself, not a spiritual. As Christ would not leave the Pleroma again at her prayer, he sent instead the Paraclete or

---

[1] As ὅρος is a boundary, so σταυρός here is not a single stake but a *fence* of stakes to guard the Pleroma.

[2] The feminine gender of the Holy Spirit among all the Judaizers is from the feminine Hebrew רוח.

[3] Col. ii. 9.   [4] κατ᾽ οὐσίαν, οὐ κατὰ γνῶσιν.   [5] Eph. vi. 12.

Soter [1] with a retinue of angels, and all power delivered
to him by Bythos and the aeons. He gave her knowledge, and set her free from her passions, which
became the ideal substance of matter. After this she
conceived the spiritual principle in the image of the
angels. Thus we have the virtual [2] origin of matter,
soul and spirit. She also put forth the seven
(heavens) which however are not the orbits of the
planets, but are personified as angels like the
Demiurge himself, who proceeded to the creation of
the actual world in complete ignorance of any being
higher than himself. After this the creation of man.
First a body of transcendental matter, then a soul of
life, and afterwards a material body. The spirit was
infused by Achamoth unknown to the Demiurge, and
only into the elect. For the sake of these came the
aeon Christ for their salvation. He had the spiritual
Christ from Achamoth, the animal Christ from the
Demiurge, but a heavenly body made with unspeakable art to be seen and handled and to be capable of
suffering : but he received no matter at all, for matter
cannot receive salvation. As for men, they are in
three classes. The carnal man is beyond the reach
of salvation ; the natural man (the common Christian)
may be saved, but only if he makes the good choice,
and even then is not admitted to the Pleroma, but
only to a middle region. The spiritual man (and by
the spiritual man they mean themselves) is not only
alone capable of full salvation, but cannot forfeit it
by any sins whatever that he may commit. He is
saved by nature, as Clement says. Forgiveness there
is none.

This is the account given by Irenaeus, which

Jesus the Paraclete as 1 Joh. ii. 1.   [2] δυνάμει.

seems to represent the ideas of the Italian school of
Valentinians. The modern reader may think the
long story too fantastic to be worth serious attention :
but we shall find meaning enough in it, and no little
depth of thinking, if we remember that it is given as
mythology and poetry, not as articles of religion.
The Eastern used personifications much as the
Western uses abstractions, as symbols of things he
could not understand. So the Eight highest aeons
shadow forth what were supposed to be the highest
attributes of deity, while the Ten and the Twelve
express those lower attributes which seem to bring
him nearer to contact with the world. The Person
and work commonly assigned to Christ is divided
between Monogenes, Christ, and Jesus or Soter,
while the cross, which is for us the symbol of atonement, is turned into the fence which guards the
Pleroma against intrusion from the grosser worlds
below. The verbal agreement with the Gospels is
great : as Irenaeus says, they used similar words with
different meanings. The system is evidently a Gnostic
reading of St. John's Prologue, in which indeed
Ptolemaeus has no difficulty in finding the whole
Ogdoad. To put the matter shortly, Valentinianism
is a restatement or spiritual interpretation of
Christianity, quite as good as some very recent ones,
and perhaps no further from historical truth. Only ;
its poetry is now out of fashion.

The chief representatives of Valentinianism in the
next generation were Ptolemaeus, Heracleon, and
Marcus, who belonged to the Western school, while
the Eastern produced Theodotus, Axionicus, and
Bardaisan of Edessa. Of these, Ptolemaeus and
Heracleon take an honourable place among the first

commentators on the New Testament, while Marcus
is represented by Irenaeus as a seducer of women and
a quack of the worst sort. Theodotus is known to
us from extracts preserved in very bad condition
with the works of Clement of Alexandria, while the
chief importance of Axionicus is that he helps to fix
the position of Bardaisan.

Ptolemaeus was the head of the Western school in
the time of Irenaeus, who gives an extract from his
commentary on St. John's Prologue. He may be
quoting a good deal more from Ptolemaeus, and
indeed his whole account of Valentinianism seems to
be of its Ptolemaic form; but this is all that we can
be sure of. Ptolemaeus is also known to us from his
Letter to Flora, preserved by Epiphanius, which gives
an interesting view of Old Testament criticism in
Gnostic hands. The Mosaic Law, says he, cannot
come from the Supreme, because it is not perfect;
but neither can it come from the devil, because it
forbids wickedness. Our Lord plainly intimates that
it contains laws of three different sorts. There are
laws given by God, like that which forbids divorce;
laws devised by Moses, like that which allows it for
fear of something worse; and laws invented by the
elders, like those which make the fifth commandment
of none effect. Of these three classes, the divine laws
fall again into three sections. We have the purely
moral commands (the law in the strict sense) which
the Lord came not to destroy but to fulfil. Others,
like the law of retaliation, were so mixed up with
evil that they had to be abolished. Others were
types and symbols, which the Saviour has transferred
from the visible and sensible to things unseen and
spiritual. To this class belong sacrifice, circumcision,

the sabbath, fasting, the passover, and such-like. The names remain, but the things are changed, for the Saviour has replaced the sacrifices of beasts by spiritual praise and thanksgiving, and fellowship and well-doing to our neighbour.[1] Similarly he commands circumcision, not of the flesh but of the heart, not sabbatical rest, but rest from evil works ; and fasting, not from meats, but from sin. Outward fasting we practise because it may be of some help to the soul if done with reason, not for the sake of imitation, or custom, or because a day has been appointed for it, and if done to remind ourselves of the true fast. The Law then was given neither by God nor by the devil, but by the Demiurge who stands between them, whom we call the Midst. He is neither good nor bad nor unrighteous, but properly righteous. He is less than God, because he is begotten, but he is greater than the devil, who is corruption and dark-ness. Let not Flora think that these are coexistent with the one true God. She shall learn another time the full doctrine of the Midst which we have received from the apostolic tradition along with the command to judge all discourses by the rule of our Saviour's teaching.

The analysis is acute, though there is no clear distinction between the statutes which were not good ordained by God and those devised by Moses. This second section of the divine laws is the weak point of the whole theory. If Ptolemaeus had ascribed them all to Moses and the elders, the rest would have been so purely divine that there would have been no need to bring in the Midst, who is only Marcion's righteous God, and an altogether unthinkable conception. The

---

[1] The reference to Hebr. xiii. 15, 16 is important.

truth is, he was wanted for other purposes, and
utilized to explain the imperfection of the Law. In
general, Ptolemaeus is sober and sensible enough, as
in his discussion of fasting : but the Gnostics were
always at their best in exoteric writings.[1]

Heracleon was a contemporary of Ptolemaeus, or
perhaps older, if he was personally known to
Valentinus. He made his reputation, not as the head
of a school, but as a commentator. We know his
works only from the quotations made by Clement
and Origen. Clement[2] gives Heracleon's comment
on Lu. xii. 8 to this effect. There is one confession
of Christ in life, another in words before a magistrate.
This latter is what is commonly called confession ;
yet it may be made by a hypocrite. Moreover, it is
not required of all. Matthew, Philip, Thomas, Levi[3]
and others never were martyrs. But the Lord is here
speaking of confession by works suitable to faith.
This he requires of all, and the other will follow upon
it if need be. Therefore does he contrast " confessing
in me" with "denying me" for the true confession
can only be made by those who are in Christ, and only
those who are not in Christ can deny him. Moreover, confession "; before men " is not simply before
unbelievers, but before men generally.

This again is a fine piece of exposition, though
Heracleon has pushed the preposition too far : and it
was much needed for times when martyrdom was too
often allowed to cover a multitude of sins. The same

---

[1] Harnack *T. U.*[2] xiv. (1904) is inclined to identify Ptolemaeus with the
teacher of the Christian woman condemned by Lollius Urbicus (Justin *Apol.*
ii. 2 : Eus. iv. 17). In this case he would be a martyr : φιλαλήθη καὶ οὐκ
ἀπατηλὸν οὐδὲ ψευδολόγον τὴν γνώμην ὄντα is a kindly judgment of him, but
not unlikely from Justin.

[2] Clem. Al. *Strom.* iv. 9 p. 595 P.

[3] Is this Lebbaeus, or is he distinguishing Levi from Matthew ?

minute care runs through his commentary on St.
John, as we see it in Origen's quotations. Thus he
notes that All things were made *through* him (διά not
ὑπό) that the buyers and sellers were in the outer
court of the temple (ἱερόν not ναός) and that salvation
is *of* the Jews, not *in* them. But his allegorical
interpretations are of the usual sort—neither better
nor worse than others—except when he* tries to read
Valentinianism into the Gospel. Thus the nobleman
is the Demiurge, the woman of Samaria's adulterous
husbands are the matter in which spiritual men are
entangled, and the whip of small cords is the power
of the Spirit. Upon the whole however the Valentinian
mythology is not very prominent in the fragments of
Heracleon which have come down to us.

We need not discuss the opinions which Marcus
thought fit to profess. His place is not with the
heretics, but with Alexander of Abonoteichos and
the rest of the quacks. Turning then to the Eastern
school and passing over the difficult questions connected with Theodotus, we come to the latest of the
great Gnostics, and one of the most interesting of
them, Bardaisan of Edessa. By his time the primacy
of Christendom had long passed from the Syrian
churches to the Greek: and if the Latin churches
were rising to claim their place in history, the Syrian
were sinking into comparative obscurity. It was the
age of Greek supremacy, when even Latin literature
was represented almost solely by the Christians for
a century and a half after Juvenal. So Syriac was
mostly imitative, and Syriac writers are few. The
chief are Tatian the Assyrian, Bardaisan and his
Marcionite opponent, the Assyrian Prepon: and of
these only Tatian thinks of throwing down the

audacious challenge, that the barbarians are better than the Greeks.

Out in the Mesopotamian desert, some two hundred miles to the east of Antioch, lay the city of Edessa, the capital of Osrhoene. It had a strong position beside the torrent of the Daisan, and was a military outpost of great importance for either Rome or Parthia, and owned a shifting allegiance to both. It was ruled for three centuries by a series of kings, mostly named Abgar, till 217, when Abgar bar-Manu was treacherously seized by Caracalla, and Osrhoene was made a Roman province. Christianity must have reached Edessa very early (though the famous letters of Christ and Abgar Uchama are apocryphal) and flourished so greatly that the last Abgar is said to have been a Christian. Bardaisan was born July 11, 154 or 155, in a high rank of life, for he was brought up with an Abgar, perhaps bar-Manu, perhaps one of his predecessors. He seems to have held a great position at the court till the Roman conquest. After the fall of bar-Manu, he appears first as a writer of Armenian history, then as an investigator of Indian religion in El Gabal's time. He died in 223.

Bardaisan's numerous works are lost. The *Book of the Laws of Nations* ascribed to him was written by his disciple Philip, so that it cannot be taken as exactly representing his own opinions, while the Bardesanist hymns which became the model of Syriac poetry seem to be the work of his son Harmonius, who had a Greek education at Athens. We cannot even be sure whether he turned from Valentinianism to orthodoxy, or from orthodoxy to Valentinianism : only his heresy is certain, and his orthodoxy was at best not of the soundest. The evidence is scanty and obscure, but it points to a docetic and generally Gnostic way of thinking, and in particular to a modified Chaldaean fatalism, as if the stars had a real influence, though not to the exclusion of nature and freewill, for men with the same horoscope turn out differently, and men with different horoscopes have the same national customs. This is the argument put into his mouth in the Laws, and may not be far from his actual belief.[1] The general tone of Gnosticism is clear, though there are no distinctive traces of Valentinianism. It may have been no more than an intermediate stage between heathenism and orthodoxy, even if it left its mark for life, like Augustine's Manichaeism.

Bardaisan was a Syrian, and had little influence on the Greek world, though some of his works were translated into Greek. But his memory was cherished in Syria. When Ephraem Syrus reached Edessa more than a century later, he found the city "grievously infested with heresies, especially that of Bardaisan." His chief trouble was with the hymns, for the Bardesanists, like the Methodists, drew their inspiration from their hymns; and we have samples enough to shew something of their quality. The *Hymn of the Soul*, given in the Acts of Judas Thomas, is much the best religious allegory of early Christian times. Its general outline is this.

When I was a boy in the kingdom of my father's house, my father and my mother sent me on a journey from the East, our country. They furnished me richly from their treasures, but they took off the

[1] Eus. iv. 30. Bardaisan addressed a book on Fate "to Antoninus"— hardly Marcus or Caracalla, though it may be El Gabal or a private person, or just possibly Severus, who was an expert in astrology.

vesture of light which was their loving gift, and
the robe of purple they had fitted to my stature.
And they made a covenant with me, and wrote it
in my heart, that I might not forget it. If thou
wilt go down to Egypt and bring the pearl that is
in the sea, which the serpent guards, thou shalt have
thy vesture of light again and be our heir with thy
brother our Second, who reigneth with us. I left
the East with two companions, for I was young, and
the dangers of the way were many. I passed the
borders of Maishan,[1] reached the land of Babylon,
entered Sarbug, and came into Egypt; and there
my companions left me. I put on the dress of the
country, that they might not suspect me. But they
gave me of their meats to eat, and I forgot that I
was a king's son, and served their king, neither did
I remember the pearl, but fell into a deep sleep.
But my father and my mother knew what had befallen me, and they called a council of all the great
men of the East. They counselled that I was not
to be left in Egypt, and they wrote me a letter,
and all subscribed it. From thy father, the King
of kings, and from thy mother, the Queen of the
East, and from thy brother our Second,[2] to our son
in Egypt, greeting. Awake, arise from thy sleep.
Remember that thou art a king's son. See into
what slavery thou art fallen. Remember the pearl.
Remember thy vesture of light: that thy name may
be written in the book of heroes, and that thou
mayest inherit our kingdom with thy brother our
Second. The king sealed it with his right hand, to
guard it from the wicked children of Babylon and

[1] Mesene at the head of the Persian Gulf, where Trajan saw the ships
leaving for India.

[2] Note the Trinity. The Queen of course is the Holy Spirit.

the rebels of Sarbug. It flew in an eagle's form and lighted down before me. And it was written in the letter even as it was written in my heart. So I remembered that I was a king's son, and I remembered the pearl, and I enchanted the dragon with my father's name, and my mother's, and my brother's. I took the pearl, and essayed me to return to my father's house. I left the filthy dress of the country behind,[1] and the letter went before me, guiding me with its light. So I went past Sarbug, and kept Babylon on my left, and reached Maishan, the mart of merchants by the sea. Then from the mountains of Hyrcania my father and my mother sent me back again my vesture of light; and behold, it was all like me, and I was all like it. It blazed with jewels and with diamonds, and all over it the image of the King of kings was figured. I took it and put it on me and adorned myself with its beauty. I went up to the gate of the palace, I bowed my head and worshipped the glory of my father who had sent it to me, and I spoke with the princes, and I was with him in his kingdom, and they gave him glory, that he had done that which he had promised me.

The *Hymn of the Soul* is Eastern; the *Pilgrim's Progress* is Western. The one is pervaded with the Eastern's joy, that he is made in the image of God; the other reflects the sad consciousness of the Western, that sin has marred that image. Each is flecked with traces of its own sectarianism, and each rises to the heights where sects are all forgotten. Bardaisan's eyes are on the eternal counsel, Bunyan's on the deeps of human wickedness. Bardaisan's is

[1] No resurrection of the body.

the grander plan : yet after all, it is Bunyan who
brings his pilgrim to the cross of Christ.

Basilides taught at Alexandria in the time of
Hadrian, so that he must have flourished about the
same time as Valentinus, who came to Rome at a
later stage of his career. He called himself a disciple
of Glaucias, who was said to have been an
"interpreter" of Peter, as Mark was. He wrote
four and twenty books of commentaries (*Exegetica*)
on " the Gospel"—doubtless meaning not so much
the narrative as the spiritual mysteries he found in
it. We are not precisely told what written Gospels
he used; only that his account of all things after
(not including) the birth of Jesus agreed with that
found in our Gospels. The statement of Origen,
that he " had the impudence to write a Gospel
according to Basilides," appears to be a mistake.

Before we can go further, we have to face the
difficulty, that one account of Basilides is given by
Irenaeus and by writers dependent on the *Compendium*
of Hippolytus, another by Hippolytus in his later
and larger work, and that these two accounts entirely
disagree. The system ascribed to him by Irenaeus
is dualistic and more or less of the Valentinian sort,
while that described by Hippolytus is pantheistic
and strongly Greek. As they both used Basilidian
books, they must be describing different developments of the teaching. But is either of them the
system of Basilides himself? and if so, which? To
decide the question, we turn to Clement, who used
the *Exegetica*, and seems constantly appealing to
its author. His evidence is rather scanty, but upon
the whole it seems to leave little room for doubt
that Hippolytus is describing the system of Basilides,

Irenaeus that of the Basilidians he found in Gaul half a century later.

In the beginning, There was, when there was nothing; and the nothing was not even one of the things that are, but frankly nothing at all. Even the "was" is an accommodation, for that which is unspeakable is above every name, and cannot even be called unspeakable. There was nothing—no matter, no substance, nothing unsubstantial, nor simple, nor compound, nor intelligible, nor sensible, nor man, nor angels, nor God. Then a not-being God willed (without intelligence or feeling or counsel or purpose or passion or desire) to make a world. "Willed" is an accommodation again, and the world is not the world of space, but a seed of a world containing all things in it. Thus a not-being God made a not-being world of things that were not. From the seed came a triple Sonship, whereof one was light, which flew straight up to the not-being God, whom all things desire. A second was gross, and flew up too, taking the Holy Spirit as wings. But when they neared the not-being God, the Holy Spirit, as an inferior being, could go no further, but remained behind as a firmament, dividing the world from things above the world. The third Sonship needed purification, and remained in the seed. From this seed came forth the Great Archon, in power and beauty inexpressible. He lifted himself up to the firmament, and in his ignorance of anything beyond it, believed himself to be the supreme lord and master, and set about the making of the heavenly or ethereal world. He also had a son much better and wiser than himself (for such was the will of the not-being God) and set him on his right hand. This is the Ogdoad, where

GNOSTICISM

the Great Archon is seated. Then from the seed
arose another Archon, much less than the first
Archon, but inexpressible too and greater than all
else except the Sonship left behind : and he too had a
son better and wiser than himself. His place is the
Hebdomad, and he is the creator of all aerial things.
But in the seed, which is our earth, all things come to
pass by nature, and it has neither ruler nor providence
nor creator—only the plan which the not-being God
planned when he made the seed.

So when the world and the things above the world
were finished, it was necessary that the Sonship left
behind should be revealed and join the others. So
the Great Archon reigned in ignorance of the mystery
which to former generations was not made known.
And the other Archon reigned too. He it was who
said to Moses, I am the God of Abraham, Isaac and
Jacob, and the name of God (the Great Archon) I
declared not to them,[1] and he inspired all the prophets.
But when the time was come for us the children of
God to be revealed, the Gospel reached every rule and
authority and lordship and name that is named. But
nothing came down from above : the thoughts of the
Sonship below penetrated upward to the Holy Spirit,
who revealed them to the son of the Great Archon,
and he to the Great Archon himself, who now learned
that he was not the Supreme. So he feared, and confessed his pride. Then the son of the Great Archon
revealed it to the son of the other Archon, and he to
his father, who also feared and confessed. So the
whole Hebdomad received the light. Then from the
Hebdomad it came down on Jesus the son of Mary.
This is what is written, Holy Spirit shall come upon

---

[1] Exod. vi. 3, as they read it.

thee—that which comes from the Sonship through the
limitary Spirit to the Ogdoad and the Hebdomad and
reaches as far as Mary. So he was enlightened, being
kindled along with the light that shone upon him—no
doubt the fire on Jordan at his baptism. So every
Sonship must ascend after Jesus above the limitary
Spirit to the first Sonship. After this God will bring
on the world the Great Ignorance, that all things may
remain as they are by nature, and desire nothing
beyond, for the desire of things beyond is the source
of pain. It will overtake the Archon of the
Hebdomad, and even the Great Archon himself: and
this is the restoration of all things.

Basilides begins from the Platonic and generally
philosophical transcendentalism, which is itself in the
main one of the ways of thinking we have classed
as Oriental, and develops it out in approved philosophical style with a highest realm of not-being, and
three descending realms of aether, air and earth,
of which only the lowest is material. So far the
system is philosophical, not religious. We reach the
Gnosticism only when we come to a doctrine of the
elect, and the work of Christ to rescue them.

Irenaeus gives a very different account of the
Basilidian system. First Mind was born from the
ingenerate Father; then from Mind Logos, from
Logos Phronesis, from Phronesis Sophia and Dynamis,
and from these again the powers, principalities and
angels who made the first heaven. From these came
the angels of a second heaven, and so on till 365
successive heavens were made. The lowest of these
is the heaven we see; and these lowest angels are
the creators of the world and of men. They were
the authors of the prophecies, and the Law in

particular was given by their Archon, who is the
God of the Jews. And because he desired to subject
the rest of the nations to the Jews, the rest of the
angels and their peoples rebelled against him. But
when the ingenerate and ineffable Father saw that
the Jews were perishing, he sent his first-begotten
Mind, even him who is called Christ, to deliver
them that believed on him from the power of the
demiurgic angels. So he appeared on earth as a man,
though he was not really such, and did mighty
works. It was not he who suffered on the cross,
but Simon of Cyrene in his likeness, while Jesus
taking Simon's form stood unseen and mocked the
Jews, and afterward ascended unseen to the Father.
Wherefore if we confess him who was crucified, we
are still in bondage to the creators of the body,
whereas we are free if we deny the Crucified.

These Basilidians formed an esoteric school with
guarded mysteries. They said that they were no
longer Jews, but something more than Christians.
They were so puffed up with their hidden knowledge
that they ate without scruple things offered to idols,
denied Christ in time of persecution, and lived just
like heathens. They used magic and incantations
and invocations and all sorts of curious arts, and
counted outward acts indifferent, even if they were
acts of promiscuous immorality. Salvation of course
is limited to the soul. These are hostile accounts,
and may be overcoloured; but there is no reason to
doubt their general truth.

Basilides and these Basilidians have little in
common beyond the use of abstract names without
reference to sex, and a general tendency to secrecy.
We have here an extreme case of disciples altering

their master's doctrine till it can hardly be recognized. The strong pantheism of Basilides is gone, and the marked Greek character of his teaching is replaced by something much more like the Judaizing and Valentinian tone dominant in the Gnostic schools of the time.   Even the ethical teaching of Basilides was too high for his followers.   Blameless as he might be himself, his doctrine of election and requirement of silence easily lent itself to the widespread tendency to form esoteric schools of heathen living and heathen immorality.   Great as the difference is, it is no more than can be accounted for by the contrast of the original teaching with the influences around it.

We come now to schools of a more heathen sort, so heathen indeed that they can hardly be counted for Christian even in the loose sense of the word which would include Basilides.   Chief of these are the Ophites and Carpocrates.   The Ophites (or Gnostics proper) appear early, and stand rather for a number of coteries than for a definite school.   The difference in the accounts of them given by Irenaeus, by Hippolytus, and by Clement and Origen, may be explained partly by lapse of time, partly by real differences of different coteries, partly by the reliance of Hippolytus on books which may have represented nothing more than personal opinions of the writers.   We need not ourselves go beyond the account of Irenaeus.

The honour paid to the serpent is not peculiar to the Ophites, for there are traces of it among other Gnostics.   It is not even the most important part of their system : but it is the part which gave the deepest offence to the Christians.   It suited well the extreme opposition to Judaism, which turned the

Old Testament upside down, thinking that if the
Creator was bad, the serpent must be good. But it
actually arose rather from heathen sources ; and these
are to be found not in Greek philosophy, but in the
baser *paganismus* of serpent-worship, so common in
the superstitions and in the mysteries of Greece, and
of the East as far as India. That however we cannot
follow here ; and indeed it belongs almost as much to
archaeology as to history. The Ophites then had a
Trinity—the God of all whom they called the First
Man, his Conception or the Second Man, and under
these a female Holy Spirit moving on the face of the
waters. Of her the First and Second Man begat the
Third Man, even Christ, who flew upward with his
mother. But the light was more than she could
bear, and a spark of it fell downward as Sophia or
Prunikos on the waters, and assumed a body which
prevented her from flying up to heaven, though
presently she reached a middle region between the
waters and heaven. From her contact with the
waters was born Ialdabaoth, and from him came
without mother a series of six powers. These seven
created the seven heavens ; and when the six strove
with Ialdabaoth, from the dregs of matter he begot
the Nous of serpent form, from whom are spirit and
soul, but also wickedness and death. Then Ialdabaoth
gave himself out for the Supreme, despite his
mother's warning from on high. But when the six
powers had created man, and Ialdabaoth had breathed
into him the breath of life, he gave thanks to
the First Man, and not to Ialdabaoth. Whereupon
Ialdabaoth created a woman to destroy him ; and the
six powers were enamoured of her, and made her the
mother of the angels. Then Prunikos sent the

serpent to persuade Adam and Eve to transgress the command of Ialdabaoth; so they ate, received knowledge of the higher powers, and revolted from Ialdabaoth, who drove them down from paradise to earth. The Old Testament becomes a long battle of mankind secretly helped by Prunikos, against Ialdabaoth and his powers. At last the Holy Spirit had mercy on Prunikos; and Christ was sent down through the seven heavens to the earth, where a pure vessel was prepared for him in Jesus, who was born of a virgin. Then Christ was united as bridegroom and bride with his sister Prunikos, and they entered into Jesus, who thus became Jesus Christ, and began to work miracles and to declare himself the Son of the First Man. But only Jesus was crucified, for Christ and Prunikos had departed from him. He survived eighteen months, teaching his doctrine to a select few. And now that Christ is received into heaven, he sits at the right hand of Ialdabaoth, receiving the souls that are his, and emptying of light the kingdom of Ialdabaoth.

A sorry rigmarole; and yet there is method in the madness. The serpent plays but a small part, though in some coteries it was identified with Prunikos herself. But in a broad way the system reminds us of the Valentinian. There is a complicated cosmogony of the same sort, and Ialdabaoth roughly corresponds to the Great Archon. But the Great Archon sins in ignorance: Ialdabaoth sins against light, and is essentially evil. We miss also the poetic colouring and the touches of Greek philosophy: the Ophite system is Eastern and prosaic.

Though we are nowhere directly told the date of Carpocrates, we know that his follower Marcellina

came to Rome in the time of Anicetus, "and ruined
many." We may therefore pretty safely fix
Carpocrates himself a little earlier — say 140-150.
He begins in the usual way with a Supreme and
demiurgic angels, the first of whom is "the
Adversary."[1] He soon reaches a thorough-going
licentiousness. The Law is the work of the angels,
and the distinctions of right and wrong are arbitrary.
It is the Gnostic's duty to defy them, for he is
not saved by works, but by faith and love. Jesus
was only a man like other men, and owed his power
to his better reminiscence of the things he had seen
with God in a former life—a clear piece of Platonism.
Other men may do as much if they remember as
much, and even surpass the works of Jesus with
works of magic. But the demiurgic angels have
the right (on complaint of the Adversary) to detain
every soul for new transmigrations till it "has paid
the uttermost farthing" by exhausting all the possi-
bilities of sin ; and it is only a few strong souls like
Jesus who are able to do all wickedness in one
lifetime. So the followers of Carpocrates were
grossly immoral, and brought much discredit on
the Christian name. So far Irenaeus.

Carpocrates married a woman of Cephallene, and
had a son called Epiphanes, who died at the age
of seventeen. This Epiphanes was a forward youth,
who did credit to his father's worthy teaching, and
after his death had a temple, and was worshipped
in his mother's town of Same with offerings every
new moon. He wrote a book "On Justice," from
which Clement of Alexandria gives an extract.
Epiphanes tells us that God's justice is founded on

[1] Mt. v. 25.

equality.   Heaven covers all, the stars shine on all
and no man can rob his neighbour of sunlight, or
seize for himself a double portion.   It is not God
who makes a difference between rich and poor,
learned and simple, male and female, freeman and
slave, ruler and subject.   Men created laws and
invented property to destroy the communism of God.
Their *meum* and *tuum* mar the harmony of the
universe.   Laws have made the thief and the
adulterer—for woman should not belong to one
man.   It is the ordinance of God that love must
be free.

   Irenaeus himself seems to have some doubt whether
his account of these men is not too bad to be true.
Of their practical immorality there need be no
question ; but perhaps they did not go quite so far
in theory as Epiphanes.   This young man has been
explained as a confusion with the moon-god, and it
is not impossible that Clement has ascribed to him
the work of an older writer ; but upon the whole
the story hangs together, and seems historical.   No
doubt Epiphanes is a strange creature to be made a
god ; but the Greeks of his time were not squeamish
in their choice of gods.   He is not worse than
Antinous.

   Marcion of Sinope flourished at Rome in the
time of bishop Anicetus ; but his first arrival in the
city must have been much earlier.   He was a well-
to-do shipmaster, and presented a considerable sum
of money to the church.   Presently he fell into bad
company—that of the Syrian Cerdo, who had already
reached Rome in the days of bishop Hyginus.   He
taught that the God of the Old Testament, being
only righteous, is not the good Supreme, who was

unknown till the coming of Christ. Marcion worked
out this idea, " blaspheming shamelessly " the God
of the Jews as a worker of evil and a lover of
wars, and moreover changeable and inconsistent in
his commands. Such doctrine found no favour at
Rome : Marcion was expelled, and his money was
returned to him. After this he seems to have been
a great wanderer (perhaps on his business) before
settling down in Rome in the time of Anicetus. At
some time or other he met Polycarp, and asked
him to recognize him. " I recognize—the Firstborn
of Satan." [1]

Polycarp was not far wrong, for Marcion was
counted a still more dangerous enemy than Valentinus.
Almost every church writer assails him, from Justin
onward ; and with good reason. Nothing shews
better the vagueness of the term Gnostic than its
application to such a man as Marcion, who entirely
denied the difference of the Gnostic from the common
Christian which the word implies. Marcion's was
a spirit of devout and sober realism which rejected
myths and allegories, and sought to build on the letter
of St. Paul. His bald literalism was utterly unlike
the poetry of Valentinus and the logic of Basilides,
and was for that reason the more attractive to the
profanum vulgus of the unimaginative, especially

[1] We need not notice the story told by Ps.-Tert. (more fully Epiph.) that
Marcion was the son of a bishop, and was expelled by his own father for
seduction before he came to Rome. The story is not told by Irenaeus or by
Tertullian (not a likely man to pass it over) and it agrees with neither his
asceticism nor his reception at Rome, nor yet with the earnest Christian
feeling we see in him. It may be too literal a rendering of the charge that
he corrupted the church.

The date of his famous meeting with Polycarp is not certain. We know
that Marcion was flourishing at Rome in the time of Anicetus, and we know
that Polycarp came to Rome in the time of Anicetus, and we naturally
connect the two facts : but we cannot be certain.

among the women, for the prominence of women is
quite a feature of Marcionism. What most impressed
him in the Gospel was its novelty, and its contrast
with the imperfections of the world and Judaism.
Surely they cannot have the same author. The hard
and righteous God of the Old Testament cannot be
the good Supreme. He is limited—does not know
where to find Adam in the garden—creates evil, stirs
up wars, changes his mind : and if none but the Son
knows the true Supreme, the prophets cannot have
known him. True, the God of the Jews is the creator,
or rather the fashioner of this world, for matter is
not of his creation, but an eternal evil which he has
not power to conquer : nor can he give more than a
limited reward to men, or rather to the Jews only—
and even on them he imposes a law which they cannot
keep. Above him stands the good Supreme in his
heavenly world, unknown in past ages. Suddenly,
as it is written in the beginning of the Gospel of
Marcion, in the fifteenth year of Tiberius Caesar the
Son of God came down (from heaven) and taught in
the synagogue at Capernaum. He came in the likeness of man, but the likeness was only apparent; and
he came to reveal the unknown Father. He was not
the Christ promised by the Creator, who was to be a
great conqueror, and to conquer for the Jews only,
whereas the Son of God was to suffer, and to suffer
for the sins of the whole world. He came not to fulfil
the Law but to destroy it, and therefore the Creator
stirred up the Jews to crucify him. His teaching
was a teaching of faith and love, and of ascetic
practice, for the body has no share in salvation. The
Marcionites renounced flesh and wine and marriage,
receiving married persons only as catechumens. The

austerity of their morals is acknowledged even by
Tertullian, and confirmed by the number of their
martyrs, for they had none of the Basilidian untruth.
No wonder they were counted the most dangerous of
all the Gnostic sects.

On this theory the Christianity of the time must
have been much falsified by Judaizers, and needed a
good deal of amendment.   Marcion set aside the Old
Testament of course, and with it the Fourth Gospel,
the Epistle to the Hebrews and the Apocalypse.   Of
the rest he selected two, which he called the Gospel
and the Apostle.   His Gospel was our St. Luke,
though not under that name, purified of everything
which connects our Lord with nature and with
history.   Leaving out the first two chapters and
sundry other passages, he was able to retain about
two thirds of it ; and the minute analysis of his results
by Tertullian and Epiphanius enables us not only to
fix the contents of his Gospel with scarcely half a
dozen verses left uncertain, but to see that he had it
in a Western text.   The theory that Marcion's is the
original Gospel and ours an expansion of it is de-
cisively refuted by the evidence of Irenaeus and the
rest, by the state of the text, by the evident reasons
for the omissions, and by the uniformity of the
language throughout our Gospel.   In Tertullian's
words, Marcion criticized with a penknife.[1]   The
Apostle consisted of ten of St. Paul's Epistles,
arranged nearly in chronological order.   The Pastoral
Epistles were wanting ; also the references to Abraham
in the Galatians and the last two chapters of the
Romans ; and that to the Ephesians was inscribed to
the Laodicenes.

[1] Tert. *Praescr.* 38 exserta et palam machaera, non stilo usus est.

The Marcionites formed a separate sect, organized apparently on the model of the other churches. The sacraments were as usual, except that baptism was refused to married persons, and perhaps occasionally performed by women. In the Lord's Supper they had water instead of wine, and seemed to have allowed the catechumens to witness the ceremony. They probably fasted like the stricter churchmen, but they shewed their opposition to the Jews by choosing the sabbath for a fast day.

Marcion's theory cannot be called successful. In some ways indeed it is more open to objection than most of the Gnostic systems. For instance, it destroys not only our Lord's manhood, but even his truthfulness, for no criticism can get rid of the fact that he claimed (on Marcion's theory, claimed falsely) to be the Christ sent by the God of the Jews. But the most radical objection is that the separation of righteousness from goodness turns both into vices.[1] Righteousness without goodness is merciless hardness, goodness without righteousness is weak good nature which slides quite easily into cruelty. The good God never punishes : he only leaves the men who are by nature carnal to the mercies of the merciless Creator. This is just as bad as the worst form of Calvinism.

It was at a real difficulty that Marcion broke down, so we need not count him like Tertullian, as worse than all the horrid beasts of Scythia. The

[1] Tert. *adv. Marcionem* i. 22 Talis et in deum Marcionis sententia dicenda est, mali permissorem, iniuriae fautorem, gratiae lenocinatorem, benignitatis praevaricatorem, quam non statim caussae suae exhibuit ; plane, si natura bonus, exhibiturus, et non accessione, si ingenio optimus et non disciplina, si ab aevo deus et non a Tiberio, imo, quod verius, a Cerdone et Marcione.

Id. 27 O deum veritatis praevaricatorem etc.

contrast of the New Testament with the Old has
been a stumbling-block in all ages. The Jews
declared that they came from different authors, and
refused the New Testament. Marcion agreed, but
rejected the Old. Orthodox writers held that the
two were not inconsistent with each other, but they
only reconciled them by a free use of allegory. To
ourselves both these methods are closed. Improved
criticism has shewn that allegory is an unsound
method, and improved science has made a final
dualism of good and evil untenable. Whatever the
world may be, it is built on a single plan. We should
be in a worse case than they that came before us,
if the improvement of criticism and science together
had not set in a new light the historical growth
of the revelation, so that we can accept the Old
Testament as a stage of it, imperfect, but good till
that which is perfect came. This is the doctrine
of the New Testament itself, as in the Epistle to
the Hebrews, and a dim perception of it was enough
to save the Early Church from the dangers of
Marcion's audacious criticism.

We have already seen among the Apologists
Tatian the Assyrian, the "founder" of the Encratites.
Though he was not of Marcion's school, he may
here be classed with him as a writer of similar spirit
and similar principles. He was a disciple of Justin,
and it was not till after Justin's death that he broke
with the church and returned to Assyria. Eusebius
places it in 172; but the dates in his *Chronicle* are
often rough. Tatian recognized one God with aeons
in the Valentinian style; but he agreed with Marcion
in his sharp opposition of the Creator to the Supreme,
in his general tone of practical and ascetic devotion,

and specially in his prohibition of wine and flesh
and marriage. Like Marcion, he was counted a
heretic in the West; but unlike Marcion, he was
honoured in the Syrian churches as the author of
the Diatessaron, or harmony of the Gospels, which
was much used in Syria till the fifth century, and
strongly influenced the text of the *dampharreshe*
which replaced it. The dispute over its character
which raged some thirty years ago has been set at
rest by the discovery in an Armenian translation
of Ephraem's commentary, dating from the fourth
century, and since then of free translations of the
Diatessaron itself into Arabic and Latin. We see
now that it was a harmony or continuous narrative
pieced together from our four Gospels, apparently
in a Western text, but without any uncanonical
material. It began with the Prologue of St. John's
Gospel, and left out the genealogies and everything
else that implies our Lord's descent from David.

The Marcionites had their divisions like others;
and they are rather maliciously exaggerated by our
chief informant Rhodon, who having himself been
a disciple of Tatian, was set against tenets which
resembled those of his former master. Thus Syneros
and the Assyrian Prepon were not really diverging
from Marcion when they spoke of three first principles
instead of two, for Marcion himself might very well
have recognized one in his eternal evil matter.
Apelles however drew nearer to the church. He
confessed but one unknown God, making the Creator
a great angel in the style of the early Gnostics, who
had made this world on the model of the heavenly
world, and made it badly, and repented of it. The
God of the Jews was a still lower being. Apelles had

taken over in full measure Marcion's dislike of the
Old Testament, and devoted a large part of his
numerous writings to the "mistakes of Moses." He
was an old man when Rhodon met him, and much
respected. "And when I said, Where is your
demonstration that there is but one first principle,
if the prophets are self-convicted of falsehood, for
they disagree with each other and tell lies and are
not consistent with themselves? he answered that
he did not know. And when I adjured him to tell
me the truth, he swore that he spoke truly. He did
not know how there is one ingenerate God, but so
he believed it is. Then I mocked him. You call
yourself a teacher, and cannot prove what you teach."
Rhodon tells the story without seeing that his own
temper contrasts badly with the charity of Apelles,
who declared that "those who put their trust in
the Crucified will be saved, if only they are found
in good works." On another point also, Apelles
came nearer to the church, for he held that the
Lord's body was real, though heavenly, so that his
sufferings were real.

After all, we owe something to the Gnostics.
There is no mean thinking in some of their strange
theories, and no little moral earnestness in others.
We cannot mistake the lofty tone of Marcion, the
noble charity of Apelles, or the genuine horror with
which Basilides and Valentinus repudiate the possibility that God may be the author of wrong and outrage.[1] Again, the asceticism of the Gnostics was as
good as that of the monks. Mischievous as it was, it
was no more than theirs the conduct of godless men.
Marcion may have been the Firstborn of Satan for

[1] Fragments of Basilides and Valentinus in Stieren's *Irenaeus* pp. 903, 912.

perverting the oracles of God ; but he is the last man who can be accused of perverting them to serve his own lusts. The Gnostics contributed a good deal to the thoughts and language of the growing theology of the church, and (though for this we owe them few thanks) they were in many directions the forerunners of mediaeval developments. Among them, for instance, we find the first traces of images, Mariolatry and transubstantiation, and of the gorgeous heathen ceremonialism which overcame the churches in the fourth century. Imperfect as their exegesis was, they wrote commentaries like those of Basilides and Heracleon, discussed the criticism of the New Testament, like Tatian and Marcion, and studied at large both doctrine and ethics. Some however of their most lasting work was of a literary sort, and of a more doubtful character. It was they more than others who shaped the apostolic history into ascetic romances whose influence is hardly even yet extinct, and they whose speculations chiefly softened the contrast of Christian literature with that of the world around.

Let there be no mistake : the contest was vital. Gnosticism undermined Christian monotheism by its distinction of the Creator from the Supreme, Christian morals by its opposition of the philosopher to the unlearned, Christian practice by its separation of knowledge from action ; and it cut away the very basis of the Gospel whenever it explained away its history. In every case it had got hold of truth on one side—the reality of evil in the world, the function of knowledge in religion, the difference between the letter and the spirit : but fragments of truth are not enough for a Gospel which is false if all truth is not summed up in Christ. Therefore there could be no peace between the Gnostic *illuminati* and the Christian churches.

This may be the place for such notice of Manichaeism as we shall find needful. It may be treated shortly, for it is an obscure subject which Western students can hardly discuss at first hand, and it is not very nearly connected with Christianity before the Nicene age. Manichaeism then is separated from Gnosticism by the fact that it places Mani above Christ. It is rather a rival religion like Islam than a version of Christianity. It arose later than Gnosticism, lay further East, and while it agreed with Gnosticism in having Persian dualism for its chief element, it differed by allowing this to be materialized by a second element of Chaldean cosmology, and throwing Christianity even more into the background than Carpocrates had done. Perhaps it was known to Mani, as it was to Mahomet, chiefly in its more degraded forms. A further influence of Buddhism is more than possible, but does not seem fully proved.

Mani[1] was born *cir.* 216 near Ctesiphon. His father was a Persian of rank, a settler from Ecbatana, and his mother was related to the Parthian Arsacidae. He laid his doctrine before Sapor I. (240-269) in that king's early years, and then undertook extensive travels in the direction of India and China. In Sapor's last years he returned to Persia and was arrested, but managed to escape. Under Hormuz I. he was in favour at the court; but Bahram I. crucified him (*cir.* 276) and began a vigorous persecution of

[1] In my account of Mani and his doctrine I have thought it better in most things frankly to follow v. Schubert *K.G.* 309-312 than to meddle with original sources which require a knowledge of sundry Eastern languages.

The latest account of Mani (with list of books) is in Gibb and Montgomery's edition of Augustine's *Confessions* p. xxi.

his followers. Their headquarters were in the East,
between Taurus and Media, where they had affinity
with Marcionites and others. They began to trouble
the Empire about 280, and the first mention of them
in the law books is the edict of Diocletian in 296;
but they did not become important before the time
of Constantine. Diocletian burned " their abominable
books"; but in the next generation the learned count
Musonianus translated them into Greek by Constantine's command.[1]

The system begins with a Persian dualism of light
and darkness, in contrast as good and evil; not
however as ideal principles, but rather as primary
elements. The First Man, begotten by the King of
Light, is worsted by the powers of darkness, and is
not rescued without leaving some of the light imprisoned in the realm of darkness. A part of this is
recovered and placed in the sun, moon, and stars
when the God of Light creates the material world.
To make sure of the rest of it, Satan begets Adam,
and puts it into him. But as this makes the light
prevail in him, he sets beside him Eve, in whom the
darkness prevails. In spite of the warnings of the
spirits of light, especially Jesus, Adam gives way to
sensual desire, and begets Seth. Thereupon begins
a struggle for the possession of men between the
demons and the spirits of light. Moses and the
prophets and the Jewish Messiah were servants of
Satan. To the prophets of light belong Seth, Noah,
Abraham, Zoroaster, Jesus, and Paul : but Jesus was
a spirit of light in the mere appearance of a man, and
the last and greatest of them all was Mani the
Paraclete. In the Elect, who wholly follow after

[1] Ammianus xv. 13. 2.

Mani, there is so complete a separation of light and
darkness that their souls are able to ascend straight
to the kingdom of light; but common believers can
only follow them after severe trials. In the end, the
souls of the unredeemed and the bodies of all men are
assigned to the kingdom of darkness, and the kingdom
of light is finally separated from it.

The Elect were distinguished from the Hearers or
Catechumens by three signs—by the *signaculum oris*
were forbidden foul words, eating of things with life,
and drinking of wine; by the *signaculum manuum*,
all business with the things of the material world
which could be avoided; by the *signaculum sinus*,
all sexual intercourse. They also had an elaborate
system of washings, fastings, and times of prayer;
and amongst their prayers were some to Mani. The
catechumens were a sort of proselytes, required to
observe only the "ten commandments" against
idolatry, witchcraft, murder, whoredom, lying, etc.,
to serve the Elect, to give them their herbs, and to
ask their prayers and blessings.

The sect was governed by the ascending orders of
Elders, Bishops, and Teachers; and above them all
there seems to have been a Pope, or Successor of
Mani, at Babylon. The public worship was of the
usual sort, but Baptism was with oil, and the Communion with bread only, and the day of the Founder's
death was observed in March.

It will be seen that nothing here is rather Christian
than Mithraic, except the names of Jesus and Paul
and the Paraclete. Even the idea of redemption,
which the Gnostics connected with Christ, is here
assigned to Mani. Except perhaps in its two
sacraments, the system is at almost every point less

Christian than Islam—in its dualism, in its rejection of Judaism, in its asceticism, in its double standard, and in the almost divine position assigned to Mani.

BOOKS

Mansel *Gnostics* ; Arts. by Hort and Salmon in *D.C.B.* ; Brooke *Fragments of Heracleon* in *Texts and Studies* ; Bevan, A. A. *Hymn of the Soul* in *Texts and Studies* ; Buonaiuti, E. *Lo Gnosticismo* Roma 1907 (excellent sketch) ; Peake, *Basilides* in Hastings' *Dict. Rel. and Ethics*; Schmidt, Carl. *Koptisch-Gnostische Schriften* (for Syrian Gnostics).

CHAPTER XVI

MONTANISM

In the same sense as Gnosticism is Christianity perverted by learning and speculation, Montanism is Christianity perverted by fear of learning and speculation. While the one refines away the Gospel into a philosophy, the other debases it into a coarse revivalism, equally opposed to the intellectual pride of the Gnostics and to the dignified traditionalism of the subapostolic church.

The author of Montanism was a convert, perhaps a converted priest of Cybele, its birthplace Ardabau [1] in Mysia, on the border of Phrygia, and its date may be roughly fixed near the middle of the second century.[2] Now Phrygia was the centre of the movement — the Montanists were often called Phrygians [3]—and the religion of Phrygia, high up the Asiatic tableland, was very unlike that of the Greek cities which lay on the coast and along some of the

---

[1] Harnack suggests Κάρδαβα. The village is unknown.

[2] The question is obscure, and historians are divided on it. We have *cir.* 130 de Soyres, *cir.* 156 Bonwetsch and Harnack (*Chronologie* i. 365 sq.) *cir.* 172 Völter and Hilgenfeld. The first date seems too early, the last is much too late, for Maximilla's death seems fixed near 179 ; and as she was the last of the three pillars of Montanism, its origin must lie certainly behind 172, and perhaps behind 156. It would be settled if we knew when Gratus was proconsul of Asia.

[3] οἱ κατὰ Φρύγας, or in Latin *Cataphryges.*

lowland valleys.   It was a hotbed of superstitions in
heathen times, and afterward of Christian heresies.
It was the Holy Land of the Montanists, the adopted
home of the Novatians, the headquarters of Marcellus ;
and even its orthodoxy differed in spirit from the
Greek.[1]   The heathen superstitions (like those of
Syria) tended at once to licence and asceticism ; but
no immorality stains the austere puritanism of the
Christian sects in Phrygia, and even their asceticism
was as far as possible from the abominations of Attis
and Cybele.   If the Montanists foreshadowed in one
direction the bold prophecy of the early Quakers, in
another they recall the timid legalism of the monks
and the Evangelicals.

Montanus himself seems to have been as insignificant a person as ever made a name in history ; but
he must have had strong followers, especially in the
prophetesses Priscilla and Maximilla.   Through them
the Paraclete spoke for the last time before Christ's
coming and the descent of the new Jerusalem on
Pepuza in Phrygia.   "After me no prophet more, but
the end," said Maximilla : and indeed the persecution
under Marcus might seem the sign of his coming, like
that of Nero a century before.   Therefore it behoved
them to have their loins girded and their lights
burning, like servants waiting for their Lord's return.
The churches were remiss, and needed bracing up.
They were delegating the universal call of Christian
men and women to mere officials, and settling down
among the pomps and vanities almost as comfortably
as if they were so many heathen clubs.   The remedy
was manifest.   As the Spirit of Prophecy had called
the churches into existence, so nothing but the Spirit

[1] *e.g.* the case of Glycerius. Ramsay *Ch. in the Roman Empire*, 443.

of Prophecy could renew them to the stricter life
which was fitting for strangers and pilgrims in these
last times. But the future must be greater than the
past. As the Law excelled the religion of Nature
and the Gospel excelled the Law, so must the dispensation of the Paraclete excel the Gospel, and be
the crown and consummation of the whole. Then at
last the church would have left its youth behind, and
reached its manhood.

It was not that the Montanists wanted to separate
from the church. Their first ideal was rather an
association within the church—a Society of Friends or
Methodists—which might be an *imperium in imperio*,
but was not an open enemy. In Phrygia, where
whole churches joined them, they regularly organized
it with stewards and financial arrangements. If the
church was worldly it was not heretical, and they
valued its ministrations—after their own. They had
no reason for separation, at least until the New
Prophecy was definitely rejected. Nor were the
bishops on their side eager for division. Some
bishops may have cast them out, and others gave
deep offence by trying to exorcise the prophetesses like
demoniacs; but others again leaned a good deal themselves to the Montanists, and a few went still further
in Chiliast fanaticism. So there was no great
question of separation for the present. But such
societies, even when the second generation softens
their first crudities, can seldom hold their ground
without developing into sects. Those without resent
their claim to be better than the church, and those
within push their peculiarities to separation. So it
has been with Quakers, Methodists and the Salvation
Army, all of whom have become practically sects;

and so it was presently with the Montanists. They
began as a local society with active prophets and on
the watch for Christ's return : they settled down at
last as a widespread sect with watch relaxed and
prophets occasional or none, distinguished from the
churches chiefly by Novatian discipline and general
rusticity.

The strength of the earlier Montanists was in their
vivid belief that the Holy Spirit was a power that
had not ceased to work spiritual wonders in the church.
But a restoration is always an exaggeration. They
claimed not simply to continue the apostolic line of
prophets after Quadratus and Ammia, but to have a
New Prophecy of more than apostolic splendour and
authority. The oracles of Montanus and the
prophetesses were the heralds of Christ's return to
reign a thousand years on earth ; and in that august
presence all worldly distinctions must be levelled, all
worldly living forborne. The gift of prophecy came
at his sovereign will, as well to women as to men.
This was orthodox, for if St. Paul had not allowed
women to teach, neither had he forbidden them to
prophesy.[1] So women play almost as great a part in
Montanism as in Phrygian heathenism. And if the
gift might come to any one, then all must be holy to
receive it. Nor would the holiness of the Gospel
suffice. Like the Law, the Gospel had allowed some
things only for the hardness of men's hearts, and in
the higher dispensation of the Paraclete such con-
cessions must be withdrawn. "The flesh had had its
play":[2] now the spirit must rule.

Gnosticism, Montanism and subapostolic Christi-

[1] 1 Cor. xiv. 34, 1 Tim. ii. 12, 1 Cor. xi. 5.
[2] Tert. de Pud. 6 Luserit ante Christum caro.

anity represent three permanent tendencies of human
nature, standing roughly for liberalism, for mysticism,
and for conservatism, with their characteristic dangers
of speculation without regard to facts, of feeling without regard to practice, and of practice without regard
to the inward witness. Each of them can therefore
be studied in its opposition to the other two. Gnosticism and Montanism contrasted sharply, while the
church endeavoured to steer between, though it leaned
more to the Montanist side than to the Gnostic.

In principle Montanism is the exact reverse of
Gnosticism. Just as the Gnostics referred everything
to man, so the Montanists referred everything to
God. Neither the one nor the other could rise to
the conception of inspiration as the meeting of God
and man, as equally the insight of holiness and its
divine reward. They degraded it, the one to godless
human reasoning, the other to a magic power over-
riding human nature. On one theory man does what
he pleases, and God is forgotten : on the other, God
does what he wills, and man is no more than a pen in
his hand. The prophet is entirely passive. He speaks
" in the Spirit by ecstatic vision," or as the Paraclete
says by Montanus, " Behold, a man is as a lyre, and
I hover round as the plectrum : the man sleeps, and
I watch ; behold it is the Lord who transports the
hearts of men, and gives them [new?] hearts." So
Maximilla, "The Lord sent me under compulsion,
willing and not willing." [1] To men who started with
such a conception of God and man and revelation,
human learning could not seem anything else than a

---

[1] These are the authoritative oracles of Montanism, and must not be set
aside as beliefs of the more ignorant Montanists. Maximilla's words resemble
1 Cor. ix. 16, but (if she is not contradicting Montanus) her point is that
she is passive in God's hands, not simply that the call is irresistible.

delusion and a snare; and the Gnostics were condemned at once for attempting to judge of revelation by reason, instead of accepting without question the plain meaning of the holy words delivered once for all from heaven. If St. John said a thousand years, must it not be a thousand years? So Gnosticism was impious presumption pure and simple, and the more completely they could contradict it, the safer they would be.

Nevertheless, the Montanists had more in common with the enemy than they knew. The likeness was partly in the conception of revelation, partly in the conception of holiness. For Christians, the Person of Christ is the full and final summing-up of truth, so that no development is possible but a fuller knowledge of that which was in Christ from the first. But the Gnostics with their speculation and the Montanists with their ecstasy agreed in adding to the Gospel things that are not in Christ, and sometimes plainly contradict his teaching. They made very different additions, but they agreed that the Person of Christ is not a final revelation.

They agreed again in the conception of holiness as ascetic, and in the resulting contrast between the enlightened or spiritual man—meaning themselves —and the vulgar or natural man, which was their description of their neighbours. Extremes meet, as usual. The Montanists might be saints, the Gnostics *illuminati*; but both stood in nearly the same relation to common churchmen. Both yielded more than the church of their time to the widespread ascetic reaction from a materialist age, and both in their several ways were more influenced by the aristocratic spirit of the ancient world.

The relation of Montanism to the church is more
complicated, because it was by no means one of
blind antagonism. The Montanists were no philosophers, but simple country folk who accepted the
historical tradition of the churches exactly as they
found it. In doctrine they were rigidly orthodox,
and even in practice they made no great changes.
Hardly one of their peculiarities but is defended by
second-century writers of unquestioned orthodoxy.
Late authors charge them with heresies and foul
immoralities: but the heresies are on questions
which in their time were unsettled, and the immoralities are only the usual slanders, summarily
refuted by the fact that nobody mentions them for
two hundred years. In fact, the churches had too
much in common with the Montanists to oppose
them very zealously. It was not at first denied
that prophecy, and that ecstatic prophecy, might
come at any time, even to women. Nor did it
seem of itself unlikely that the Holy Spirit should
extend the laudable custom of fasting, or impose
a sterner punishment on gross offenders, or forbid
the more or less discredited practice of second
marriage. Nobody doubted that Christ's coming
might be very near, or that the thousand years'
reign of the saints *might* prove literal. Even the
defiant spirit of martyrdom preached by the
Montanists would have had an enthusiastic admirer
in Ignatius. At first it seemed answer enough to say
that these particular prophets were false prophets : the
questions of principle only came to the surface gradually, and were never fully understood in early times.

The Montanists had a good deal to say for their
view of the world. They may have been too much

of pessimists, as reformers of the conservative sort commonly are; but the moral inferiority of their own age to the apostolic was dramatic, if not entirely real. Apostles and prophets raised up by God had given place to bishops and elders appointed by men; and the laity were putting off the royal dignity of the universal priesthood on officials. If we cannot safely say how far this state of things was a real decline from the past, the Montanists were certainly right in thinking it unsound; and they looked to the right quarter for the remedy, in an outpouring of the Spirit from on high. Nor were they mistaken in their belief that such an outpouring might be as real a power of life in their time as it ever was at Pentecost. But the natural man will not believe in the Spirit of Pentecost unless he sees the gifts of Pentecost. The man of little faith must have signs and wonders of one sort or another. True, the Montanists were not specially greedy of miracle: such marvels as they tell of are rather special judgments on wickedness than proper miracles.[1] But so much the more they looked for the visible sign of prophecy, and that in its commonly accepted[2]

---

[1] Like Tertullian's tales *de Spect.* 26 of one woman who returned from the theatre with a demon, and of another who did not survive her visit five days, or *de Idol.* 15 of a man grievously punished in a vision because his slaves had crowned his door with flowers, though he was himself away, and rebuked them when he came back.

[2] It seems evident that the Montanists only stated the current view of prophecy in their own time when they made it ecstatic. Athenagoras entirely agrees with them, Justin comes dangerously near them, and so do others, from the *Teaching* onward. There is really nothing on the other side till after the rise of Montanism. Then we have the treatise of Miltiades (if that be the right reading Eus. v. 16.) περὶ τοῦ μὴ δεῖν προφήτην ἐν ἐκστάσει λαλεῖν; and Clement of Alexandria makes ecstasy the mark of a false prophet. This ecstatic view is simply the heathen μαντεία; and its prevalence in spite of St. Paul's warning (1 Cor. xiv. esp. 32.) is significant in many directions.

form of ecstasy. Combining this with the belief
still not uncommon that Christ would very soon
return, they got a dispensation of the Paraclete
resting on the Gospel no doubt, but superior to
it and at certain points amending it. However
orthodox the Montanist might be,[1] his first allegiance
was given to the Paraclete and the "New Law,"
not to Christ and the Gospel.

What then was the message of the Paraclete,
and wherein did the righteousness of the New Law
exceed the righteousness of the Gospel? The points
of difference are three, concerning fasting, marriage
and church discipline. These we will take in order.
The early Christians took over from Judaism the
practice of fasting, and the bishops even commanded
fasts, though they followed Christ's teaching[2] to the
extent of leaving a good deal of liberty to the
individual. The full scheme of strict piety (probably
carried out by few) was to keep Easter with a festal
season till Pentecost, to hold *stationes* (partial fasts)
on Wednesdays and Fridays, and to keep the fast
of Good Friday,[3] which was already developing in
the direction of Lent. To this the Montanists added
two weeks (less Saturday and Sunday) of dry meats.[4]
Later writers mention other fasts, and they may be
right for later Montanists; but these are all that
Tertullian admits; and his witness is decisive for his
own time. These however the Paraclete made a law.

---

[1] Tert. *de Jej.* 1 Hi paracleto controversiam faciunt, propter hoc novae
prophetiae recusantur, non quod alium deum praedicent Montanus et
Priscilla et Maximilla, non quod Jesum Christum solvant (1 Joh. iv. 3 λύει)
nec quod aliquam fidei et spei regulam evertant, sed quod plane doceant
saepius jejunare, quam nubere.

[2] Mt. ix. 14-17 is decisive, that a church which makes fasting a *law* is
acting *ultra vires*.   [3] Tert. *de Jej.* 14.

[4] The ξηροφαγίαι meant abstinence from soups and succulent fruits.

With regard to marriage, the Montanists leaned more than the church to asceticism. If they did not forbid it like some of the Gnostics, they seem to have been more decided than the church in ranking marriage below virginity. Tertullian already has something of that unwholesome dwelling on the physical fact which did so much harm in later times; and many of his arguments against a second marriage are just as good against a first. He expresses nobly the Christian view of marriage as a blessing; yet the ascetic view is never far off, that it is little better than fornication with a sort of licence meant only for the weak. Second marriage however the Montanists definitely forbade. It was very commonly regarded as a more or less discreditable concession to the flesh, and Athenagoras goes the length of calling it a respectable adultery. The position indicated in this phrase is that of the Montanists, who forbade it on the ground that marriage is a contract for eternity. Here again the Paraclete contradicted Christ, for the point of his answer to the Sadducees is precisely this, that marriage is a relation for this life only, " till death us do part." So too St. Paul takes it, stating that the widow is free to marry again, and actually wishing the younger widows to do so.[1]

Concerning penance: we can now take up the whole subject again. Christ's teaching is clear. Forgiveness is free, in the sense that repentance (the new mind, not torments of remorse, and still less satisfaction) is all that God requires—and unlimited, in the sense that it is as free as ever to the man who has sinned until seventy times seven. Furthermore, if God's

[1] Lu. xx. 34-36, Rom. vii. 2, 1 Tim. v. 14 (widows especially, as the context shews).

forgiveness is the model he sets forth to men, and if
God's punishments are only "the goodness that leadeth
us to repentance," and even in the other world are
purely remedial,[1] it follows that church discipline has
no right to go beyond the reformation of the offender.
As soon as we are sure of that, others will cease to
need protection from his bad influence. This is the
principle on which St. Paul deals with the Corinthian
offender. If they are satisfied of his repentance, he
directs them to restore him unconditionally, warning
them against driving him to despair; and if he delivers
Hymenaeus and Alexander unto Satan, it is not that
they may be damned, but "that they may learn not
to blaspheme."[2]

But Christ's teaching was too simple for men who
lived under Caesar's rule, and measured God's mercy
by Caesar's justice. However, all were agreed that
the church has no concern with sins committed before
baptism, except to warn the convert against them,
and to make him give up any evidently sinful ways of
living. Even after Baptism, it was as impossible for
the church as for the state to punish sins as sin, and
therefore all sins. All that could be done was to
single out some sins as gross scandals, and expel these
worst offenders till they came to a better mind.
Before long, penitence was required to be shewn in the
outward form of penance—sackcloth and ashes, mourning, fasting, asking intercession of the brethren,
beseeching the elders[3]—and Tertullian only expresses

---

[1] Rom. ii. 4. Mt. xxv. 46 εἰς κόλασιν (not τιμωρίαν) αἰώνιον. κόλασις is
remedial even in Acts iv. 21—teach them not to tell lies about a resurrection,
as Caiaphas would have said.

[2] 2 Cor. ii. 5-11, 1 Tim. i. 20.

[3] Tert. de Poen. 9. The ὄλεθρος τῆς σαρκός to which St. Paul delivers the
Corinthian offender was taken to be penance.

the current opinion when (here again contradicting
Christ's repeated teaching) he refuses to believe that
penitence can be real without penance. But proofs
of penitence before long became punishment—so
long for such a sin—and the idea that these ascetic
observances are of themselves meritorious easily led
to a belief that penance was not simply a *satisfactio*,[1]
but a satisfaction, not only to the church for the
scandal caused, but to God for the sin committed.
So grew up that fatal confusion of crime and sin
which made possible the inhuman penitential system
of the third and fourth centuries, and even now in
Latin countries practically replaces the idea of sin
against God by that of disobedience to the church.

Penance was imposed by the church itself, and
naturally by the bishop when he became its representative. In Tertullian's time he seems to have
dealt summarily with the lighter offences. The
confessors however, who held a quasi-official position
in the church, had a great influence till Cyprian's
time, and their intercession was not lightly refused.
But, at least in the third century, it seems to have
been the bishop who pronounced the sentence, and
the bishop who received back the penitent by the
laying-on of hands when the penance was completed.

There seems to have been little doubt before
Novatian's time, that the church "had authority to
forgive"[2] any sin whatever. So much even the
Montanists formally allowed. But on what conditions?

[1] *Satisfactio* is a form of *solutio*—the destruction of an obligation, and
does not of itself mean that the penance is an equivalent or payment for
the sin.
[2] The dangerous ambiguity will be noticed. Does the church forgive the
scandal against itself or the sin against God? But we can leave it till it
comes to the front in Cyprian's time.

The tendency has always been to limit Christ's free gift to the grace of Baptism, and after it to make forgiveness depend on some sort of good works— which is one way of denying that Christ died for our sins. And surely God's honour requires satisfaction as much as Caesar's honour, and the more exacting the good works of penance can be made, the better it will be vindicated. The natural man takes much better care of it than God himself. So there was a strong party of opinion that if gross offenders were not to be summarily expelled, it was at any rate impossible to make their penance too severe. So utterly did they forget St. Paul's warning. So far as we can judge from our scanty information, the confessors rather inclined to leniency, and the bishops generally moderated between them and the zealots; but the general issue of the discipline controversies was that while even the worst sinners were in the end admitted to penance, this penance was made so cruelly severe that in the fourth century its chief results were the discouragement of baptism, the manufacture of hypocrites, and the general embitterment of party spirit.

Meanwhile said the Paraclete by the Montanist prophets, "The church has power to forgive sins; but I will not do it, lest men commit other sins." [1] This refusal to use the power of forgiveness made it necessary to divide the graver sins into remissible and irremissible. It was agreed that God might forgive both; but it was not expedient for the church to forgive the latter. But on what principle were they to make the division? It is a return to paganism when one outward act is declared to be *in itself* more

[1] Tert. *de Pud.* 21.

sinful than another : but if an essentially absurd division is to be made, it can only be done by assimilating sin to crime, selecting the acts which do most harm, and perhaps taking a hint from our Lord's list of the unclean things that proceed out of the heart.[1] So they got their catalogue of seven "more heinous and utterly ruinous sins which cannot be forgiven—murder, idolatry, fraud, denial of the faith, blasphemy, and of course adultery and fornication, and any other violation of the temple of God. For these sins Christ will plead no more ; these sins no man that is born of God will ever commit, and no man who has committed them shall be a child of God." [2] If this is not a slander on Christ's mercy, it is hard to say what would be. This however is the Montanist position, and it makes nugatory their admission that God may forgive even these sins. Here again the Paraclete has contradicted Christ.[3]

These three would seem to be the only points on which the Montanists altered the recognized practice of their own time. Tertullian's objection to Infant Baptism is not a fourth, for we have seen that Infant Baptism was an open question long after Tertullian's time. But it is to be noted that his arguments— e.g. Why should such a burden be laid on infants ?— depend largely on the broad distinction, drawn more broadly by Montanists than by others, between sin before and after Baptism. If the matter is put on that ground, we must simply choose between trust in

---

[1] Mt. xv. 19.   [2] Tert. de Pud. 19.

[3] It is worth notice that the seven "capital" sins (which include those "deadly" sins which the Church of Rome will not forgive without confession to a priest) are not identical with the seven "irremissible" sins of the Montanists, which the church cannot prudently forgive at all. They agree in a practical denial of Christ's mercy ; but they have little more in common.

him who welcomed the little children, and took them up in his arms and blessed them ; and the Montanist fear that of such as sin after Baptism, he may not be willing to save to the uttermost all that come to him. Is there any limit to his mercy but impenitence ?

Upon the whole, Montanism was blameless as touching orthodoxy, and not very schismatic in practice—less so than Methodism near the end of Wesley's lifetime. It had real merits as a protest which was needed on behalf of spiritual religion against the growth of a mechanical officialism and the layman's forsaking of his royal calling to a higher priesthood than that which offers sacrifices for sin. It had seeming merits also, for there must have been many who looked more or less kindly on its busy revivalism, its enthusiastic expectation of the Lord's return, and its sturdy defiance of an ungodly state. Its ecstatic theory of prophecy seemed to many no more than the honour due to God, while its asceticism, its extra fasts, its penitential rigour and its condemnation of second marriage would be at worst mistakes in the right direction. The most doubtful practice was the employment of women : and even this might be defended, for the Montanists did not suffer them to teach in church or to perform any ministerial act whatever ; and surely there was no great harm in letting them tell their spiritual experiences—after service only—to a select few.[1]

---

[1] Tert. *Virg. vel.* 9 *Non permittitur mulieri in ecclesia loqui, sed nec docere, nec tinguere, nec offerre, nec ullius virilis muneris, nedum sacerdotalis officii sortem sibi vindicare.* This in his Montanist days : before this *Praescr.* 41 *Ipsae mulieres haereticae, quam procaces ! quae audeant docere, contendere, exorcismos agere, curationes repromittere, forsitan et tingere.* He gives the Montanist practice (some would call it an evasion) in *de Anima* 9 *Est hodie soror apud nos revelationum charismate sortita, quas in ecclesia inter dominica sollemnia per ecstasin in spiritu patitur ; conversatur cum angelis,*

Even this was full of danger, told as it was in
regular meetings and not in the natural intercourse
of life; but the deadly mischief was done when they
were encouraged to look for visions, and those visions
(after "diligent testing" by sympathetic hearers)
were allowed not only to forbid or enjoin in the
Spirit's name things which Christ left unforbidden or
uncommanded, but to forbid or enjoin on principles
directly opposed to Christ's teaching. This was
anarchy. It set aside the Gospel as effectually as
Gnosticism, and we rather wonder why it did not
more generally lead to crying scandals. The Montanists would seem to have been like the early
Methodists, essentially a sane and earnest people
with occasional excesses kept in bounds by strong
and sober chiefs. They had their martyrs too, some
not of the sort who provoke their fate by fanatic
insolence. Blandina herself is not a nobler martyr
than the Montanist Perpetua. With all their faults,
they were a living force in Christendom. They had
indeed the Spirit of Christ, but not as they fancied,
in their mischievous ecstasy.

The men of their own time did them both more
and less than justice. Setting aside partizans and
heresy-hunters like Apollonius, we find that common
opinion passed over too leniently the practice and even
the theory of Montanism, finding the chief offence
in its claims to spiritual authority. This was just
offence, both to Greek moderation and to Christian
soberness. Yet clearer Christian thought would not

---

interdum cum domino, et videt et audit sacramenta. . . . Post transacta
sollemnia dimissa plebe . . . solet nobis renuntiare quae viderit, nam et
diligentissime digeruntur, ut etiam probentur. Elsewhere he speaks of a
Montanist church which had seven virgins waiting for visions, and doubtless
not in vain

have failed to discover in Montanism, behind its
theory that the Spirit in the church may rightly set
aside Christ's teaching, the subtler endeavour of ascetic
scepticism in all ages to improve that teaching in the
direction of greater fancied purity and holiness.

We can see at once the powerful attraction of
Montanism for the Phrygian country-people. It
seemed to give them the life that is in Christ, and to
give it in their own Phrygian form of wild revivalism.
So from its holy centre at Pepuza Montanism
spread rapidly through the Phrygian villages. But
Phrygian nature is human nature too, and a deep
wave of spiritual excitement was running through
the Empire in the tranquil days of Titus Antoninus.
Wandering philosophers gathered crowds to their
sermons from the steps of the temples, wandering
priests of Cybele and Isis held "missions" in every
village, and the Montanists only gave a less unworthy
answer to the widespread craving for a religion of
feeling. So the doctrine spread in Asia too, and with
little change from Asia to Thrace and Gaul and
Rome and Africa. They must have reached Rome
and the Rhone Valley before 177, when the confessors
of Lyons and Vienne sent Irenaeus with a letter
against [1] them to Eleutherus of Rome. In Africa we
find Montanists in abundance about 203 (Perpetua,
Tertullian) and may fairly suppose that they had not
found Carthage harder to reach than Lyons. It will
be noted at once that the spread of Montanism was
in the West, for we hear little of it in Greece and

[1] A decision which Eusebius v. 3 calls εὐλαβῆ καὶ ὀρθοδοξοτάτην must have
been against the Montanists, not in their favour. The confessors cannot
have had much sympathy even with the asceticism, if "it was revealed to
Attalus" (Eus. l.l.) that Alcibiades (name disputed) was "not doing well in
refusing the creatures of God."

beyond the Taurus. Phrygians and Eastern Celts were an island in the Greek World. Their affinities were with the West. In strong emotionalism they were near akin to Moors and Western Celts, and their legalism was not alien to Rome herself. The historical significance of Montanism lies chiefly in this Western affinity. In the East it was reinforced in the next century by Novatianism from the West, and enabled to hold its ground for a couple of hundred years longer on the tableland of Asia; but in the end it passed away without leaving any serious traces on the Greek world around it. Like Christianity itself, it perished from the land of its birth; but while Christianity took a Greek form, Montanism became Western by adoption, and became Western with very little change. It fell in with Western thought, won over the first great Western writer, and has left its traces in the Western churches deep and clear to our own time.

There are three great stages in the history of Montanism—an Asiatic, a Roman, and an African. As soon as it reached Asia, the churches held many conferences over the new opinions,[1] and we can hear the echoes of much stormy controversy in the writers quoted by Eusebius. The decisions of the conferences are said to have been unfavourable; but they were not decisive. Either the rejection and expulsion of the Montanists is overstated,[2] or there was a strong party on the other side. The next stage is the discussion of Montanism in 177 by Bishop Eleutherus at Rome. As all opinions found their way sooner or later to that great centre of discussion, we need not

---

[1] Anon. *ap.* Eus. v. 16. The details given by the *Libellus Synodicus* are late and uncertain.

[2] Anon. *supra.* He is quite capable of representing local or partial expulsions as general.

assume that the Montanists were appealing from
Asiatic decisions to the judgment of the central church
of Christendom. The thing is not unlikely, but we
cannot be sure. Of the discussion we know only
that the confessors in Gaul sent a letter against[1] the
Montanists by the hand of Irenaeus. The decision
however of the church at Rome cannot well have
been altogether against Montanism, for we know that
it was more or less an open question at Rome till its
definite rejection in Tertullian's time. The third
stage of the history is mainly African, and gathers
round Tertullian. It was he who made Montanism a
great and lasting power in the church which rejected it;
so we can leave its further history till we come to him.

The first great result of the Montanist controversy
was that Chiliasm fell more or less into discredit,
and the unsettling expectation of Christ's immediate
return was commonly laid aside.[2] So far, this was
pure gain. Montanist Chiliasm descended naturally
from the apocalyptic aspirations which surrounded
the Lord and his disciples; and it suited the *naïve*
effort of early times to take the revelation as literally
as possible. But it had deeper roots than these.
When the natural man is in earnest, he is apt
to be impatient. In common life he mistakes rudeness for honesty, and force for strength; in politics
he cuts the knot by calling for a dictator: and when

---

[1] *Supra.*

[2] It was probably much less unsettling in the first century than in the
second. Warneck *Living Forces* 276 acutely says, "The eschatological
outlook had great results in the early church; it makes little impression
on any heathen Christians I have known. The reason may be that many
preachers are themselves little affected by it: but the deepest reason
probably is that the greatness of the gift they have received makes them
calm in prospect of the judgment of the world. The simple child-like trust
in the strong Saviour hardly allows fear of the final judgment."

he comes to religion, he expects to see with his own eyes some sudden and dramatic intervention from on high to right the wrongs of the world and do poetic justice on its evil-doers. The Lord himself was under no such illusion. More than once he plainly hinted that his church would have a long career before his second coming. That coming would be sudden, and the day was unknown to the Son himself; but at all events it was not in any near future.[1] So too St. Paul warns the Thessalonians that the day is not at hand, so that they must not let any immediate expectation of it disturb the higher duties of the common work of life. In the main his warning was obeyed, for though such an expectation was a real factor of Christian life in early times, it was never more than a subordinate factor. Whatever the theory might be, the practice of the churches was another matter. If there were occasional outbursts, there was no general enthusiasm of that sort.

But crude literalism and unspiritual impatience insisted nevertheless on looking for the Presence in the clouds of heaven as a piece of news that might be reported any day. It was a distinct gain for Christian life when this unwarranted hope was checked by the failure of the New Prophecy. It was only checked. Iranaeus is as crude as Papias

---

[1] As in the Seed growing silently, or the Unjust Judge. In the latter (Lu. xviii. 8) ἐν τάχει must mean *suddenly*, not *soon*, for the whole parable turns on the fact that the avenging would be long delayed. If then we take Apoc. i. 1 the same way, we bring both into line with his many warnings that his coming will be sudden.

St. John certainly contemplates his coming not only as a historical event (vi. 51) but as a continuous process (vi. 33, i. 9, governing Apoc. i. 8). If so, the apostles were not mistaken when they expected one great coming (the judgment of Jerusalem) in their own lifetime. But St. Paul at any rate had discovered the false perspective of the question in Mk. xiii. 4 before he wrote 2 Thess.

on this matter, and there was a good deal of
Chiliasm in the rustic churches of the next age.
Indeed it is a common feature of spiritual excitement
in all ages, and has littered the whole course of
church history with false predictions that the end
was very near.   But the gain was not without its loss.
Men who refuse to advance to the higher cannot
even keep the lower as a living faith.   If the last
Coming and the last Judgment were rightly relegated
to some distant future, so much the harder was
it to see that Christ has comings and judgments
here and now—that not only the great scenes of
history but the common things of common life are
as truly comings and judgments of the Lord as is
the dawning of the day of doom.   The failure of
Montanism did much to fix on Western Christendom
that deist conception of God as a King departed
to a far country which empties the world and
common life of that which is divine and holy, and
restores it but in part, through the mediation of
the church his representative, and by the ministry
of sacraments and works of law.

A second result which the Montanist controversy
left behind was a deep distrust of Prophetism in
all its forms.   In this way the third century was
an age of disillusion like the eighteenth in England.
The fiery preachings of Puritanism were flouted as
enthusiasm ; and in course of time that word was
given a wider meaning, as men passed from a rejection
of claims to special and immediate inspiration to
a general condemnation of all impassioned speaking
in religion.   If things did not go so far as this in
early times, they went in this direction, and the
distrust of enthusiasm lasted longer.   It was as

hard as ever to believe in the Spirit of Pentecost without the signs of Pentecost. The failure of Montanism did much to discredit every form of prophecy; and the failure of Prophecy barred every plea of inspiration, and helped to bar every plea of conscience which was not consistent with the actual order of the church. It threw even preaching into the background for a thousand years, and helped to form the mediaeval conception of the priest's duty—to say masses and to be a spiritual director, but by no means to preach. There were great preachers in the West—Ambrose, Augustine, Leo; but these were all bishops, and all early: but preaching was not common after their time before the twelfth century, except for missionary or crusading purposes, and even in the later middle ages it was chiefly done by bishops and friars. It may be that the Latin church did wisely for the times of ignorance: yet an important side of Christian teaching was obscured after the failure of Montanism, and never came to light again till mendicants and mystics began to prepare the way for the preaching of the times of the Reformation.

A third result must be noted. After the apostles were gone, the prophet remained a link with the past, for there could be no break with it while the words of the Spirit came from the lips of living men. But when prophets also were extinct, the church began to draw broad and deep that contrast of the apostolic age with later times which ever since has fascinated it. Henceforth that age shone out with unearthly splendour, consecrated alike by marvels that were real, and by a seamless unity that was imaginary. It seemed treason to the wonder-working

Spirit of the past to imagine that "greater works than these" were being done in the humdrum toil of a degenerate age. But men who will not see the greater works must have the lesser: and if they cannot get true miracles, they will manufacture false. So from the third and fourth centuries we see a new craving for marvels, no doubt rooted in the past, but still different in kind from the old romance and superstition which the Christians could hardly help sharing with their neighbours. After Constantine's time the church could freely convert to pious uses the rich stores of heathen legend and superstition.

But the brighter the halo of legendary purity that shone around the apostolic age, the greater the stress that had to be laid on the regular ministry of the church and on its connexion with that age. Now that the ministry of gifts was at an end, the official ministry seemed the one mediator with an absent King, the one power that could bring him back to bless his church. So they began to magnify their office: and they did well, if Christ is not with the two or three, unless they are gathered in the bishop's name. Step by step from this age onward Christ's minister is advanced forsooth to a dignity Christ never gave him. First he is turned into a priest to offer sacrifices, then a material sacrifice is invented for him to offer, then the whole work of the Spirit is shut up into his ministrations. No grace but in the visible church, no salvation outside it. Nothing remained but to "compel them to come in." The entire mediaeval system from the Papacy downward is no more than a natural development of the unbelief which knows no working of the Spirit but one transmitted by outward ordinances from a distant past : and to this development the failure of Montanism gave a greater impulse than the defeat of the Gnostics or the conversion of Constantine.

Books

De Soyres *Montanism and the Primitive Church* ; Bonwetsch *Montanismus*. See also Ch. XXII.

CHAPTER XVII

IRENAEUS

WITH the last quarter of the second century came a crisis in the church. New dangers were pressing which the old forms of teaching did not fully meet. Now that there were Christians who called themselves philosophers, Christianity was discussed like philosophy, and became a theme of eager controversy. There were Gnostics of all sorts inside and outside the churches, revelling in the luxuriance of allegorical interpretation, and Montanists within and without the churches met them with a fanatic literalism, while educated and thoughtful heathens looked on with mixed and curious interest, comparing not only the sects with each other but Christians generally with the Stoics and Cynics who also preached an overcoming of the world, and with the adherents of those Eastern worships which like the Gospel promised everlasting life to all believers.

Meanwhile the spirit of the subapostolic churches was the spirit of the apocalyptic church of Ephesus. In works and in labour and in patience it was blameless; but it had left its first love. Its tone was given by the elders who overlived St. John. They spoke not only with the natural influence of age and dignity, but as the last survivors of apostolic times

and seemingly the last holders of their miraculous
gifts.　Men like Polycarp looked more commonly
backward to their memories of St. John than to the
strange thoughts that were stirring a younger generation.　They stood like soldiers at their posts.　The
Lord had set them there, and it was not for them to
ask him why.　Their task was to preach and iterate
the historic Gospel, and to hand down the witness
delivered to them of the things which Christ had
said and done : and this they were content to do
without following far the deeper thoughts of apostolic
writers.　Polycarp was right enough in his rejection
of Marcion ; but he was not the man to see that the
church had something to learn, even from that Firstborn of Satan.

To do them justice, they did learn from the
contest with heresy a good deal that was practical.
We have seen how the resistance to false teaching
was organized in institutions.　We have seen how
the loose government of the apostolic age was centred
in the bishops, how the sacred books were formed
into the canon of a New Testament, how the essential
facts of the apostolic teaching were summed up in
simple professions of faith and diligently taught,
how the bishop in every church was made the official
guardian of the historic tradition, and how the
churches learned to confer together when points of
doubt arose.　It was fully understood that they
were bound each and all to guard the deposit of
the faith, and these measures greatly strengthened
their organization for the purpose.　But the difficulty
was one which no mere institutions could fully
overcome.　It was a great thing to organize and
fix the traditional teaching and bring home the facts

of the Gospel to all its converts : but the interpretation of the facts was not thereby settled. What was
to be done if Valentinus found an esoteric meaning
in the record of the Gospels, or if Marcion set it
aside as a mutilated or false account of Christ?
They claimed to be at least as good Christians as
others, and their claim called for a reasonable answer.
Excommunication was only the logic of a majority,
which is a form of the *argumentum baculinum*.
Authority is not evidence, but at best a call to
consideration and a presumption of evidence; and
in this case the authority itself was the matter
in dispute. No theories of Christianity but those
which set truth and reason at defiance can
evade the appeal to history and criticism for the
verification and interpretation of current teaching.
Tradition was outworn the moment its meaning was
disputed; and there was no resource but to fall
back on the written documents of the Old and New
Testament which came with the revelation. There
was now no other means of ascertaining what Christ
had really delivered to his church. The appeal then
from tradition to Scripture is the constant method
of the Greek writers from Irenaeus and the School
of Alexandria till the decay of free thought after
the fifth century. Each new opinion as it came
forward was tested by Scripture; and according as
it stood the test was either accepted like Origen's
theory of the eternal generation, or rejected like
Gnosticism and Arianism.

The problem was threefold. In the first place,
it was not fully settled what the authoritative documents were. In the case of the Gospels, any doubt
might have been serious, for almost all other memory

of Christ seems to have perished early. The scraps
of genuine tradition otherwise preserved are astonishingly meagre. We have ourselves a fringe of
uncertainty round the Canon, even of the New
Testament, for few students will venture to place
the Second Epistle of Peter quite on a level with
that to the Romans. But in the second century
there was more or less uncertainty about five catholic
Epistles and that to the Hebrews, though the
Apocalypse does not seem to have been questioned
till Chiliasm fell into discredit; and various sects
of Gnostics quoted apocryphal books of their own,
or disputed (though hardly on critical grounds) some
of the commonly accepted books. Even their
opponents do not always seem clear about the
authority to be assigned to the *Shepherd* or the
Teaching. The four Gospels however, the Acts,
the thirteen Epistles of St. Paul, two catholic
Epistles (1 Pet. and 1 John) and the Apocalypse,
were acknowledged by almost all teachers but
Marcion; so that though there was still a good
deal of work to be done, the range of doubt was
not enormous.

In the second place, principles of interpretation
had to be settled. Assuming for instance the
authority of St. John's Gospel, how far must we
limit ourselves to the literal meaning of his words?
If allegory is to be admitted at all, why not the
Valentinian theory of aeons? Of course it contradicts
the current tradition: but does it also contradict
Scripture? If so, how can we shew that it does?
Questions like these were part of the general
education question of the time, about the interpretation of sacred books. The heathens had exactly

the same trouble with Homer, for he was not to
them an ancient poet only, but an inspired teacher,
whom they used very much as we use our Bible.
Homer was the text-book of the schools, and a
quotation from Homer was commonly clinching.
But how was he to be interpreted? There were a
few who kept severely to the letter; others found
rationalizing explanations for the scandals of a
literal interpretation, and others made allegory a
key to everything. It seemed no more than proper
respect for an inspired teacher, to take for granted
that his words must have some deeper meaning,
especially when otherwise they would be trifling or
immoral. Moreover, the use of allegory enabled
them not only to get rid of a good many scandals
about the gods, but to read into Homer almost
anything they wanted in the way of morals or
philosophy, or sometimes even science, much as some
friends of ours find everything in the Bible.
Allegorical methods suited equally the tendency of
the later philosophers to move the gods out of the
way, and the devout endeavours of men like Plutarch
of Chaeronea to revive their worship in a purer form.
They had been freely applied by Philo to the Old
Testament; and the rabbis were as ready as the
allegorists to draw out mysteries of every sort from
words and letters. So the Christians fell in with
the stream. Though there is no genuine allegory
in the New Testament, St. Paul's application of the
story of Hagar comes very near to allegory, and
the argument of the Epistle to the Hebrews is easily
confused with allegory by careless readers. But
from Barnabas and Clement onward its use is
constant. The more speculative of the Gnostics

revelled in allegory without limit; and even the
most reverent of their opponents could not help
feeling that if there is any revelation at all in
Scripture, it must not be limited to what was
consciously present to the mind of the writers. If
allegorism was forbidden, they must give up the Old
Testament to Marcion.   There must be some distinction between the letter and the spirit; and till
it was more clearly seen that revelation is progressive,
allegory was the best way of reconciling the admitted
divinity of Scripture with its undeniable imperfections.   It gave the necessary protest on behalf of
truth and right, that what is certainly unworthy
of God is in any case incredible.   It was a stage
in the history of exegesis, good till something better
was discovered.   True, it turned the Old Testament
into a book of pious riddles, and parts of the New
fared little better : but it was really the best that
could be done.   So if we leave out extremes like
Marcion and the Montanists, there was a general
agreement for the use of allegory.   But then came
the question, how it was to be used, and what limits
were to be assigned to it.   The Gnostics had given a
very successful demonstration that limits of some sort
were needed.   What were they to be, and where were
they to be placed ?

The third problem was wider still.   As usual, the
Gnostics had essayed it already; and as usual, their
work was more beacon than guidance.   What is the
relation of the Gospel to human learning generally ?
A mere philosophy might be content to float in the
clouds, a mere religion to grovel on the earth; but
a revelation from heaven is bound to satisfy the
intellectual as well as the moral needs of men by

giving some reasonable account of the world of
thought into which it comes. It may be that man
is unable by searching to find out God; but if
revelation is possible, as it must be unless God is
unable to find out man, no fact of this world
can be meaningless. A revelation which appeals to
the image of God in man is bound to satisfy the
intellect to the extent of shewing something of the
unity of plan which the unity of God implies in
history and nature as well as in the life of the
individual.

This then was the great threefold problem which
faced the churches. It had been pushed aside for
two generations, partly by the practical needs of
Christian life in the growing churches, partly by
the conservative timidity which shrank from going
beyond the letter of the traditional teaching, but
partly also by sheer need of time before a measure
could be attempted of the stupendous facts of the
historic incarnation. If love could recognize the
true light at once, reason needed time to ponder
them. Now however the question could no longer
be put off. It was already clear that churches which
dare not face this world's learning are well on the
way to lose that world's life. The problem had been
shaping for some time, and a good deal of preparation
had already been made for it. The literature of the
middle of the second century (except Justin) is
mostly lost; but we may glance at the chief writers
who prepared the way for Irenaeus.

Papias of Hierapolis appears to have been somewhat older than Polycarp, so that he may be dated
roughly 60-140. He was a disciple of John the
Lord's disciple; but it is not clear whether this John

was the apostle or the elder.[1]   In either case he was
a friend of Polycarp, and much respected by Irenaeus
and others as "an ancient man," and a great
champion of Chiliasm.   Eusebius has a low opinion
of him ; but Eusebius was impatient of his Chiliasm,
and plainly does him less than justice.   He wrote
nothing but five books of Expositions of passages
of Scripture relating to the Lord.[2]   Some of these
may have been Old Testament prophecies, but others
were certainly taken from our Gospels.   On the first
two he makes important statements, and his use of
the First Epistle of St. John is sufficient proof
(besides other evidence) that he also used the fourth
Gospel.   Of the third there is no trace ; but we cannot expect to see everything in the half-page or so of
fragments now extant.   The importance of Papias is
that he is the first orthodox commentator, and that
he illustrated his comments with traditional sayings
of the Lord, which he had gathered from the hearers
of the Lord's disciples, of whom Andrew and Peter,
Philip and Thomas and James, John and Matthew
and others were dead, while Aristion and the elder
John were still alive.   This must have been *cir.* 100.
He was quite right in thinking that if he could get
genuine traditions of the Lord, they would be more

[1] Irenaeus says it was the apostle, but Eusebius quotes his Preface, which
points to the elder ; and Eusebius is the more accurate writer of the two.
On the other hand, Irenaeus may have had other information, and we might
accept it without hesitation if we could be sure that it came from Polycarp.

[2] Chief fragments in Eus. iii. 39 λογίων κυριακῶν ἐξηγήσεις can only mean
"Commentaries on (certain) oracles relating to the Lord." It cannot be
translated "a narrative of the words of the Lord"—which would require τῶν
λόγων τοῦ κυρίου διήγησις.   E. A. Abbott and others have entirely failed to
shake Lightfoot's position here.   The theory that he was writing a rival
Gospel is not worth discussing.   His contemptuous reference to the statements of books and to "the gentlemen who had so much to say" is much
better referred to the treatise of Basilides On the Gospel in four-and-twenty
books than to our Gospels.

to the purpose than the endless books of Basilides
and the Gnostics. His work was most likely very
unequal. A story which Irenaeus seems to quote
from Papias is, as Eusebius would say, more or less
fabulous : but if Ewald is right in believing that the
story of the woman taken in adultery is that which
Papias chose to illustrate the next words,[1] Ye judge
after the flesh ; I judge no man, we must admit that
it is admirably chosen.

Justin's importance in this direction lies partly
in his development of the doctrine of the Logos on
the lines of Greek thought, partly in his treatise on
Heresies, which set the example and gave much of
the material to the later works of Irenaeus, Hippolytus
and others. Heresiology now came in as a depart-
ment of history.

Hegesippus, apparently a converted Jew, visited
sundry churches (including Corinth) about the middle
of the second century, coming to Rome in the time
of Anicetus, and living there till that of Eleutherus
(cir. 160-180). His work seems to have been rather
polemical against heretics than directly historical,
though it contained important historical material.
From it Eusebius quotes accounts of James the Lord's
brother, of Simeon the son of Clopas, of the grandsons
of Jude, of Antinous, and of the origins of heresy.
There is no reason for counting him an Ebionite.
Thus Hegesippus was a precursor rather of Eusebius
himself than of Irenaeus, though the first beginnings
of Church History may be seen in the chronicler
Bruttius,[2] who " lived near the time " of the persecution of Domitian, and therefore before Hegesippus.

Claudius Apollinaris was a successor, perhaps the

[1] Joh. viii. 15.   [2] On Bruttius, Lightfoot *Clement* i. 46 *sq.*

immediate successor, of Papias at Hierapolis. He
wrote against Montanus, and an Apology to the
emperor Marcus. He gave the Christian version of
the Thundering Legion, whether in the Apology or
elsewhere. His importance in this connexion is in
his discussion of the disagreement of the Gospels
concerning the day of the Crucifixion. Similarly the
writer of the Fragment of Muratori on the Canon,
which is best placed near this date (*cir.* 170) lays
stress on the difference in the *principia*[1] of the
Gospels, and explains that it does not concern
our faith, because the main points of the narrative
are the same in all.

Dionysius of Corinth (*cir.* 170) is known to us as
the writer of letters to sundry churches, in which he
commented on passages of Scripture. But the best
representative of literary activity in this period is
Melito of Sardis (under Marcus). He lived in the
odour of sanctity, and is counted by Polycrates in
190 as the latest of the " great spirits of Asia." The
titles of twenty-two of his works, given by Eusebius,[2]
cover an enormous range. Some of them are directly
controversial, against heathens, Montanists, and
Marcion, others deal with a variety of anthropological
and dogmatic questions, and others again are exegetical and practical. Only a few fragments remain.
The chief of these are a passage from his Apology to
the emperor Marcus, in which he represents the
Empire and the church as twin growths, and pleads
for peace between them : his catalogue of the scriptures
of " the Old Testament" (implying a New Testament
Canon) : and the first sentence of his treatise Con-

---

[1] Are these simply *points of view* or rather *beginnings*—that the Gospels
begin so differently ?   [2] Eus. iv. 26.

cerning Easter, in which he states that the dispute
broke out at Laodicea about the time when bishop
Sagaris was a martyr.

There was therefore much more literary activity in
the generation before Irenaeus than we might suppose
from its scanty remains. But after all it seems to
have been at best fragmentary ; and it was no longer
enough to clear up isolated questions without a more
comprehensive scheme. The Gnostics had fairly
raised the questions; but though they had done
something for the exegesis of Scripture, their work
was in general a failure, because they never fairly
reckoned with history and human nature. Irenaeus
appears to have been the first who took the whole
problem in a broad way, and strove to solve it by
criticism and not by speculation.

In some ways Irenaeus stands midway between the
simplicity of subapostolic teaching and the philosophy
of the Alexandrian School. As a disciple of Polycarp,
he leans more to the former, and indeed has less than
Justin of the Alexandrian, and more of the Western
tone of thought. The Roman Clement's moderation
is more congenial to him than the Alexandrian
Clement's wide sympathy. Yet he is a much deeper
thinker than Justin. If he speaks less of the Logos
as the teacher of the nations, he sees much more
clearly the meaning of the Incarnation as bringing
new life to nations and to men. Christ became like
us that he might sum up all creation in himself. So
Irenaeus understands the problem of his own time
very much better than his predecessors. Though he
has no liking for the speculations of the Gnostics, and
hardly understands their subtle ways of thinking, he
does his best to describe their systems truly, sparing

no pains to get his information accurate, and then fairly meets them on the ground of Scripture, discussing the historical origin of the canonical books, and shewing in detail their inconsistency with the Gnostic theories.

We may take it that Irenaeus was a native of Asia, and that he was born about 130.[1] We do not know whether his family belonged to Smyrna; but he came under the influence of Polycarp in early life, and remained under it for a considerable time. He seems to have left Smyrna before Polycarp's death in 155. That he was in Rome at the time may be doubtful, but the decided Roman cast of his thought makes it likely that his visits to the city were neither few nor short. We next find him in 177 as a presbyter at Lyons in Gaul under Pothinus the bishop, whose long life of more than ninety years linked on to the last apostles in Asia.[2] When

---

[1] The age of Irenaeus is fixed on one side (a) by his connexion with Polycarp ἐν τῇ πρώτῃ ἡμῶν ἡλικίᾳ, which cannot mean less than early manhood, so that he must have been say eighteen or twenty some time before 155; (b) by the elderly tone of his letter to Florinus, which implies an age of scarcely less than sixty in 189. On the other side, we have no hint that Florinus was then extremely old; and Florinus was at least half a dozen years older than Irenaeus. He need not have been much more, for half a dozen years are enough to make the difference between the growing boy and the promising young official. These indications converge about 130.

Much difficulty has been caused by his words to Florinus ap. Eus. v. 20 εἶδον γάρ σε παῖς ἔτι ὢν ἐν τῇ κάτω Ἀσίᾳ παρὰ Πολυκάρπῳ λαμπρῶς πράττοντα ἐν τῇ βασιλικῇ αὐλῇ καὶ πειρώμενον εὐδοκιμεῖν παρ' αὐτῷ. If this means that the emperor was himself in Asia, the choice will lie between Hadrian in 129, which is much too early, and Pius in 154, which seems too late. We may however, (a) suppose an unrecorded visit of Pius about 141, or (b) follow Lightfoot's suggestion (Ign. i. 448) that the proconsular court of T. Aurelius Fulvus in 136 might be called imperial half a century later, because Fulvus became emperor in 138 as T. Antoninus Pius. But surely this is too early. It would seem better (c) to take ἐν τῇ βασιλικῇ αὐλῇ as not of necessity implying the emperor's own presence (so Lipsius in D.C.B. Art. "Irenaeus"). Then it will be nearly what the epitaphs of a later time express by militavit in palatio of a civilian—that Florinus was then a promising young official.

[2] There is no early authority for the statement that Pothinus also came

Pothinus perished in the persecution, Irenaeus took his place. He seems to have held it for twenty years or more, and to have died in peace.

Irenaeus is an eminently representative man, giving evidence as he does from personal knowledge of Asia, Rome, and Gaul, and resting on the teaching of Polycarp (who had certainly known St. John) of Pothinus, and of another elder who belonged to the ancient worthies.[1] Papias he does not seem to have known personally, though he was familiar with his book. A better witness to the beliefs and practices current in the middle of the second century can hardly be imagined. So his action when Blastus raised the Easter Question at Rome about 190 was that of a mediator. On one side he wrote to rebuke Blastus for stirring up strife : on the other he sent a grave admonition to Victor of Rome, with whom he personally agreed, reminding him that the question was not one of essentials, so that it was not right to refuse communion to the Easterns for nothing more than a diversity of practice, especially one on which their predecessors Polycarp and Anicetus had been content to differ.

But Gnosticism did touch essentials, and in its Valentinian form was making progress in Gaul, so that Irenaeus threw himself heartily into the controversy. Not that Irenaeus was a mere zealot. He looks on heresy with neither the impulsive horror of Polycarp nor with the bitter scorn of Tertullian,

---

from Asia ; but it is quite likely. In any case he must have been old enough (as far as years went) to remember apostles.

[1] Some of his references are doubtless to the written work of Papias. But at least two passages—(a) *Talia quaedam enarrans presbyter reficiebat nos et dicebat* (b) *Hujusmodi quoque senior apostolorum discipulus disputabat*—imply personal intercourse, and therefore a *presbyter* other than Papias. It may of course be Polycarp, but Irenaeus does not say so.

but with the deliberate aversion of a student who has convinced himself of its mischievous and often immoral tendency. His great work—the five books of the *Refutation of Gnosticism* (ἔλεγχος καὶ ἀνατροπὴ τῆς ψευδωνύμου γνώσεως)—cannot be more precisely dated than by the fact that the third book was written before the death of Eleutherus of Rome *cir.* 189. We have the original only of a part of the first book, and of sundry fragments (mostly important) preserved chiefly by Hippolytus and Eusebius. Fortunately the work is complete in a rude Latin translation used by Tertullian, and therefore nearly contemporary. So closely does it follow the original that we can often restore the Greek with a very small margin of uncertainty.

He begins with general remarks on the Gnostics as "bad interpreters of things well said," and soon comes to Valentinianism, giving slight accounts of other schools. He denounces its dualism, its arbitrary interpretation of Scripture, its mercenary and immoral practice, and its too practical distinction between the spiritual and the natural man. In the second book he comes to close quarters with the Valentinians, and in the third he develops his argument from Scripture. We know, says he, the doctrine of our Salvation only through those by whom it was delivered to us, first in preaching, then in written works. He then describes the origin of the four Gospels, and goes on to the argument from tradition. Whether the Lord taught Valentinianism or orthodoxy, he must have delivered it to his disciples, and they to theirs, and so on. For instance, here is the succession of the bishops of Rome; and the single life of Polycarp actually covered the

whole distance from apostolic times to our own.
Now we all teach orthodoxy. If the Lord taught
Valentinianism, there must have been a change
somewhere ; and the Gnostics are bound to shew
when and by whom it was made. He illustrates
the exclusive authority of four Gospels and no more
by the famous simile of the four quarters of the
heavens. Upon the whole, his appeal is to the four
Gospels as verified by criticism, and to their doctrine
as handed down by an unbroken succession of bishops
as teachers in the churches.

The fourth book is on the same lines ; but here
he chiefly has in view Marcion's doctrine that the
Father revealed by Christ was not the God of the
Jews, so that his general theme is the relation of
the Law to the Gospel. But in the course of his
argument he touches many other questions, like
the nature of inspiration, the work of the Spirit,
the reality of freedom, the purpose of the Incarnation.
And all along the way he scatters, not indeed the
brilliant epigrams of a Tertullian, but sentences which
fairly rival them as food for thought. Perhaps no
later writer has given a more striking view of the
Lord's Supper as our great sacrifice of thanksgiving
for the gift of life in this world and that to come ;
" but the altar is in heaven, for thither we direct
our prayers." For as the earthly bread after consecration is no longer common bread but bread with
a blessing—an earthly and a heavenly element—so
our bodies receiving that blessing are no longer
corruptible, but have the hope of resurrection to
life eternal. As the bread joins our spirits to our
mortal bodies, so the blessing joins them to the
everliving Lord. How can the flesh perish when

it feeds on Christ by thanksgiving?[1] The fifth book
goes on with the resurrection of the body, and passes
on to a Chiliastic exposition of the last things, illustrated from Papias. He discusses the Number of the
Beast, noticing the various reading (616 for 666)
and proposing solutions — ΕΥΑΝΘΑΣ, LATEINOS,
TEITAN—but adopting none of them. But it is a
little earlier that he gives his measured judgment
of future punishment as eternal, because the good
things of God being eternal, the loss of them must
also be eternal.[2] He is not enough of a mystic
to ask whether the eternal may not be measured by
something else than time.

Of the other works of Irenaeus we need say but
little. None of them have reached us complete but
the recently discovered *Demonstration of the Apos-
tolical Preaching*, which we have discussed already.
We have a piece of his letter to Florinus, and fragments it would seem of his *de Ogdoade*, of his
treatise against Blastus, and of other works. But
the only fragments which call for special notice
are those published by Pfaff in 1715 from a MS.
in the Royal Library at Turin. They seem very
much in the style of Irenaeus; but Pfaff's account
of the MS. is not satisfactory, and it had somehow
vanished from the Library in 1749. Harnack sets
them down as forged by Pfaff; but perhaps it is
safer simply to leave them under grave suspicion.
There is however one more document which may
just possibly be the work of Irenaeus—the Letter of
the churches of Lyons and Vienne. True, it is not
ascribed to him by Eusebius; but he may have
written in the name of the churches like Clement,

---

[1] *Haer.* iv. 18, v. 2.   [2] *Ibid.* v. 27.

without ever naming himself. Nor does it agree
with the modest disclaimer of literary skill at the
opening of the *Refutation*. But after all, the letter
is no way rhetorical: its power is that of simplicity
and sincerity, of dignity and self-control: and it is
just this dignity and self-control which is so marked
in Irenaeus. He might very well have written the
letter, but it would be going much beyond the
evidence to say that he did write it.

BOOKS

See on Ch. XV.

CHAPTER XVIII

THE EASTERN EMPERORS

AFTER Commodus the Empire enters on a new stage of its history. From Vespasian's time to that of Marcus it had been ruled by a series of good administrators, all of them peaceable but Trajan, and all but Domitian willing to govern in harmony with the Senate and society. History can scarcely shew such another line of rulers as the four successors of Nerva, who so worthily sustained the honour of the Empire for more than eighty years. Nor did the wasteful reign of Commodus appear to have done any incurable evil. The provinces were loyal, the legions irresistible as ever. They had renewed the glories of Trajan beyond the Tigris, and avenged the disgrace of Elegeia by the sack of Ctesiphon. If the Germans had reached the Hadriatic for a moment in the days of the great pestilence, they had long since had their answer on the Elbe. There was neither thought nor dream as yet that Rome would ever bow for need to the barbarians. If the Empire was visibly overstrained, even Commodus had suffered no great disaster; and now that he had to be put out of the way like Domitian, there was a Nerva ready to take his place in the consul Helvius Pertinax.

Though Commodus was put out of the way

successfully enough, his death was like Nero's in letting loose the forces of anarchy. Pertinax turned out a Galba, not a Nerva. He was a brave and worthy general, and his resolute economy might have done wonders in quieter times. Even in his short reign, he did enough to shew that the Empire was still far from bankruptcy. One of his edicts allowed any one who pleased to take up uncultivated land and have it for his own (tax-free for ten years) on condition of cultivating it.[1] But Pertinax was not a true statesman. He looked to the senate and people of the republic, and hurried on his reforms without seeing that there was a military problem behind the financial. The praetorian guards were masters of the situation; and after the pampering of Commodus, it was a fatal error to provoke them with sordid parsimony before he had made sure of his position. The new Augustus could only face the mutineers with Galba's courage, and meet his fate with Galba's dignity. In eighty-seven days from the murder of Commodus, the throne of the world was vacant again.

From this point the course of events might almost have been foreseen. The praetorians were on the spot, and promptly sold the purple to the highest bidder. The purchaser was a respectable official named Didius Julianus, who had succeeded Pertinax in the consulship and in the proconsulate of Africa. But Didius was not the man to succeed him in the Empire also. He shewed no great ability, and sank almost without an effort under the infamy of his elevation. In sixty-five days he too had passed away.

---

[1] Like Hadrian before him : such a policy is significant.

The legions lay almost as they did in Nero's time. Three great armies lined the three great frontiers of the Rhine (with Britain), the Danube, and the Euphrates, and were now commanded by Clodius Albinus, Septimius Severus, and Pescennius Niger. There were seven legions on the Rhine, nine on the Euphrates; but the six or seven on the Danube had now grown into twelve, so that Severus was not only the nearest but the strongest of the rivals. He marched straight on Rome, put down Didius and secured the senate, disbanded the praetorians, temporized with Albinus, and in a month marched eastward to fight with Niger. The strife was deadly, but the army of Syria was never a match for the legions of the Danube. Niger was driven steadily back, till the battle of Issus (Nov. 194) made Severus master of the East. Only Byzantium remained, where Caecilius Capella held out desperately for nearly two years after Niger's death. The destruction of its walls by Severus was regretted half a century later, when the Bosphorus lay open to the Goths. Only Albinus and the army of the Rhine had still to be reckoned with; and their defeat in the great battle of Lyons (Feb. 197) left Severus master of the Empire.

Lucius Septimius Severus was a soldier raised to power by the soldiers, and frankly dependent on them. The revolt of Avidius Cassius had shewn their contempt even for Marcus; and now they had an emperor after their own heart. No philosopher was Severus, nor sot nor weakling senator, but an iron soldier who could guard the majesty of Rome. He shares with Aurelian the glory of recovering both Syria and Gaul from civil war; but he is the only emperor who in one campaign pushed down the Tigris to the sack of Ctesiphon, and in another rose almost from his deathbed to fight his way through the Caledonian morasses to the shores of the northern sea. His reign was grim and terrible. If he flattered the senate, it was only for a moment. He scarcely cared to hide his contempt and hatred of those elegant and obsequious nobles, and put to death more than forty of them without trial. Never yet had the Empire been so ruled with a naked sword. Yet the great soldier was very far from being a mere soldier. He judged causes as diligently as Marcus, filled his council with great lawyers like Papinian and Paul, and has left his mark on almost every page of the Digest. African though he was, with Phoenician for his native language, and an accent he never got rid of, he mastered Latin and Greek, studied at Athens, wrote his own memoirs, and shewed a good deal of taste for literature, and even for sight-seeing in Egypt. There is a touch of Hadrian's restlessness in his words, " I have been all things, and nothing has last answered."

The Christians were no great losers by the death of Commodus. No doubt they had their share of the troubles, as at the siege of Byzantium,[1] but nobody had much leisure to persecute them during the civil wars. Though it is not likely that Pertinax was thinking much about them when he stopped the *quaestiones majestatis*, his action must have given them some relief. Nor was Severus himself specially

---

[1] Tert. *ad Scap.* 3 *Caecilius Capella in illo exitu Byzantino : Christiani gaudete ! exclamavit.* The excitement of a desperate defence may well have roused heathen superstition : and the Christians in the city were very likely lukewarm in the matter. They cannot have had much interest in refusing to accept Severus as *de facto* emperor.

unfriendly to them.   If he was decently respectful to
the gods, he gave his real belief to the stars, married
Julia Domna on the word of the astrologers, and was
himself no mean astrologer.   The old Roman ideas
which had caused so much persecution were foreign to
a Phoenician of Africa with a Syrian empress at his
side—and that empress a liberal eclectic like Julia
Domna.   Severus was moreover at enmity with the
Senate, which was the focus of Roman conservatism.
He had no more quarrel with the Christians than
with any one else who lived peaceably, and did not
meddle with sedition.   He allowed them about his
person, protected them from the mob, and was not
moved even by the scandal of senatorial men and
women whom he knew to be Christians.   So says
Tertullian ;[1] and there are facts enough to show that
his account is fairly true.

So the peace continued, such as it was, and subject
to local breaches, as in Africa in 197.   If Severus did
not set the law in action against the Christians,
neither did he repeal it.   They remained exposed as
before to popular fury, and the governors did much
as they pleased in the way of mitigating it or otherwise.   If the Christians were better off than in the
days of Marcus, they were by no means unmolested.
The persecutions in Africa were serious enough to call
forth more than one of Tertullian's writings, including
of course his great *Apology* in 197 : and its difference
of tone from Justin's is not entirely a matter of personal

---

[1] His son Caracalla (*b.* 188) had a Christian nurse (Tert. *ad Scap.* 4) and
a Jewish playmate (*Hist. Aug.* Car. 1).   Severus himself was healed with oil
by Proculus a Christian, whom he invited to the palace and kept till his
death.   Men and women of senatorial rank were known to be Christians, yet
praised and protected by him (Tert. *l.c.*).   Prosenes the *procurator patri-
monii* of Commodus seems to have been undisturbed till his death in 217
(Wilmanns 1285, discussed by Friedländer *Sittengesch.* i. 188).

character.   In some ways however Hippolytus *de
Antichristo*, written just before Severus began active
persecution in 202, is even more significant of
Christian feeling.   There had always been two
tendencies in relation to the Empire.   The two great
apostles preached submission and obedience, and were
followed by Clement of Rome : the writer of the
Apocalypse breathes defiance, and is followed by
Ignatius.   Upon the whole however the church of
the second century respected the persecuting Empire
as a power ordained of God.   Ignatius and the
Montanists are clearly in a minority.   If apologists
like Justin tend to overstate their friendliness, the
sufferers at Lyons and Vienne shew no traces of disloyalty.   To Melito the Empire is the foster-sister of
the Church, born at the same time and growing up
along with it, while Irenaeus closely follows the lines
of St. Paul, and sets aside the dangerous question of
the number of the Beast.   The Empire is still to him
a power that works for righteousness.   But now
comes a change.   The long years of utter insecurity
are telling on Christian temper.   If Tertullian still
repeats the language of St. Paul, he repeats it with
an accent unknown to Irenaeus, and Hippolytus (his
work seems esoteric) takes a sterner view than his
master did.   The Empire is not indeed Antichrist, for
the judgments of the world are only partial hitherto,
so that the end is not yet.   But Rome is the fourth
beast of Daniel, the restraining power of St. Paul.
Two centuries of her empire are past already, and she
will break up into nations long before the other three
are finished ; and from those nations cometh Antichrist.   The number of the apocalyptic beast cannot
be anything else than ΛΑΤΕΙΝΟΣ.   Even now the

Empire is the image of Antichrist's kingdom; its
Caesar-worship is the spirit of Antichrist, its gathering
of the nations into one realm is a devilish caricature
of the all-gathering church of God.   Here is a defiance
less passionate indeed than that of Ignatius, but more
thoughtful and quite as resolute : and we may be
sure that Hippolytus only put in words the thoughts
of many.[1]

Upon the whole however the churches had tolerable
peace for the last twenty years of the second century ;
and some of them even obtained legal recognition in
an indirect way.   We have seen the likeness of the
Christian churches to the clubs which abounded in
the Empire.   The general law was that clubs of the
poor (*collegia tenuiorum*) might meet monthly for a
levy of contributions, and oftener for purely religious
purposes,—provided always that there was no breach
of the senatus consultum against forbidden clubs.
Whether this law had become obsolete or not, Severus
renewed it in a rescript of his own, not later than
198.   Here was a chance for an able man like Victor
of Rome or Tertullian.   These *collegia tenuiorum*
were mostly burial clubs, and burial clubs needed no
special permission from the authorities.   If therefore
the churches were constituted into burial clubs, they
would as such obtain legal rights, including that of
holding property; nor would this corporate recognition be affected by the fact that individuals practised
an unlawful worship.   So Tertullian[2] pictures the
churches as clubs.   " We are a corporation, not a

---

[1] I have not thought it needful to discuss generally the eschatology of
Hippolytus, or even to distinguish carefully the statements of his *de Ant.*
from those of his commentary on Daniel, which was written during the
persecution.   But it must be noted that Hippolytus always leans to the
sterner view of things.   [2] Tert. *Apol.* 39.

gang of plotters. We meet for prayer, and we pray
for the emperor and the good estate of the Roman
world. Our presidents get their place by merit, not
by money, for we do not sell things divine. Such
common chest as we have is maintained by monthly
contributions, moderate and voluntary, for neither do
we buy things divine : and it is not spent on feasting,
but on the relief and burial of the poor, on our
orphans and old folk, and on our people who are in
trouble for their faith. Even our feasts are sober and
religious. If all this is like the forbidden clubs, then
we deserve to be forbidden along with them."

The church of Rome as a burial club! It was a
strange guise, though less strange than that of the
revolutionary club, assumed by Oberlin for the church
of the Ban de la Roche. Nor was it so strange in
early times. The care of the dead was a very solemn
duty with the ancients, and Roman law protected
without regard to persons every place where they were
laid. The bodies of criminals were seldom refused
to relations, or even to strangers like Nicodemus and
Joseph ; and it was the very last outrage of persecution [1] to scatter the ashes of the martyrs—to defeat
forsooth their hope of resurrection from the dead.
Jews and Christians buried their dead instead of
burning them, and buried them amongst their own
people. Thus the vaults of notable Christians like
"Lucina" or Antonius Restitutus became burial
places for their relations and dependants ; and before
church buildings became common, these burial places
were the chief visible possessions of the Christians.
The mobs which cried "Away with their burial places"

[1] In the persecution of Lyons and Vienne Eus. v. 1 *ad fin.* and occasional
cases in Diocletian's time Ditto viii. 7, *Mart. Pal.* 9.

in Tertullian's time [1] had churches to destroy less than half a century later.[2] Thus the guise of burial clubs was not so strange then as it would be now.

As soon as Severus was free from danger in the West, he found it necessary to spend nearly five years (summer 197-May 202) in the East. The Parthian war was his main business; but the Jews also had given trouble serious enough to furnish an excuse for the Senate to decree a Jewish triumph to his son Caracalla. Hadrian had endeavoured to stamp out Judaism by entirely forbidding circumcision, but Pius had limited the penalty to proselytes, and Severus now renewed his law in 202.[3] "He also forbade conversion to Christianity." Of course the old laws remained in force, and the new rescript might help to revive them; but in itself it struck at none but converts. It marks a certain change in the policy of the emperors, as though they were beginning to think it the first necessity to stop the further spread of the unlawful worship. Thus it is the first of the special measures against particular classes of Christians which so broadly distinguish the persecutions of the third century from those of the second.

Our records of the persecution are as usual most

[1] Tert. *ad Scap.* 3 *Areae non sint.*

[2] Passing over Clem. Al. p. 228 ἐξ ἐκκλησίας as no more conclusive than 1 Cor. xi. 18 ἐν ἐκκλησίᾳ, we find the first traces of churches in (1) Tert. *Pud.* 4 *non modo limine, verum omni ecclesiae tecto submovemus* (2) The great church at Edessa destroyed by a flood in 201 (3) *Hist. Aug.* Alexander 49 (cannot be dated nearer than 222-235) (4) Min. Felix Oct. 9 if we read *sacraria* (also Alexander's time) and (5) Origen *in Matth. Comm. Ser.* 39 *ecclesiae incensae sunt* (under Maximin 235-238).

[3] *Hist. Aug.* Sev. 17 *Judaeos fieri sub gravi poena vetuit.* This must be limited to actual circumcision, for we read Eus. vi. 12 of one Domninus, who betook himself in time of persecution to "Jewish ἐθελοθρησκεία" (not θρησκεία) which seems to mean that he became a proselyte of the looser sort, who were not circumcised.

Then Spartian adds *idem etiam Christianis sanxit.*

imperfect.   We hear of Natalius as a confessor at
Rome,[1] and Asclepiades at Antioch;[2] but the only
martyrs better known to us belong to Alexandria
and Africa; and in both groups we see clearly the
new aim of persecution to put down conversions.
The policy had succeeded against the Jews : why
should it not be equally successful with the Christians ?
Severus forgot first that Jews cared much less than
Christians about proselytes, then that Christianity
satisfied the monotheistic drift like Judaism, and
satisfied it better.

At Alexandria the catechetical school bore the
brunt of battle.   Clement stood his ground manfully,
though he " saw martyrs daily "; but presently there
came a great scattering, and when there seemed no
more work for him to do in Alexandria, he retired to
Palestine.[3]   The post of danger was seized by a
youth of eighteen : but that youth was Origen.   His
father Leonides was one of the first victims the year
before, and Origen would have rushed into court to
declare himself a Christian, if his mother had not
prudently hid his clothes.   As the property of
Leonides was confiscated, his family was reduced
to poverty, and Origen became for a while dependent
on a rich lady of Alexandria, though even then he
refused to worship with Paul of Antioch, her chaplain
and adopted son, whose heresy he detested.   But he
had not been Clement's disciple for nothing.   When
the catechetical school was closed, some zealous
heathen students — among them the future bishop

[1] Eus. v. 28.

[2] Eus. vi. 11.   Neumann p. 166 adds Alexander (of Jerusalem) : but it
seems better to put him later.

[3] The consideration he enjoyed later is sufficient proof that this was no
unworthy flight.

Heraclas—applied to him for teaching; and before long he was formally appointed head of the school by bishop Demetrius. His disciples were in great danger : seven of them were put to death. Women were not spared, for Herais the catechumen was burned. Origen himself challenged his fate, and escaped with difficulty from the mob : but the authorities must have shut their eyes to his defiance.

To this time belongs the story of Potamiaena, which was a famous memory in the time of Eusebius. When after many tortures she was threatened with dishonour, she replied with "words which they consider impious," and was haled away straight to execution—a slow death of boiling pitch poured over her. On the way she was shielded from the hustling and insults of the crowd by Basilides the officer in charge, who was himself a disciple of Origen, though still a heathen. She thanked him for his kindness, and promised to reward him before long. Some time after this, Basilides was asked for an oath on some business or other, and answered that it was not lawful for him to swear, because he was a Christian. When they found that he was in earnest, they brought him into court, and he was remanded to prison, where he told the brethren the cause of his sudden and astonishing change. Potamiaena had appeared to him three days after her death, placed on his head a crown of victory, and told him that she had obtained favour for him with the Lord, and would soon receive him. So they baptized him, and he was beheaded next day. And she appeared to others also, and converted them too.[1]

[1] Eus. vi. 5. Eusebius vouches for these stories, and there is nothing unlikely in them.

As Roman law did not allow the execution of a virgin, dishonour was the legal preliminary to a capital sentence. The daughter of Sejanus is one case

In Africa the persecution claimed a still nobler victim than Leonides. Some time before Mar. 7, 203 a group of five catechumens was seized. Vibia Perpetua was a young matron, Revocatus a slave with Felicitas his "companion"—Roman law disdained to call her his wife. The others were Saturninus and Secundulus. A few days later their friend Saturus joined them of his own accord; for Montanist enthusiasm was high in Africa, and the persecution did not calm it. Perpetua's was a divided house. Her mother and aunt and two surviving brothers were Christians, so that her old father stood alone in his heathenism, and his distress was time after time her sorest trial. As we hear nothing of her husband, we may set him down as heathen too. For a while Perpetua herself tells her simple story of their baptism in the first days of their detention, and " the one prayer for endurance which the Spirit gave me after it." Then to prison. Such darkness! and heat, and crowding, and rudeness of the soldiers. But " the blessed deacons who ministered to us " bought them a daily airing in a better part of the prison; and when she got her infant to stay with her, " it straight-way became a palace to me." Then her brother bade her ask a vision from the Lord to shew how these things should end. She asked; and that night she saw a ladder reaching up to heaven, beset with swords

---

in point. A well-meaning heathen judge might even think he had done a good work, if the threat saved life by securing obedience to the law.

As regards Basilides, there is nothing unlikely in his gentleness to Potamiaena, in the statement that he was Origen's disciple while still a heathen, in his refusal to swear, or in the vision of Potamiaena to him and others. Her death may well have made an immense impression on those prepared to receive it.

Neumann *Röm. Staat* 165, 292 rejects the stories. His argument seems sufficiently answered by Augar *Die Frau in römischen Christenprozess*.

and knives, and guarded by a dragon at its foot.
Saturus went up first; then Perpetua, stepping on
the dragon's head; and the Good Shepherd welcomed
them in the gardens above. The trial follows, and
the procurator Hilarianus condemns them all to the
beasts. Then a vision of her little brother Dinocrates
in evil case, who was dead of cancer. So she prayed
for him; and " on the day we were kept in the stocks,"
she saw him again drinking the water of baptism and
rejoicing. The last night but one she hears herself
called to the amphitheatre. No beasts are there, but
a hideous Egyptian wrestles with her. She treads
him underfoot, and leaves like a conquering gladiator
by the Gate of Life. " So I understood that I was not
to fight with beasts, but with the devil; but I knew
that I should have the victory." Saturus has a
bolder vision. The victory is won, and angels bear
away their spirits to a paradise of trees, where the
host of heaven is waiting for them. There they find
the martyrs who were burned before them; and in
" a place whose walls were as built of light" the
Ancient of Days receives them, and wipes away their
tears. But Optatus the Bishop mourned outside;
and when Perpetua began to talk with him in Greek,
the angels drove him away, saying, Let these alone;
and if ye have quarrels amongst you, forgive one
another. And they rebuked him, saying, Amend
thy people, for they quarrel like the factions of the
circus.

Perpetua lays down her pen the day before the
games—"let him write the rest who will"—and
Tertullian himself[1] takes up the story. Secundulus

---

[1] So Robinson *Texts and Studies* i. 47; and his case seems as well made
out as we can expect.

died in prison, and "by God's grace escaped the beasts."
Felicitas was great with child, and they sorely feared
that " their good companion " would not be delivered
in time to suffer with them; but on their earnest
prayer she brought forth a girl two days before the
games, "which a certain sister reared as her own."
The "free supper" of the condemned on their last
night they turned into an *agape*; and when gazers
crowded in—Mark us well, said Saturus, that you
may know us in the day of judgment.   " The day of
their victory shone forth; and they went out to the
amphitheatre as if to heaven, trembling it might be
with joy, but not with fear," Perpetua with bright
step and flashing eyes, Felicitas rejoicing to come
" straight from the midwife to the gladiator."   To
Hilarianus, as they swept in triumph past him,
" Thou art our judge : God is thine "—a defiance for
which they were scourged at once.   Saturninus was
torn by one bear, but another meant for Saturus would
not come out of his den.   " For the girls, the devil had
prepared a savage cow to suit their sex " : but even
the savage mob was horrified to see the milk trickling
from the young mother's breasts.   So they were given
gowns.   Perpetua was tossed first; and as she came
to herself, she drew her gown over her and fastened
her hair, " for it was not fitting that a martyr should
seem to mourn."   Then she raised Felicitas, and the
two stood hand in hand, the matron and the slave,
alike faithful unto death.   The mob itself was touched.
They were remanded to the Gate of Life, as if
their victory were won, though not that they might
live, and a bold catechumen ministered to them.
When will they want us for that cow? said
Perpetua, as waking from an ecstasy.   In the last

round of the games Saturus was covered with blood
by the first bite of a leopard. *Salvum lotum!* Good
luck of your bath! was the brutal jest. At last the
butchery. They rose and gave each other the kiss of
peace, came to the slaughter, and passed under the
knife in silence. Only Perpetua cried out at the
first clumsy stroke, and then guided the raw gladiator's
unsteady hand to her throat. "It may be that so
great a woman could not have been killed, had not
she herself been willing."

There is something here even more significant than
the lofty courage of Perpetua, which forms the front
of the story. From first to last she never dreams
that Revocatus and Felicitas are less than her equals
and companions in Christ. Enthusiasm might have
nerved the matron and the slave apart : but no mere
enthusiasm could have joined their hands in death.
The mischievous eccentricities of Montanism are as
dust in the balance while we watch the mighty working of the power of another world in which not only
the vulgar fear of death is overcome, but the deepest
social division of the ancient world is utterly forgotten.

It were well if we could rest here at the noble
story of Perpetua, for the student has no harder task
than that of seeing a time of persecution in the clear
light of truth. The dangers of a false perspective are
as real as those of prejudice, and less generally recognized. We do well to fix our eyes on its heroic
scenes, for the man who looks coldly on them is far
sunk in baseness. By all means let the martyr stand
out in his glory, and let many a weakness be forgiven
him if he needs it : but let not history forget that
persecution has a squalid background of cowardice,
disorder, bitterness and fanatic enthusiasm. Its

general influence is bad.   If it weeds out the time-servers and the weak, it hardens the strong for evil as well as for good.   The break-up of regular church government is the opportunity of unquiet spirits ; and if the old quarrels are sometimes forgotten in the grandeur of the contest, new disputes more often grow up round them.   The sobering influence of regular religious life is ill replaced by the excitement of secret meetings and the demoralizing strain of an ever-present sense of danger.   Small wonder if manly resolution passes into wilfulness—if men fling out defiance to persecutors and false brethren, and judge hardly the weakness they have themselves overcome —if they strengthen themselves with pride and bitterness, and allow free course to the enthusiasm which seems needed to sustain them in their heavy trial. This is the familiar background of every persecution : and though some of its features are better seen in the times of Decius and Diocletian, we can trace most of them in those of Severus.   The great discipline questions were only just raised as yet by Montanism ; but we have seen the confusion of the church of Alexandria, the defiances of Origen, the visions of Perpetua and her companions.   We read also of other strange enthusiasms.   Judas the commentator brought down the seventy weeks of Daniel to the tenth year of Severus, and there stopped as he thought just before Antichrist's coming : so deeply had the stirring of the persecution disturbed the minds of men.[1]   A bishop in Syria led out his flock to the wilderness to await Christ's coming; so they wandered in the mountains till the governor seized them for brigands, and only the efforts of his Christian wife prevented a

[1] Eus. vi. 7.

widespread persecution.   Another in Pontus was
three times warned in a dream that the day of judgment would come the next year; so they left their
lands untilled or sold their goods till the return of the
year covered their prophet with shame.   But by that
time many of them were beggars.[1]

Hard as the trial was for the African churches, it
passed away like others.   The rescript of Severus was
gradually forgotten, and in his last years there was
peace.   The grim emperor died in Feb. 211, and left
his sons at deadly enmity.   They had some thoughts
of dividing the Empire at the Hellespont, but Roman
feeling was not yet ripe for this.   Before long the
knot was cut by murder : so Geta died, and Bassianus
reigned (211-217).   Severus Antoninus, to give him
his official name, utterly belied the gentle promise of
his childhood.   He was a mere soldier, " more cruel
than his cruel father."   His murders were wholesale
among the Roman nobles, and great was the massacre
with which he punished the scurrilous mob of
Alexandria.   He cared only for the soldiers, spared
no money to secure their favour, and was hated by
the rest of the world.

As regards the Christians, things drifted.   Caracalla (to give him his nickname) began by recalling
the exiles : and some of these may have been
Christians.   If there is a doubtful story that he put
to death bishop Alexander of Baccanae in Etruria, we
have no reason to set him down as a special enemy of
the Christians.[2]   The only serious persecution came
in Africa, early in his reign, and seems to have

---

[1] Hippolytus *in Dan.* iv. 18, 19.

[2] The story as it stands in so gross a legend that a residuum of truth is
hardly worth the search.

originated in the great camp at Lambaesis. On the
occasion of a largess, the soldiers used to come up
with crowns on their heads to receive it. Even the
Christians did the same, though the wearing of crowns
was a pagan custom, disapproved by so moderate a
man as Clement of Alexandria. Only one of them
refused to wear his crown, carried it in his hand,
avowed himself a Christian, and was no doubt
punished according to law. Tertullian enthusiastic-
ally defends him in his treatise *de Corona*, though
we can see that Christian opinion was mostly against
him. But when persecution spread to Carthage itself,
he addressed a sober remonstrance to the proconsul
Scapula. " We are not afraid of you, but rejoice in
condemnation rather than acquittal. It is for your
own sake that I write. We worship the one true God
of Nature, and you do wrong to make us sacrifice to
your gods, for it is the natural right of every man to
worship what he believes in. We are good citizens
who pray for the emperor—we never were mixed up
with Albinus, or Niger, or Cassius—and reverence
him as greater than the gods his creatures, and second
only to the true God. Nor will you slay the innocent
with impunity. Signs are not wanting of the wrath
of heaven. Remember the rains which ruined last
year's harvest, the northern lights which lighted up
the walls of Carthage, the eclipse which scared the
assembly at Utica. Remember the fate of our first
persecutor Vigellius Saturninus, who lost his sight—
of Claudius Lucius Herminianus in Cappadocia, who
was eaten of worms—of Caecilius Capella, who
perished in the ruin of Byzantium. So you gave
Mavilus of Hadrumetum to the beasts, and then
came the rains—may it be a warning to you. In any

case you need not be so cruel. Even stern judges
have shrank from work of this sort. Cincius Severus
for example taught the Christians how to answer in
court. Asper declared his disgust in open court, and
let a man go when the torture was hardly begun,—
and that without making him sacrifice. Pudens tore
up the accusation when he found that a man had been
riotously seized, and refused to hear the case.
Severus himself deliberately protected us, and so did
Marcus after his deliverance in Germany. We are
blameless; and our reward is that you burn us. The
governors of Numidia and Mauretania are content
with the lawful punishment of the sword. But look
to yourself, for we are not afraid. Even Arrius
Antoninus was daunted when the Christians in Asia
defied him in a body. What will you do if the
Christians of Carthage defy you in their thousands?
You will have to decimate the city. Spare yourself, if
you will not spare us. Our Master you cannot touch,
but those you count your masters are only mortal
men. But our sect shall never fail. The more it is
smitten, the more it grows, for every one who is moved
by our patience to inquiry straightway becomes our
follower."

The most striking feature of the age of Severus is
the change in heathenism which prepared it for its
last great conflict under the standard of Neoplatonism
with the Gospel. The earlier stages of it are represented by the four great women of the house of
Severus—Julia Domna and her sister Julia Maesa, and
Maesa's daughters Julia Soaemias and Julia Mamaea.
They belonged to the old royal family of the priests
of El Gabal, the sun-god of Emesa in Syria; and

though their house was fallen from its high estate, they were still a power in the land. Julia Domna had beauty and culture, ambition and ability, and was no cipher of an empress even by the side of Septimius Severus. She contended on equal terms with the favourite Plautianus, and surrounded the emperor with Syrian counsellors. Paul and Ulpian were her countrymen, and Papinian was her relative. But while Severus lived, she was rather the centre of a literary circle of an eclectic sort, whose chief ornament was the sophist Philostratus, whom she commissioned to write the life of Apollonius of Tyana. Her power reached its height when Severus was dead. She saw indeed her favourite son Geta slaughtered in her arms ; but she did not therefore refuse to come to a sort of understanding with Caracalla. He let her govern as she pleased, provided she found him money, and did not meddle with his life among the soldiers. So it is to Julia and her Syrian lawyers that we must ascribe the extension of the Roman franchise in 212 to all free inhabitants of the Empire. It was done for mere fiscal purposes, but none the less it marks an epoch. The work of obliterating the difference between Romans and provincials begun by Julius Caesar was completed by Julia Domna. If Rome had long been the world, henceforth also the world was Rome. But Julia's most important activity was on the side of religion ; and to understand this we must survey the state of heathenism in her times.

The scepticism of the decaying republic was only the religious unrest of an age of change, so that it vanished as the Empire settled down. Even in the upper classes it was not universal, and the masses it scarcely reached at all. It never disturbed the stately

round of the ancient ceremonials.   The old gods of
Rome never ceased to be supreme above the crowd
of upstarts.   There were flamens, and augurs, and
pontiffs as of old ; and the proudest senators felt
honoured by admission to their sacred colleges.   The
knights of Rome rode year by year to Vesta's door,
and the holy virgins still watched the perpetual fire
on Vesta's hearth.   The Arval Brethren still performed
their immemorial sacrifices, and the Salii danced to
chants whose ancient cadences no living man could
understand.   When the cloud of scepticism had
passed away, the old gods of Rome seemed standing
where they stood before.   Many a nation had been
blotted out from under heaven, but the primaeval
rituals were scarcely changed   Pagan Rome too could
cry her *Semper eadem.*

Nevertheless, a mighty change had overtaken
them.   They went into the cloud as gods of the city,
and they came out as gods of the Empire.   The
worships of the world were melting down together,
as in some vast crucible.   There was a great variety
among them.   The many-breasted Artemis of Ephesus
was not the virgin Artemis of Athens, the Ashtoreth
of Carthage was not the Juno of Italy, and the Baals
of Heliopolis and Emesa were very unlike the Roman
Jupiter.   So there was a great confusion when Greek
and Latin names were given wholesale to the gods of
all the nations.   It was partly under cover of these
civilized names that the crowd of Eastern gods came
in—the *Mater Deûm* from Phrygia, then Isis and
Serapis from Egypt, and later still the Sun-god
Mithra from the further East.   As the gods of
Greece had invaded Rome since the time of the
Tarquins, so now the gods of the East were being

fused with those of Greece and Rome together. The merchants, the soldiers, and the slaves brought in strange worships in spite of the earlier emperors ; and the later emperors themselves went after them. Commodus and the house of Severus were devoted to Serapis, and every man did that which was right in his own eyes in choosing to himself gods from the motley crowd of national divinities. "They sought them gods from all quarters, and made them their own." Only two forms of worship were everywhere the same—Christianity, which was not the worship of a national god, and was for that reason in particular forbidden : the other was the official worship of Rome and of the dead and living Caesars.

If the first century was partly sceptical, the second and third centuries not only were religious, but became more and more religious. Serious men turned more and more to religion in the deepening gloom of the declining Empire, and the common people listened gladly to the sermons of the wandering philosophers, and the " missions " of the wandering priests of divers mysteries. They looked peradventure for something more reasonable than polytheism, certainly for something more definite than scepticism, more comforting than philosophy—something that would give them purity in life, patience in the time of trouble, and above all assurance of atonement in the hour of death. In a word, the search for a new religion, which had been going on since Plato's time, was coming to an issue. What was it to be ?

The old philosophies were dead. Sceptics and Epicureans were becoming impossible, and Stoicism was a failure. There were no Stoics after Marcus. The movement was on three main lines. Some strove to

cleanse the old mythologies and return to the simple
faith of the old heroic times, others sought comfort
in the warmer worships of the East, while a few
forswore the gods, and gave themselves heart and soul
to the Galilean. The first line is conservative, the
second implies a considerable change, while the third
is a revolution, though a revolution which alone could
truly satisfy their needs.

The conservative movement can be traced back to
the first century in Apollonius of Tyana, who died at
a great age in the reign of Nerva. If there be any
truth in the romance of Philostratus, we may see in
Apollonius a religious reformer who preaches one
Supreme to be worshipped above and through the lower
gods. Sacrifices might be offered to these, but not to
the Supreme. He is the Ineffable, who needs nothing
at our hands, and accepts neither sacrifice nor offering.
A moral life is needed to clear our sight, Pythagorean
asceticism to give the higher intuition ; for communion
with the Supreme is not by prayer, but by the
"higher word" of ecstasy and trance. Here is
Eclecticism sketched out already, with its lofty
doctrine of one transcendent God confused and defiled
by this unlimited licence to worship other gods " before
him," and at best made sterile by this fencing-off of
all approach to him but by the way of ecstasy. A
few mystics may be able to live in that thin moun-
tain air, but meaner men will always prefer the warm
and pestilential swamps of superstition. Eclecticism
might be monotheistic in theory, but for most men it
was in practice as crass a polytheism as anything that
had gone before it. They chose them gods according
to their fancies, and the grand monotheism was forgotten.

The devout and cultured Plutarch of Chaeronea (*cir.* 48-125) was neither a mystic nor one of the meaner men ; yet he followed similar lines, though with a difference. The Supreme is there, but his power is limited as in Plato by the intractable qualities of matter. The gods are there, and they are all good, but their worship is more than a duty—it is a joy and a blessing. Ecstasy is there, but it is only one way out of many in which the Supreme reveals himself to men ; and the preparation for things divine is not by Pythagorean asceticism, but by the detachment and quiet of a moderate and reasonable Platonism. Though Plutarch is not counted among the saints, no writer of the ancient world comes nearer to the Christian model of kindliness and stainless purity in common life without ascetic pride and sourness. The trouble was that the scandals of worship could not all be explained away, and the scandals of mythology could not all be allegorized into something edifying, so that he had to introduce an order of demons to do the dirty work of heaven which is unworthy of the gods. These are the authors of all the scandals, and they will harm us if they are not propitiated with the ancient ceremonies. Thus even Plutarch is unable to escape the deliberate worship of spirits of evil.

We may pass over others, like Nigrinus, Dion Chrysostom, Apuleius, Numenius, who were all labouring in their several ways for the reform of heathenism. Even Apuleius may fairly take a place, though a low place, in the list. He is made indeed of rather base metal, and utterly lacks the lofty purity of Plutarch ; yet still he strove to throw a passionate devotion into the service of his gods.

Speaking generally, the divine immanence preached

by the Stoics was giving place to the dualism of a
reviving Platonism.   The Oriental thought which
Stoicism had limited to ethics was now overspreading
theology too, and was presently to dominate politics
also for a thousand years and more.   As the Empire
was the *pis aller* of ancient society, so Byzantinism
was the *pis aller* of the Empire, and the Papacy the
pis aller of Latin Christianity.   Meanwhile men felt
more and more that there must somewhere be some
divine Power which cannot finally refuse all answer
to the great and bitter cry that comes up from earth
to heaven.   If Olympus was unworthy to represent
him and reason unable to find him out, and even
Caesar's earthly providence could not reveal him, it
did not follow that he could not be reached at all
Philosophy and superstition must be more thoroughly
examined ; and even barbarian thought was not to be
despised in this dire necessity.   So the last great
effort of the ancient world to find out God by searching took two directions, and yet was one.   On one
side it essayed the heights of heaven ; on the other
it called infernal powers to aid :—

Flectere si nequeo superos, Acheronta movebo.

There was a real connexion between the philosopher
and the theurgist (or magician).   They had the same
general view of religion, constantly tended each to
imitate the other's methods, and finally coalesced in
the vastest system of religion ever devised by human
thought.   The later Neoplatonists felt that philosophy
is a poor thing without some more direct access to
the gods, while the *de mysteriis* aspires to be a
defence of theurgy on grounds of reason.   The
philosopher's awe of truth passed easily into the

incantations of the theurgist. To the one, the old philosophies were broken lights of higher truth ; to the other, the old worships were symbols of a better. In that age of decay, everything seemed to speak dimly of a mysterious Supreme far off from men, represented by philosophers as his prophets, by gods and demons as his agents in the world—satraps and proconsuls, as Celsus calls them. Even Christianity might (with some straining) be fitted into such a scheme as this. So the current of the time set back to monotheism, but to a monotheism never fully disentangled from the maze of polytheism. No heathen thought ever reached the first word of true monotheism—I am the Lord thy God : thou shalt have no other gods before me—in my presence.

In fact, there was a power in these Eastern worships which no deistic monotheism was likely to overcome. There may have been much sophistry among the philosophers, much ignorant superstition in all classes ; but the movement as a whole was a vast advance on the old unspiritual religion of the state. Aspirations to a higher life and cravings for true communion with higher powers were things unknown to the religion of Numa ; and these the Eastern worships in their measure satisfied. In this they were all much of a muchness. Thus the devout women who worshipped Isis were very like the devout women of Roman Catholic countries. With a good deal of running after fashions, a little asceticism and much formalism and ignorance, though probably much less bigotry, their religion was in the main genuine and zealous, and often a cleansing power in life.

In the second century the worships of Isis and

Serapis were predominant, but that of Mithra
came to the front in the third. There was a true
moral element in the worship of Mithra the all-
seeing, the author and protector of life, Mithra the
purifier, the giver of immortality. A great catholic
church of Mithra overspread the lands from Persia
to Britain, especially along the great rivers where
the legions lay. It had regular and irregular clergy,
ascetics and mendicant friars, and divers orders of
faithful men. It had regular divine service three
times daily, and a yearly round of festivals culminat-
ing in the Birthday of Mithra (Dec. 25), with
meetings for worship and processions of noisy
votaries. It had its mysteries too, and surrounded
them with the impressive splendour of stately rituals
and vested priests and blazing lights. It had a
catechumenate of fasting and preparation for a
sacrament of baptism, while the mystic seal of
Mithra marked on the candidate's brow, in token
of his promise to be a "soldier" of Mithra to his
life's end. But he refused the offered crown, for
"Mithra was his crown." Then came a common
meal and sacrament of bread and water (afterwards
of wine) at the "holy table," in memory of the
last meal of Mithra here on earth, before the Sun's
bright chariot carried him away to heaven. It had
confession too, with penance and absolutions; it
had sprinklings of holy water and anointings with
holy oil, and in uncouth lustrations of the blood
of bulls and goats it recognized a promise of re-
generation to life eternal.

What wonder if men preferred the magnificence
of Isis and Mithra to the beggarly worship of the
early Christians? At last the divergent aspirations

of superstition and philosophy seemed to blend in adoration of the all-seeing Sun as the worthiest image of the Supreme.   Mithra, Baal, Helios, Jupiter —as men might chance to call him,

$$\pi o\lambda\lambda\hat{\omega}\nu\ \dot{o}\nu o\mu\acute{a}\tau\omega\nu\ \mu o\rho\phi\grave{\eta}\ \mu\acute{\iota}a,$$

the Sun-god reigned in heathenism, and gathered round him all the failing powers of the ancient world to final battle with the power that is not of this world. In the sign of King Sun the last heroes of heathenism from Aurelian to Julian went forth to battle; and Constantine himself took many years to learn that the Sun-god's cross of light is not the cross of Christ.

We may draw a veil over the hideous immoralities often mixed up with the worship of Mithra, worthily represented in the doings of the emperor El Gabal. They were but the old abominations of Baal and Ashtoreth in the plain of Aven.   Mithraism had too much disorder and indiscipline, too much asceticism and quackery, too much trust in outward forms, to be other than largely immoral in practice, though its tone seems to have improved in the fourth century.   Even its theory will not bear comparison with the Gospel. Mithraism was indeed a stately tree; but it welcomed every unclean and hateful bird to shelter in its branches.   Mithra was not a jealous god, and allowed his votaries to practise any foul worships alongside of his own.[1]   The very grandeur of Mithraism was a fatal weakness, for it never was able to make the Supreme stand out clear from the crowd of lesser gods who seemed to swell his train.

---

[1] Thus the *Taurobolia* belonged rather to the worship of the *Magna Mater*.

It had no effective principle of unity, but was practically little more than a confused agglomeration of all the superstitions, *quotquot toto orbe coluntur.* Above all, between Christ and Mithra is the gulf of death. It is historically evident that the power of the Gospel is in the cross of Christ; and just this was wanting in Mithraism. Whenever the wise men of the world were pleased to construct a Gospel, they always left out this—and they were quite right in doing so, if there is no sin of the world which needs to be taken away. If Mithra has his Last Supper, he ascends to heaven straightway after it. Can we wonder that the Unconquered Sun went down before the Galilean?

But the fullest illustration of the scandal of the cross may be found in the Life of Apollonius, written by Philostratus at the command of Julia Domna. It is practically the Gospel rewritten to satisfy such objections as those of Celsus: and that it was more or less intended for something of the sort seems hardly doubtful.[1] Apollonius is not a Jewish carpenter, but a well-born Greek who learns his wisdom (so far as he needs to learn it) in the approved way, from the sages of India and Ethiopia. He knows the thoughts of men, and (unlike Christ) is continually predicting the fortunes of those he meets. Many of his miracles read almost like those of Jesus of Nazareth; but they are not told in the bald way of the Evangelists: they are decked out with an immense amount of elegant rhetoric. But the most striking contrast is in the closing scenes. Apollonius is not betrayed by a false disciple (as if he could not have seen through a Judas) but accused

[1] So in fact it was used by Hierocles in the Great Persecution.

like Socrates by enemies before Domitian, and allows
himself to be shaved and put in fetters. In prison
he takes his feet out of the fetters for a moment to
shew Damis that he can do it, and sends him on to
meet him at Dicaearchia. At the trial he rebukes
Domitian in open court, and when challenged to save
himself by miracle, vanishes before the eyes of all the
grandees of Rome. In the evening he appears to
Damis at Dicaearchia, and soon afterwards mysteri-
ously disappears from the earth. This at once recalls
the objection of Celsus, that Jesus ought to have
vanished from the cross, and Origen's reply, that if
it had been so written, Celsus would have objected
again, that he ought to have vanished before. Both
in statements and omissions, the contrast of the Life
of Apollonius with the Gospels is the contrast of
heathen pride and rhetoric with the simple truthfulness and insight of the Christian writers.

The Eastern frontier of the Empire was insecure
through most of the third century. Parthia was
dangerous even when she was torn by civil war, and
the restored Persian kingdom (from 226) was for two
generations an overmatch for Rome. Besides this,
the peoples beyond Mount Taurus were restless, from
Armenia to Egypt, and some were willing to look
eastward for deliverance from Rome. Things did
not settle down till after the peace of 297. Caracalla
dealt with the situation in his own vigorous way.
First he cowed Egypt with a great massacre at
Alexandria; then he seized Abgar bar Manu of
Edessa by treachery, and made a province of his
kingdom; then he captured Vologaeses of Armenia,
and sent him prisoner to Rome. By this time he

was involved in war with Parthia;[1] but he could not do much more than desecrate the tombs of the Parthian kings at Arbela before he was assassinated by the craft of the Praetorian Praefect Macrinus (Apr. 8, 217). As the other Praefect Oclatinius Adventus refused the purple, Macrinus was hailed emperor.

M. Opellius Macrinus was a Mauritanian of low birth and moderate ability. He suffered a great defeat from the Parthians, and had to obtain peace by payment of a great sum of money, and on conditions which practically meant the surrender of Armenia. His policy however was wise and healing. He stopped the prosecutions, and endeavoured to reform the army. But instead of disbanding the soldiers, he kept them in winter quarters in Syria, and they grew disaffected. Julia Domna sought a voluntary death after the fall of her house, but her sister Julia Maesa retired to Emesa with her two daughters, Julia Soaemias and Julia Mamaea, and their two young sons, Bassianus and Alexianus, the future emperors El Gabal (Heliogabalus) and Severus Alexander. Bassianus the son of Soaemias held the family priesthood of El Gabal, the Sun-god of Emesa; and his handsome form was very much admired. So when a rumour was spread (and Maesa proved it with golden arguments) that he was really the son of Caracalla, the idol of the soldiers, they caught it up with enthusiasm, and proclaimed him emperor. Macrinus fled like Antonius at Actium, in the crisis of a hard-fought battle, and El Gabal reigned in his stead.

To the student of church history El Gabal is

---

[1] Dio lxxviii. 1 and Herodian iv. agree that he demanded the daughter of Artabanus with a view to annexing Parthia. The great massacre ascribed to him by Herodian is quite in character with him; but the silence of Dio seems fatal.

a man of special interest, because he is the first
emperor with a definitely *religious* policy. Augustus
found religion a useful support for the state : but El
Gabal sought first the kingdom of Baal. His mother
was a Jezebel for whoredoms in the palace, and he
was himself a very saint of the foul Canaanite sort.
He was the priest of El Gabal, and valued the
empire of the world only as a means of bringing all
men to the worship of his god. In this he was a
precursor of Constantine, who would certainly have
been glad to see the whole world Christian. Of
course there is difference enough between the third
and fourth centuries, between Christianity and Syrian
Sun-worship, between Constantine and a vicious boy,
though they had the same general aim of making
an Eastern worship supreme. Therefore there was a
difference in their methods. Constantine stood for
monotheism and for virtue, denouncing idols and
destroying immoral temples, but officially respectful
to heathenism, and only committed to Christianity
on his deathbed. El Gabal's was a frantic syncretism.
He brought the sacred relics of Rome, the palladium
itself included, to the splendid temple of the Sun-god
on the Palatine, married him with infinite pomp to
the Ashtoreth (Juno Caelestis) of Carthage, and
placed all the gods of Olympus in subjection to him.
Constantine avoided Rome, and never lost the respect
of the army : El Gabal flaunted his Syrian superstition before the Senate, and exhibited his unmanly
abominations to the soldiers. Roman pride revolted
against a Caesar who wore the diadem and demanded
Eastern adoration ; and Roman decency was shocked
by the enormities of a fouler beast than Commodus
or Nero. The army became restive. At first they

were satisfied with removing the vile creatures who
" made him a greater fool than he was already ";
but when he provoked a fresh mutiny, they killed
him as incorrigible (March 222).

The Christians remained in peace, for El Gabal
had little to do with them. Even the legend-mongers
have resisted the temptation to turn him into a bloody
persecutor. A single saying connects him with them.
He said that the religion of the Jews and the
Samaritans, and the worship of the Christians, ought
to be transferred to the temple of the Sun-god.[1]
This may have been meant for a friendly invitation;
but it is enough to shew that El Gabal would soon
have come to persecution, if the Christians had been
unfortunate enough to attract his serious attention.

Alexianus and Mamaea contrast brightly with El
Gabal and Soaemias. No scandal taints Mamaea's
fame; and hardly another of the long line of emperors
is as amiable as the unfortunate Severus Alexander
—for this was the imperial title given to Alexianus.
He was not fourteen; so he grew up under the
guidance of Mamaea and the Senate; and they must
have governed fairly well, for the years of regency
were years of peace. In fact, the senatorial restoration lasted to the end of Alexander's reign, for he did
everything in concert with the Senate and its com-
mittees, and gave it an important share in the conduct
of affairs. Alexander's high sense of duty is like that
of Marcus, and there is a touch of pedantry in it,
though he was no Stoic. A gracious and kindly
sovereign he was; implacable only to thieves and
peculators, and to the creatures of " the unclean

[1] *Vita Heliog.* 3 *Jud. et Sam. religiones et Christianam devotionem.* The
change of word may possibly be significant.

beast," as he called El Gabal. Nor did his high
literary culture make him any the less a brave and
hardy soldier, though like Marcus he was a poor
general. His chief public weakness was his too open
dependence on his mother, for he was neither remiss
with the army nor wanting in moral courage. On
the contrary, his discipline was only too severe; and
his severity seems to have helped his ruin. Yet after
all it was rather the violence of weakness than the
firmness of strength, for it did not keep order. The
soldiers fought with the citizens for days together in
the streets of Rome, and slaughtered the Praefect
Ulpian in the emperor's own presence; and he could
not punish the murderer without making him governor
of Egypt in order to get him away from Rome.
Alexander could retrench the squanderings of El
Gabal; but he was not the born ruler needed to
restore the discipline of the army destroyed by
Severus and Caracalla, and such chance as he had
was ruined by his failure in the Persian war. His
end is obscure : the one thing certain is that he
perished with his mother in a mutiny near Mainz
(March 235).

Severus Alexander contrasted as a Roman with El
Gabal and his foreign superstitions. The black stone
went back to Emesa, the image of Juno Caelestis was
restored to Carthage, the palladium returned to the
keeping of the Vestals—if it had ever left their
keeping, for they boasted of having given El Gabal a
counterfeit. Alexander's official religion was blameless, for he went up weekly to the Capitol, and was
often at the temples; but his personal devotion was
given rather to the saints and heroes of the past. In
his private chapel, along with the deified emperors,

were statues of Apollonius, of Christ, of Abraham,
of Orpheus, and of others like them; and these he
devoutly worshipped every morning.[1]

Alexander was genuinely religious, though his
eclecticism was not quite of the usual sort. When
cooks and Christians disputed a piece of waste ground,
he awarded it to the Christians, on the ground that
any sort of divine worship[2] was better than a cook-
shop. If he is no Christian, he knows something
about the Christians, and takes a friendly interest in
their religion. We have got a long way from the one
contemptuous allusion of Marcus to their "mere
obstinacy." Christianity is now too strong for a
conspiracy of silence, though it is still ignored by
Dio, and even by Macrobius at the end of the fourth
century. Hippolytus addresses an Exhortation to the
empress Severina, probably the Vestal Julia Aquilia
Severa, married and divorced by El Gabal.[3] Origen
was sent for by Mamaea at Antioch (rather 232 than
218) and stayed with her for some time. Alexander
cannot have seen much of martyrs, though the
legends give him a few, including St. Cecilia. One
saying he learned "from Jews or Christians"—*What
thou wouldst not have done to thyself, do not thou to
another*—he often used himself, and often chose for
the crier's proclamation when punishments were going
on. So too he posted up the names of intended
governors and invited objections to them, saying it
was a scandal that Jews and Christians did this in

[1] *Vita Alex.* 29 *si facultas esset, id est, si non cum uxore cubuisset*—a curious touch of asceticism in the genial Alexander.
[2] *ib.* 49 *melius esse, ut quemammodumcumque illic deus colatur.* Rather a god than God.
[3] The Syriac Fragments are למה ממאיא (πρὸς Μαμμαίαν) but there is no evidence that Mamaea had the name Severina. See Caspari *Quellen* 392-3.

the ordination of their priests, while it was not done at the appointment of governors, to whom the lives and fortunes of men were entrusted. The Christians flourished in the palace, and flattered themselves (at least in the next generation) that Alexander was one of themselves.

The mutiny in which Alexander perished was the signal for half a century of confusion. The new emperor was a soldier like Septimius Severus, but without a vestige of culture. C. Julius Verus Maximinus (235-238) was a rude Thracian peasant, the son of a Gothic father and an Alan mother. Strange tales are told of his gigantic size and strength;[1] and there must have been some foundation for them. Maximin owed his first promotion to Severus, kept honourably aloof from the usurper Macrinus and the vile El Gabal, and proved himself one of Alexander's best generals. Of his reign we have none but hostile accounts : yet a bitter enemy admits that he "sometimes did justice," and tells us how he refused Eastern adoration in the true old Roman style. "The gods forbid that a free man should kiss my feet." His rough manliness contrasted well with Alexander's culture and El Gabal's vileness. If he never came to Rome like a civilized emperor, he smote the Germans with such a destruction as kept the Rhine fairly quiet for the next twenty years. But he was nothing more than a good soldier. Both his position and his own character urged him to reverse the policy of Alexander, and therefore to pamper the soldiers like Caracalla, and to govern by cruelty and terror. The Senate accepted him only because they

---

[1] Thus we need not believe that he commonly drank five gallons of wine and ate forty (sometimes sixty) pounds of meat.

were not able to fight him. They hated him from
the first for his barbarian birth and general rusticity,
and he despised them for culture and cowardice.
Herodian and Capitolinus are no doubt unfair to him;
but there can be no question that Maximin was bad
enough at best, and that well-grounded suspicion
made him a savage tyrant.

To the Christians he could not but be hostile.
True, he had little of the aristocrat's contempt for
them, perhaps no serious policy of any sort; but he
hated all men who had been in favour with Alexander.
Yet he did not raise a bloody persecution. We hear
of no executions. We are told that Pontianus and
Hippolytus (apparently the rival bishops of Rome)
were exiled to the malarious island of Sardinia, and
that Pontianus, and apparently Hippolytus also, died
there. We learn something more from Origen's
Exhortatio ad martyrium. His friends Ambrosius
and Protoctetus were arrested; but the former at any
rate seems to have escaped without losing even his
property. There were also the usual outrages, as
when the mob revenged an earthquake on the
Christians by burning their churches; and there was
a persecution in Cappadocia under the *praeses*
Serenianus. For these however Maximin was not
directly responsible. His own attack was limited to
the officials[1] of the churches: and this is significant
of a change in the character of persecution. Hitherto

---

[1] Eus. vi. 28 Μαξιμῖνος . . κατὰ κότον τὸν πρὸς τὸν Ἀλεξάνδρου οἶκον ἐκ
πλειόνων πιστῶν συνεστῶτα διωγμὸν ἐγείρας, τοὺς τῶν ἐκκλησιῶν ἄρχοντας
μόνους ὡς αἰτίους τῆς κατὰ τὸ εὐαγγέλιον διδασκαλίας ἀναιρεῖσθαι προστάττει.
Neumann (*Röm. Staat* 211) shews from the usage of Eus. that these ἄρχοντες
are not the bishops only, but the clergy generally. Thus Maximin was the
precursor of Decius in his particular attack on the clergy, which Valerian
and Diocletian (each in his second edict) developed into special measures
against them.

the clergy had run no greater danger than others, except in so far as that they were likely to be better known than others : henceforth they were deliberately singled out for attack. As Severus had struck at the converts, so now Maximin and his successors struck at the clergy.

But it soon ceased to matter what Maximin did or left undone. Early in 238 there was a rising in Africa in favour of the old proconsul Gordian, which the Senate hailed with delight. It was put down as soon as the third legion marched on Carthage from Lambaesis ; but now the Senate was committed to a struggle of life and death with Maximin. The empress strove in vain to mediate. Maximin was devoted *more majorum* to the infernal gods, his creatures in Rome were butchered, and the defence of Italy was organized. So ably was this done that we can hardly mistake the generalship of the *princeps senatus*, the future emperor Valerian. Two emperors were chosen, Pupienus and Balbinus, the one a rough soldier of low birth, to conduct the war, the other an elegant senator for civil affairs. Military and civil powers were at last divided as the Senate always wished to divide them ; and no practical change was made when the army in Rome insisted on adding to them young Gordian, the proconsul's grandson, a boy of fourteen, as a third emperor. Maximin came down on Italy, breathing revenge and slaughter ; but the country was laid waste before him, Aquileia held out stoutly, and before long the hardships of the campaign led to a mutiny. Maximin was killed by his own soldiers.

The Senate did not long enjoy its victory. Within three months another mutiny carried off Pupienus and Balbinus, and young Gordion reigned alone (238-244). The reign is obscure, for here ends the narrative of Herodian, and here begins a gap reaching to the capture of Valerian in the *Historia Augusta*. As we hear nothing of Gordian's dealings with the Christians, we may safely take it that he troubled himself very little about them. The one outstanding fact is that his want of success in the Persian war enabled his *Praefectus Praetorio* Philip to supplant him (early in 244).

M. Julius Philippus (244-249) was the son of an Arab sheikh, and is the last of the Oriental emperors. Nearly all his successors came from the Illyrian countries where the legions of the Danube were recruited. His reign also is obscure. We hear of a few mutinies and rival emperors; but the chief new feature of it is the increasing pressure of the Goths on the Danube, and its only conspicuous event is the magnificent festival of the thousandth year of Rome in 248. To the Christians he was so friendly that rumours arose that he was a Christian himself. They are mentioned a dozen years or so after his death by Dionysius of Alexandria,[1] and later by Eusebius, though neither seems to warrant them : and here the silence of Eusebius is decisive, for he knew the letters of Origen to Philip and his wife Otacilia Severa, which must have made it quite clear whether the emperor was Christian or heathen. Considering the eagerness of the Christians to claim every emperor as friendly, it was only natural that a friendly emperor who corresponded with Origen should be claimed as a convert. Philip was certainly not baptized : and if

---

[1] *ap.* Eus. vii. 10 οἱ λεχθέντες ἀναφανδὸν Χριστιανοὶ γεγονέναι cannot mean any but Alexander and Philip.

we do not entirely reject the story told by Eusebius and Leontius [1] of his exclusion from the church by Babylas at Antioch for the murder of Gordian, we cannot accept it in anything like this form.   Philip was a heathen in his official action : and if curiosity led him to the church at Easter, the simple fact that he was not baptized would explain his exclusion from the more solemn parts of the service.

Here then we see Christianity almost on the steps of the throne : the heathen reaction is yet to come.

[1] Eus. v. 34.   Leontius in *Chron. Pasch* 503 Bonn. Eus. begins κατέχει λόγος, and names neither Antioch nor Babylas.   Chrysostom (who wrote at Antioch) names Babylas, but not Philip.

Books

Réville Jean *Religion à Rome sous les Sévères* Paris 1886 ; Neumann K. J. *Staat u. Kirche bis auf Diocletian* Bd. I (all publ.) Leipz. 1890 ; Cumont *Textes et Monuments* 1896 (for Mithraism) ; Robinson J. A. *Perpetua* in *Texts and Studies* ; Bigg C. *Neoplatonism ; The Church's Task in the Roman Empire* ; Dill S. *Roman Society from Nero to Marcus Aurelius* ; Fuchs C. *Gesch. des Kaisers L. Septimius Severus* Wien 1884 ; Schultz O. *Der römische Kaiser Caracalla* Leipz. 1909 ; Canney *Apollonius* in Hastings' *D.R.S. and Ethics* ; Cumont *Oriental Religions in Roman Paganism* 1911.

CHAPTER XIX

THE SCHOOL OF ALEXANDRIA

THE relation of Alexandria to Greece is like that of Constantinople to Rome, as her greatest colony, and nearly her last.   In his choice of a site, the genius of Alexander may rival that of Constantine.   Alexandria lay near the Canopic mouth of the Nile, on a tongue of land between Lake Mareotis and the sea.   Opposite was the Pharos Island, connected with the city by a huge mole nearly a mile long, with a port on each side.   It was the largest commercial city of the East. Antioch might nearly equal it in size and surpass it in the beauty of its situation and the splendour of its buildings, though all Syria could shew nothing to match the mighty pile of the Serapeum.   But nowhere in the wide world could so vast and multifarious a crowd be found of traders and sailors and craftsmen of every sort.   If most of them were Greeks, Jews or Egyptians, hardly a language spoken under heaven was missing from the Babel of the quays of Alexandria.   She had many a merchantman carried by the monsoons to India, and many a great corn-ship sailing into Italy.   Her commerce ranged from Barygaza to the Pillars.   Her populace was the most turbulent in the Empire; as scurrilous as that of Antioch, but with an Egyptian savagery

of its own.   Caracalla's great massacre in 216 was
not unprovoked.   Heathen Alexandria tore in pieces
Philopator's concubines; Christian Alexandria tore
in pieces bishop George and the philosopher Hypatia.
The mob was always ready for murderous outrage
—to hunt the Jews in Caligula's time, to lynch
the Christians in Philip's days, to slaughter prisoners
in the siege of the Serapeum under Theodosius.   The
herdsmen of the Delta were hardly less ferocious;
once they cut up and ate a Roman centurion: and
similar doings were not unknown in the religious
feuds of the cities further up the Nile.[1]   So the
government had to keep a jealous eye on Egypt,
for Rome depended on her corn supplies.   Augustus
gave her no lordly senator as *legatus,* but a mere *praefectus* of equestrian rank, and allowed no senator
to set foot in the province without permission,
Egypt was Caesar's business only.   Under stricter
administration there was less room for lawless riots
against the Christians, so that the tumults in Philip's
time (248) are the more ominous of the coming
Decian reaction.   Meanwhile philosophy and learning
flourished from the first round the great Library of
Alexandria and the college of the Museum with the
Fellows who ate at its table.   In the Greek age the
learning of the ancient world was fairly summed up
at Alexandria by Eratosthenes and Aristarchus, and
in Roman times by Ptolemy and Athenaeus.   The
tradition of learning was worthily continued on the
heathen side by Ammonius Saccas (Plotinus rather
belongs to Rome) and Hypatia; on the Christian by
Clement and Origen, Athanasius and Cyril; and its
last traces only died away with John Philoponus in

---

[1] Ombi and Tentyra Juv. *Sat.* xv.

the sixth century. So long was Alexandria a chosen
home of learning. And if thought was free throughout the Empire for those who conformed to the
Roman ceremonies, it was nowhere more expansive
than at Alexandria. Greece had thrown open her
doors to the world, and even barbarian religions
were eagerly discussed in the cosmopolitan city by
the Nile.

The early history of the church in Alexandria is
obscure. It claimed St. Mark for its founder; but
we have no clear evidence on the matter. However,
the Gospel made rapid progress in the busy turmoil
of this "ant-hill of men," and was more than usually
influenced by the heathen thought around it. Thus
Alexandria was a natural centre for Gnosticism. It
was the home of Basilides, of Carpocrates, of Valentinus. They seemed to have made the church their
own : yet from the church of Alexandria came
the movement which conquered Gnosticism. We
must look back to the beginning to see what that
movement was.

When Christ our Saviour says, I am the way, the
truth and the life, he claims to be himself the way in
which all must walk, the truth for which all must
seek, the life by which all must live. Hard as the
saying is, it cannot mean less than this. He must
be served with mind as well as heart and soul, if he
is not only a teacher of truth, but himself the final
truth which informs and constitutes all truth in
heaven and earth. Thus the Gospel is theoretical as
well as practical, though most of all a power of life.
It had an intellectual element from the first. The
inquirer needed some intellectual effort even to follow

the story of the Saviour's life, or to get some notion
of the Trinity in whose name he desired to be
baptized. So much teaching as this was needed for
the humblest applicant. But if this was as much as
the officials of the church were bound to give to all,
individuals here and there would feel called on like
Aquila and Priscilla to expound the way of God
more perfectly to some—and they were quite free to
do it, for there was no idea yet that only the clergy
ought to be teachers. It was but an outcome of the
missionary zeal inseparable from healthy Christian
life. So Christian teachers gathered scholars round
them like the heathen philosophers. In some places
no very advanced teaching might be needed; but at
Alexandria the inquirer would sometimes be a cultivated student like Pantaenus or Clement, whose
questions might touch the deepest mysteries of the
Gospel. In this case the teacher also would have to
be a cultivated student, a match for the literary men
of the Museum. Hence the school tended to assume
a literary form, and seems to have had no official
connexion with the clergy till it was taken up by
bishop Demetrius in 203.[1]

Four times in four distant ages the truth of Christ
has had to be defended from a great and deadly
enemy inside his church. Each time the Spirit of
Christ has pointed away from a church entangled
in traditionalism to the living voice of Scripture;
and each time fresh strength has come from a fresh

[1] So de Faye *Clém. d'Alex.* He points out (*a*) how Clement p. 322 had
to "hunt out his Sicilian bee (Pantaenus) hidden in Egypt" (ἐν Αἰγ. θηράσας
λεληθότα)—which seems to shew that he was not an official teacher, (*b*) the
informal way in which the restored school in 202 gathered round Origen, as
the first capable teacher the heathen inquirers could meet with.

These considerations seem to shew that the school arose in an informal
way. Similar needs gave rise to similar schools at Antioch, Edessa, Caesarea.

revelation of the ever-living Person of whom
Scripture speaks. The first of these crises was the
contest with Gnosticism, the second that with
Arianism; the Reformation was the third; the fourth
is the great scientific controversy opened by the
Deists, which seems gathering to its hottest battle in
our own time. In every age of revolution God is
putting forth to the world some new revelation; and
the church that will not receive it—from that church
shall be taken even that it hath. It may keep its
worldly pomp, its priests may be as gods, its state-
craft a marvel to the world; but its life is gone. To
the second century was given a wider view of Christ
which hallowed all knowledge; to the fourth a higher
view of Christ in the divine fulness of his eternal
Sonship, to the sixteenth a nearer view of Christ as
dealing singly with us all, not through some infallible
human authority; and now to the twentieth century
is borne a deeper view of Christ as not the giver and
revealer only, but the personal ground of truth and
law in earth and heaven. Thus the School of
Alexandria marks the first of the four great returns
to Christ which have kept his church a living power
to this day.

Its central thought was already given by St. Paul
to the Colossians—that all aspirations are fulfilled in
Christ. Though the false teachers at Colossae are
Judaizers, not Gnostics, they shew us the ideas from
which Gnosticism arose in the next generation. Like
the more earnest of the Gnostics, they had a deep sense
of the fulness of God, of the greatness of the chasm
between God and man, of the need of knowledge, of
the duty of rising to the unseen. All this was good
and true; but they went wrong through forgetting

that it is all fulfilled in Christ already.   He it is who
reveals the fulness of God and fills the chasm without
the help of angels.   In him all the treasures of
knowledge are hidden, and in him we can rise to
the unseen without an ascetic "philosophy," which
indeed is valueless to check the carnal nature.[1]

This is the general answer of the Gospel to
Gnosticism and the thoughts allied to it in every age,
and the Alexandrians had only to work it out with
reference to the particular needs of their own time.
The problem, as we have seen, always involves the
relation of the Gospel to the current ideas of religion
and philosophy ; and at the end of the second century
this was necessarily a Greek problem.   Christendom
was by this time chiefly Greek, for the Latin churches
of the West were in their infancy, and the Syrian
churches eastward had sunk into outliers of the central
mass ; and both Latins and Syrians leaned on Greek
thought.   Greek was the language of commerce, and
Christianity moved on the lines of commerce, so that
all the leading churches, Carthage excepted, were
Greek.   Education (except in law) was wholly Greek
in method and mostly Greek in substance, so that
literature in the second century was almost entirely
Greek, except in Roman Africa.   Philosophy also was
Greek, for Rome shewed no originality in that
direction.   Cicero adapted Panaetius, the emperor
Marcus put down his private thoughts in Greek.
The Latins had a hard struggle with their stiff unspiritual language before they could even formulate
their faith in terms of Roman law.   The Greeks on
the other hand had cultivated philosophy for centuries,
and wielded a language of unrivalled subtlety and

---

[1] Col. ii. 23 (Lightfoot).

precision. If it had lost something of its elegance and classic purity since the great days of Athens, it had gained in richness and was as flexible as ever. Like English in our own time, which has lost something of its Elizabethan strength and dignity, it tended to simpler constructions and shorter sentences, and was therefore all the better fitted to be the common language of culture all over the Empire. It was historically unavoidable that the old balance of Israelite and Greek and Roman should be as distinctly overweighted by the Greek in the second century as by the Latin in the thirteenth—only, the mistakes of the Greeks were somewhat less disastrous.

The Gospel was helped even more by the crumbling of the Greek mythology than by the crumbling of the Greek language. The Greeks had always drawn gods and men together, and in doing so they were more right than they knew; but they so mismanaged their theology that if the world was full of gods, the gods were full of human weakness and human vice. There might have been something divine in the idea of gods

From above
Descending to enjoy our mortal love.

Did not the Lord himself enjoy, and promise to reward the love of those who had continued with him in his temptations? But the Greeks were thinking of sense: the legends which joined gods and men in lawless amours were utterly debasing. They were a scandal to serious men from Xenophanes onward, and gave the man in the street his excuse for "thinking that lust is godliness."[1] Their demoralizing influence is no way exaggerated by the Apologists. Again,

[1] Clem. Al. *Protr.* p. 53.

the consecration of the dead to deity may imply some recognition that benevolence and self-sacrifice are not less divine than the intellect and beauty which the Greeks were now more ready to worship.[1] Every now and then it may have been so, for the heroes are sometimes better than the gods.   But the deification of living men did as much as the legends to debase the idea of God to the level of common sinners.   It is positively lower than beast-worship; for if the beasts were the likeness of gods, they were not commonly supposed to be themselves gods as the men were.   Besides, as Clement says on behalf of the Egyptians, "Even if they are beasts, they are at any rate free from" the foulest vices of men.[2]   The custom was old enough in the East; but in Greece it was very significantly begun by the deification of Lysander after the fall of Athens in 403 B.C.   Plato replied by sharply separating the gods from the world of practical things; and in this the later philosophers mostly followed him, for the God whom the Stoics brought back into the world was not in the image of man, but a mere personification of Fate.   But the current of political servility and vulgar flattery was too strong for the philosophers, so that deification soon became a cheap compliment for the great.   Rome understood better than the Greeks Homer's old problem of the difference between gods and men, for *deus* is a much more definite word than θεός, though she too had deified legendary kings.   But Romulus was the last of them, and she never deified the heroes of the

---

[1] Well put by Firmicus Maternus *de errore Prof. Rel.* 7, *amat enim Graecorum leuitas eos qui sibi aliquid contulerint uel qui consilio aut uirtute se iuuerint diuinis appellare nominibus, et sic ab ipsis beneficiorum gratia repensatur, ut deos dicant, deos esse credant, qui sibi aliquando profuerint.*

[2] Clem. Al. *Protr.* p. 33 εἰ καὶ θηρία, ἀλλ' οὐ μοιχικά κ.τ.λ.

republic. Flamininus was a god in Greece; but Scipio was no more than a man at Rome, and even Sulla was only *Felix*, not *Augustus*. So Rome followed slowly, and in the main reserved the honour to the emperor alone of living men, for in him her glory was incarnate. A few of his near relations might have that glory reflected on them; but the worship of a mere favourite like Antinous was rather Eastern and Greek than Roman. That of the emperor himself was doubtless fashion; but it was also a genuine worship sustained by a real belief. If deification was pressed on the dictator Caesar by a servile senate, it was almost forced on his successors by the grateful provinces. Now if this characteristically Greek confusion of men with gods, and of the worship due to God with the honour due to men, became the greatest of hindrances to the Gospel, the truth which underlay it proved one of its greatest helps, because the Greeks were prepared to see the possibility of the Incarnation, and to realize the old gospel of Genesis, In the image of God made he man, on which the revelation through Christ, and in the end all knowledge whatever depends. For this reason the Greeks were able to deal much better with the problem than the Latins. If they never quite got over Plato's error of resolving sin into ignorance, they at least began at the right end, with the sinless man and not with fallen men, and from the eternal deeps of Wisdom rather than from the intruder and destroyer Sin.

We may now trace the life and work of Clement at Alexandria. Origen represents a further development, and is best reserved for a later chapter.

Athenagoras the Apologist is said to have been the first great Alexandrian teacher; but a story which rests on the authority of Philip of Side is at best doubtful. We are on firm ground when we come to Pantaenus (*cir.* 180) though even of him we know but little. He may have been a Sicilian by birth;[1] but in any case his heathen training was that of a Stoic philosopher. At one time he went to preach in "India"—a term loosely used of almost any country that could be reached by way of the Red Sea—where he is said to have found Christians already settled, with a Hebrew Gospel of St. Matthew brought to them by the apostle Bartholomew. His writings have perished almost to the last fragment, and of his work at Alexandria we know little more than that Clement was his pupil : and the teacher of Clement must have been a man of power.

Titus Flavius Clemens was a Greek, apparently an Athenian, and may have been a descendant of some freedman of Flavius Clemens the cousin of Domitian, consul in 95. A son of heathen parents, born *cir.* 150, he searched for truth in sundry lands, wandering from Greece to Southern Italy, and thence in the East, and studied under divers teachers before he lighted on the last and best of them lying hidden at Alexandria, where he "hunted out the true Sicilian Bee" Pantaenus.[2] Here then at Alexandria he settled down as a teacher and became a presbyter of the church, and here he did his life's work, not leaving the city till he had trained the still greater Origen, who was to take his place. His life was that of a quiet student, which gives little scope for a biographer. We do not even know whether he had a wife. But

---

[1] Clement p. 322 Σικελικὴ τῷ ὄντι ἡ μέλιττα. But it may be no more than a metaphor.

[2] Clem. Alex. p. 322. The allusion is almost certainly to Pantaenus.

when the terror of persecution returned in 202, and the school was scattered, and he saw martyrs falling round him daily, he had no call of duty to remain at Alexandria.   A few years later, about 211, his old friend Alexander of Jerusalem mentions him as still living in a letter to Origen, and perhaps later still, sends him to the church of Antioch with a letter of congratulation on the election of its new bishop Asclepiades.   After this we hear no more of him.

Clement has fared better than Pantaenus, for several of his writings are preserved—the *Protrepticus* in one book to the heathen, the *Paedagogus* or *Tutor* in three books for the ordinary Christian, and the *Stromateis* or Miscellanies in eight for the Gnostic or advanced Christian.   To these must be added the *Quis dives salvetur*, from which Eusebius quotes the story of St. John and the brigand; and the obscure *Excerpta ex Theodoto*.   These are all that need now concern us.[1]   The work, says he, of the divine Logos is to bring men by steps first out of heathenism to the knowledge of Christ, then to the practice of right living, then to the full knowledge of truth.   First he exhorts, then he trains, then he teaches.   The *Protrepticus* and the *Tutor* represent the first two stages, but Clement never reached the third, for the *Stromateis* (or Carpet bags) is no book of doctrine. Speaking roughly, for so rambling a work is not easily described, it is on the training needed by the advanced Christian for the teaching to follow.   It corresponds rather to the *Tutor*, which is on the training of the common Christian for his humbler station ; but it is

---

[1] Only one other work by Clement is of any consequence—the Ὑποτυπώσεις or Outlines, in at least seven books—a commentary on the books of N.T., including Jude and the other Catholic Epistles, and adding Barnabas and the Apocalypse of Peter.   Fragments only : fullest account in Eus. vi. 14.

naturally thrown into a different form, and deals more with character and principles, less with commands and practice. In fact, it was an afterthought, and rambled on to an unforeseen length. In the sixth and seventh books he encroaches on his unwritten Third Part by drawing his portrait of the ideal Christian, much as the Stoics used to draw their portrait of the wise man. The eighth however is a treatise on logic, which may have been meant to form part of the doctrinal work, but in any case has nothing to do with the first seven books.

Clement is by no means a great writer, if greatness requires a clear and definite system worked out with logical thoroughness. In this respect he compares badly with some of the Latins. Cyprian, for instance, is clear and logical enough. Given his premises, there is not much fault to be found with his conclusions. He changed indeed his position on the practical question of the *lapsi*, and altered more than once his practical measures accordingly ; but his theological system is in the main as clear and self-consistent as Calvin's. From first to last it is emphatically " definite teaching," whatever else it be. Quite otherwise Clement's. He is very commonly a little hazy, and not always logical. He is not given to the analysis of ideas, and accordingly falls into sundry inconsistencies, occasionally even delivering downright contradictory opinions. After due allowance for the intentional desultoriness and unfinished condition of the *Stromateis*, which seems never to have been finally revised, and for his eclectic and therefore fragmentary and heterogeneous philosophy, it must be admitted that Clement's mind is very far from orderly. Again, his learning is great, though much of it (like other learning of his time) is not first-hand,[1] and it is a little too much for him, so that there is a good deal of pure pedantry about his excellent advice on the conduct of life. Here also the comparison is not to Clement's advantage. In a few cases Cyprian shews very bad taste; but he scarcely ever fails in practical good sense, or lets his learning run away with him. The difference is that of the lawyer from the academic teacher, of the man of the world from the theorist.

For Clement is a student and a mystic, not a practical statesman. He has a harder task than Cyprian, for his thoughts are incomparably deeper, and harder to form into a harmonious combination. A logical system is easily constructed by forcing everything into subordination to a single dogma, or by putting a convenient quantity of truth into legal form, and ignoring the rest. Any sect can do as much as this; and the narrower the shibboleth, the better it serves the purpose. The difficulty begins when we try to grasp the many-sided mystery. Words and thoughts break down, and the vail of sin is over us. Truth may be fully expressed in life, but not in logical forms. We may have true knowledge; but the truth we apprehend in life we cannot comprehend in words. Narrow thought may be perfectly clear; but on the noblest a summer haze must always rest. The logical completeness of a system is enough to prove that it is not only imperfect as all thought must be, but well satisfied with its imperfection— which is the note of Pharisaism in all ages.

Clement was a philosopher in the time of his ignorance, and remained a philosopher when he had

---

[1] Bigg *Chr. Platonists* p. 46. Bibliography in de Faye *Clém.* 312.

found like Justin true philosophy in Christ. But he is more of an apologist for philosophy than Justin. Earlier writers either left philosophy on one side or strove to shew that the Gospel is consistent with it, but piety had now taken alarm at the rise of Gnosticism —a great and growing danger—so that Clement was in opposition to the general feeling of his own time. He represents not the church even of Alexandria, but the best thought inside the church. The Gnostics had subordinated religion to philosophy, and with such disastrous results that the simpler sort of Christians would now have nothing to do with philosophy or logic, and looked on learning generally as little else than a hindrance to piety. In strength and weakness, the average Christian of Alexandria was not unlike the narrower Evangelical of a century ago. He had the same reality, the same charity, the same love of long dull services, the same strange enthusiasms, the same timid clinging to rule, the same cowering terror of every new thought. From learning, says Clement, he abstained "like the beasts which have no understanding." He feared it like the song of the Sirens, lest it should enchant him. Had not St. Paul spoken meanly of the wisdom of the world, and warned us against philosophy and vain deceit? What was the need of learning? Would not bare faith suffice? Celsus hardly caricatures these men when he represents the Christians as saying, Do not examine; only believe. Learning is a bad thing. The greater the fool, the greater the sinner, the better the convert he makes. If words like these are a slander on Christ, they do no great injustice to the Orthodoxasts of Alexandria. Western pietism was even more cowardly, as we see from Tertullian's argument that search for truth is a mere confession of apostasy, because we found truth at our conversion and have no need to seek further, unless we have lost it again.[1] So limited and definite a thing does truth seem to him.

Clement could deal fairly with this narrow fear, for he recognized the truth behind it—the supreme value of the revelation, and the real danger of sinking it in philosophy like the Gnostics. He therefore secures the supremacy of revelation at the outset, by his definition of philosophy. He means by it no particular system, but all doctrines of any school " which teach righteousness and scientific knowledge of piety." [2] He is himself an eclectic. His idea of God is almost as much Platonic as Christian, his doctrine of the Logos is deeply coloured by Philo, and his morality floats between Christian love and Stoic ἀπάθεια.

He knows indeed quite well the imperfection of philosophy. At best its guidance is but partial, for only Christianity covers the whole of life. Moreover, it is full of the devil's sowings. The Sophistic art of which the Greeks are so proud is the wisdom of the world against which St. Paul warns us; for it is careless of truth, and tends to rhetoric and strife. Rightly did Plato call it an evil art, and Aristotle complain that it undertook the whole work of wisdom without doing it.[3] The Greeks are hunters of phrases and admirers of oratorical tricks. They go astray after music, geometry, grammar and especially

---

[1] Tert. Praescr. 8-11. This however is not his usual position. It is only one of the mischievous sophisms of the de Praescr.

[2] p. 338 δικαιοσύνην μετὰ εὐσεβοῦς ἐπιστήμης ἐκδιδάσκουσα. Clement cared only for the ethical side of philosophy.

[3] p. 339.

rhetoric—they are bewitched with these servant-girls, and neglect Philosophy their mistress.[1] Clement quite understands the faults of education in his own time, though he is himself too much of a rhetorician to escape them.

But of true philosophy—for he does not count the ungodly Epicureans and such-like " tares "—he always speaks with profound respect. Even where he does not follow Plato, he counts him " something like inspired," and never criticizes him. Plato himself never held more firmly the first axiom of philosophy —the supremacy of truth. " The true death is that which separates the soul, not from the body, but from truth." No Christian writer before him, and few for ages after him saw so clearly the first postulate of philosophy—the unity of truth in all its range. " The way of truth is one, and into it as a never-failing river flow the streams on either side." [2] In love of truth Clement is no whit behind the chiefest of the heathen ; for the Lord had not borne witness to the truth in vain. We cannot go wrong, says he, if we refer all good things to Providence, whether they be Christian or heathen. Was not the skill of Bezaleel [3] the gift of God ? Is not this wisdom manifold ? [4] Now philosophy is good, for it makes men good : therefore it comes from God. To deny this is almost to deny particular providence, and to make the devil more benevolent than God. True, the law was given direct from heaven : but philosophy was equally given by God, though it was not given through angels, but in the way of consequence from his

[1] p. 332.   [2] p. 331.   [3] p. 330.
[4] p. 331 πολυποίκιλον τὴν σοφίαν τοῦ θεοῦ πολυμερῶς καὶ πολυτρόπως διὰ τέχνης, διὰ ἐπιστήμης, διὰ πίστεως, διὰ προφητείας, τὴν ἑαυτῆς ἐνδεικνυμένην δύναμιν εἰς τὴν ἡμετέραν εὐεργεσίαν.

primary gift of reason. It was given to the Greeks just as the law was given to the Jews,[1] to be a training and a preparation—a stepping-stone—for the Gospel, so that it was a real revelation and a justifying[2] covenant with God, giving them a true knowledge of him, even if it was a dim knowledge. Just as common studies help towards Philosophy their mistress, so does philosophy itself help towards wisdom, for philosophy is the study of wisdom, and wisdom is the knowledge of things divine and human, and their causes. If then human learning has its use in things divine, piety must be a reasonable service; so that Clement agrees with the Gnostics against the Orthodoxasts in thinking that the Gospel may be and ought to be presented in a philosophical form. The true Gnostic, he says, must be a man of learning. If his own words ring differently from Scripture, he tells us[3] that they draw life and inspiration from Scripture and truly represent its meaning.

So philosophical indeed is Clement that some have done him the injustice of doubting whether he is not more philosopher than Christian. The glowing peroration of his *Protrepticus* ought to have made that reproach impossible:[4] yet his heart is more

[1] p. 823.   [2] p. 762.   [3] p. 829.
[4] Harnack *What is Christianity?* E.Tr. 216. "We can still feel from his writings that this scholar, although he was absolutely steeped in speculative ideas, and as a thinker reduced the Christian religion to a boundless sea of 'doctrines'—a Greek in every fibre of his being—won peace and joy from the Gospel, and he can also express what he has won and testify of the power of the living God. It is as a new man that he appears, one who has pressed on through the whole range of philosophy, through authority and speculation, through all the externals of religion, to the glorious liberty of the children of God. His faith in Providence, his faith in Christ, his doctrine of freedom, his ethics—everything is expressed in language that betrays the Greek, and yet everything is new and genuinely Christian."

Christian than his reason. He starts from the
current philosophical conception of God as the highest
abstraction and simplicity, to be reached by removing
not only body parts and passions, but all relations
and qualities. He has no natural relation for instance
to ourselves; and the proof of his goodness is that he
cares for us notwithstanding, for we have nothing to
do with his essence or nature, but are simply creatures
of his will.[1] Such a God ought to be utterly inscrut-
able : but Clement does not see that this doctrine
flatly contradicts the Gospel. Were such the true
conception of deity, there could be no historic Incarnation. He is equally shocked by the Stoic doctrine
of God's immanence "even in the basest matter,"
and by the Epicurean denial of any gods who care for
the world at all. Nay rather, God is good, as Plato
said. If he permits evil, he is not therefore its author
as the Gnostics maintained he would be, for the fault
of it is in ourselves. There is no predestination to
good or bad. The will is free both ways till it either
reaches the highest state in perfect following of grace,
or sinks to the lowest in perfect slavery to sin. We
sin as Adam sinned, and for the same reasons of
ignorance and fleshly weakness; but our sin is no
way dependent on his. It is wholly our own fault,
and God is in no sense its author. But we must not
think with the Stoics—he might have added the Lord
himself—that God's virtue is like ours.[2] If he is good,
he is not good by nature (for that would subject him
to necessity) but because he wills to be good.[3]
Clement has not overcome like Athanasius the
dilemma, that we must choose between caprice and
fate.

[1] p. 467.   [2] p. 798. Cp. Matt. v. 48.   [3] p.855.

But given a purely transcendent God, he needs a mediator of some sort to connect him with the world. In the *Timaeus* of Plato the Soul of the world partakes of both the ideal and the material world. Some of the later Jews filled the gap with angels, and most of the later philosophers filled it with demons, as ministers on earth of the Supreme. But Philo took up the Stoic doctrine of divine forces working in the world, and identified them with the Platonic ideas. Then he summed them up in the Logos, which is the mind and will of God, the creator and indwelling sustainer of the world. The conception was more Platonic and Stoic than Jewish, though it has points of contact with the Old Testament and the Targums. But was the Logos divine or creature, attribute or person! Philo wavers helplessly before the dilemma, that if the Logos is God, he is a second God ; and if not, then God acts himself after all. So he leaves the question unsettled. The one thing certain is that the Logos cannot be in any sense human. Then comes St. John, starting not from the Greek side, but from the Jewish דיי מאמרא (Memra), which is the medium of God's communication with men, and sets the philosophers at defiance one and all by his witness that the Logos was incarnate in Jesus of Nazareth. Clement combines the philosophical vagueness of Philo with the historical precision of St. John : but while Philo is thinking chiefly of cosmology and metaphysics, Clement follows St. John in looking on the Logos rather as the revealer of God and the teacher and trainer and saviour of men. His manhood is a little hazy—Clement is not free from docetism—but his premundane personality is definite, and his work stands out clearly in the gift of knowledge and immortality [1]—the Greek conception of eternal life.

Clement was too much of a philosopher to dispute the Gnostic distinction between knowledge and faith; but he accepted it with an important reserve. The two were related as knowledge to opinion in Plato, that is as reality to appearance. But whereas with the Gnostics the reality had no organic relation to the appearance, Clement held firmly to the historic revelation, and allowed no speculation to tamper with its facts. Faith, he says,[2] is the compendious knowledge of essentials, and knowledge is the strong and sure demonstration of what is received by faith. It is a higher stage, for faith in Clement (unlike St. Paul's) is a religion of hope and fear, whereas knowledge works by love: yet faith is necessary for all men, and also sufficient. He quite overlooks the inference, that a religion which is not of love is enough for salvation—much less does he deliberately maintain it like the modern church of Rome. Indeed he gives higher views of faith, as "a deliberate anticipation or assent of piety," or as "a power of God, being the force of truth."[3] These come nearer to St. Paul; but Clement wavers as usual. The *Tutor's* training may be austere and puritan, but it is not ascetic. Spiritual men are not a select few "saved by nature," as the Gnostics held. All that have put away sin are spiritual men, for we were all enlightened in Baptism, and received

[1] On Clement's doctrine of the Person of Christ Bigg *Chr. Platonists* 63-75. We need not here pursue it further.

[2] p. 865.

[3] p. 432 πρόληψις ἑκούσιος, θεοσεβείας συγκατάθεσις, quoting Hebr. xi. 1, and p. 434 προαιρέσεως κατόρθωμα—all Stoic words. So too p. 454.

the knowledge of God.[1] The knowledge is no doubt
only in germ; but everything is in that germ, as
the tree is in the grain of mustard seed. He that
hath the Son hath already life eternal. There is
no such difference of children and perfect as the
Gnostics fancy. We are all children as being under
the Tutor's guidance, who trains the true Gnostic
with mysteries, the faithful with good hopes, the
impenitent with correction. Yet we are all perfect,
for we have all received the perfect gift. Every one
can "philosophize," whether man or woman, child
or slave, Greek or barbarian, learned or simple.
The youngest is not too young, and the oldest is
not past learning. Virtue is the same for all, and
every man of righteous purpose belongs to the
church [2]

Knowledge must rest on faith—"if ye believe
not, neither shall ye understand" [3]—and be worked
out in life. It has to be won not by mystic trance
but by thoughtful toil, and perfected by patient
and earnest practice. "He that will enter the shrine
must be pure." Sin before baptism was done in
ignorance, and its forgiveness is the light given in
Baptism, by which we avoid sin; for it is no true
repentance which needs often to ask forgiveness for
offending often. Though Clement seems nowhere
formally to discuss the doctrine of the Atonement,
he rightly sees that forgiveness has to root out sin,
not simply to remit its punishment. That punishment indeed he regards like Plato as purely remedial.
It is for the good of him that is punished: "it leads

---

[1] pp. 112, 116.
[2] pp. 590, 899. Contrast the Latin *extra ecclesiam nulla salus*.
[3] Isa. vii. 9, lxx.

to conversion, and desires rather the repentance of the sinner than his death."[1] And he rightly sees also that atonement is not needed to appease an angry God, but to give sinners full assurance of his love, and strength to conquer sin. "Everywhere the barrier is not God's wrath, but man's impurity."[2]

Thus the moral difference of Clement's ideal Gnostic from the ideal of the Gnostics is the difference of light and darkness. He was a false Gnostic who taught that we are to overcome sin with sin, as if we could live in sin without being defiled by sin.[3] Even the common Christian of the *Tutor* avoids sin, if only from fear; and the true Gnostic has a higher motive. Fear, says Clement, by which we abstain from sin is the first stage of Christian life; then comes hope, by which we aspire to the best things; and love is the final stage. We become Christian by the first, Gnostic by the second, and the third is Gnostic perfection,[4] for perfect love casteth out fear. Knowledge not only purifies the heart, as the Stoics tell us, but opens out the deep things of Scripture, and gives a higher character to goodness. The true Gnostic's life is all prayer, though not always uttered prayer, for he prays in all his works; all virtue, for his every act is a moral success;[5] all steady progress beyond earthly passions and desires, till he ceases not only to commit sin but to feel temptation. His aim is not moderation in them, but deliverance from them.[6] At last nothing remains to disturb him but the bare needs of nature;

---

[1] pp. 139, 764.   [2] Bigg *Chr. Platonists* 74.
[3] p. 490.   [4] pp. 457, 866.
[5] p. 796 κατόρθωμα, the Stoic word.
[6] p. 778 : not Peripatetic μετριοπάθεια, but Stoic ἀπάθεια.

and the perfect Gnostic, the Lord himself, was free from even these. He felt neither joy nor sorrow, and ate and drank not for need, but only to confute docetism[1]—and to confute it in vain, so far as this passage of Clement is concerned.

The Gnostic is passionless as a Stoic Philosopher, loving as a Christian saint. He will not pray for earthly things; he is well content with all that comes to pass. To the image of God in which we were created he adds the likeness of God which we have to win for ourselves; and this likeness Clement understands in a Christian way of moral likeness, without clearly seeing its difference from the intellectual likeness preached by Platonism. The Gnostic omits nothing that can help him to win that likeness. He is used to poor fare and independence. He is grave and sober, needing few necessaries and troubling himself no further, and not seeking even these as specially desirable, for he counts knowledge the one thing needful. He is patient, lives justly, rules his passions, "cuts away desire," swears rarely, speaks the truth unless a lie be needed in a medicinal way,[2] and is beneficent in word and deed to the utmost of his power. He is a holy priest of God who needs no ordination by men to offer the spiritual sacrifice of prayer, and a true elder of the church, though he sit not in the elder's chair. His entire life is a holy festival, with prayer and praise and reading of the Scriptures before meals, psalms and hymns at meals and at bed-time, and prayer again by night.[3] "He then who has first moderated his passions and then trained himself to be passionless, and developed to the beneficence of Gnostic perfection, is equal to the

[1] p. 775.   [2] p. 863.   [3] pp. 860-61.

angels here on earth. Luminous already, and like the sun shining in the practice of beneficence he speeds by righteous knowledge through the love of God to the holy mansion, to be an abiding light, unchangeable for evermore." [1] He is "a god walking in flesh," [2] a knower of God, and a sharer of his immortality. "This is the true athlete, who in the great racecourse of this fair world wins the crown of true victory over all passions. The president of the games is God all-sovereign, the giver of the prizes is the only-begotten Son of God, while angels and gods are spectators, and the contest in all its varied forms is not against blood and flesh, but against the spiritual powers of stormy passions working through the flesh. He that overcomes in these great struggles and overthrows the tempter in the contests he seems to bring upon him is the winner of immortality. For God's decision is not to be deceived when he pronounces his most righteous judgment." [3]

Upon the whole, Clement's teaching is like Marcion's in being a return to St. Paul; but it is not a blind reaction from Judaism like Marcion's. It is like the Reformation in returning to St. Paul; but Clement is not narrowed and embittered as the Protestants were by their hard and demoralizing struggle with the bottomless treachery of the catholic reaction. If the Orthodoxasts are poor creatures beside the Puritans, the Gnostics themselves were less profoundly immoral than the Jesuits. Thanks partly to the Roman peace, partly to the freedom of thought at Alexandria, partly to his own studious and uncontroversial temper, Clement was able to combine intensity of Christian purpose with a philosophical detachment hardly

[1] pp. 792, 866.   [2] p. 894.   [3] p. 839.

possible in modern Europe till the wars of religion began to abate. It is not accidental that the next great return to Plato followed the Peace of Westphalia. So his work is a many-sided endeavour by careful and scholarly study of Scripture and philosophy to bring all human learning into its due connexion with the revelation through the Word, and so to work out more fully the universal significance of the revelation itself. The problem which the Gnostics attacked by speculation in the interest of cosmogony Clement essayed by philosophy in the interest of religion ; and with better results. If he could not shape his materials into a clear and rounded system like Cyprian's, he has left us guiding thoughts of a higher order than carnal theories of carnal churches.

The plan was a noble one, and it is not surprising that Clement could not fully work it out. But his mistakes are personal failures rather than faults in the plan itself. In the first place, his mind is neither very clear nor very orderly nor very practical. In short, he is neither reasoner enough nor man of the world enough. Then again his scholarship was weak, for he had not even Origen's slight knowledge of Hebrew, so that he could not use the Old Testament to much purpose, or generally get beyond the unsound allegorical exegesis of his time. Above all, he could not shake off the weaknesses of Greek philosophy. With all his insistence on the image of God in man, he still thinks of God too much as purely trans- cendent. So, though his true Gnostic is a noble character, but for the hideous blot of the " medicinal lie "—itself a legacy of the philosophers—he is too intellectual, too detached from the relations of life, too much given to the Stoic ἀπάθεια. Surely he has not reckoned with the guile of sin who strives rather to overcome it by direct and solitary efforts than to crowd it out by faithful use of his appointed training in common life.   With all his greatness, Clement reflects everywhere the weakness of his own time. The philosophical conception of God as purely transcendent struggles in him with the immanence implied by the Incarnation, the emptiness of abstract being with the goodness revealed in Christ, the aristocratic spirit of heathenism with the universalism of the Gospel, Platonic contempt of the body with its Christian consecration, Greek confidence in education with the subtleness of sin.   Though Clement had perhaps a wider view than later writers of the vast range of difficulties, he was not the man to see his way through them.   No man ever more nobly welcomed the true light whose ever-present coming lighteth every man ; but a darker and ruder age than Clement's was needed to bring home to men by dire experience the gospel of the Lamb of God, which taketh away the sin of the world.

BOOKS

Bigg C. *Christian Platonists of Alexandria* ; Westcott (Bp.), Art. *Origen* in *D.C.B.* ; de Faye C. *Clément d'Alexandrie*, Paris 1898 ; Clement *The Seventh Book of the Stromateis* Ed. Hort and Mayor.

CHAPTER XX

ORIGEN

IF the greatness of a man is to be measured by the fascination of his ideas for the best men of later ages, Origen will rank second to Augustine only, if to him, in the history of Christian thought. His daring speculations were not left unchallenged even in his lifetime, and soon became the subject of controversies which are spread over the next three hundred years. In the fourth century indeed Nicenes and Arians were equally anxious to claim for their own side the great Alexandrian scholar. Eusebius is devoted to him, Athanasius mentions him with all respect, the Cappadocians go very much on Origen's lines, while Hilary and Ambrose in the West, and Augustine through them, were influenced by him. Marcellus and Epiphanius are not much to balance these. But from the reign of Arcadius onward Origen became more and more suspected. The controversies are a dreary and often a disgraceful history : but the judgment of a declining church was truly given by the anathemas launched against him in Justinian's time. Yet his influence never perished. In a long course of ages almost every great Christian thinker has more or less turned to thoughts which were thoughts of

Origen ; and the signs of our own time seem to shew that the advance of the future will rather follow the lines of Origen and Athanasius than those of Cyprian and Augustine.

The transition from the second century to the third is well marked by the fact that Origen— despite his heathen name—is the first great writer of Christian birth.[1] The Christians were ceasing to be sojourners in the world looking daily for the coming of the Lord. They were settling down as citizens of the Empire, and in the peace thereof they had their peace. The defiance of Ignatius was hardly echoed but in times of persecution, and not often then. Even Tertullian prayed for the delay of the great catastrophe that was to end the age.[2] Visions were becoming possible of a world which was not entirely hostile, and of a victory over it which was not purely spiritual. Christian and heathen thought were influencing each other more actively, and the time was come for a more systematic and philosophical presentation of Christian doctrine. The subapostolic writers seldom touched it directly, the Apologists only dealt with its defence against enemies, and even Clement of Alexandria had rather rambled over the vast field than endeavoured to plan it out. Origen was the first who attempted to survey the whole scope of revelation and work out systematically its relation to the whole range of human knowledge.

For the Gospel is neither a religion nor a philosophy but a revelation : and the revelation is Christ —in his Person, not simply through his teaching.

---

[1] Polycarp (and perhaps Polycrates) are hardly worth excepting.
[2] Tert. *Apol.* 39 pro mora finis.

But if it is not to remain a barren mysticism of personal feeling and nothing more, some sort of a religion will be needed to connect it with human life, and some sort of a philosophy to bring it into relation with human thought. And the more explicit the philosophy the better, for there is always more danger in taking principles for granted than in thinking them out. To put it shortly, the Gospel is of a Son of God made man for us men and for our salvation; and this is folly to the natural man. So even those who accepted it often thought it needed toning down. Either he was not in any full sense the Son of God, or else he did not truly become man. So we see the two great forces whose action and reaction determined the main lines of Christian thought in the Eastern churches which took the lead from the second century to the seventh or eighth.

It is a long and complicated history; and when we watch it year by year its details are interminable; but we see the progress as we pass from one age to the next. One result is reached after another, and then the contest is renewed on a narrower field. The whole scene divides into two main parts— a Trinitarian period ending at the Council of Constantinople in 381, and a Christological which comes down we will say to the fall of the last Monothelete emperor in 713. The first period divides into three sections very roughly corresponding to the second, third and fourth centuries. First Ebionism and Gnosticism are diametrically opposed. Of the two natures in Christ, Ebionism entirely denies the reality of the divine, Gnosticism that of the human. In a second stage Ebionite and

Patripassian Monarchianism are the combatants, and
each admits the reality of the other element while
reducing its significance as much as possible. A
third stage shews Arianism and Sabellianism (or
at least Arianism) each striving to do justice to
the other side, yet each so emphasizing its own
side that the effort is an utter failure. Thus by
the time of the Council of Constantinople it was
fully agreed that Christ was truly divine and truly
human; and the contest had to be fought out on
the narrower Christological field. Given the two
natures, what was their relation to each other?
Those who would have denied the divine nature in
past times now put it as far from the human as
they could, that the lesser might not be over-
powered by the splendour of the greater; and those
who in past ages would have denied the human
nature now mutilated it or joined it as closely as
they could to the divine, for the very purpose that
the lesser might be lost in the greater.

In the last years of the second century the first
of these stages was coming to an end, and the
defeat of Ebionism on one side, and of Gnosticism
on the other, was preparing the way for the decisive
conflict of the Nicene age. The Lord's own disciples
may have been slow to see the stupendous truth
that the carpenter of Nazareth was indeed the Son
of God, for us men and for our salvation come down
from heaven; but when they did see it, they
preached it not as a dogma they had agreed upon,
but as a fact they had witnessed. It was that which
they had heard, which they had seen with their eyes,
which they had gazed on and their hands had
handled of the word of life. The thing was true,

and must be true, whatever might be the philosophical difficulties involved in it.

So the Christians began from the fixed position, that "we must think of Christ as God," and worship him as such. But when they passed from personal knowledge to tradition, they found it harder to forget that history has a philosophical side. Some simply refused the question, as some do now; and some found relief, as some do now, in the suggestion of the Gnostics, that what had been taken for history was mostly parable; but in the course of the third century the difficulty shaped itself into a tremendous dilemma. Either Christ is in the fullest sense divine, or else he is not. If he is, the Christians worship two gods: if he is not, they worship a creature. Either way there was no escape from the charge of polytheism. Hitherto they had chiefly insisted on the true deity of Christ in answer to Ebionites who denied it entirely, and to Gnostics whose conception of deity did not rise above the heathen. But now they had to make their choice. If they ceased to worship Christ, they ought to give up calling themselves Christians: if they worshipped even the highest of creatures, they confessed themselves idolaters. On one plan the Gospel was emptied of everything that distinguishes it from philosophy, while the other sank it straight to paganism. The Christians however had no intention of taking either plan. Christian logic was strong, that if a divine Person is needed for creation, redemption must be beyond the power of a being who is less than in the fullest sense divine; Christian testimony was unwavering, that the Man of Nazareth had claimed to be the Son of God, and proved it by doing the works of God; and Christian

experience, that life divine is flowing from the risen
Son of Man, is a final certainty for those who have
it.   Yet it was impossible to set aside reason by
refusing indefinitely to deal with the teaching of the
philosophers and the common sense of the vulgar,
that one who is man cannot be God ; and if he were,
he would be a second god.

In the course of the second century there was a
general reaction of Christians and pagans in the direction of monotheism, and Christians generally were
coming round to the belief that the deity of Christ must
be subordinated to the unity of God.   This might be
done on two theories, leaning respectively to Ebionism
and to Gnosticism, but not going the full length of
either, for neither the manhood nor the deity was
now denied outright.   If they started from the
historic manhood of Jesus, they might explain the
deity by some divine power dwelling in him : or if
they started from the deity, they might explain his
Person as no more than a temporal and temporary
manifestation of the one God, the Father.   On one
theory the divine power had no organic relation to
the man Jesus ; on the other his manhood stood in
no organic relation to the one God revealed in him.

The first class (dynamistic monarchians) are
chiefly represented by the Alogi, Theodotus, and
Artemon.   The Alogi of Asia have their name from
their rejection of the Logos doctrine of St. John, and
of his writings generally—an anomalous position in
the early Church.   Like the Gnostics, they claimed
to be sound Christians ; and like most of the Gnostics,
they do not seem to have been ejected from the
churches, though Epiphanius of course counts them
heretics, and puns on their name (ἄλογοι, irrational).

They seem to have been influenced rather by opposition to the Montanist doctrine of the Paraclete than by the differences they noticed between the Fourth Gospel and the Synoptists. But they never were a school of any importance.

Theodotus the leather-worker came from Byzantium to Rome about 190. His doctrine was almost Ebionite. Jesus was a mere man, most pious and righteous, born of the Virgin Mary by the overshadowing of the Holy Spirit. On him came the Holy Spirit, the Son of God, at his Baptism; and so he became the Christ, and worked miracles. But he was not God, though some of them said that he was so after his resurrection. Bishop Victor excommunicated them; but in the time of Zephyrinus his followers set up a church of their own under the guidance of Asclepiodotus and another Theodotus, a banker, and had for their bishop a confessor named Natalius at a salary of 150 denarii monthly — till some visions frightened him back into the church. Still they formed a school. As says the writer quoted by Eusebius,[1] "They fearlessly criticized (ρεραδιουργήκασι) Scripture, set aside the rule of the ancient faith, and knew not Christ in their search, not for what Scripture says, but for some pretence of argument in proof of their ungodliness—and on this they worked laboriously. . . . They forsake the Scriptures of God and practise geometry, as we might expect from men who are from the earth and speak from the earth, and know not him that cometh from above. Euclid is studied with anxious care by some of them, Aristotle and Theophrastus are much looked up to, and Galen (this is a fact)[2] is actually

---

[1] Eus. v. 28. [2] Eus. ίσως de re certa as Mart. Pal. ix. 13.

worshipped by some of them. That those who use
the arts of the unbelievers to establish their own
heresy, and adulterate the simple faith of the
Scriptures with the craft of the ungodly do not even
come near to faith, is more than I need say. Therefore they laid hands on the Scriptures without fear,
professing to correct them." All this is astonishingly
modern, though the Orthodoxasts of Alexandria
would have quite appreciated it.

Little is known of Artemon, though he seems to
have been living *cir.* 267, when the synod which
deposed Paul of Samosata sarcastically bade him
write his letters of commendation to Artemon. He
seems however to have maintained not only that
Christ was a mere man, but that this was the
doctrine of the churches till Victor's time. A
completer inversion of history can hardly be imagined
—it seems of itself to prove that he lived long after
Victor's time.

We now turn to the other class (modalistic
monarchians) who denied the distinction of the Son
of God from the Father, making Christ an appearance
of the one God in some special form. Noetus of
Smyrna, late in the second century, taught that " the
Father himself endured birth, suffering, and death
in the flesh," so that his followers were called
Patripassians. Of this way of thinking was the
confessor Praxeas, who came to Rome apparently in
the time of Bishop Eleutherus,[1] and not only stirred
him up against the Montanists, but pushed him in
his dislike of Theodotus into something like Patripassianism. So, says Tertullian, " Praxeas managed

---

[1] It is an open question between Eleutherus and Victor, at least as regards
Montanism.

two businesses for the devil in Rome. He drove out
Prophecy and brought in heresy, put to flight the
Paraclete and crucified the Father." When he came
on from Rome to Carthage, he was attacked by
Tertullian, who then held the intermediate stage of
accepting the Montanist oracles without leaving the
church.   Meanwhile the disciples of Praxeas at
Rome gained over bishop Zephyrinus, and the
presbyter Callistus, who managed him.   But this
caused so much confusion in the church that Callistus
was forced to take up a mediating position when he
became bishop himself in 217.

The original teaching of Sabellius is not easy to
trace, for he became the chief anathema of the con-
servatives in the next century, so that everything of
a modalistic sort was counted Sabellian. In spite of
his date in the time of Callistus, Sabellius belongs
rather to the Nicene cycle, for he extended modalism
to the whole Trinity.   According to him, the one
God is the father, who expands himself into the Son
and the Holy Spirit; or sometimes it is the one God
who speaks at different times as Father, Son, or Holy
Spirit, so that there are three aspects of one divine
Person, like body, soul, and Spirit in man, or three
activities of the one divine Person, like the roundness,
light, and heat of the sun.   How far he himself
identified these different times with those of the Old
and New Testaments and the church respectively is
more than we can say.   But in any case the Trinity
is purely economic and temporal, and corresponds no
doubt to the needs of this world, but to nothing in
the eternal world.

This then was the state in which Origen found the
problem.   The chief advance since the time of

Irenaeus was that Tertullian had brought it into closer connexion with history by gathering it round the eternal Sonship rather than the doctrine of the Logos. This also made more clear his premundane and real personality, though it also fell in with the tendency to press the subordination of the Son to a denial of his true deity. If Origen failed to solve the problem, he cleared up some of its worst difficulties, and brought the question to a point from which the next great thinker was able to see his way through it. Athanasius had only to go one step beyond Origen, though that step was the most momentous in the entire history of Christian thought, for by it the dominant heathen conception of God as abstract and simple was renounced as inconsistent with the historic facts of the Gospel. But the great work of Origen was not so much his particular theories like the eternal generation of the Son of God or the pretemporal fall of souls as the vast foundation laid by his unwearied toil for the studies of many generations. As critic, as commentator, as scientific theologian, he struck out lines which the scholars who came after him could not choose but follow. If his name was anathematized, his influence remained even in the middle ages. It is as evident in the teaching of Ambrose and Augustine as in the sensuous mysticism that was built upon his treatment of the Song of Solomon : and much of the best thought of happier times is a conscious or unconscious return to thoughts first thrown out by Origen.

A student's life is not likely to be eventful, and we can soon run through the chief facts of it.

We have already traced his life to the execution of his father in 202. As the property of Leonides

was confiscated, Origen found himself destitute with
six younger brothers, of whom we hear no more. His
first refuge was with a wealthy lady of Alexandria;
but he cannot have been very comfortable there, for
he "observed the rule of the church"[1] too strictly
to meet with civility the heretic Paul of Antioch,
whom she harboured as her philosopher or chaplain
and adopted son. Origen however had received a
careful training in the ordinary liberal education of
the time so that he was able before long to make his
living by teaching secular literature.

He was soon called to a more special work. The
catechetical school had been dispersed by the persecution, and the departure of Clement left it without
a teacher. So some heathens applied to Origen for
Christian teaching, and a new school grew up round
him. Six of his disciples—one of them a woman—
perished in the persecution, but the school grew
larger and larger. It did not long remain on the
old informal footing, for bishop Demetrius now
brought it into official connexion with the church.
The need of supervision was greater than in Clement's
time, for Origen was still a youth of eighteen, and
sadly wanting in wisdom and moderation. He
courted his father's fate by the open and public
support he gave to the martyrs, and so provoked the
mob that he could not have escaped if the authorities
had cared to take him. He also practised the
severest asceticism, living on a pension of four
obols a day, which he had procured by the sale of
his books of secular literature. He pushed his
austerities till his constitution nearly broke down,

[1] Eus. vi. 2. The hatred of heretics was quite strong enough in the
third century to explain the persecutions of the fourth

even taking literally the Lord's words of those who
have made themselves eunuchs for the kingdom of
heaven's sake,[1] and carried it out in a literal sense
upon himself. These were excesses of youthful zeal,
and seem to have caused little offence at the time.
Bishop Demetrius would seem rather to have given
him encouragement. Perhaps his judgment was not
very different from that of Eusebius, whose admiration is tempered in this one case with a clear though
mild disapproval. Yet the act was condemned not
only by Roman law but by the better feeling of
Christian men expressed by the Nicene Council.[2]
Origen himself was brought by the teaching of life
to a better mind on this question, but he never got
rid of the general ascetic taint. If he utterly lacked
the Christian cheerfulness of Clement, the reason is
not simply that he had a deeper sense of sin, but
also that he was less of a Greek than Clement on
a class of questions where the mind of Christ was
less unworthily represented by the better sort of
heathenism than by the asceticism which was clouding
over the churches.

Meanwhile his work expanded. Men and women
flocked to him from morning till night, and in the
end he was forced to divide the work, giving the
more elementary part of it to his disciple Heraclas,
and keeping the more advanced students for himself.
So passed some thirty years of unremitting toil.
Origen was still in favour with bishop Demetrius,
and his reputation spread far beyond the bounds
of Egypt. At one time he was summoned to confer
with the governor of Arabia,[3] at another he was

[1] Mt. xix. 12.   [2] Canon 1.
[3] Mamaea's summons is perhaps best placed about 232.

at Rome; and again when he left Alexandria for awhile (216) during the tumults of Caracalla's time, and stayed at Caesarea, the Palestinian bishops asked him to expound Scripture publicly before them. Demetrius took deep offence at this, declaring it quite irregular that a layman should expound in the presence of bishops. It may already have been the custom at Alexandria that he should not: but there was no such rule in Palestine, and Origen's friends, Alexander of Jerusalem and Theoctistus of Caesarea, had no difficulty in naming other churches where the practice was allowed.[1] Demetrius treated it as insubordination, and angrily recalled him to Alexandria; but presently things seemed to settle down much as they were before.

His work still widened Origen was now a referee of churches and a spiritual counsellor of high authorities. It seemed unfitting that so great a man should be no more than a layman; yet years passed on, and Demetrius never ordained him. However, about 230 Origen took a journey to Greece on the business of the churches, and in the course of it was ordained by his friends at Caesarea. Demetrius was quite right in counting this a much worse offence than the other, for it was a public censure on himself. Whatever his reasons might be for an omission which must have been deliberate, they were here openly set aside. What they were, we do not know. Origen's rash act may have been one of them,

[1] It will be noted that the question is of the layman's right to expound in the presence of bishops, not of his right to preach at all. The latter seems to have been undisputed till the fifth century, and was granted in principle even in the middle ages, for monks were licensed to preach, and monks were often laymen.

In any case an Alexandrian custom was not binding on Palestinian bishops, or on Origen either when he was at Caesarea.

though it might seem to have been long ago
condoned; but more likely the old bishop had never
quite trusted his brilliant catechist. The relations
of an eminent man to his official superior are delicate
at best, and in this case there seems to have been
neither tact on one side nor forbearance on the
other. Origen's discourtesy let loose the envy of
Demetrius. But when he called a council of bishops
and presbyters, they refused to go beyond the
just and obvious decision, that Origen must leave
Alexandria. Had this contented Demetrius, all
would have been well. But it did not content
Demetrius. He called another council of bishops
only, and packed it till he obtained an excommunication of Origen—and a division in the churches.
The sentence was enforced in Egypt and recognized
in the West; but it was disregarded by the churches
of Palestine, Arabia, Phoenicia and Achaia, in which
Origen was best known.[1]

So Origen betook himself to Caesarea in 231;
and thenceforth Caesarea was his usual home. He

[1] The excommunication of Origen is an obscure question, because Eusebius
refers us for information to his *Apology for Origen*, which is lost, so that we
have to depend on scraps preserved by Photius. The misdeed of Origen's
youth was no doubt brought up against him; but it cannot have been the
real reason, or at least the effective reason for the action of Demetrius.
Most likely both sides were much to blame. Origen's conduct is not likely
to have been a first case of discourtesy, while the rancorous violence of
Demetrius looks like an explosion of long-cherished jealousy.

The strongest point against Origen is the fact that he was not recalled
by his own disciple Heraclas, who so soon succeeded Demetrius as bishop.
Heraclas may for aught we know have been an active enemy of Origen;
or he may only have thought that he could not recall him without fresh
troubles from the Orthodoxasts or from Origen's own indiscretion. This
last was probably good reason for the action of Heraclas, and we may hope
it was his motive.

Neither did Dionysius recall him when he became bishop in 247. But
we cannot lay stress on this, for the lapse of seventeen years must have
greatly changed the situation.

must have left the city for a short time in 232,
if this was the time of his visit to the empress
Mamaea at Antioch. A few years later we find him
fled from the persecution of Maximin to the
Cappadocian Caesarea. With the return of peace
he resumed his work in Palestine, corresponding
with the emperor Philip and the empress Otacilia
Severa, and going to a council in Arabia, where
he convinced Beryllus of Bostra of the error of his
ways and brought him back to orthodoxy. Of his
sufferings in the Decian persecution we must speak
hereafter.

Origen was well satisfied to be a student and
teacher. His lectures were unwritten, for he had no
wish to be a literary man, and no desire to leave
anything behind in writing. It was not till 218 that
he found a wealthy friend in one Ambrosius, whom
he had converted from Gnosticism. Ambrosius
pressed him to write, and provided him with seven
stenographers who worked with him by turns,
besides seven copyists and sundry girls to make fair
copies. So from 223 onwards came out a marvellous
series of works. Epiphanius tells us that there were
six thousand of them; but it is at any rate certain
that the extensive works remaining are only a small
part of what was written for him. They fall into the
three main divisions of textual criticism, exegesis and
doctrine.

Textual criticism was as much needed then as it
is now. The text even of the New Testament was
in a bad state, and Origen's revised copies were in
much esteem for a long time. Yet he does not seem
to have reached a genuinely critical method, tending
as he did to lean on majorities of MSS., and to make

the language more classical. But his most remarkable work was done on the Old Testament. The
Hexapla, upon which he laboured for many years,
gave in six parallel columns the Hebrew, the Hebrew
in Greek letters, the LXX, and the translations of
Aquila, Symmachus and Theodotion. So vast a work
as this is of course lost; but fortunately the LXX
column was copied at Caesarea by Eusebius, and of
this considerable fragments remain.

The exegetical works consist partly of Scholia on
difficult passages, partly of Homilies, or series of
sermons going through most of the books of the
Bible, partly of commentaries proper, dealing at length
with exegesis. The chief of these, and the most
characteristic of the writer, is the commentary on St.
John; though that on St. Matthew is preserved in
part, and that to the Romans in a Latin translation
by Ruffinus.

Of his chief doctrinal work, the *de Principiis*
(Περὶ ἀρχῶν), we shall have to speak presently, his
contra Celsum we have already seen in connexion
with the Apologists, and his practical works, *de
Oratione* and the *Exhortatio ad martyrium*, we
need only mention.

A work which cannot well be classed is the
Philocalia, a collection of extracts from his writings
made in the next century (before 379) by Basil and
Gregory of Nazianzus. It treats first of Scripture—
of inspiration, and of the rude and unclassical style
which conceals great mysteries; of its difficulties, and
of the duty of studying even the passages over which
the heretics have made cavils, and of the need of
philosophy and other preparatory discipline. Then
come answers to some of the objections of Celsus as

that Scripture is meanly written, that Christianity is full of heresies, that the Christians preach folly and ignorance, that Jesus cannot be God if he had a mortal body, that the world is made rather for beasts than for men. Then come chapters on freewill and on fate, that matter is not the cause of evil, that foreknowledge does not destroy freewill, and discussions of difficulties like the hardening of Pharaoh's heart, and It is not of him that willeth.

With all his learning, with all his width of view, with all his boldness in speculation, with all the subtle fervour of his piety, even Origen has his limitations. Besides his want of imagination, he was hampered in some directions by the slightness of his Hebrew scholarship and the current overestimate of the LXX, and in all directions by the allegorism, the transcendental philosophy and the ascetic leanings of the time. The methods of criticism had still to be settled, and no one man can do the work of centuries. But Origen was everywhere the pioneer ; and even in the haste of his dictation an intellect so learned and so subtle could not move without scattering thoughts to be ripened in later ages, like the famous motto of Butler's *Analogy*. Whatever his faults, all history can shew no more true-hearted, pure-minded and laborious seeker after truth than Origen.

It must not be supposed that Origen stood alone in the world, any more than Shakespeare did. With all his greatness, he was only the greatest of many students in his time. Schools like those of Alexandria had grown up in Edessa, Bardaisan's home, and at Caesarea. Alexander of Jerusalem formed a library in his own city of Aelia Capitolina—to give it its

official name. The other Caesarea in Cappadocia was
the refuge first of Clement, afterwards of Origen
himself; and Asia was still a home of Christian
thought and controversy, though its pre-eminence in
the second century had passed away. The interest
of Christendom, gathered no longer to Ephesus and
Smyrna, but to the great cities of Rome, Carthage,
and Alexandria, and even the foundation of Constantinople never brought it back to Asia.

One of these scholars is worth mention here.
Sextus Julius Africanus was an old officer of Septimius
Severus, who lived at Emmaus in Palestine in the
time of El Gabal and Severus Alexander. He seems
to have been a man of rank, and was attracted to
Alexandria by the fame of Heraclas, and came into
relations with Origen himself. His Κεστοί has the
distinction of being the only known work of early
Christian literature which is not directly religious.
Its fragments touch all sorts of questions, and shew
an omnivorous learning and an omnivorous credulity
worthy of the elder Pliny. Perhaps he was not yet
a Christian when he wrote it. But Africanus did
better work than this. If he was not absolutely the
first Christian chronographer, he stands midway
between Bruttius and Eusebius. His five books
brought down the chronicle of the world to the reign
of El Gabal, and was much used by Eusebius and
later writers. There was also a letter of his to
Aristides on the disagreement between the genealogies of our Lord; and a letter to Origen on the
History of Susanna. Africanus disputes its genuineness on thoroughly critical grounds, and has much
the advantage of Origen, who merely pleads the
authority of the LXX, and is not shaken even by the

double pun,[1] which to most minds is clinching proof that it was written in Greek.

Origen was beyond comparison the greatest scholar and the greatest teacher of his time. If Clement was the father of Christian literature, Origen was the first who systematically surveyed the vast field and set the problems and traced the lines of future work on exegesis, dogmatics and homiletics. The Eastern writers did very little that had not been sketched out by Origen. Yet his mere learning, vast as it was, by no means forms his highest qualification, for there is something that must rank even higher than his subtle intellect and marvellous fertility of thought. No man since Plato had formed a nobler conception of education. It was not for Origen either the battle of empty declamation and idle sophistry the Greeks so often made it, or the undigested mass of marketable information which seems the modern fashion, but a systematic training of all the mental powers for the highest of all studies. Like Socrates, he thought it more important to root out prejudices and clear up confusions of thought than to communicate as many facts as possible. He believed like Clement, though with a clearer perception than Clement, not only that all truth in heaven and earth comes from Christ and leads up to Christ, but that the fulness of human nature is needed to reach the fulness of truth, and that the fulness of truth is needed to reach the fulness of Christ. No doubt his conception of human nature was debased alike by Greek intellectualism and by the ascetic ideals of his time. But this means only that he was a man of his own age, and could not shake off all its limitations. Even Plotinus

---

[1] *Hist. Sus.* 54-59 πρῖνον . . πρίσαι . . σχῖνον . . σχίσαι.

fared worse, though he is the greatest of Greek thinkers after Aristotle. At all events Origen was one who strove to bring learning in its widest range to bear upon the work of training all the faculties of human nature.

So Origen's conception of education was of the widest. He had laid his own foundations broad and deep. He was no mean student of literature and scripture before his father's death and then for nearly fifty years he laboured on with *adamantine* energy. His inspiration was a pure and fearless love of truth, and every gift of intellect was his, except imagination. With all his subtle thoughtfulness and fertile fancy, he had nothing of the imagination which makes the past a living present. Perhaps the toil of teaching chilled it, as it often does. But he soon learned to put Scripture before philosophy, and draw all his studies this way, selling his books of secular literature for a pension of four obols a day, on which he was able to live.[1] And his studies were sundry. Heretics and heathens came to his lectures, and he read heretic and heathen books, to the scandal of many. He even undertook the toil of learning Hebrew, though he never got beyond a superficial acquaintance with it, which will not for a moment compare with the scholarship of Jerome. To perfect himself in philosophy, he attended the lectures of Ammonius Saccas, the first of the Neoplatonists. As Porphyry says from his heathen point of view, " Origen was a Greek brought up on Greek literature, but wrecked himself on the barbarian doctrine (Christianity) to which he

---

[1] Sixpence a day is decent fare for an ascetic in a cheap country like Egypt, and represents a fair capital sum. Origen must have made some money by teaching.

went and sold himself and his learning, living like a Christian and contrary to the laws; but in his opinion of things earthly and divine he played the Greek, though he subordinated Greek learning to foreign fables. For he constantly studied Plato, Longinus, and others (including the chief Pythagoreans), and he used the writings of Chaeremon the Stoic, and of Cornutus; and from these he learned that figurative method of interpreting the Greek mysteries which he applied to the Jewish Scriptures." [1]

He might no doubt have learned it from the Stoics, but we have no reason to think he did. With Philo and Clement before him, he had no occasion to look for heathen models. The point to notice is that Porphyry treats Christianity exactly as the Apologists treated heathenism. He will allow no excuse of allegory for the scandals of the Bible, and is as anxious to derive the good things of the Gospel from philosophy as the Apologists are to trace back the good things of philosophy to Moses—And this is something more than a *tu quoque*, for the arguments of controversialists on all sides are shaped by the exegesis of their own time, so that they always have a good deal in common, especially in the things they take for granted.

Education in the Eastern provinces of the Empire was not unlike the education of our own Public Schools some half a century ago, before the intrusion of Science on the old Classical training, which indeed had been shaped on Greek models in the sixteenth century, and had since been little changed. Great as the differences were, the principles were much the same. There was of course no Greek Testament on

---

[1] *ap.* Eus. vi. 19.

Sundays and no Nowell's Catechism for Monday
mornings. There was also no Latin, for Latin in
the East was studied rather for the practical uses
of officials and lawyers than as a general means of
education, and the Greek which remained was not
the dead language it is to us, so that there was no
translation from and into Greek. Yet both Translation and Composition were well represented in the
schools. What answered to Translation was the lower
stage of teaching, which they called Grammar. It
was much more than what we call grammar, for it
included the study of language, of antiquities, and
of exegesis, especially of the passages in which the
poets gave their moral teaching. In short, it meant
all those questions of scholarship and subject-matter
which a modern editor would elucidate with notes or
references. It was in theory an excellent grounding :
in practice it was treated very perfunctorily. The
chief stress was laid on the Rhetoric which formed
the second part of the course. This consisted of
recitations, compositions and discourses, and answered
very fairly to the Composition side of the Public
School, for the compositions and discourses had to be
on classical subjects and in classical language. We
know what the zealots of Composition were some
fifty years ago—boys with a marvellous command of
Greek and Latin words, and not only ignorant but
contemptuous of everything else. The education of
the third century must have tended in the same
direction ; and two further circumstances increased
the evil. One was the greater attention paid to the
arts and tricks of rhetoric and oratory : for the other,
these elegant amusements were more the fashion of
grown men than they ever were in England. They

were the serious occupation of senators, and the
admiration of the literary coteries. Pliny and
Symmachus were quite as proud of their literary
trifles as of the work they did for the state. We
read of a Praetorian Praefect of Illyricum, who liked
nothing better than to come and preside all day at
some great literary tournament of this kind : and he
was not singular in his taste. Words were everything, matter nothing ; and the evil went on increasing. A system which began by resolving
education into rhetoric and sophistry naturally ended
in smothering rhetoric itself under the meaningless
affectations and absurd bombast which make its last
representatives almost unreadable. It is a relief to
turn from the empty conundrums and literary in-
sincerities of Ennodius to the rude Latin of Gregory
of Tours, who at any rate has something to tell us.

The Christians had the same education as their
neighbours. Many were converts ; and there was not
yet much distrust of heathen education for Christian
children. The schools were open to all comers, for
heathenism had no articles of faith, while even the
Orthodoxasts of Alexandria distrusted rather learning generally than heathen education in particular.
The chief difference was the instruction given to
catechumens and the educative influence of the
Sunday services : and these went far to balance the
general defects of the system. Truth was not to the
Christian a thing to be speculated upon and argued
over and trifled with, but a thing revealed once for
all in Christ. So he had a more definite and concrete
standard of truth than the heathen, and a higher and
more practical sense of duty to truth—for none but
the Christian had to witness of truth at the risk of

life. He might set forth truth with all the arts of rhetoric; but truth he would set forth, for he could not play the sophist.

So Origen saw clearly the central weakness of education. The time was spent in polishing tools for work, and the work was never done. So broadly, his plan was to take the usual course of Grammar and Rhetoric, and then add first Philosophy, and then Theology as the only studies worthy to complete all this preparation. If he did not escape the danger on the side of rhetoric, at any rate he greatly mitigated it by subordinating the Rhetoric to the study of truth in its highest forms.

Origen's method has now to be more fully described.[1] Having abandoned secular literature, he had to do with inquirers and students, and could frankly lead up all his teaching to Theology. He began with logic and the training of thought, studying the character of his disciples, criticizing their crude ideas, laying open the fallacies which misled them, and guiding them into habits of accurate and careful thinking. It was not a pleasant process for them, but they loved him notwithstanding. So Gregory tells us; and he speaks from experience. The second period was devoted to Physics, beginning with geometry and arithmetic, and going on to astronomy. The third stage was philosophy, or rather moral science, for he took it like the Stoics on the practical side: nor did he confine himself to Greek thinkers, but used barbarian help whenever he found it useful. This then was the training he deemed necessary before beginning the study of Theology.

[1] Chief account by Gregory of Neocaesarea.

Of course it was intended for students only under Origen's own supervision. No doubt many of the simpler sort received only the plain teaching they might have had anywhere.

Origen's doctrine we shall best survey by seeing how he states it in his *de Principiis*. Though this, as we have seen, was written at an early stage of his literary activity, it gives his ripe opinions, and so fully covers the ground that we can get no more than secondary additions and corrections from the rest of his works, chiefly from the commentary on St. John. Unfortunately it is preserved in the Latin of Ruffinus, who was apt to think that anything heterodox was a corruption, and needed to be set right. We can however check his divagations by the Greek of certain passages preserved in the *Philocalia* and in the *Acts* of the Councils, and by Origen's deliverances elsewhere. Upon the whole, there is no great margin of doubt as to what his opinions really were.

He begins by professing his belief in the teaching of the church, and that nothing outside that teaching can be received as an article of faith. What questions then are settled by it, and what left open? Origen replies by setting forth the rule of faith. Now the rule of faith is not a creed. A creed is a summary of necessary Christian teaching sanctioned by authority for local or general use as a profession of Christian faith or a standard of Christian teaching, whereas a rule of faith is a similar summary set forth by private persons in their own words for the edification of their readers. Irenaeus and Tertullian had given sundry rules of faith; and now Origen gives another. Its substance is this.

The apostles plainly taught—First, that there is

but one God, the creator of all things out of nothing,
a just and good God, the Father of our Lord Jesus
Christ, and the author of Law and Gospel, Old and
New Testament. In the second place, Jesus Christ
who came into the world was begotten of the Father
before every creature. He was the minister of
creation : and at the end of the ages he emptied
himself and was incarnate, becoming man while still
remaining God as he was before. His body was like
ours, except that it was born of the Virgin and the
Holy Spirit. He truly suffered, truly died, truly rose
again and ascended into heaven. Thirdly, the apostolic
tradition associates the Holy Spirit in honour and
dignity with the Father and the Son. Whether the
Holy Spirit is begotten, or whether he is to be
regarded as a Son of God, is an open question : the
one thing taught without hesitation is that he is the
giver of all inspiration both before and after Christ's
coming.

The church teaches also that the soul is endowed
with a life of its own, and shall hereafter pass into
eternal life or eternal fire according as its work shall
be. Another undisputed part of church teaching is
the freedom of the will. Outside powers may urge
us to good or evil ; but they cannot constrain us,
whatever the astrologers may say. The church
leaves it undecided, whether the soul is transmitted
by generation, or originates in some other way ; and
in the latter case, whether it is ingenerate or not, or
whether it is infused into the body from without.
As touching the devil and his angels, the church
teaches their existence, but not their nature or the
manner of their existence, though it is most commonly
believed that the devil was once an angel, and that

his angels are angels seduced by him. Another point of church teaching is that this world was created at a definite time, and will one day be dissolved by its native corruption. But what there was before this world, or what there will be after it, is left uncertain. The Holy Spirit has given to the Scriptures not only that meaning which is manifest, but a spiritual meaning which is commonly overlooked. The whole church is agreed that the Law is spiritual : but its spiritual meaning is unknown, except to those endowed by the Holy Spirit with wisdom and knowledge. Though the word *incorporeal* (ἀσώματος) is not found in Scripture, it is a well-known conception of the philosophers : but if it be asked whether God is incorporeal, we cannot certainly answer the question. Finally, whether sun, moon and stars are animated beings or not, is more than we can be sure of.

The converse of Origen's rule of faith is his classification of heretics. The heretic is one who professes belief in Christ, and yet errs on some fundamental question. First, there are Gnostics who make the Creator (who is the God of the Old Testament) some other being than the Father of our Lord Jesus Christ. Next come three groups of heresies concerning the Person of Christ. Ebionites and Valentinians deny his divinity, and even his pre-existence, making him only a son of Joseph and Mary. Others (Docetists) accept the virgin birth and the rest of the history, but reduce them to appearance without reality. Others again (*e.g.* Beryllus of Bostra) hold that he had no personal existence before the incarnation, and no divinity of his own after it, so that the Person incarnate was really the Father. Then there are others who make two Gods of the Holy Spirit, by

distinguishing the inspiration of the Old Testament
from that of the New. All these make shipwreck of
faith upon the doctrine of the Trinity : and to these
we must add the dualists who hold that all souls are
not of the same nature, making an *original* difference
between the spiritual and the natural man, and so
denying the freedom of the will. These six groups
of heretics correspond very nearly to the questions he
treats as settled in his rule of faith, for he does not
seem to think it possible for persons professing belief
in Christ to deny the life of the soul, the existence of
the devil and his angels, the finite duration of this
world, or the existence of a spiritual sense of Scripture.
On this last point he was not far wrong in fact, for
Marcion was an undoubted heretic, and the Montanists
were at best suspected.

The first thing that strikes us in Origen's rule of
faith is its incompleteness as a scheme of doctrine.
Like all the Eastern creeds, it hardly gets beyond the
doctrines of the Trinity and the Incarnation. Nothing
is decided about the Sacraments, the Atonement or
Justification, or even about the church to whose
tradition he appeals. All these are controversies of
other ages, in which the Greeks took little or no part.
Even the one question—that of free will—which looks
like an anticipation of Latin controversies, is not
really such, for the heretics in view are Gnostics, not
Pelagians, and the question at issue is not whether
all men are disabled by original sin, but whether some
men were created incapable of receiving the things of
God.

Origen's rule of faith is given as the Confession of
the Christian man, in the same sense as the Articles
and Liturgy are the Confession of the English cleric.

If it gives a decision, that is binding: if not, the question is open, and a man is no heretic for any opinion he may have upon it. So we look for the special features of Origen's own theology to the four questions which he expressly states to be open. Two of these will not detain us. Origen made no great advance on the doctrine of the Holy Spirit; and indeed to ourselves the relation denoted by procession is an even greater mystery than that denoted by generation—except that we believe it to be different. Again, it was a fair question for the ancients, whether sun, moon and stars are animated beings. It is so implied in much primitive belief, and such was the opinion of the Greek philosophers from Thales to Plato, and perhaps of Aristotle too. The Stoics and Philo had something of the sort, and this was the old Chaldaean doctrine which even more than Persian dualism shaped the heathenism of the third century. Origen himself leaned that way, though for the West the matter was settled by the prudence of Augustine, who pointed out that Scripture leaves the question undecided. But the other two questions, on the origin of the soul and the existence of past and future worlds, bring us to the heart of Origen's own theology.

Origen starts from the fact that this world is created and therefore has a beginning and end in time. But we cannot suppose that God does nothing outside those limits. If he is παντοκράτωρ (all-ruling, not almighty) he must always have subjects to rule. Hence there must be an indefinite series of created worlds covering the whole range of time from beginning to end. And as worlds, so souls must have been created in the beginning—and created equal, for inequality is injustice not to be imputed to God.

The present inequality—the difference of angels and
men and devils—must be caused by the free action
of the souls in the successive worlds they have passed
through. In each world God rewards each soul
according as its work has been in the last world.
One exceptional soul held to God with such perfect
faithfulness that it could be chosen for the soul of
the incarnate Lord himself. In general however
the souls which held to God are angels who now do
nothing evil, while those which fell away are devils
who now do nothing good, and between them are
men who do both good and evil. But however souls
may rise or fall, they cannot in any case lose their
freedom. An angel will fall if he gets tired of goodness, and the devil himself has the possibility of
rising, though some even of human sinners have no
forgiveness in this world or the next world. So the
whole is one vast universe of immortal souls rising
and falling each by itself in successive worlds.

This is not the Pythagorean transmigration of
souls, for Origen draws a clear line between man and
beast. A bad man may sink into a devil, but he
cannot be born again as a beast. A more serious
objection can be made, that there is no finality in a
process where the highest is never above the fear of
falling, and the lowest never below the hope of rising,
and where for all that yet appears, a fall is as likely
as a rise. Such a system is like the recurring cycles
of the Stoics, which build up nothing that will not be
destroyed by the next conflagration. Taken by itself,
it is no better than the reincarnations of the Buddhist
karma, except that Justice is personal and not
impersonal. It mocks the Christian hope of resurrection to life eternal, and shuts out the promise of the

restoration of all things. Had he allowed for the cumulative force of habit, he might have been able to shew that there is something higher as well as something lower than freedom. In the end, the good might have been for ever fixed in goodness, but also the evil for ever fixed in evil. He does indeed occasionally speak of the punishment of the wicked as never ending; but the main current of his thought sets quite another way. And if he had further allowed for the fact that creation is for good and not for evil—for God and not for Satan—he might have maintained that while goodness may be eternal, wickedness cannot endure for ever.

It will be noted that his main scheme is vitiated by a false conception of divine justice, as if it were not enough for a man to be judged by what he has and not by what he has not, but each must have no more and no less than his neighbour, except in just reward or punishment of his doings in the past. Instead of setting this right, he tacks on a corrective, which at any rate makes the scheme Christian. That corrective is his faith in the infinite and boundless virtue of the Atonement. The mechanical process of divine justice—for it is nothing more—is not his whole philosophy of religion. High over all rules the love of God which guides men not as for this life only, but for the endless ages of the future, and searches out the deepest sickness with the sharpest remedies, as every good physician does. How this consists with the unbending law of justice is more than we can say; but no Christian man can doubt that so it is. Christ died not for men only, but for angels and for devils also. The ransom was duly paid to Satan; and who will now set limits to the mighty working of redeeming love? The process that seemed mechanical is a process of purification worked out from age to age and cycle to cycle; and the love which leaves the ninety and nine sheep at their pasture to seek for the one that is lost will never rest till in this world or another or in yet another of the worlds to come the very last of the souls that sinned is for ever gathered to the Saviour's arms.

Though Origen's thought is so largely shaped by opposition to the fatalism of the Gnostics, his main scheme reminds us of the Gnostic cosmologies. It is marked by the same aspiration to other worlds, the same intellectualism, the same contempt for the body, and the same endeavour to save God's justice. It has all the philosophical advantages of thorough-going individualism, and gives fair explanations of original sin and of this world's inequalities; and we can appreciate better than our fathers its stern insistence that every man's lot in the present is the fruit of his doings in the past. A scientific unbeliever of our time might almost adopt the scheme for his own, if once he came to see that natural consequence is as direct a work of God as any miracle can be. On the other hand, it has all the philosophical difficulties of an unqualified individualism. It allows nothing for inheritance, takes no account of mankind as an organic whole, makes the body no more than a coat which wears out and is cast aside, and has to tone down the idea of sin like the philosophers to some-thing purely negative. Origen does not even make the best of his own principles, for with all his insistence on human freedom, he does not see like St. Paul that the variety of men makes their variety of lot a question not of divine justice, but of fitness for divine purposes. These are serious objections ; and not one of them is removed by his Christian confidence in the unbounded power of the Atonement. That remains an excrescence on the scheme, though we cannot doubt that it was nearer to the life by which he lived. The heart may make harmless the errors of the head, but it cannot of itself correct them. Taken as a whole however Origen's is a noble scheme for all its faults, and just its noblest feature is its worst offence to men of little faith. Its grand confidence in all-embracing all-redeeming love divine was too bold even for the larger number of Eastern churchmen, while the timid legalism of the West hardly understood it enough to anathematize it. I think Cyprian never mentions Origen : and his silence is significant.

BOOKS

Westcott (Bp.) Art. " Origen " in *D.C.B.* ; Prat (S. J.) *Origène* Paris 1907 ; Keim *Celsus.*

CHAPTER XXI

THE ROMAN CHURCH

HITHERTO our work has been mostly in the East. The writers we have had to mention were all Easterns but Clement and Hermas, and even they wrote in Greek. Now however we come to Western writers and a Western form of Christian thought. We are not yet called upon to deal with it fully; and indeed we cannot till we have seen more of the characteristic developments of East and West. Suffice it for the present to say that Greek and Latin Christianity bear the marks of Greek and Latin religion and literature, and are related to each other accordingly. The one is philosophical and speculative, seeking after knowledge, and tending to resolve revelation into philosophy. The other is legal and practical, holding to the faith once received, and tending to convert the revelation into law. Gnosticism and Arianism are characteristic of one, Montanism and Pelagianism of the other. The Greek divines and bishops who culminate in Origen and Athanasius are the true successors of the Greek philosophers and orators; while the Latin bishops and divines, from Tertullian, Cyprian, and Augustine to Leo and Gregory, carry on the succession of Roman lawyers and statesmen towards the mediaeval popes.

Where then was the first great centre of Latin Christianity ? We look to the church of Rome, and we look in vain. Its history indeed to the end of the second century is obscure. Clement and Hermas belonged to it, and Ignatius wrote to it; but they tell us very little about it. We have a list of bishops, of whom Telesphorus only was a martyr. We have also the visit of Polycarp, a sentence or two from the answer of Dionysius to Soter, and a few references to the arrival of heretics like Cerdon, Marcion, Valentinus, and Marcellina : and this is about all that we are directly told. Even the laborious work of recent years has been spent on the early history rather of the creed than of the church of Rome.

Nevertheless, we can say for certain that the church of Rome was more Greek than Latin, and remained so for a long time. St. Paul writes in Greek to Rome, Clement writes in Greek from Rome; and almost every document connected with the Roman church before the Nicene age was written in Greek. The chief exceptions are the works of Novatian, and a few of the genuine letters and spurious treatises which have come down to us among the writings of Cyprian. The early bishops of Rome bear Greek names, with Clement, Pius, and Victor the only exceptions in the first fifteen. Even the Liturgy was at first in Greek, as we see from survivals like *Kyrie eleison* ;[1] and we hear of no great Latin preacher at Rome before Leo I.

But if the church of Rome was not the centre of Latin Christianity—we shall find that across the sea at Carthage—it was the centre of Christendom as a

---

[1] When Polycarp held the service at Rome, he would probably hold it in Greek.

whole. Its central position was fully recognized by
Irenaeus, and became more and more definite as time
went on till the rise of Constantinople. In the first
place, Rome was the capital, and the only apostolic
see in the West.[1] So she exercised the full influence
of a great and wealthy church with a noble fame for
world-wide charity. From the first—the practice was
old even in Soter's time—she sent her gifts to the poor
and to the confessors in the mines all over the Empire.[2]
Then again, the Roman church gained strength from
its close relation to the emperor. The palace was
always its stronghold, and "they of Caesar's household" were its chiefest leaders. Scenes which did not
mean much in the provinces might at Rome be the
signal for the ever-threatening struggle of life and
death with heathenism. Moreover, Rome was the
natural link of East and West. As a Greek colony
in the Latin capital, it was the representative of
Western Christianity to the Easterns, and the
interpreter of Eastern thought to the Latin West.
For all these reasons Rome was the natural centre of
discussion. Her orthodoxy was unstained. Whatever heresies might flow like the Syrian Orontes to
the great city, no heresy ever issued thence. The
strangers of every land who found their way to Rome
and the tombs of the great apostles were welcomed
from St. Peter's throne with the majestic blessing of
a universal father. "The church of God which so-
journeth in Rome" was the immemorial counsellor of

---

[1] Plutarch de Romanorum Fortuna 316 F. Rome made by Τύχη and
Πρόνοια into πᾶσιν ἀνθρώποις ἑστίαν ἱερὰν ὡς ἀληθῶς καὶ ὀνησίδωραν καὶ πεῖσμα
μόνιμον καὶ στοιχεῖον ἀίδιον, ὑποφερομένοις τοῖς πράγμασιν ἀγκυρηβόλιον σάλου
καὶ πλάνης, ὥς φησι Δημόκριτος.

Ath. Hist. Ar. 34, p. 288 μέχρι τῶν ἐκεῖ τὴν μανίαν ἐξέτειναν· καὶ οὐχ ὅτι
ἀποστολικός ἐστι θρόνος ᾐδέσθησαν, οὔθ' ὅτι μητρόπολις ἡ Ῥώμη τῆς Ῥωμανίας
ἐστὶν εὐλαβήθησαν.   [2] Eus. iv. 23.

all the churches; and the voice of counsel slowly passed into that of command. When Rome spoke in Eastern controversies, she commonly had the West behind her; and then her voice was decisive. She spoke for the West on Arianism and Monophysitism, and therefore she conquered; she spoke only for : herself on Pelagianism and the Three Chapters, and then she was powerless.

There are legends in abundance about the beginnings of the Gospel in Rome, but the truth is lost in impenetrable obscurity. It was not brought there by one of the Twelve, and probably not by the strangers of Rome returning from the Day of Pentecost. More likely it came with some nameless Jewish traders whom business brought to Rome. The first trace of it may be the " continual disturbances " in the Jewish community in the time of Claudius (cir. 52). If "at the instigation of Chrestus" is a confused report of disputes about the Christ, we may be pretty sure that Christianity was the bone of contention. Our next trace comes from an unexpected quarter. Tacitus tells us how Pomponia Graecina, the wife of Aulus Plautius, the first Roman general in Britain, was accused in 57 of " foreign superstition," and handed over to the judgment of her husband and relations, by whom she was acquitted. This Pomponia had put on mourning in 43 for Julia the daughter of Drusus, one of Messalina's victims, and was admired for her courage in doing so. For forty years she lived a "melancholy" life.[1] Whether she was indeed the Lucina of the catacombs must be left in doubt; but her "melancholy" life is just the description Tacitus might give of Christianity, and no

[1] Tac. *Ann.* xiii. 32.

other "foreign superstition" is likely to have brought her into danger.

We get our next view of the Roman church from St. Paul's Epistle of 58.   It is a mixed body of Jews and Gentiles, perhaps in nearly equal numbers, and can boast of "notable apostles" in Andronicus and Junias.   But it is not yet organized as a single church : it consists rather of a number of small "churches" which have grown up in different parts of the city.   St. Paul's visit (61-63) must have done as much for the consolidation of the church as for the spread of the Gospel.   We can already recognize its strongholds in the palace and the Praetorium.   Then came the fiery trial of the Neronian persecution, and St. Peter's visit in its later stages.   After this we have nothing for five-and-twenty years but the shadowy names of Linus and Cletus, who appear as its first bishops in the list of Hegesippus.[1]

We learn very little from Clement in 96.   He speaks indeed of "the sudden and repeated calamities that have befallen us," and significantly reminds the Corinthians that "we are in the same lists" of persecution as "the good apostles" and Nero's victims : but for the rest, we can only say that the Roman church was in better order than the Corinthian, and that the bishop appears nowhere in the letter.   It is the church which speaks throughout, and even the church claims no jurisdiction over Corinth.   In the language of the diplomatists, it does not intervene, but simply tenders its good offices for the restoration of order.

---

[1] Lightfoot *Early Roman Succession* in *Clement* i. 201-345.   Irenaeus calls Cletus Anencletus ; which may have been his real name.

We may pass over the apocryphal *Acts* of Linus.

Some twenty years later Ignatius[1] addresses the
church of Rome as "having the presidency in the
district of the Romans . . . . having the presidency
in love"—*i.e.* as the chief church in that district,
and as famous for its good works. The words refer
to the church, not to the bishop, and they do not
seem to imply jurisdiction over even the neighbouring or suburbicarian churches. There is no sign of a
bishop in the letter, much less of a universal bishop.
For the rest, we gather only that there were Christians with influence at Rome, and that there was no
active persecution going on at the time.

Of the next six bishops—Euarestus, Alexander,
Xystus, Telesphorus, Hyginus, Pius—who cover the
first half of the second century, we know only that
Telesphorus was a martyr, and that Pius held "the
chair of the church of the city of Rome" while his
brother Hermas wrote the *Shepherd.*[2] If Hermas
was a slave, as he represents himself, his brother the
bishop was most likely a slave too, or at best a

[1] Ign. *Rom.* 1 ἥτις προκάθηται ἐν τόπῳ χωρίου Ῥωμαίων . . . . προκαθημένη
τῆς ἀγάπης. It will be noted that χωρίον is a *small* district, and that the
presidency is of love, not law.

Bardenhewer would do well to give some proof of his round assertion
that "the word ἀγάπη often signifies in Ignatius the entire community of
Christians" (*Patrology* 33 E.Tr.).

[2] This statement of the Muratorian Fragment would fix the *Shepherd cir.*
140, and suits generally the character of the book. The difficulty is that
Hermas is directed to send the vision to Clement for communication to the
churches. Either (*a*) Clement is the writer's contemporary, and we must
shift the date to *cir.* 100. So Zahn : and there is no strong internal evidence against this. Or (*b*) there must have been a second Clement acting as
Foreign Secretary to the church of Rome. This is not impossible, especially
as Clement must have been a fairly common name in the church ; but upon
the whole, it is not likely. Or (*c*) Hermas deliberately lays the scene of his
vision some forty years back. This seems the best alternative ; but whether
we adopt (*b*) or (*c*), the *Shepherd* will be evidence for the state of the Roman
church *cir.* 140. An earlier date is forbidden by the reference to Pius, a
later by the absence of any allusion to Gnosticism, which became very active
in Rome a few years later.

freedman. Yet from the *Shepherd* we get little information about the church of Rome. Even its government is not clearly indicated, for though Hermas usually speaks of the elders as its rulers, there are a few places where he may be referring to bishops, though even here it is never certain that he means bishops in the later sense of the word. His own opinions would have been described half a century later as leaning to Montanism. He makes much of fasting, allows but one repentance, and evidently looks forward to a great persecution and the end of the age. Of course this is not Montanist doctrine, for Montanism did not yet exist; but it shews more or less of the Montanist temper. We cannot say how far this temper prevailed in the Roman church; only that it was not dominant. Hermas no doubt speaks for a party; but he clearly does not speak for the church of Rome in general.

Meanwhile Rome was becoming the centre of discussion. Thither came every man who had a new doctrine to propound, and there he strove to obtain recognition for it. The Syrian Cerdo came in the episcopate of Hyginus, Valentinus and Marcion a little later, and Marcellina "destroyed many" in the time of Anicetus. Thither came also, for sojourn or for residence, Justin and his disciple Tatian, Hegesippus, Polycarp and his disciples Florinus and Irenaeus, and perhaps the enigmatical Avircius of Hieropolis.[1] There cannot have been many forms

---

[1] The doubt is not whether Avircius came to Rome, but whether he was Christian or heathen. On one side stand Ramsay, Lightfoot, Zahn, Hogarth, Duchesne; on the other Harnack (*T.U.* xii. *Abercius Inschrift*) and von Schubert (*K.G.* 191).

The question is delicate. If Avircius is a heathen, his language is deeply coloured by Christianity—the Shepherd, the Fish, Paul as companion (or example) the wine and the bread—for Harnack does not seem successful

of thought, Christian or heathen, which had not adherents in Rome.

The next three bishops are known to us by their relations to other churches : of the church of Rome itself in their time we hear next to nothing. Anicetus is known only by his friendly dispute with Polycarp, Soter by his Letter to the church of Corinth, which was publicly read like Clement's. The answer of Dionysius praises the church of Rome for its ancient custom of world-wide liberality, and for the fatherly welcome received by "the brethren who go up" to Rome.[1] He also speaks of Rome and Corinth as being the joint foundation of the two great apostles. Clement had already joined their names, and so had Ignatius, but this is the first distinct statement that the church of Rome had them for its founders. It cannot be strictly true, for we know that it was not in the proper sense founded by either of them, though both may have done much to organize it. But from this time forth it is the accepted story.

The next bishop Eleutherus had been deacon to Anicetus—the first of the long line of archdeacons of Rome which reaches down to Hildebrand. In his time Irenaeus brings out vividly the primacy of Rome as the focus of discussion among the

in shewing that these are not Christian. On the other hand, if he is a Christian, he gives his words touches of heathen colouring, and avoids clear and definite Christian language. Upon the whole, he seems much more likely to have been a Christian. He is writing poetry, good or bad ; and in that age Christian ideas could hardly be put into poetry without borrowing the poetic dress from heathenism. Moreover, it was prudence in an age of persecution not to put them on public monuments without veiling them under phrases which might pass as heathen ; and that this was very commonly done we see from the inscriptions at Eumenea. And if Avircius was a Christian at all, nothing seems gained by supposing him heterodox.

[1] Eus. iv. 23.

churches. His argument, as we saw before, is that
if the apostles taught Gnosticism, some later bishop
in each church must have gone astray into common
Christianity. Now look over our lists of bishops,
and tell us who they were. But it would be too
long to give the lists of all the churches; so we
give only that of "the very great and ancient and
universally known church founded and established
at Rome by the two most glorious apostles, Peter
and Paul. . . . For unto this church, on account of
its more powerful lead, every church (meaning the
faithful who come from all quarters) must needs
resort; since in it that tradition which comes from
the apostles has always been preserved by those
who come from all quarters."[1]

After the Gnostics the Montanists came to Rome.
They must have been making a stir in 177, for in
that year Irenaeus was sent by the confessors at

[1] Irenaeus *Haer.* iii. 3 *Ad hanc enim ecclesiam propter potentiorem* (or
potiorem) *principalitatem necesse est omnem convenire ecclesiam, hoc est, eos
qui sunt undique fideles, in qua semper ab his, qui sunt undique, conservata
est ea quae est ab apostolis traditio.*

The Greek is lost, and it is not easy to say whether *principalitas* refers
to age or dignity : but in any case it is impossible to translate—"With this
church must agree every church, meaning the faithful who are everywhere."
First, *convenire ad* is strange Latin for *to agree with*. Second, *necesse est*
(not *oportet*) is not of that which ought to be, but of that which must be so,
and cannot be otherwise. Now it was plain necessity that the faithful would
often have business in Rome ; but it is absurd to say that a church *cannot*
disagree with Rome. Next, it is not *ubique* but *undique*. The faithful are
not living everywhere, but coming from all quarters—to Rome, no doubt.
Again, the last clause is not to be omitted, or got rid of by putting on *in qua*
the impossible meaning *in communion with* (*e.g.* Bardenhewer *Patr.* 121 E. Tr.)
nor is there any sense in referring it to *omnem ecclesiam* without putting
unnatural meanings on *necesse est* and *convenire ad*. It is clearly local ; and
the meaning is that the faith of the Roman church is continually refreshed
and kept true by the strangers from all parts of the world, whom their
occasions bring to Rome.

See Bright *Roman See in the Early Church* 30-36. So Langen *Gesch. röm.
Kirche* i. 171. Their Greek parallels seem conclusive on the meaning of
convenire ad.

Lyons with a letter to Eleutherus. The letter must have been in the main against the Montanists, though perhaps not very decidedly so. The position taken by Eleutherus is a disputed question. Tertullian tells us that a bishop of Rome had already recognized the Montanist prophets and drawn up letters of peace to the churches of Asia and Phrygia when he was persuaded by the confessor Praxeas to recall them. Praxeas brought an evil report of the prophets from Asia, and appealed to the authority of (more than one of) the bishop's predecessors. That bishop may be either Eleutherus or Victor; and it is not easy to decide between them. Upon the whole however it is unlikely that the question of the prophets did not come to an issue at Rome till a dozen years or more after Maximilla's death: and this consideration seems to turn the scale in favour of Eleutherus.[1]

Bishop Victor (189-199) is the first of the grand series of statesmen who have held the Roman see. He ranks in line with Julius I. and Leo the Great, with Calixtus II. and Hadrian IV, with Sixtus V. and Leo XIII. We have seen his intercession with Marcia, and the skilful use he made of the rescript of Severus. Yet he made a great mistake in dealing with the Easter Question, which Anicetus and Polycarp had left unsettled. Up to that time the Roman bishops had kept the Sunday, but left the strangers who came to Rome to do as they pleased. Soter and Eleutherus would seem to have been less friendly to the Quartodecimans; but the controversy did not blaze up at Rome till the peace of the church was disturbed by a Quartodeciman zealot named

[1] Tert. *Prax.* 1, discussed by Harnack *A.C.L.* i. 375.

Blastus. By this time the Quartodecimans had fallen
out with each other, and many councils in sundry
regions had pronounced for the Sunday. Victor had
nearly all the churches behind him, except those of
Asia : yet he met with general condemnation when
he tried to make the prevailing custom a law of
the church.

If Victor was a thorough Roman, it does not
follow that he was a modern pope born out of due
time. He is not laying down the law, that a custom
must be observed by all churches because it is the
Roman custom. The dispute was very troublesome,
especially in such a resort of strangers as Rome was,
and the provocations of Blastus had not made things
easier. And now that the Quartodecimans had been
so generally condemned, Victor had some reason for
thinking the time come to put an end to the old
scandal by enforcing the all but universal custom of
Christian churches on the few that insisted on going
their own way. He forgot only what most of his
successors have forgotten, that there can be no true
unity without diversity. The preachers of uniformity
have always been the chief makers of division.

Our information about the Roman church in the
first quarter of the third century comes mostly from
Hippolytus. Tertullian gives important help, but
Eusebius does not seem to know much more than the
names of Zephyrinus and Callistus, and the work of
Gaius against Proclus the Montanist. He mentions
Hippolytus, but does not know where he was bishop,
and gives the titles of some of his works, though he
does not appear to have read them—in fact, Hippolytus is the most obscure of all the early church
writers, and the worst of the many difficulties con-

nected with him gather round his relation to the
Roman see.

Hippolytus then was born not much before 160,
for he lived till nearly 236 ; nor much after 170,
for he was an influential presbyter at Rome under
Zephyrinus (199-217). His birthplace and family
are unknown, and of his education we can only say
that he was a disciple of Irenaeus—no doubt at
Lyons, *cir.* 185-195. But his learning was enormous,
wherever he got it : he has no equal but Tertullian
among the early Westerns. He was in favour with
bishop Victor ; but under Zephyrinus he was in
opposition to the dominant influence of Callistus.
About here (*cir.* 200-210) may be the date of his
Syntagma, or account of 32 heresies from Dositheus
to Noetus, which was directly or indirectly used by
Ps.-Tertullian, Epiphanius, and Philaster. Callistus
became bishop (217-222) on the death of Zephyrinus ;
and Hippolytus gives a very hostile account of his
life and policy. Of the next bishops, Urbanus (222-
cir. 230) and Pontianus (*cir.* 230-235) we hear very
little, though most likely it was Pontianus who held
the Synod at Rome which ratified the condemnation
of Origen at Alexandria. During this interval
Hippolytus wrote his *Refutatio* (*Philosophumena*)
which may be taken as a much enlarged edition of
the *Syntagma* with new material and considerable
changes, as we have seen with reference to Basilides.
At last we come to an entry in the Liberian List
of 354. "The bishop Pontianus and the Presbyter
Hippolytus were deported to Sardinia, a pestilential
island, in the consulship of Severus and Quintianus
(235). In that island Pontianus laid down his
office Sept. 28, and Anteros was chosen in his place

Nov. 21 of the same year." The deportation was of course by Maximin, not by Alexander. Exiles in Sardinia were not expected to live long; so it was probably in the next year (Aug. 13) that bishop Fabian, who had already succeeded Anteros, laid to rest the remains of Pontianus in the cemetery of Callistus, and those of Hippolytus by the via Tiburtina. On that spot a statue (perfect except the head) was found in 1551. The bishop is seated in his chair, and round it are inscribed the names of his works, his Easter cycle of sixteen years, and a calculation by it of Easter for seven cycles (222-333). As the cycle went wrong from 237, this must be the latest date for the statue—an altogether unique honour for a Christian of early times.

But now comes the question, Who was Hippolytus? A bishop certainly, for so he tells us : but of what city ? Nobody seems to know. His connexions are with Rome, and less certainly with Portus at the mouth of the Tiber.[1] But he was certainly not bishop of Rome; and the silence of Damasus (366-385) and Jerome is unaccountable, if he was bishop of Portus. So Lightfoot made him bishop, not of Portus, but of the foreign population in Portus. But though the theory is Lightfoot's, it seems untenable. Such a position as he assigns to Hippolytus would be not "exceptional" only, but unique in early church history. But the fatal objection is that the Liberian List and Damasus call him presbyter, not bishop.[2]

---

[1] We may dismiss the Bostra and Aden theories as mere blunders.

[2] Lightfoot (*Clement* i. 435) endeavours to parry this by making presbyter a title of honour, like The venerable Bede, or as he calls his own teacher Irenaeus the blessed presbyter. But surely *Pontianus episcopus et Hippolytus presbyter* is a contrast of office ; and the definite *H. presbyter* in an official notice is not parallel either to the general οἱ πρεσβύτεροι or to the particular ὁ μακάριος πρεσβύτερος.

Further, Hippolytus tells us that "on the death of
Zephyrinus, Callistus thought he had got what he
was hunting after, and rejected Sabellius for fear of
me," and how the rascal had the impudence to "set
up a school in opposition to the church," and per-
sistently speaks of his "school," as he would speak of
the school of any heretic. All is fairly clear if
Hippolytus was the rival of Callistus for the Roman
see itself—the first antipope. In that case outsiders
would take his own word for it that he was a bishop,
while officially he would be no more than a presbyter
at Rome. The only real difficulty is that the schism
is not mentioned by later writers; and this is not
insuperable. The schism must have lasted till 235,
as we see from the way the rival bishops are coupled
in exile. Yet Hippolytus must have been reconciled
in the end to the Roman church, for she counts no
other antipope among her worthies. The natural
inference is that the two bishops resigned together in
Sardinia. If the schism was ended in this friendly
way, its memory would soon be effaced by the rise
of Novatianism, with which indeed pope Damasus
confounds it.[1]

Clearly the guiding power in Rome was Callistus,
not Hippolytus. If Hippolytus had the learning,
Callistus had the statesmanship, and carried the
church with him. The account of him given by
Hippolytus is nearly as follows :—

The heresy of Noetus was supported by Callistus,

[1] Lightfoot's other argument is that Hippolytus would not have failed
definitely to state his claim to the Roman see. But was it not enough to call
Callistus pointedly the head of a mere school in opposition to the church ?
Nor was it necessary for him to deny that Callistus was the "lawfully
constituted bishop of Rome." His contention was that however lawfully
constituted a bishop might be, he lost all moral claim to his office by such
offences as those of Callistus, and ought to be deposed.

a crafty schemer who governed the ignorant Zephyrinus, and was hunting for the succession to his chair.
He actually got Zephyrinus to make publicly a
Patripassian declaration, and called us ditheists for
opposing it. So we will tell the story of his life, that
it may discredit his heresy. Callistus then kept
a bank for his master Carpophorus, a Christian of
Caesar's household. When he " had made all the
deposits to vanish," he tried first flight, then suicide,
but was seized and sent to the mill like a wicked
slave. As death was better than this, he promised to
get back some of the money, and tried to get the
credit of a martyr by making a disturbance in a
Jewish synagogue. The praefect Fuscianus did not
put him to death, but he did the next thing to it.
He scourged him and sent him to penal servitude for
life in the mines of Sardinia. Some time afterward
Marcia, willing to do a good work—for she was the
pious concubine of Commodus—sent for the blessed
Victor, who was then bishop, and obtained from him
the names of the confessors in Sardinia. Callistus of
course was not on the list, but he contrived by
prayers and entreaties to get his freedom with the
rest. Victor was much annoyed at his return, and
endeavoured to abate the scandal by sending him to
live at Antium on an allowance. After Victor's death,
Zephyrinus brought him back from Antium, set him
in charge of the cemetery, and made him his chief
adviser—and flatterer. On the death of Zephyrinus,
thinking he had got the bishopric he was hunting for,
he expelled Sabellius for unsound teaching : but this
he only did for fear of me, and to get rid of the
current charge of heresy against himself. When hard
pressed on both sides, he scattered blasphemies right

and left, blundering badly between Sabellius and Theodotus, and set up a school of his own in opposition to the church. He was the first who devised a way of yielding to men in their sensual pleasures by saying that by him sins were forgiven to all men. So the bad consciences, the outcasts of the sects and our own excommunicates, filled his school. He laid down the law that if a bishop sinned, even a sin unto death, he ought not to be deposed. In his time began twice-married and thrice-married men to be made bishops, elders and deacons; and if one of the clergy married, he kept his office as if he had not sinned. For this Callistus quoted, Who art thou that judgest another man's servant, Let the tares grow together with the wheat—the sinners in the church—and the clean and unclean beasts in the ark, saying it must be so in the church. So he got a good school of sinners. He even allowed women who did not wish to lose their rank by a legal marriage with a man below them to have any one they pleased (whether slave or free) for a companion, and counted that a marriage. In his time was first impudently attempted a second baptism.

This is an enemy's account, and no doubt does Callistus a good deal of injustice; yet it seems honestly given, and the broad facts must have been too notorious to be much falsified. We may take it then that Callistus was a slave, and that he was unfortunate—Hippolytus does not say fraudulent—in his banking. The brawl in the synagogue must be somehow misrepresented, for it is clear that Callistus was most commonly counted a true confessor. He may or may not have been on Victor's list; but if he was not, there must have been many who thought

injustice had been done him.   Nor need his removal
to Antium imply any special dislike on Victor's part.
The bankrupt was in any case best out of the way,
and he could hardly be employed in Rome against the
will of his old master Carpophorus.   It is not every
bankrupt who fails for want of talent; and his influence over Zephyrinus is better explained by real
ability than by mere gifts and flattery, if only because
a favourite of that sort is too generally obnoxious to
have a chance of the succession.

Like most of the Roman bishops, Callistus was
more statesman than saint.   The very violence of
Hippolytus proves that he was a successful bishop;
and the changes he made may not have been unwise.
First comes his action with regard to penance; and
on this we have the evidence of Tertullian.   "I hear
that an edict has been published, and indeed a
decisive one.   The Pontifex Maximus forsooth, the
bishop of bishops, issues his edict : I remit the sins of
adultery and fornication to those who have done
their penance."[1]   That is to say, Callistus has issued
a declaration as authoritative in substance as an
emperor's edict, and even more summary (*et quidem
peremptorium*) in tone.   In this he sets forth his
personal dignity as bishop of Rome, in virtue of which
he presumes to restore church communion to all who
have committed sins of the flesh (a few abominations
no doubt excepted) if they have shewn their penitence
in the prescribed form of penance (*exomologesis*).
Thus unchastity is removed from the list of unpardon-
able sins, leaving only idolatry and murder.   The
change was doubtless good policy, for it brought the
sinners to the church of Callistus.   It seemed a sad

[1] Tert. *de Pud.* i.

decline to rigorists like Hippolytus, who would permanently refuse communion to all gross sinners. The contest had still to be fought out over the *Lapsi* : but the change would have to be made, if the church was ever to be more than a pietistic sect. After all, it was one step nearer to the spirit of Christ when sinners were received, even to inhuman penance, than when they were for ever shut out and surrendered to the powers of evil.

Another change made by Callistus marks the first clear divergence of church and civil law on social questions. The Roman law of marriage reflected the strong class feeling which survived the Empire. A man might marry his freedwoman, and a woman might marry her freedman, though such marriages were not considered very decent; but there could be no marriage of a slave, even with another slave. Senators however and their near relations were not allowed to marry low women, much less freedwomen or slaves. The law was no doubt difficult to enforce, for the relation of a *concubina* (morganatic wife) was outwardly very like an immoral relation which Society did not seriously condemn. Callistus now decreed that if a woman of high rank formed a permanent connexion with a man of low birth, with a freedman, or even with a slave, such connexion should be recognized by the church as a lawful marriage. Here again Callistus was in advance of his time. Unequal marriages and marriages with freedmen might pass with more moderate men than Hippolytus, and the marriages of slaves among themselves were recognized (subject to master's sanction) but even Christian opinion was not yet prepared to sanction marriages between slave and free.

The other complaints of Hippolytus are also
coloured by his rigoristic leanings. Thus he states
the extreme practice of forbidding the ordination of
digamists and the marriage of ordained persons as
if it were the undisputed law of the church. His
complaint that Callistus forbade the deposition of a
bishop guilty of deadly sin probably means that
Callistus did not agree with him on what constitutes
deadly sin. The second baptism which was attempted
(Hippolytus does not say by Callistus) must be the
rebaptism of heretics who came over to the church;
and the attempt must have been a failure, for we cannot set aside the clear and definite statement of bishop
Stephen, that rebaptism neither was nor ever had
been the custom of the church of Rome.

BOOKS

Lightfoot *Apostolic Fathers* ; Langen *Gesch. der römischen Kirche* ; Rolffs *Indulgenzedict d. Kallistus.*

CHAPTER XXII

AFRICA—TERTULLIAN

SEPARATED from Europe only by the sea, but from
Egypt and the Soudan by some twelve hundred miles
of desert, lies what the Arabs call the Island of the
West. Behind the rocky coast which faces Spain is
a belt of fertile lands, and beyond it the hills slope
upward to the Atlas range, then southward and
downward to the Sahara. In prehistoric times the
mountains ran without a break from Spain to Sicily
and Crete, and even to the Taurus and the Lebanon;
but now their ends sink down to meet the coast
where it turns abruptly south to the Syrtes. This
trend of the coast is what gives its matchless grandeur to the site of Carthage. Even Constantinople
has no more commanding position than the Queen
of the West beside her noble bay, overlooking the
Italian seas from the shelter of the Hermaean Cape,
and resting on the thickly peopled valley of the
Bagradas behind her, in fertility unsurpassed by that
of the Nile itself.

If the historical connexions of Egypt are with
Asia, north-western Africa belongs even geographically
to Europe. The separation from Spain and Sicily is
a thing of yesterday, so that plants and animals differ
very little across the sea. Even the foreign element

in Roman Africa is much more Asiatic than Ethiopian.[1] The desert is the barrier, not the sea. Even the climates intermingle. Algiers is as wet as Europe, while the glowing coast of Murcia ripens dates like the African oases.[2] The Berber aborigines look like Europeans, and are utterly unlike the Semite or the negro, or even the Egyptian. Their tall and sinewy forms, often with blue eyes and flaxen hair, have given rise to many a legend of children of the Vandals in the recesses of Mount Aures, or of Gothic fugitives in the Canaries : yet their vivid and emotional temper reminds us rather of Gauls or Phrygians than of the solid Teutons. It is not for want of courage that they never played a leading part in history. The Numidian cavalry turned the scales of war for Hannibal at Cannae, for Rome at Zama, and nearly gave her a Moorish emperor in the ruthless Lusius Quietus. After five-and-twenty centuries of foreign rule, they still remain the basis of the population ; and Islam itself has never been able to seduce them into Arab nomadism and polygamy.

The Phoenicians were the first of their foreign masters. They came as traders, and their power was never strong except along the coast and round Carthage. They were hard masters, cruel and selfish, so that the fall of Carthage was a great deliverance for the Berbers, who under the dynasty of Massinissa nearly developed into a nation. Yet Phoenician literature and civilization survived for ages by the

[1] Most *e.g.* of the Mollusca of Algeria are found in Spain or Sicily, and the rest resemble those of the Anatolia and Syria ; but with those of the Soudan they have almost nothing in common.

[2] Bp. Collins tells me that they need careful irrigation, and are not equal to the African. Still, even this seems more than can be done on the African coast.

sea, from Leptis Magna to the Pillars. The emperor Severus spoke Phoenician, his sister spoke no Latin, and even in Augustine's time Phoenician was the language of the rustics near Hippo. The Alonim and Alonoth of Carthage were still worshipped in Roman times, public sacrifices of children lasted "till the proconsulship of Tiberius," [1] and El Gabal brought the Queen of Heaven to Rome as a bride for Jupiter Capitolinus.

The Romans came in as destroyers, with more than Punic treachery ; and for a whole century the ruins of Carthage were a parable of a neglected province. In spite of Caius Gracchus, the finest site in Africa remained a waste. Only after Juba's presumption had been crushed at Thapsus was the dictator Caesar able to cover it with a Roman colony. Roman Carthage grew fast like Roman Corinth, and before the third century stood next to Rome herself as the greatest city of the West. A new life was in the land. Roman roads ran from Carthage to the Pillars and to the edge of the desert, and even across it to Alexandria. Roman yeomen tilled the fertile soil, and Roman nobles settled in their midst. If Rome had won her conquest foully, she learned to use it nobly. Africa rivalled even Gaul in the number of her cities, and in the splendour of their buildings. Only the native tribes of Aures and the desert were neglected. Vast camps indeed like Lambaesis and Gemellae held the frontier, and Roman forays might pierce far south across the Atlas or to Fezzan : but no effort was made to civilize the dweller of the desert. So back he came "like the desert sands" whenever

[1] Tert. *Apol.* 9, best interpreted of a proconsul in the second century, served perhaps by Tertullian's father.

Rome was weak, and his incursions nearly ruined the province long before the Vandals conquered it.

Meanwhile Roman Carthage was a splendid restoration of the old Phoenician city. Eshmun and Tanith came back to temples on the Byrsa, the quays were once more full of commerce, and the ships of Carthage covered the seas as in the olden time. No garrison was there, for the legion which held Africa was quartered at Lambaesis till Constantine removed it to the rock of Cirta. But a Roman proconsul had his palace on the Byrsa, and the city was Roman— not Phoenician, not Greek like the other great cities of the Empire, but Roman. Not its lawyers only, but its rhetoricians and philosophers (poets it had none) wrote Latin, and a stately amphitheatre provided Roman pleasure for its people. Yet with all this, Carthage was not quite like Rome. The Greek element of its life may have been smaller, but the dominant Latin was never quite natural. The mincing elegance of Apuleius and the rugged boldness of Tertullian are alike in this. From Phoenician[1] peradventure or Berber came a certain un-Roman strain of intensity which ran through the superstition and sensuality of the place—for Carthage was as vicious and as frivolous as other great cities. Athletes and singers, actors and rope-dancers were the men it delighted to honour. The great ladies had more

[1] The Phoenician element in African Christianity seems underestimated by Benson *Cyprian* p. xxxv. True, Cyprian's bishops (and martyrs too) nearly all bear Roman names. But (1) Some of the earlier martyrs (Namphamo, Miggin, Guddenis, Nartzallus) are clearly natives. (2) Some who bear Roman names may have had native fathers, as we frequently see in the *Sufetes* of the towns. (3) Some such influence seems needed to explain the admitted peculiarities of African Christianity. If the African church was so thoroughly Roman, why was it not more like the Roman? The weakness of Donatism at Rome may be as significant as that of Arianism. I am not seeking to deny Benson's general position ; only to qualify it.

influence than their sisters at Alexandria, and were
not behind them in careless luxury. The great
landlords gave themselves, not indeed commonly to
gross excesses, but even less to manly virtue. They
lived for elegance and selfish pleasure.[1] Meanwhile
capital was locked up in palaces of luxury, free
labourers were disappearing, and the yeomen's farms
were swallowed up in ever-growing stretches of
grazing land. Slavery and rotten economics and
rampant vice were preparing the way for the nomads
of the south.

How and when Christianity came to Roman
Africa is unknown. We may guess that it came
from Rome, and we may be sure that it came early,
and that it had Greek beginnings; but information
we have none about its origin, or even about the
first century or more of its history. Fronto of Cirta
tells us little, and may have Italy more in view than
Africa, while Minucius Felix is better placed after
Tertullian than before him. The reference of Apuleius
to the Christians is disputed, but in any case he gives
us little that is definite. So we first get sight of the
African churches in the proconsulship of Vigellius
Saturninus, which covers the opening of the reign of

[1] As samples of the great Roman nobles, we may take the description of
the two Gordians in Africa by Capitolinus *Gordiani tres* 6 (*Gordianus*) *erat
. . . canitie decora et pompali vultu . . . oculis ore fronte verendus . . .
moribus ita moderatus ut nihil possis dicere, quod ille aut cupide aut in-
modeste aut nimie fecerit . . . vini parcus, cibi parcissimus, vestitu
nitidus, lavandi cupidus, ita ut et quarto et quinto lavaret aestate, hieme
secundo.*

19 (*Gordianus junior*) *fuit vini cupidior, semper tamen undecumque conditi
. . . cibi parcus . . . mulierum cupidissimus* (scandalous details) *. . . vixit
in deliciis, in hortis, in balneis, in amoenissimis nemoribus . . . vestitu
cultissimus, servis et omnibus suis carus.*

They were much the same a century or two later *e.g.* in Gaul, Dill *Roman
Society in the Last Century of the Western Empire* 115-223 "Very pleasant,
but somewhat self-indulgent and frivolous."

Commodus. The first of the African martyrs was Namphamo of Madaura, a Phoenician by origin ; and a few days later came the Scillitans (July 17, 180). Some years after this, we find Christianity flourishing with astonishing vigour. The original Greek element is long ago swamped, and the churches, like Carthage itself, are in the main Latin, with a strain of Phoenician. The Christians were not only numerous in the cities —there may have been some thousands in Carthage— but had spread to the villages, and reached the native Berbers and the edge of the desert. But the Africa of this age is Tertullian's Africa. Fronto and Apuleius are insignificant beside him, and Cyprian himself is no more than a pale copy of " the Master." Tertullian has no equal in Latin Christendom before Augustine.

Quintus Septimius Florens Tertullianus was born about 155-160. His father was a centurion[1] and a heathen : of his mother he tells us nothing. He had the usual literary education, of course beginning with Homer : but for Latin the fashion of the time was archaic. Fronto preferred Ennius and Cato to Virgil and Cicero. Then came rhetoric, both Greek and Latin, for Tertullian wrote in both languages : after- wards the legal studies which have left their mark on almost every page of his work. Whether he was the great lawyer Tertullianus whom we meet in the *Corpus Juris* is more than we can say. He read the poets, and cared little for them, practised rhetoric, and despised it, studied philosophy, and railed at it ; but all his conceptions are shaped by law and Stoicism. Then he seems to have been in Rome throughout the reign of Commodus, or at any rate

[1] Jerome *de Vir. ill.* 53.

at its beginning and end; and at some time he seems
to have paid a visit to Greece.

So far Tertullian was a heathen, frequenting the
games, perhaps more or less of a Mithraist, and
living much the same life as others. The date of
his conversion may be about 195, but afterwards he
became an elder of the church. His wife was also
Christian, but we do not know whether he married
her as such.

His conversion seems to have been caused rather
by the sight of Christian constancy than by any
search for truth in Justin's style, or by the reading
of Christian books—for he tells us that nobody reads
them till he is already a Christian. However, it
came as a shock which filled him with a deep horror
of all the works and ways of heathenism, a nervous
dread of everything that might countenance idolatry,
and a firm determination to keep the church free
from everything even pointing to that greatest of all
sins. So Tertullian was a rigorist from the first, and
a prince among rigorists. In weight of learning he is
no unworthy match for Clement of Alexandria, in
literary skill and force of character he far surpasses
him, and in strength of conviction he is not behind
him. He lacks only Clement's fairness, moderation
and width of view. Augustine himself is not more
full of the vivid phrases that live for ever; and all
history can shew no greater master of irony and
invective. For Tertullian has neither charity nor
even common justice for an opponent, and nothing
of Clement's reverence for truth as the mystery of
God which we can truly know, but only know in
part. Controversial questions are quite clear to him.
Truth is an item of church property, and he is counsel

for the defence against heretics and heathens. So
he is everywhere the keen lawyer who uses every
argument that will tell, and appeals to every passion
that will serve his purpose.   Irony and sarcasm and
paradox and downright special pleading alternate
with grand bursts of eloquence and long stretches of
solid reasoning.   His stern uncompromising sentences
come like blows of a hammer crushing everything
before them : for mercy is a word he understood no
better than the Stoics.   He was a Montanist in temper
long before he accepted the oracles of the New
Prophecy.   Tertullian was no friend of publicans
and sinners.   To him the Gospel is a rigid law, and
the heinous sinner is once for all beyond the reach of
mercy.   Christ will plead no more for him,[1] and wrath
shall come upon him to the uttermost.   Forgiveness
is not until seventy times seven, but after Baptism
not even once.   The heretics he fought were many and
dangerous ; yet is not Tertullian himself among the
worst of them, when he slanders Christ as merciless ?

This is Tertullian in his usual and characteristic
mood ; but it is only fair to say that he is com-
paratively mild in some of his earlier and more
devotional writings, where he has no special enemies
in view, and shews himself fully sensible of the evil
done him by his gusts of passion.   Even as late as
213 his remonstrance to Scapula is written with
perfect dignity.   But in general the bad habit
steadily grows on him, till his latest works are
monuments of Montanist narrowness and want of
charity.   Yet even these are full of power : only
Tertullian could have written them, and Tertullian
only in the bitterness of his old age.

[1] *de Pudicitia* 19 (Montanist).

The date of his adoption of Montanism is uncertain, but it did not for some years lead to a rupture with the church. The time of his death is equally uncertain; but we must put it well after 220, if Jerome is right in telling us that he lived to extreme old age. There is no reason to suppose that he was a martyr.

We will now review some of his treatises, taking those which may throw light on the man himself and on the times in which he lived.

We will begin with Tertullian at his best, in the *de Oratione*. Jesus Christ, the Spirit, Word, and Reason of God, gave a new form of prayer to the disciples of the Testament, because the old ordinances no longer held good, now that the new grace had renewed all things from carnal to spiritual. Short as it is, it is a summary of the entire Gospel. Then he goes through it clause by clause. We take a sample. "After God's name, God's will, and God's kingdom, he makes a place for prayer for earthly needs, for the Lord had already laid down the rule, Seek ye first the kingdom, and then all these things shall be added to you; though we rather understand, Give us this day our daily bread, in a spiritual sense. For Christ is our bread, because Christ is life and bread is life. I am, saith he, the bread of life, and a little before, The bread is the Word of the living God, which came down from heaven. Again, his body is counted to be in bread—This is my body. Therefore in asking for our daily bread, we ask for a perpetual continuance in Christ, and that we may never be separated from his body. But because the word may be taken in a carnal sense, it must not be so taken without regard to religion, and specially to the spiritual discipline, for he commands that bread be asked for, which is the one thing believers need, for after the rest the Gentiles seek." His summing-up is too brilliant to be omitted. "How many duties are here ticked off. The honour of God in *Father*, the testimony of faith in *Name*, the offering of obedience in *Will*, the remembrance of hope in *Kingdom*, the prayer for life in *Bread*, the confession of debts in *Forgive*, the dread of temptation in *Lead us not*. What wonder? Only God could teach how he wished to be prayed to." After this, we may add other prayers, but we must be free, not only from anger against a brother, but from all disturbance of mind. But we need not first wash our hands like the Jews (who notwithstanding are never clean) or take off our cloaks as the heathens do. Nor is there any reason for sitting down when we have finished, unless it be a childish imitation of Hermas. Again, we ought not to make known our fasting by forbearing the kiss of peace, though it is another matter at the Passover (Good Friday) when we all fast openly. So too it is a mistake, though a common one, to abstain from the sacrificial prayers on the half-fasts or *stationes*, on the ground that the fast will be broken by receiving the Lord's body. If the fast is a service devoted to God, will not the Thanksgiving bind it closer to God? Will not your *station* be more solemn if you have stood at God's altar? But if you take the bread and reserve it to eat at home, you can attend the sacrifice without breaking the fast.[1] Women without exception must be veiled at the common prayers. There are a few

[1] It will be noted here (1) that the fast is here at most a laudable custom, not a binding ordinance, (2) that this reservation differs entirely from the later custom. Instead of depending on the doctrine of the Real Presence, it is rather inconsistent with it. But neither does it agree very well with the

who abstain from kneeling on the Sabbath ; but for ourselves, we follow the tradition of standing only on the day of the Lord's resurrection and in the season of Pentecost. As for prayer at the third, sixth and ninth hours of the day, these are good habits, though there is no precept enjoining them : still it is becoming for believers not to take food or enter the bath without prayer. After mentioning some minor practices, he concludes with a noble description of the efficacy of prayer, beginning, Prayer is the spiritual victim which has abolished the ancient sacrifices.

We take next a rather later work, which deals with more thorny questions, where however Tertullian still (by comparison) shews good sense. The subject of the *de Idololatria* is the limits of Christian liberty in common life in a heathen world ; and this, like the observance of Sunday in later times, is a hard question for those who determine Christian duty by legal rules. He begins then by saying that idolatry is the worst sin of mankind, because it includes all others. The idolater is a murderer of himself, an adulterer and a robber of God. Idol-makers must not be admitted to the church, for God forbids us even to make an idol, for making one *is* worshipping it. The brazen serpent is the exception which proves the rule. Yet these men are received in the church, and even chosen for the ministry ! " The Jews laid hands on Christ but once : these men wound him daily," when they deliver the Lord's body with unclean hands. These hands deserve to be cut off.[1] The astrologer is as bad, and the schoolmaster or

---

idea of communion, on which it does depend. In short, it seems a superstition pure and simple.

[1] Probably these cases were few : but the scandal would be great.

teacher of literature no better, for he has to explain
all about the gods, and to keep their festivals.   The
disciple however is not bound to do either, and some
literature we must have.   It is therefore lawful to
learn, but not to teach literature.[1]   In general, no
art or trade which is a help to sin is free from the
stain of sin.   One of his instances is the seller of
incense.[2]   As for the festivals of the heathen, both
faith and discipline forbid us to rejoice then ; and if
money is usually paid or received on those days, we
must choose other days.   The command to rejoice
with them that do rejoice refers to brethren, not to
heathens.   Illuminations on state occasions are idolatry
too.   " Christ said, Let your works shine ; but now
all our shops and gates shine."   The lamps before
your doors and the laurels on your door-posts are an
honour to the multitudinous gods who preside over
entrances.   I know of a brother who was grievously
punished in a vision, because his slaves had crowned
his door : yet he was away from home, and on his
return reproved them.   So strict (he might have said
unjust) is God in dealing with us.   But as regards
private festivals, of putting on the *toga virilis,*
betrothals, weddings, namings, I think there is no
danger in the whiff of idolatry mixed up with them.
All these are innocent—God curses nothing in the
way of dress, except a man in woman's clothes.   We
may attend even if there is a sacrifice, provided we
do not come for the sacrifice.   But as for helping
at a sacrifice, as by handing the wine or prompting
the sacrificer, that is flat idolatry.   Any public

[1] Exactly Julian's position, that Christians must not teach the classics.
It is a form of the general fallacy, that it is dishonest to teach anything we
do not take literally.

[2] Yet he says *de Cor*. 10 that he uses incense to abate a stink.

office is quite impossible for a Christian. Can he
avoid sacrificing or countenancing sacrifice, farming
out victims, providing for the care and revenue of
temples, giving games and presiding over them,
not even taking oaths or judging any man for life
or character, or punishing any man? The thing is
impossible. Similarly the soldier: and even if he
can escape compliances with idolatry, the soldier's
promise is inconsistent with the baptismal promise.
The centurion may have been a believer; but in
disarming Peter the Lord disarmed every soldier
from that time forth.[1] When the law forbids us to
name false gods, it does not mean such casual mention
as, I live in Isis Street; nor does it forbid me to call
a man Saturnus, if such be his name. It is the
naming them as gods which is the sin. Thus we
must not say, By Hercules: and if the heathen say,
Jupiter be angry with you, we must not answer,
Nay, with you. Christ lays down the law that
we are not to swear at all, and it is not enough
to forbear swearing in words. An oath written
in a deed is still an oath; and if you sign it,
you cannot say that you have not sworn. "Amidst
these rocks and inlets, these shallows and straits
of idolatry Faith makes her voyage with her sails
filled by the Spirit of God, safe if cautious, secure if
watchful."

We come now to his "most plausible and most
mischievous book," the *de Praescriptionibus*. Its
perversities are more serious than those of the *de
Idololatria*, because he is not now seeking a middle
course between carelessness and scrupulosity in

[1] He forgets Cornelius. In *Apol.* 42 he speaks of Christian soldiers as a
matter of course.

Christian practice, but resting the whole defence of
Christian doctrine against the heretics on a gross
fallacy of argument. He abandoned this fallacy
(along with some others he here lays down) when he
joined the Montanists: but it is so simple and so
plausible to the natural man that it has always been
the staple of distinctively catholic theology. He
begins then with general denunciations of heresy, and
traces its doctrines to philosophy. Thus the Valentinian aeons come from Plato. The God of Marcion
is Stoic. When the soul is said to perish, that is
a note taken from the Epicureans, and when the
restoration of the flesh is denied, that is the common
belief of all the philosophers. From the philosophers
come the curious questions—Whence is evil, and
why? Whence is man, and how?—and the latest
problem of Valentinus—Whence is God? From
enthymesis and *ectroma*, of course. What have
Athens and Jerusalem in common? the academy and
the church? heretics and Christians? We who believe in Christ need ask no further questions, for we
believe that there is nothing further which we ought
to believe. "Seek, and ye shall find," was spoken
only to the Jews; and in any case, we who have
found the truth cannot seek further without confessing
that we have lost it. If we keep the rule of faith,[1]
other questions are open to curiosity, and minister
only to curiosity. Heretics must not be allowed to
appeal to Scripture, for when the apostle commands
us to reprove them, he forbids us to argue with
them : and indeed such argument leads to nothing
but confusion of mind and loss of temper.

[1] Roughly, the Apostles' Creed *plus* the inspiration of the Old Testament
and eternal fire for the *profani*.

We shall get a more satisfactory method if we take it as a matter of law. Whose property then is Scripture ?   Jesus Christ sent his apostles who founded churches ; and from these churches we have our tradition of his teaching.   Here then we enter our demurrer (*praescriptio*) that (whatever the heretics may have to say) no teachers can be received but those Christ sent, no doctrine accepted but what is proved by means of those churches.   All contrary teaching may be summarily set down as false.   The apostles knew everything, and taught everything, and the churches did not mistake their teaching. If Galatians and Corinthians went wrong, no doubt they were set right : and they cannot all have gone wrong together unless the apostles taught them wrong.

Truth is older than error, and the churches are older than Marcion and Valentinus.   If these men are new apostles, let them produce their new gospel, and prove it with miracles.   If they are disciples of the old, let them tell us the origin of their churches, and trace back the succession of their bishops to some apostle, or to some companion of the apostles who did not turn heretic.   We can do it, they cannot : and as for their doctrines, they are precisely those exposed and denounced by the apostles.   If this be so, heretics must not be allowed to appeal to Scripture, for we can shew on independent grounds that they have nothing to do with Scripture.   For if they are heretics, they are not Christians ; and if they are not Christians, they have no right to Christian Scriptures. These are our property ; we have long been in possession : by what right do you disturb us ?   We are the heirs of the apostles.   We keep the deposit according to the terms they laid down in their testament, you they disinherited as strangers and enemies. Heresies are inspired by the devil, and come very near to idolatry, for they are just as much his work. After further complaints of the way in which they treat Scripture—"Marcion criticizes with a pen-knife"—he gives a lively account of their disorderly worship, no doubt referring chiefly to the Marcionites. "In the first place, it is uncertain who is catechumen, who full Christian. They come up together,[1] they pray together—heathens also, if any come in. They throw their holy things to dogs and their pearls (though they are but shams) to the swine. They will have it that the destruction of order is simplicity, and our care of order they call pandering. They give the kiss of peace indiscriminately to all, for with all their differences, they make no difference amongst themselves, so long as they are all agreed in their conspiracy against the one truth. They all promise knowledge. Their catechumens are 'perfect' before they are fully taught. Even their women— how pert they are! They have the impudence to teach, to dispute, to exorcise, to promise cures, perhaps also to baptize. Their ordinations are random, hasty, unstable. Sometimes they choose neophytes, sometimes men of the world, sometimes our renegades—to bind them by vanity, since by truth they cannot. Promotion is nowhere easier than in the camp of rebels, where the mere fact of being there is a merit. So one is bishop to-day, another to-morrow; a man is deacon to-day, reader to-morrow; elder to-day, layman to-morrow, for they

---

[1] To *see* the "mysteries" only, for even Marcion could not have allowed heathens to partake of them.

put sacerdotal functions even on laymen." They
have no reverence even for their own chairmen; and
this is why they are scarcely troubled with schisms—
because they have no obedience. Schism itself is
their only unity. Most of them have not even
churches—forlorn creatures that they are. We all
know their dealings with magicians in plenty,
vagabonds, astrologers, and philosophers— all of them
gentlemen given to curiosity. This is their reading
of, Seek and ye shall find. The work concludes
with a piece of irony audacious even for Tertullian.
Our Lord himself addresses the heretics—" I committed my gospel and the rule of discipline once for
all to my apostles; but as you forsooth were not
likely to believe it, I thought it well to make some
changes here and there. I promised a resurrection,
even of the flesh; but on second thoughts, perhaps
I could not fulfil it. I declared myself born of a
virgin; but afterward I thought that rather scandalous.
I called him Father, who makes the sun and the
rains; but another father has adopted me now, to my
great advantage. I forbade you to listen to heretics;
but in that I blundered."

All this is magnificent as declamation and invective; and large parts of it are quite true, though
he has evidently mixed up the misdeeds of different
sects as a satire on heresy generally. But the fallacy
of the argument is evident. He assumes first that
the revelation is a definite body of doctrines and
practices so fully given to the apostles and delivered
by them to the churches that the Holy Spirit cannot
have any fresh light to throw on it, or at any rate will
give none to those who for any reason are outside the
visible churches. He further takes for granted—

precisely the question at issue — that the actual
teaching of the churches exactly represents that of
the apostles. In a word, he ignores history, and that
on both sides—the teaching of God in history, and
the varieties and changes of men summed up in
history. Again, he assumes that tradition is always
in accord with Scripture; but he requires this to be
believed without proof, for there is no way of proving
it without the appeal to Scripture which he forbids.
The direct and practical mischiefs of the argument
might have been less if tradition had been limited
to those historic facts of which every particular
church is a witness and keeper, though even then
Christianity would have been rested on a false
basis and made impossible of rational reception;
but the extension of tradition to sundry doctrines
and practices without allowing them to be verified
by Scripture and sound learning is nothing short
of a rejection of Christ in favour of the particular church authority we think fit to choose for
ourselves.

In truth, the *de Praescriptionibus* is a piece of
special pleading, and Tertullian does himself less than
justice in it. In other works he continually meets the
heretics on the ground of Scripture, and challenges
them to prove their doctrines from Scripture. His
five books against Marcion begin with a little abuse
—Marcion worse than all the horrid beasts of Scythia
— but soon become a continuous argument from
Scripture. A few years later, when his acceptance
of the oracles of the Paraclete had practically
made him a schismatic, he shattered the sophistry
of the *de Praescriptionibus* with a single great
saying, which echoed in the Latin Church for

centuries — Our Lord called himself Truth, not
Custom.[1]   Even Tertullian learned something in
schism.

[1] Tert. *de Virg. vel.* 1.

BOOKS

Neander *Antignosticus*; Noeldechen *Tertullian* Gotha 1890 ; Glover
Conflict of Religions.

CHAPTER XXIII

DECIUS AND VALERIAN

FOR more than half a century the churches had a tolerable peace, from the reign of Commodus to that of Philip. Doubtless the fires of persecution only smouldered, and ever and anon some outbreak, even in the friendly reign of Philip, reminded them that Rome was still their enemy. Yet the situation seemed improving. The Christians were more in number, and better known. They belonged to all ranks of society, and claimed the ablest literary men of the time. They were no Brahmins or hermits, but lived in the world and frequented the streets and markets like other men.[1] They were found to be worthy citizens like their neighbours, but for a few quakerish eccentricities. So the old scandals died away, and the violence of mobs abated. We hear of no riots after the time of Gallus, and the later persecutions of Valerian and Diocletian were set on foot by the government. Meanwhile the Christians found favour in the highest quarters. First Commodus, then Severus and his successors leaned to Eastern worships. So they were left unmolested, and rather protected than otherwise. The

[1] Tert. *Apol.* 42

only break is the short reign of Maximin; and after
that Philip returned to the Eastern policy. The
surface signs were those of peaceful progress : yet
the hardest struggles were still to come.

Even in Philip's time a careful observer might
have seen that danger was near. Earnest men like
Cyprian would read the signs of coming judgment in
scandalous bishops, caballing clergy and a laity quite
at home in a world of rampant sin. Some storm of
persecution was needed to cleanse the church. There
was truth in this view of things, though it was too
darkly coloured. An outsider might have seen almost
as much. Toleration rested not on law, but on the
favour of Syrian emperors ; and the Syrian emperors
had not been successful. El Gabal had been swept
away for his insolent defiance of Roman feeling ; and
the cautious eclecticism which Alexander failed to
carry through was not likely to fare better in Philip's
more ambitious hands. The Empire was visibly sinking into some abyss of disaster. Macrinus, Alexander
and Gordian had all been failures in the East ; and
the steady pressure of the Goths on the Danube
was hardly less alarming than the growth of Persia.
Even the splendid festival of the thousandth year
of Rome in 248 had a touch of sadness in it as
a reminder of a glorious past, and must have stirred
many hearts to indignation against the un-Roman
degeneracy which seemed ruining the Empire—and
against the Christians most of all as the worst of
degenerates. Murderous riots in 249 at Alexandria[1]
were a sign of things to come. The heathen reaction
only wanted a leader ; and a mutiny in Pannonia
supplied one. Philip fell in battle at Verona (249,

---

[1] Eus. vi. 41.

about Sept.[1]) and Trajanus Decius reigned in his
stead.[2]

The new emperor was no barbarian like Maximin.
Without reaching the saintly fame of Marcus which
overawed the Christians, Decius appears to have
been a noble type of Roman virtue. His military
reputation was hardly shattered by the catastrophe
of the Gothic war; and we have no reason to doubt
his dignity and general mildness, and earnest wish
to restore the grand old Roman virtues. Zosimus
gives him a splendid character, and even the
Christians have nothing against him but the
persecution—and that was the natural expression
of his Roman zeal.[3] He was a Trajan fallen on
evil days, and he endeavoured to go back to the
systems of a better time. Soldier though he was,
Decius worked in harmony with the senate, and

---

[1] Philip was living Aug. 29 : Decius is reigning Oct. 16.

[2] Some words seem needed on the thorny question of the credibility of
Pollio and Vopiscus—for the other writers of the *Hist. Aug.* concern us less.

We may set aside at once the attempt of Dessau to make the whole
series the work of one forger in the time of Theodosius.   There is no reason
to doubt that the Lives were written in the times of Diocletian and Constantine, and put together in their present form *cir.* 330.   It is agreed on
all hands that they are as poor stuff as ever passed for history, and that
Pollio and Vopiscus wrote the poorest stuff of all.   But is it poor history or
little better than romance ?

As the letters of the kings on the capture of Valerian are evident forgeries,
there is no *a priori* reason why the rest of the letters and documents should
not be forgeries : but it does not summarily follow that they are forgeries.
Each case must be taken on its own evidence, and even a forgery is often
good evidence on side questions.   But I fear the conclusion will very
commonly be adverse.

A protest however must be entered against some of the arguments.
Thus the conversation of the praefect Tiberianus with Vopiscus at the
Hilaria is dismissed as invention because Tiberianus was not praefect at the
Hilaria.   Surely it is not common sense to take for granted that a most
inaccurate writer cannot possibly have put down the wrong festival.

[3] Decius not led (Eus. vi. 39) by hatred of Philip.   He seems (Zos. i. 21)
to have been quite loyal to Philip, and was set up by the army against his
will.

even endeavoured[1] to restore the censorship in the person of Valerian.[2] The mere attempt is enough to stamp him as a dreamer like Julian. In fact, under the name of a republican censor he was creating a second senatorial emperor for civil affairs.[3]

Very soon an edict (the first *edict* against the Christians) struck the churches the most terrible blow they had ever yet sustained. Its exact wording is unknown; but it must have required all persons generally to sacrifice before a certain day. The object was to make as few martyrs as was possible, if only Christianity was rooted out. For this purpose there was an ascending scale of compulsion,

---

[1] Trebellius Pollio *Val.* 5, 6 dates the election of Valerian by the senate Oct. 27, 251. Schiller *Röm. Gesch.* i. 807 rightly shifts this to 250, on the ground that Decius was dead before Aug. 28, 251. To his arguments may be added the impossibility (if Decius was alive as late as Oct. 27) of getting in the reigns of Gallus and Æmilianus before the return of the third legion to Africa. It was sent back by Valerian, and a squadron of it reached Gemellae Oct. 23, 253. This by the way is one of the arguments which fix Valerian's own election to the Empire for 253 and not 254.

[2] This division of powers, reserving civil affairs to the senate, was always the senatorial ideal. There was something like it under Pupienus and Balbinus; and it is very strongly shewn by the letters (genuine or not) in Vopiscus *Tacitus* 18, 19. The fact that Decius permitted it is enough to shew his senatorial leanings.

[3] The Decian persecution is ascribed by v. Schubert (Möller *K. G.*[2] 286) to Valerian as Censor, while Decius is taken for a mere soldier, busy with the Goths throughout his reign, who practically had nothing to do with it. Against this view:

1. Decius was at Rome during the active part of the persecution, and it dropped when he left for the front in Oct. 250.

2. Valerian was a general in the field at the time of his election as Censor in Oct. 250: and if he then returned to Rome, he carried on no active persecution.

3. If Valerian was the real persecutor, v. Schubert has to admit that "he gave the lie to his whole past" by his friendliness to the Christians when he became emperor. Yet even when he turned persecutor again, the Christians never hinted that he had been their worst enemy before.

4. The persecution of Valerian is such a contrast to that of Decius, not only in spirit but in some special characters, that the two can hardly be the work of the same hand.

leading up to the severest tortures. A stedfast
refusal was not at first always followed by execution, except in the case of bishops. When all tortures had been exhausted on Celerinus, he was kept
nineteen days in the stocks, and then set free.[1] A
while later the confessors were by the emperor's order
simply left to die of famine in prison.[2] The persecution was quite as horrible in character as that of
Diocletian, though its victims appear to have been
fewer, for we hear of no wholesale massacres like that
of the city in Phrygia.

We need not follow it into details. It reached all
classes, for women, and even boys were not spared.
But the main attack, like Maximin's, was on the
clergy. Bishop Fabian of Rome was one of the first
victims (Jan. 20, 250) and the persecution prevented
any choice of a successor for more than a year.
Cornelius was not elected till Mar. 5, 251, after
Decius had left Rome for the Gothic war. Babylas
of Antioch died in prison, and so likewise the old
confessor Alexander of Jerusalem, and even the
charmed life of Origen was struck at last. His age
and learning were not spared. He was not indeed
put to death, but carefully kept alive under refined
and long-continued tortures, of which he died soon
after the end of the persecution. Dionysius of
Alexandria was rescued from the soldiers by some
country people; Gregory of Neocaesarea and Cyprian
of Carthage hid themselves—though not for want of
courage.

The Decian persecution is the first which can
fairly be called general. Others originated in re-

[1] Cyprian *Ep.* 39. So the boy Dioscorus at Alexandria Eus. vi. 41.
Other cases.   [2] Cyprian *Ep.* 22.

scripts to particular officials, and were too short or too unequal or limited to special classes : but Decius issued a general edict and put it in vigorous execution throughout the Empire.   His plan of operation is shewn by some recently discovered *Libelli*, or certificates of sound heathenism put in by some villagers and their wives near Alexandria.[1]   They are addressed to the local commissioners who were added to the local magistrates in order to enforce the sacrifices.   They state that the undersigned have always sacrificed to the gods, and now "in your presence, according to the commands" have poured libations and tasted of the victims ; in witness whereof they desire the commissioners to countersign the document.

This is systematic and thorough work, reaching to villages, to individuals,[2] and even to women.   It succeeded well at first, as persecutions usually do when the government has common sense enough to make recantation easy.   It is far harder to resist at first than at a later stage, when each successive martyr swells the growing tide of enthusiasm which often gives new strength to those who began with utter failure.   At first apostates are many, martyrs few.   So in the Decian persecution.   It was skilfully planned, it took the churches by surprise, and it found many unworthy brethren whom the long peace had tempted into them.   So the crowd of renegades was particularly scandalous.   These were of sundry sorts, for the authorities cared little how a man

---

[1] *Th.L.Z.* 1894 pp. 38, 162.   The former *libellus* is dated June 26, which must be in 250.   More than twenty have now been discovered, and are edited by Paul M. Meyer, *Die Libelli aus der decianischen Christenverfolgung*, Berlin 1910.   All dates preserved are June-July 250.

[2] Dion. Al. *ap.* Eus. vi. 41 ὀνομαστὶ καλούμενοι.

denied Christ, so that he did it in one way or
another.   There were actual apostates who offered
sacrifice in open court to the gods or the emperor
(*sacrificati*) or cast incense on the altar (*thurificati*)
and commonly poured libations and ate of the victims.
Some of them did it willingly, or even impudently,[1]
rushing it might be to the forum of their own accord,
" others came pale and trembling, as if they were
themselves going to be the victims, so that the whole
crowd mocked them as plain cowards who dared
neither die nor sacrifice." [2]   Others gave way after
a few days' imprisonment, and others again yielded
only to severe torture.   There was also a class of
virtual apostates who without doing in person anything directly idolatrous, either put in for themselves
or accepted from the magistrate certificates that they
had sacrificed (*libellatici*),[3] or else had their names
enrolled as having sacrificed (*accepta facientes*).[4]   If
a slave or a heathen friend made satisfactory declara-
tions on behalf of somebody who " was unable to
appear," the magistrate was not likely to examine
them too closely.   Thus there were many ways of
evasion.   In Diocletian's time some were brought to
the altars and dismissed, or allowed (perhaps for a
consideration) to slip past them without sacrificing,
while others had their protests silenced by violence,
perhaps not unkindly meant.[5]   The virtual apostates
appear to have been much fewer at Alexandria, where
the riots in Philip's time had warned the waverers, than
at Carthage, where the offenders were in thousands,
and gave rise to more than one serious controversy.

[1] Like Repostus of Tuburnuc, who persuaded most of his flock to follow
his example.   Cyprian *Ep.* 59. 10.
[2] Dion. Al. *ap.* Eus. vi. 14.
[3] Cyprian *Ep.* 55.   [4] Cyprian *Ep.* 30.   [5] Eus. viii. 3.

The Decian persecution made a deeper impression on the churches than any other since Nero's time. Once more the whole power of the Empire seemed put forth to crush them. Small wonder if it gave new life to the old fearful expectation of Nero's return and the end of the world. Commodianus (of Gaza?) is an obscure and neglected writer; yet he gives us a view of Christian thought which we cannot get from more elegant authors. As he seems a well-read man, we must not set down the rudeness of his verses to pure want of culture like the prose of Celerinus. Both in their uncouth form (they scan by accent only) and in their rustic language they rather seem a deliberate appeal to the common people like that of Gregory of Tours.[1] The first interest of the *Carmen Apologeticum* is that it is the earliest Christian poem in Latin which we can date. It seems to fall in the year 250.[2] Next is the writer's rather colourless doctrine, which in some ways resembles the popular Christianity of the Nicene age. He holds indeed firmly, the divinity of Christ

[1] Greg. Tur. *Proem.* ; *philosophantem rhetorem intellegunt pauci, loquentem rusticum multi* is the reason he gives for writing rustic Latin.

[2] Ebert dates the *Carmen* in 249. But if the persecution is imminent (or already begun) we must place it at the end of the year, or in the next year if written in Syria.

The first book of the *Instructiones* was written earlier, yet after Cyprian's first two books of *Testimonia*—say not before 247. The second was later, and *pace* Ebert, I cannot help seeing in *Acr.* 6 a distinct reference to the Novatian quarrels. The *subdola pax* of *Acr.* 25 may be the last months of Decius : hardly the early years of Valerian, still less those of Gallienus, in which *persecutio flagrat* would be absurd.

See Ebert *Litt. d. Mittelalters* i. 88 and *Abhandlung* : also Harnack *A.C.L.* ii. 433.

It is right to add that H. Brewer (S.J.) in his elaborate *Kommodian von Gaza* (Paderborn 1906) dates the writer *cir.* 466, after the death of the emperor Libius Severus. His arguments will need a work almost as elaborate as his own to do them full justice ; but my own impression of them (*pace* Dr. Sanday) is not favourable.

—indeed his heterodoxy is far more Sabellian than Arian; but he lays the stress on monotheism and morality. Just now however we have to do with his rude Chiliasm. The six thousand years, he says, are ending; and the seventh persecution[1] is the sign of the end. It is already knocking at the door. But soon the Goths will burst across the Danube, and with them comes Apollyon their king to put down by arms the persecution of the saints. Rome is captured. Goths and Christians are as brethren, but the senators and the rest of the idolaters suffer persecution five months. Then comes a Cyrus back from hell, even the old Nero who slew the two apostles, to deliver the senate. Away with the enemies of Rome! cries the senate to Nero; and thereupon a dreadful persecution rages for the appointed three years and a half. Then the Jewish Antichrist brings from the East the swift and ruthless Persians and a mighty host. The Euphrates is dried up before them. He slays Nero and his two Caesars, and compels the Roman army to worship him. Back they come in fury, slaughter every man in Rome and burn the city with fire, so that no trace of it is left. "So she mourns for ever who boasted she should live for ever."[2] Then the conqueror goes to Judaea, works lying wonders, and is joined by the Jews. He declares himself immortal. As Nero ruined Rome, so this Persian ruins the world. At last the Jews repent and turn to the Most High, who brings back the lost ten tribes from beyond Persia. Of these an idyllic description is given. No lies are there, nor any hatred. No

[1] The Decian persecution *is* the seventh in the list of Orosius; but Commodianus rather means the "seventh" for the completing number.

[2] l. 923 *luget in aeternum, quae se jactabat aeterna.*

mourning of parents for children lost, nor sorrow
for the dead like ours.   They eat no living flesh,
and shed no blood.   No foul sins are found among
them, no fevers hurt them, nor bitter cold.   They
are righteous and strong because they keep the law
with a true heart.   At the head of these God makes
his progress to Judaea.   The whole creation blossoms
and rejoices, and welcomes them with fountains
springing everywhere.   The clouds bow down to
shade them from the sun, the hills are levelled under
their feet.   Away rushes Antichrist to the quarters
of the North to gather his hosts to battle; but angels
fight and overcome him, and cast him into the lake
of fire.   His captains are made slaves to the righteous.
Then God comes to Zion, fire from heaven destroys
the wicked, and the trumpet sounds for judgment.[1]

Uncouth and fantastic as the vision is, it shews
us a new turn of Christian thought.   Hitherto St.
John's defiance of the Empire has hardly found an
echo but in Ignatius.   For others, the powers that be
are ordained of God.   Irenaeus and Hippolytus, and
even Tertullian, sharply distinguish Caesar from the
Antichrist who is to follow him.   Be the Empire
what it may, it is still the restraining power which
hinders the revelation of the Man of Sin, the bulwark
which delays the horrors of the end of the world.
With all his thirst for vengeance on the heathen, even
Tertullian shews no disloyalty to the Empire.   But
now we note a change.   How long, O Lord? is ever
the cry of the persecuted : and when the fight is
hardest, the spirit of the Covenanters and the
Camisards is not far off.   The high-wrought feeling
and the stern apocalyptic denunciations of Commo-

[1] *Carmen* 791-1002 (condensed).

dianus are not uncommon in history : the sign of the
times is not so much these in themselves as the fact
that there are Christians who turn with hope and
longing to barbarian invaders, and delight in looking
forward to the destruction of Rome by Goths and
Persians.

Still we must not make too much of it.   The
Christian churches might be wanting in public spirit,
but they were never generally disloyal.   The spirit
of rebellion was called out by the persecution of
Decius, and died away with it.   Even in Diocletian's
time its traces are faint, and none can be found in
the reign of Julian.   Melito's teaching was always
more congenial to the churches than that of Ignatius ;
and in the fourth century it became in the hands of
Prudentius a philosophy of history.   " The Scipios
worked for Christ," the glorious career of Rome
was ordained of God, and the Christian Empire
was its worthy consummation.   But to return to
Commodianus.

The trumpet had sounded indeed, though not for
the day of doom.   The world was not passing away,
nor even Rome—only the enemy of Christ.   Had
Decius lived longer, it may be that his vigour would
have brought the long contest with the church to an
earlier decision, and a worthier Caesar than Galerius
would have signed the capitulation of the Empire.
But Decius was not given time to work out the
persecution to its natural result.   The Gothic war
demanded his attention ; and the persecution was
practically at an end the moment he left Rome for
the army in the autumn of 250.   This is significant.
Had there been much genuine popular hatred of the

Christians, some attempt would have been made to keep it up. Instead of this, it drops by common consent. The Roman confessors are set free before March 251, and by April Cyprian is back in Carthage, and holding a council. Public opinion was coming round at last to the conclusion that the Christians were harmless people. The riots in Philip's time were nearly the last of the riots against them. We shall see a few more when the pestilence breaks out; but after these we hear no more clamours of mobs for Christian blood.

The Goths ought not to have been very serious enemies. Their numbers availed little against Roman discipline, and fortified towns they never could take without treachery inside the walls. Mutiny and treachery were the danger, rather than the enemy. Decius had scarcely left Italy when Julius Valens was proclaimed emperor by the mob at Rome. The policy of Decius was the senate's, not the mob's. Valens was soon put down; but the Goths repulsed Decius from their camp, and soon after surprised and scattered his army. Thereupon Priscus the governor of Macedonia betrayed Philippopolis to them, and set up for emperor. Once more Decius attacked the Goths as they were returning with their plunder through the marshes of the Dobrudscha; and once more treachery decided the battle. Trebonianus Gallus the governor of Moesia (it is said) held back his troops, and the rest of the army was cut to pieces. Decius fell fighting, and his body was never found (Summer 251).

No such disaster had befallen Rome since Varus and his legions were destroyed in Germany; and this time an emperor was among the slain. The wreck

of the army gathered to Trebonianus Gallus as the
nearest capable man ; and the senate gave him
Hostilianus the young son of Decius as a nominal
colleague.   Gallus must have been a good soldier,
and he had beaten the Goths before ; but instead of
fighting them now, he patched up a shameful peace,
and hastened to Rome.   There he found a dreadful
pestilence.   Unlike the plague of 167, which the
legions of Marcus brought back from the East, this
one came down the Nile on Egypt, and thence spread
westward, returning on the wasted provinces at
intervals for twenty years.   It was equal to the
former plague in virulence.   It swept away more than
half the population of Alexandria ; and in one of its
returns five thousand people are said to have died at
Rome in a single day.   Wars and famines helped the
ruin ; but the worst of the work was done by the
plague.   The Empire never recovered, for the rotten
economics and still more the rotten morals of
heathenism made the repair of its ravages impossible.
Even the interruption of industry and the destruction
of capital [1] were less ruinous than the blight upon the
human harvest.

Whatever might be his merits as a soldier, Gallus
was a weak emperor, and soon became unpopular.
At first he gained some applause by his care for
the burial of the meanest victims of the plague ;
but before long all sort of charges against him
were eagerly welcomed.   He had betrayed Decius,
he had paid tribute to barbarians, he had poisoned
Hostilianus—who died in the midst of the pestilence.
Though Gallus was hardly strong enough to have

---

[1] Perhaps Fustel de Coulanges *L'Invasion germanique* 191 makes a little
too much of these.   His analysis of them is masterly.

a policy of his own like Decius, the Christians did not escape persecution. Their action in the plague, at least under the guidance of Dionysius and Cyprian at Alexandria and Carthage, is a noble story of tenderness and courage. Among the heathen, despair and greed and selfishness ran riot. In Carthage forgery and poisoning and corruption of justice were the order of the day, and robbery and murder disdained concealment, for no man thought of punishing them.[1] In Alexandria men deserted their friends at the first signs of sickness, and fled from their nearest relations, and cast out the sick half dead in the streets, and left the dead unburied like refuse—anything whatever to escape contact with death.[2] In the midst of all this cowardice and selfishness, the Christians alone shewed hope and courage, clinging to each other, and boldly visiting the sick, and ministering to them continually. They cared not for the burial only but for the nursing, and that not of Christian sick alone, but of all without distinction. They paid the penalty of well-doing in such crowds of deaths, that as they said, the greeting of mere civility, "I am thine off-scouring," was turned into a grim reality.[3] Meanwhile the hasty multitude saw only that the Christians refused to offer the atoning sacrifices to Apollo Salutaris which an imperial command enjoined on all men. Once more the cry was raised, "Cyprian to the beasts," and his old friend Demetrianus distinguished himself at Carthage as an inhuman

---

[1] Cyprian *ad Demetr.* 11.   [2] Dionysius *ap.* Eus. vii. 22.

[3] 1 Cor. iv. 13. It is tempting to take περίψημα with Benson *Cyprian* 244 as a nickname in heathen use: but the words (Dionysius l.c.) τὸ δημῶδες ῥῆμα, μόνης ἀεὶ δοκοῦν φιλοφροσύνης ἔχεσθαι, seem to require the meaning given above.

persecutor.   Elsewhere the storm seems to have been
less violent, and we cannot be sure that it reached
Egypt at all.   Cornelius of Rome however was exiled
with many of his flock, and other bishops may have
shared his fate.   His successor Lucius was relegated,
though this was after Gallus was dead, but promptly
restored by Valerian.[1]

Before long the Goths came back into Moesia, but
only to be defeated by the new governor Aemilianus,
who was thereupon saluted emperor, and made straight
for Rome.   Gallus marched out as far as Interamna,
sending Valerian over the Alps to collect another
army.   But there was no serious fighting.   Gallus
was killed (May 253) by his own soldiers, and
Aemilianus wrote to the senate that he left the
government to them, and would be their general—
the very division of powers the senate was always
aiming at.   Meanwhile Valerian had been hailed
emperor in Rhaetia ; and he too made straight for
Rome.   Again there was no fighting.   The army
took Aemilianus at his word, that he was only the
senate's general, judged him unfit to reign, and sent
his head to Valerian (Aug. 253).

Publius Licinius Valerianus was an elderly senator
of ancient family and blameless life—a model of
Roman dignity and antique virtue.   He must have
made his mark in Alexander's time, for he was
princeps senatus as early as 238, when the senate
was defending Italy against Maximin.[2]   When Decius

---

[1] Dion. Al. (Eus. vii. 1.) does not say that it reached Egypt, for τοὺς ἱεροὺς
ἄνδρας . . . ἤλασεν may perhaps be satisfied by the exile of two successive
bishops of Rome. Cornelius died in exile at Centumcellae, and his successor
Lucius was chosen June 25, 253. His immediate relegation must have been
the work of the senatorial party in the three months of Aemilianus, his
restoration that of Valerian. He was buried Mar. 5, 254.

[2] Capitolinus *Gordiani* 9.

left the choice of a censor to the senate, they hailed
Valerian by acclamation as the worthiest of the
Romans. So far he might seem the very man to
take up the policy of Decius. But Valerian was
a soldier too, and more soldier than senator. At
one time he held the command of the third legion—
one of the highest distinctions in the service.[1] He
was in the camp with Decius at the time of his
election to the censorship, and next appears as a
general of Gallus; and now he is raised to power by
the three united armies as their protest against the
sloth of Gallus and the subservience of Aemilianus
to the senate. All parties may have accepted him
gladly; but the fact remains, that Valerian represents
not the senatorial policy of Decius, but the military
opposition to it.[2]

Valerian was an able ruler, and the disasters of
his reign must not blind us to the greatness of his
work. Unfortunate as he was himself, he laid a
foundation others could build on. The need of the
moment was to restore the discipline of the army;
and much was done for it by Valerian. No emperor
ever had a keener eye for merit in his officers, and
none ever gathered round him a more brilliant school
of generals. Much of his work was undone by his

---

[1] So he seems to say himself, Vopiscus *Probus* 5. Even if the letter is
forged, it may be trusted on this point.

[2] This view of Valerian seems forced upon us by the circumstances of his
elevation. It also best explains (1) the utter difference between his treatment of the Christians and that of Decius. He begins by restoring the
exiles, shews them marked favour for several years, and when he does turn
against them, he persecutes in a very different temper. It also explains (2)
the wisdom he shewed in his choice of generals. In this perhaps no emperor
ever excelled him. After all allowances, Claudius, Aurelian and Probus,
Macrianus, Ballista and Successianus, Regalianus, Ingenuus, Postumus and
Aureolus are a group of generals who would have done honour to any age of
the Empire, and they were all trained by Valerian.

successor, the clever and erratic Gallienus, whose
suspicions and implacable cruelty drove nearly every
able governor to revolt in simple self-defence : yet
Claudius and Aurelian survived the civil wars to
restore the sunken Empire.

In his real relation to the Christians, Valerian
reminds us of Severus and Diocletian. If he had no
sympathy with Christians as such, he was willing to
be on the most friendly terms with individuals. He
began with the recall of Lucius and the exiles.
Before long his house was full of Christians, who
were so kindly treated that they called it a house of
God. " Not even the emperors who were said to have
openly become Christians (these must be Alexander
and Philip) shewed them such open good-will and
favour." [1]

Presently there came a change—Dionysius ascribes
it to the influence of Macrianus his finance minister.
Macrianus was one of the most distinguished soldiers
of his time, " the first of the generals" of Valerian ;
and he misled the old emperor into Egyptian magic
and unholy rites of homicidal superstition. So says
Dionysius ; and indeed there was much to which
Macrianus might have appealed. The Empire was
in a dreadful state when Valerian marched eastward
in 257, though the worst was yet to come. Its
frontiers were broken through on all sides. The
Franks had forced their way right through Gaul
into Spain. Dacia was lost in 256. The Goths on
land swept over Illyricum and Macedonia ; by sea
they captured Trebizond and threatened to join
hands with Sapor, who had taken Antioch in 256,

---

[1] Dion. Al. *ap.* Eus. vii. 10. The picture may be a little overdone : but
it must be substantially true.

and was making a Persian province of Armenia. Even Africa was raided by the Berbers of Mount Aures and the desert. In the midst of calamities which gave tenfold force to the old appeal of Celsus, that every good citizen should support the emperor with all his strength, the great corporations of the Christians even yet maintained their selfish isolation. Not a hand would they lift to save a sinking world. Nay, some of them were more than half inclined to welcome Goths and Persians as heaven-sent avengers of their slaughtered saints—the traitorous miscreants whom the justice of the past had fitly punished. Was it not high time to put some check on these disloyal societies?

Decius had begun with this conviction : Valerian only came round to it, and therefore worked it out differently. Though his first rescript (in 257) is lost, we can see its general purport. He begins like Decius by ordering that "all persons not following the Roman religion must conform to the Roman ceremonies." But we find no endeavour to compel obedience by torture; and for the first time the penalty of disobedience is not death. Though bishops are specially aimed at, as in the time of Decius, the better class of them like Dionysius and Cyprian escaped with deportation,[1] while meaner victims, at least in Numidia, had to suffer the usual hardships of penal servitude in the mines. Cyprian's own exile was to Curubis, a lonely but not unpleasant seaside town some forty miles from Carthage. The edict further directed that the Christians were not to hold assemblies or to enter cemeteries on pain of death. This last provision was new. The government had

---

[1] Not including confiscation. Benson *Cyprian* 466 *n.*

at last found out the catacombs. Hitherto they had
been largely protected by the general reverence of
heathenism for the burial of the dead : but now the
Christians were to be hunted out of their last
retreats.

The latter part of the edict must have been loosely
executed, for we hear of no capital sentences, though
some of the exiles died in the mines. But persecutors
cannot stop where they please; and Valerian was
soon driven on to a severer measure. Xystus of
Rome had somehow escaped arrest : and now (June
29, 258) he ventured to transfer the remains of the
two great apostles from the Vatican and the Ostian
Road to the catacombs. This open honour to ring-
leaders of the sect was a bold step at any time, and
just now a peculiarly audacious defiance of the edict
which forbade the Christians even to enter the
catacombs.[1]

The second rescript of Valerian, which reached
Rome early in August, seems to be his answer to the
challenge Xystus had thrown down. It orders " that
bishops, presbyters and deacons be punished
summarily; but that senators, *egregii viri* and
Roman knights should lose their dignity, and moreover be deprived of their property; and if they
persisted in being Christians when their means were
taken away, they should also lose their heads; that
matrons should be deprived of their property, and
sent into banishment; but that they of Caesar's
household,[2] whoever of them had either confessed

---

[1] In this paragraph and the next I closely follow Benson *Cyprian* 479-487.
If Valerian was within eighteen days of Rome, the case seems clear.

[2] The *Caesariani* were lower officials of the Fiscus in the times of Diocletian
and Constantine : but we are in the year 258, and it is not easy to see why
this one class of minor officials should be singled out for special punishment.

before or should now confess, should have their property confiscated, and be entered on the lists and sent in chains to Caesar's estates "[1]—to the worst form of slavery.

Severe as this rescript is, it is far from coming up to the edict of Decius. It inflicts death on none but clergy and men of rank, and lets off common Christians (at least so far) unpunished. On the other hand it is the first graduated scale of penalties we have met with ; and the influence of panic may be traced in its reversal of the principle of Roman law, that men of rank ought to escape with lighter and less shameful punishments than the common people suffered for the same offences. Valerian's aim is plainly to destroy the Christian corporations, and to root out Christianity from the higher classes. It would cease to be dangerous if it could be reduced to a floating superstition of the vulgar.

This edict at all events was meant for use. It had scarcely reached Rome when Bishop Xystus was found teaching in the catacombs, and put to death on the same spot with four of his seven deacons. But even a bishop of Rome may be overshadowed by a more illustrious martyr. Cyprian was summoned from Curubis to Carthage by the new proconsul Galerius Maximus. But when Galerius found himself too unwell to leave Utica, he sent for Cyprian to come there. As this did not suit Cyprian's plans, he hid himself. He was quite ready for death, but at Carthage among his people, not at Utica. When the proconsul reached Carthage, Cyprian was arrested in his own house, and brought before him next morning (Sept. 14). The trial was short, for the

[1] Cyprian *Ep.* 80.

offence was flagrant and avowed : and soon the dying
Galerius read the sentence "that Thascius Cyprianus
be beheaded with the sword." A great company
followed to the place of execution, for all men felt
that a great career was ending. Even the executioner
was overawed and utterly unnerved, and the commanding centurion had to give the fatal stroke.[1] So
fell Cyprian; and the proconsul Galerius Maximus
died a few days later.

We know little of the persecution elsewhere. This
time however there seem to have been very few
renegades. Decius had thoroughly weeded the
churches; and since his time there had not been
enough of settled peace to attract many converts of
the unstable sort. It was ended like that of Decius
by a great catastrophe. Sapor had captured Nisibis
and Carrhae, and was besieging Edessa when Valerian
came to his relief. The campaign is obscure; but we
hear of defeats, of treacheries, of the ravages of the
plague ; and at last Valerian was reduced to parley
with Sapor, who seized him by treachery. The
emperor was never heard of more. Rumours came
of his unworthy treatment; but whatever the truth
of these may be, Valerian was henceforth dead to
Rome. After him came his son Gallienus.

For awhile the East seemed lost. The Persians
captured Antioch again, then Tarsus, then came
streaming through the passes of Mount Taurus down
on Caesarea Mazaca. There they found a brave
resistance ; but the place was taken by treachery,
and flying squadrons of cavalry spread terror and
destruction to the shores of the Propontis and Aegean.
But these were only raids. Roman courage was

[1] A detail first noted by Benson *Cyprian* 506.

unbroken, and Sapor himself hardly dreamed of solid conquests. Edessa stood like an island in the sea—neither Persian nor Saracen could ever storm her virgin walls—the legion camped at Samosata formed a rallying post, and before long Ballista checked the Persians in Cilicia. So Sapor gave the order for retreat. Then rose Odenathus, chief of the senate of Palmyra, gathered to him the Arabs of the desert and the wrecks of the legions, drove Sapor across the Euphrates, recovered Carrhae and Nisibis, chased him down the Tigris, and routed him before the walls of Ctesiphon itself. The exploit was worthy of Trajan or Severus. Odenathus had saved the East.

Hardly less splendid was the work of Postumus, who set up for emperor in Gaul. Franks and Alamanni were driven out, the line of the Rhine secured, peace and prosperity recovered. It was a Gaulish Empire; yet not such a Gaulish Empire as Civilis would have set up two hundred years before, for Gaul was Roman now, but a Roman Transalpine Empire which lasted till Aurelian's time.

In general cleverness and versatility, the emperor Gallienus reminds us of Hadrian : and he was not wanting in energy and courage. His defeats of Ingenuus and Aureolus are no mean achievement. Yet after all allowance for hostile evidence, Gallienus was a poor burlesque of Hadrian. His fits of sloth were ignoble and long, while his cruel suspicions forced his generals into revolt, and his implacable revenge drove every revolter to desperation. So confusion became worse confounded. Postumus held the West, and Zenobia the widow of Odenathus was "Queen of the East"; but from Asia to the Alps

the provinces were overrun by Goths and Alamanni,
devastated by the plague and torn by civil war. The
Gothic vikings came past the ruined walls of
Byzantium, at one time to devastate Bithynia, at
another to the sack of Ephesus and Athens, and only
stopped in sight of Italy. Slave-risings in Sicily,
tumults in Alexandria, a permanent rebellion in
Isauria, are but episodes of the tragedy. The Empire
seemed melting away. At last in 268 the generals
took serious counsel for a second time. Gallienus
was put out of the way like Aemilianus, and the
task of restoring the shattered Empire was placed in
the hands of Claudius.

The Christians at any rate owed something to
Gallienus. If he was no special friend of theirs, much
less was he their enemy. The empress Salonina may
have been a Christian. The rescripts of Valerian
were at once revoked, and more than revoked, by a
public edict. This is lost; but we can see its purport
from the rescript [1] which put it in force in Egypt
after the defeat of Macrianus in 261. The address,
To the bishops, of itself recognizes the government of
the churches, and the restoration of the places of
worship (and afterwards of the burial-places) can
only have been made to the corporations of the
Christians. Here then at last was practical toleration: and though the common law of the Empire
was not repealed, and might be made an excuse for
occasional persecution, there seemed little reason to
fear that it would ever again be generally put in force.

[1] Eus. vii. 13.

BOOKS

Benson *Cyprian*; Schoenaich *Die Christenverfolgung des Kaisers Decius*
Jauer 1907.

CHAPTER XXIV

THE DISCIPLINE QUESTIONS

BEFORE we come to Cyprian, let us look back on the growth of church government in the second century and the first forty years of the third. Apostles and Prophets and Evangelists have long since disappeared, unless the Prophet may still be traced in the humble Reader, and the Ignatian ideal is so far realized that a single bishop stands at the head of the presbyters and deacons of each city. All Christian meetings except of heretics are under his authority, and that eucharist is held valid which is offered by him or with his permission.[1] He is also the official guardian of doctrine (in *this* sense the successor of the apostles) and the chief administrator of the church in his city ; the centre of its unity, and its representative to other churches and the outer world. The presbyters have lost something of their independence, for they have long ceased to govern without the bishop ; but they have taken over from him the chief part of the pastoral work of the growing churches, and still co-operate with him (as indeed they do to this day) in the ordination of their colleagues. The deacons are drawn closer to the bishop by the growth of church business, while

---

[1] Ign. *Smyrn.* 8.

274

the widows are beginning to give place to virgins; but the laity retain most of their former power, for even the bishop is commonly chosen by the entire church.   But the eucharistic priesthood of the laity is becoming forgotten in an official (not yet a sacerdotal) ministry, and the rule is beginning to form which ended in the layman's exclusion from the government of the church.   Thus the bishop has become a king in his church, though so far only a constitutional king, for his presbyters are still an effective council, the laity speak with weight, and the confessors in time of persecution have a great and independent influence.

But we are on the eve of changes.   The first great contribution of Latin thought to Christian history was a new theory of the ministry and of the church in general, which forms the greatest break between the apostolic age and the Reformation. The Nicene decision, which seemed at the time so revolutionary, was only a necessary protection for a vital doctrine; and even the Hildebrandine papacy, utterly as it is opposed to Cyprian's own teaching,[1] was after all the form into which his theory was finally thrown by the logic of circumstances; but the theory itself is nothing less than a recast of the Gospel in heathen moulds.   In one sense indeed it was only a continuation of the process we have already traced.   If the laity were losing their personal interest in church affairs, it was best that the bishop should become a Tudor despot, little hampered by constitutional forms.   It is also likely enough, humanly speaking, that the strong confederation of the churches which called out the last

---

[1] To discuss the Roman forgeries after Benson would be to slay the slain.

attacks of the Empire was also their best defence
against it, just as the papacy was the best defence
of the Western churches from feudal anarchy. But
Cyprian claims for the bishop a sacrificing (no
longer a purely eucharistic) priesthood, and a *jus
divinum* essentially different from the divine sanction
given to the " powers that be " of every orderly
government.

Both claims were new. The New Testament
gives no hint of any such priesthood to be held
by Christian men, though there was no other
worship in the world without it.[1] Even the
Pastoral Epistles nowhere mention it as a function
of the Christian ministry, and the Epistle to the
Hebrews repeatedly and expressly reserves it for
the Lord himself. Clement of Rome indeed compares
the Christian ministry to the Jewish priesthood,
but only as a model of order : the names and the
offices he carefully distinguishes. Ignatius and
Polycarp are silent; and Justin's comparison is not

---

[1] I cannot follow the logic of Mr. B. J. Kidd's reply (*Journ. Theol. Studies*
xii. 483) that the New Testament does indicate " a sacrificing priesthood to
be held by Christian men." The question is of a sacrificing priesthood,
implying something else than the sacrifice of praise and thanksgiving
which all Christians are bound to offer, though none but ministers may offer
it officially. It will be enough to notice three of Mr. Kidd's main arguments.
(1) Granted (what may be true in matters of religion) that λειτουργεῖν
"always means ministering *in an office*," we cannot summarily take for
granted that the office of the prophets and teachers in Acts xiii. 2 was not
prophecy and teaching, but a sacrificing priesthood. (2) Granted again
that priesthood is a possible function of stewardship, he still needs to prove
that a *sacrificing* priesthood is a *necessary* function of stewardship before he
can argue :—Stewards, therefore priests. (3) His parallel of the table of
the Lord with the table of demons is rightly taken from St. Paul : but it
directly contradicts the argument he founds on it. The heathens did not
sacrifice on their table, but feasted on it in memory of a sacrifice already
offered on an altar elsewhere. If therefore St. Paul is right, we do not
sacrifice on the Lord's table, but feast on it in thanksgiving for a sacrifice
already offered on an altar elsewhere.

of the presbyter but of the layman, and that not
to the priest but to the high priest. Irenaeus and
Clement of Alexandria recognize only a moral priesthood of saintliness, not an official priesthood of
sacrifice ; and this is substantially Origen's view,
though he sometimes calls the bishops priests, and
(only once, and then with hesitation) equates
presbyters and deacons to priests and Levites. The
direction in the *Teaching*, to give the firstlings to
the prophets, "for they are your high priests," will
not bear the weight of a literal application even
to the prophets ; and the statement of Polycrates
that St. John "was made a priest, and wore the
mitre," is almost certainly metaphorical. So we
come to Tertullian, the first writer who habitually
uses priestly words of the Christian ministry, and
even to draw conclusions from the Jewish priesthood,
though Hippolytus follows before long. Yet his
view of it cannot be really sacerdotal, for he not only
lays heavy stress on the priesthood of the laity, but
insists that the functions of the ministry belong
of right to the whole congregation, and are only
entrusted to officials for convenience ; so that the
bishop cannot be more than the mouthpiece of his
church.[1] As regards the *jus divinum*, it will be
enough to repeat that even Ignatius never claims
it for him.

[1] The statement of the case in Lightfoot's *Exc. on the Christian Ministry*
is still unshaken. Thus Gore *Chr. Ministry* 196-200 seems to think it enough
to prove (what nobody disputes) that the presbyter may be called a priest
in *some* sense ; and then—does he really slide over the essential difference
between the eucharistic and the sacrificing priest without noticing it ? Surely
there is also a difference between historical developments which (like the
abolition of slavery) only carry out the plain teaching of Scripture, and
those which run counter to its elementary ideas, like Mariolatry, image-
worship, or the Cyprianic theory.

But if it was not easy to turn the bishop into a sacrificing priest, it was even harder to provide him with the something material which a priest must have to offer. Scripture admits no sacrifice that Christian men can bring but that of thanksgiving : and this is the deliberate language of all Christian writers before the Nicene age— Cyprian excepted—whenever they speak of sacrifice.[1] It is their constant boast that they have no material temple nor altar nor sacrifice. When therefore they speak of the bread and wine provided for the Lord's Supper as an offering or sacrifice, they must mean that it is an offering of thanksgiving. So in fact they always explain it, as shewing forth the union of body and spirit, in which the Holy Spirit consecrates our food to nourish the body, and through the body nourishes our spiritual life of thanksgiving. Indeed, it cannot be anything else than a thank-offering, so long as it is offered by the people or in their name. So no attempt was ever made to change it : the novelty was in making it a mere preparation for the real sacrifice. Hitherto the bishop in the people's name presents the elements as a thank-offering ; but now he goes on to offer them a second time as a sacrifice. This theory we first trace in Cyprian, though even he hardly gets beyond a rehearsal or imitation of the sacrifice on Golgotha.

[1] It may suffice to quote Irenaeus *Haer.* iv. 18. 6 *Offerimus autem ei, non quasi indigenti, sed gratias agentes* (εὐχαριστοῦντες) *dominationi ejus, et sanctificantes creaturam . . . . Sic et ideo nos quoque offerre vult munus ad altare frequenter sine intermissione. Est ergo altare in caelis, illuc enim preces nostrae et oblationes nostrae diriguntur, et templum,* etc. Tertullian *adv. Jud.* 5 *Quod non terrenis sacrificiis sed spiritalibus Deo litandum sit, ita legimus* (Ps. li. 19. 14) *Itaque quomodo carnalia sacrificia reprobata intelleguntur* (Isa. i. 11) *ita spiritalia accepta praedicantur* (Isa. v. 11 *sq.*, Mal. i. 11).

The doctrine is a commonplace. The Apologists insist on it as a

However, in Cyprian the new theory of the church is well developed. He did not invent it to meet the needs of the Novatian controversy, for it is clearly laid down in his earliest letters;[1] and indeed there is no sign that he ever seriously troubled himself to think out the ideas on which it depends.[2] He takes them like a practical man from the air about him, assumes them to be not only true but self-evident, and concerns himself only with their practical applications. Yet they are not only new but essentially heathen, though the mischief is masked in his own case by lofty gifts of practical charity and complete sincerity. Cyprian is a saint—none can doubt it— yet his general conception of religion is more heathen than Christian. As the heathen god's favour is strictly limited to his worshippers, so God's grace is strictly limited to the visible church. "He cannot have God for his Father who has not the church for his mother. If he could escape who was outside the ark, he too will escape who is abroad and outside the church. The Lord warns us, saying, He that is not with me is against me."[3] For the "aliens" there is

---

principal difference of the Gospel from heathenism; and it is frequently emphasized even in the Nicene Age.

[1] Cyprian *Ep.* 1 *quando singuli divino sacerdotio honorati et in clerico ministerio constituti non nisi altari et sacrificiis deservire et precibus adque orationibus vacare debeant.*

Ep. 3 (Contempt of the bishop compared to the sin of Korah) . . . *Apostolos id est episcopos et praepositos Dominus elegit, diaconos autem . . . apostoli sibi constituerunt episcopatus sui et ecclesiae ministros. Quod si nos aliquid audere contra Deum possumus qui episcopos facit, possunt et contra nos audere diaconi a quibus fiunt.*

[2] How little Cyprian can be regarded as a serious thinker may be seen from *Quod Idola* 5 *Regna autem non merito accidunt, sed* sorte *variantur.* It does not occur to him that this is an utter denial of Providence.

[3] Cyprian *de Unitate* 6. He quotes Mt. xii. 30 as early as *Testim.* iii. 86 (*schisma non faciendum, etiamsi in una fide et in eadem traditione permaneat qui recedit*). Note the quiet transfer to the church of our Lord's *personal*

nothing but wrath and the damnation of hell fire for ever.[1] No thought comes to Cyprian that a Spirit of God may be moving over the face of the darkness of this world's ignorance and sin. As the idol's favour was dispensed by his priests, so God's grace is dispensed by the bishops—for Cyprian counts the bishops alone as priests, while the presbyters are merely the Levites who minister at the altar.[2] No thought comes to Cyprian that it was the very work of Christ to do away all human mediators who might presume to offer sacrifice for their fellow-sinners. As a Roman magistrate held a defined authority by regular transmission from its last holder, so must it be, and so forsooth it always must have been, in the Christian ministry. Thus sound doctrine ceases to approve the ministration, and the outward succession guarantees the soundness of the doctrine, so that the legal questions of a valid succession become vital. No thought comes to Cyprian that he who raised up Elijah the Tishbite, or the Forerunner, may any day raise up a Luther or a Wesley to do the work unfaithful bishops have left undone.

Cyprian starts from the unity of the church : and this is not a spiritual unity of faith and hope in its ever-living Head, but the visible unity of a visible society. It was first built on one, Peter to wit, that

---

claim. The right quotation would have been Mk. ix. 40 ; but I do not find that he ever uses it.

[1] Cyprian *ad Demetr.* 22 quoting Mal. iv. 1 (with *alienigenae* for the Vulg. *superbi*), 24.

[2] This important point must be noticed. He is generally careful to use sacerdotal words only of the bishop, Levitical of the presbyter. So Benson *Cyprian* 33 ; C. H. Turner, *Camb. Med. Hist.* i. 157. At the same time there are a few cases where he uses *vacerdos* of the presbyter and apparently even (*de Lapsis* 25) of the deacon, so that in these instances it seems to be used in a general way of the clergy, not as a deliberate claim of sacrificial powers for presbyters. I owe this point to Mr. A. C. Jennings of King's Stanley.

it might be shewn to be one, though an equal
authority was afterwards given to all the apostles.
The church is one, and the episcopate is one and
undivided, for each part of it is held by each bishop
for the whole.[1]   Thus there is a government ordained
of God—an aristocracy of coequal bishops, for within
the limits of faith and unity, every bishop was
independent in his own diocese.   God's grace is
given through the bishops and to the church alone.
They are his priests who alone can offer sacrifice,
while the presbyters minister as Levites : and "the
sacrifice we offer is the Passion of the Lord." [2]   The
bishop's power is from above, not from below ; and
he rather represents God to the people than the
people to God.   So instead of being elected by
the people in the presence of the presbyters and the
neighbouring bishops, he must now be elected by the
bishops of the province in the presence of the people,
according to the law of Moses.[3]   In fact, the Christian
priesthood differs from the Jewish in nothing but its
permanence.   The old law of the priest was meant
all along for the bishop, and resistance to him is the
sin of Korah.   He is Judge in Christ's place ; [4] and
whoso is an alien from the bishop is also an alien
from Christ.   A wise bishop will "do nothing without the counsel of his presbyters and deacons, and
the consent of the people" [5]—such was Cyprian's
own rule from the first—but this is grace, not right,
for he is not accountable to them.   He listens as a
Tudor king listens to his Council ; but in the end he
decides the matter for himself.

[1] Cyprian *de Unitate* 5.   [2] Do. *Ep.* 63. 17.
[3] Cyprian *Ep.* 67. 4 ; quoting Num. xx. 25, 26.
[4] *Ibid.* 59. 5 ; *vice Christi*, and *vice sacra*, as was said of the Emperor's
deputy.   Note this and the bishops *of the province* above.   [5] *Ibid.* 14.

The Cyprianic theory has long since drifted from its Cyprianic moorings. No church but Rome now lays down the doctrine that there is no salvation beyond its own limits. No church now holds that all outside baptism is null. No church now counts the presbyter as a Levite. On the Roman theory he is only the bishop's deputy; but it is still the essence of his office to be a priest, and not a Levite. No church now declares all bishops equal, for even the orthodox East is organized in patriarchates, mostly by national churches. Least of all does any modern church require its bishops to be elected by their comprovincials in the presence of their people. Could Cyprian have foreseen these changes, he might have lamented them as revolutionary; yet they were but the modifications made in this theory by the logic of circumstances. The extension of the priesthood to presbyters was a necessity, when the bishop ceased to be the chief pastor of a manageable congregation in a city and became the spiritual ruler of a vast establishment. The inequality of bishops did but recognize the fact that Rome was greater than Velitrae, Caesarea than Sasima. Even the change from election by comprovincials to nomination by pope or king was the natural result of conflicts that were bound to arise between a catholic church and particular governments. Subject then to necessary changes and natural developments, the Cyprianic theory as modified by Augustine and completed by Roman bishops has shaped the history of the Western church for centuries, and deeply influenced both the orthodox East which never accepted it, and the protestant North which rejected it. Some of its rigid conceptions are as clear in Calvinism as in the church of Rome.

For Cyprian himself, his nearest modern likeness is in some of our great English churchmen. They are born rulers—men of intense activity, yet of grave and winning gentleness, men of princely dignity and perfect temper ; as quick as any lawyer to judge of men, and as skilful organizers as any merchant-prince. Such was Cyprian. Yet somehow we feel that we never quite get at the real man. He moves in matters of administration, and takes the deeper questions for granted. It is not merely that he does not like to study principles : he will not face them when they call for a decision. He takes his system unexamined, and allows himself to be absorbed in it ; and the system is not quite Christ's. *Pro ecclesia Dei* is more in his heart than ἐν Χριστῷ. With all his winning qualities, we partly miss the noblest fire of all, which shines so gloriously in many a lesser man. Cyprian had no such commanding gifts of intellect as Athanasius to obscure his piety : yet he does not so often make us feel that he is saint as well as ruler.

Early Christian writers rarely tell us anything definite about the thoughts and struggles of their heathen days. Their eyes are fixed on the light before them, and seldom turn back to the darkness they have left. We get a few words from Tatian, Clement of Alexandria, and Commodianus ; but only Justin tells the tale of his conversion—how the old man by the seashore kindled in his soul the living fire. If we want more than this, we shall find it only in the romance of Clement of Rome. So Thascius Cyprianus meets us only as a convert. We know neither his parents nor the place and year of his birth ; nor does he tell us himself what sort of a heathen he had been or how he became a Christian. He lives in the new life received in baptism,[1] and thinks no more of the old. We may say without much risk of error that he was born of well-to-do parents about 200 : but we know for certain only that about 246 he was a lawyer in Carthage with a fame of eloquence and a character for culture and refinement which he never lost even in heathen society. It was only a dirty joke which called him Coprianus. The conversion of such a leader of men was an event in Africa, and the old presbyter Caecilian might sing his *Nunc dimittis* when he had brought Cyprian into the fold. The new convert began by selling most of his farms[2] for the poor. His beautiful gardens followed, though they were bought by friends and restored to him. Meanwhile he studied Scripture, and what seems to be his first work was two books, soon followed by a third, of *Testimonia* from Scripture.[3] He was also a diligent student of his great predecessor Tertullian. Little as he had of Tertullian's massive power of thought, no man was better fitted than Cyprian to translate " the Master's " rugged sentences into elegant and flowing Latin.

Bishop Donatus died soon after. Cyprian was still a novice, and some objected on that ground ; but many thought him clearly marked out for the post by his energy and practical wisdom. Public opinion was soon made up, and his own resistance was vain. So Cyprian was duly consecrated " Pope " of

[1] *ad Don.* 4.

[2] *Vita* 2, reading *tota prope praedia* e conj. Westcott in Benson *Cypr.* 8 note.

[3] As Benson says, the collection would task even a lawyer's memory—if he made it himself. But Rendel Harris (*Expositor* Nov. 1908) holds it to be copied from some earlier manual.

Carthage, and took possession of the bishop's chair.[1]
Unfortunately five influential presbyters remained
unsatisfied, and formed an organized and pertinacious
opposition.

It was no sinecure that Cyprian had undertaken.
Carthage was as full of enthusiasms and as full of
scandals as ever, and was not improved by the long
peace it had enjoyed since the early years of Caracalla. Almost the first thing he had to deal with was
a grave abuse of holy women and holy men living in
the same houses or even in the same rooms together
in a spiritual relation which nothing but marriage
can set free from scandal. No more dangerous form
of enthusiasm can be imagined. We cannot greatly
blame Cyprian if he "forgot himself," and wrote for
once in his life an angry letter :[2] but he put down
the practice by methods whose energy was only equal
to their indecency. Before long the work of peaceful
reform was interrupted by the Decian persecution ;
and Cyprian went straight into hiding (January 250).
This was a bold step, for it looked like cowardice,
and at first was taken for cowardice, as by the Roman
presbyters. Yet though Cyprian for the moment
compared badly with their martyred Fabian, he was
right in thinking that just then his life was more
useful than his death. If Decius aimed at disorgan-
izing the churches by striking first at the bishops,

---

[1] Between June 248 and Easter 249.

[2] *Ep.* 4 *Pomponio.*

The continual recurrence of the scandal of the συνείσακτοι (*subintroductae*,
agapetae) from about Cyprian's time when purposes began to harden into
vows, is most significant. Cyprian, Basil, Gregory of Nyssa, Ambrose and
Chrysostom had to deal with it officially. Council after council condemns
it (*e.g.* Antioch *cir.* 267, Elvira, Nicaea), and in the fifth century the civil
power was called in to enforce the prohibition ; yet the practice continued.
If unnatural vows are made, there is no avoiding scandals without bolts
and bars.

it was not wise for the bishops to play into his hands by throwing their lives away. Cyprian's time was not yet come.

Meanwhile questions were arising which called for his utmost wisdom. The crowd of renegades, as we have seen, was very great at Carthage. But many of these had only been carried away by the first panic, so that before long a crowd of suppliants was moving heaven and earth to get back into the church they had renounced. Some wiped out their disgrace by facing the magistrate afresh, and were honoured as true martyrs for a courageous death. Others meekly accepted their ignominious penance, though there was no certainty that the church would ever shew them grace. But many were less patient. Might not some intercession avail? Weight had always been given to any letters a martyr might leave behind, recommending particular cases to the bishop's favourable consideration at the return of peace. This was the old custom, reasonable and orderly, though even this was liable to abuses;[1] but before long the malcontent presbyters took upon them summarily to restore the offenders, without waiting for the bishop's consideration, or even for the martyr's death. Worse abuses followed. Some indeed of the confessors were modest enough. Mappalicus left letters only for his mother and sister, Saturninus gave none at all, and Celerinus interceded only for his fallen "sisters," Tecusa[2] and Candida. Others were less scrupulous. One Lucian issued letters in numbers, first in the name of Aurelius, an illiterate confessor, then in that of

---

[1] Abuses pictured by Tert. *de Pud.* 23.

[2] *ap.* Cyprian *Ep.* 21. See Benson *Cyprian* 74. We cannot be quite sure that they were more than spiritual sisters of Celerinus.

Paul, a martyr who (so he said) had left him directions to use his name.   A single letter sometimes included a whole household, and letters were issued in thousands, and even found their way into the market.   The answer to Cyprian's repeated requests " that some regard be had to the law of the Lord and the Gospel " [1] was a truly comprehensive letter by Lucian's hand. " All the confessors to Pope Cyprian, greeting.   We do you to wit that we all have given peace to all persons who shall bring you a satisfactory account of their doings since their offence ; and we desire that this decree be by you communicated to the other bishops." [2]

This was a *reductio ad absurdum* of the whole system of letters.   Even if it were wise and right to pass over all offences on the simple condition of later good behaviour, it was not right for the confessors to take upon them the government of the churches.   Of course the offenders ignored the clause which seemed to reserve a discretion to the bishops, and besieged them with clamours for immediate restoration.   The weaker bishops yielded—it was invidious to discriminate cases—and the stronger found every discord in their churches inflamed to fever heat by Lucian's reckless amnesty.

The root of the mischief lay deeper than Cyprian or any of his enemies clearly saw.   The restoration of a penitent necessarily conveys the pardon of the church for any offence against itself : but does it equally convey God's forgiveness of the sin?   Distinct as the two ideas are, they were (and are) much confused. No doubt the better class of Lucian's friends had a

---

[1] "The Gospel" in Cyprian (in this connexion) generally means the strict discipline.   [2] The letter is Cyprian *Ep.* 23.   He discusses it *Ep.* 27.

right feeling that there are no limits to God's mercy, just as the Novatians at the other extreme were right in saying that the church is holy: yet neither Cyprian nor any of his enemies could see through the dilemma. If Christ receiveth sinners, there must be plenty of them in the church: yet how can that be, if the church is holy? The error was the error of the Western church. The Lord's personal claim—"he that is not with me is against me," had been construed into he that is not with *us* is against us: and his solemn warning—he that disbelieveth is condemned, was turned into a doctrine that whoever dies outside a certain visible society shall without doubt perish everlastingly. Outside the church there was no salvation. Justin indeed believed that God had not left himself without a witness among the heathen, and the Alexandrians made the maxim harmless by their refusal to limit the church to the visible society: but to the Latins (Augustine perhaps excepted) all this was mere evasion. Cyprian, for instance, was in this way quite as hard as any Calvinist. Baptism would save the infant, and martyrdom the catechumen, for the "baptism" of blood ranked even higher than Christ's ordinance of water: but as for one who never heard the Gospel, or one who wandered into heresy, or died out of communion with the bishops of the church— no innocence, no virtue, no repentance, not even death for Christ would in the least avail to save him from the everlasting fire of hell. On this theory, church pardon and divine forgiveness are closely linked together. The negative side is obvious, that God forgives none to whom the church refuses pardon; and the positive side lay very near in practice, that whomsoever the church pardons, God forgives.

Small wonder if men's brains reeled, when they took to themselves the awful power of dispensing to their fellow-sinners a pardon without which there was no forgiveness in the world to come. Cyprian leaned at first to severity.[1] It was the tradition of the past, it had the support of Tertullian, and it undeniably represented a principle that needed to be maintained against the indiscriminating laxity of the confessors. But he was too wise to be pushed into an extreme by his own supporters. As they leaned forward towards rigour, Cyprian drew back towards mercy. If he was as fully committed as any one to the false theory of the church which was the root of the mischief, he had more wisdom than others to pick his way from one step to another. First he reserves the whole question for quieter times, meanwhile restoring only those who had letters, and those only in the hour of death, but excluding none from hope. Later on he establishes a clear distinction between the grosser offenders and the rest, and in the end he secured the ordinary enactment of a pardon in terms almost as comprehensive as those of Lucian's lawless amnesty.

Meanwhile he was a fugitive bishop at a difficult crisis, with confessors and offenders and a strong party of his own presbyters allied against him. Nor was his provisional plan likely to escape objections. It was of course clear that all the cases must be reserved for quieter times, if any such distinction was to be made among the offenders as justice required. But if the letters of the confessors were to have any

[1] *Testimonia* iii. 28 *non posse in ecclesia remitti ei qui in Deum deliquerit* (quoting Mt. xii. 32, Mk. iii. 28, 1 Sam. ii. 25) is exactly what Novatian might have written.

weight at all, the party of laxity might fairly complain that there was no logic in limiting it to the hour of death. Zealots of another sort would find offence in his noble confidence that God would care even for those who died outside the peace of the church. Cyprian was at any rate learning something from the awful scenes around him : would only he had never fallen back from the *Crede et manducasti* to which the storm of persecution had lifted him. But if his plan was not quite logical, it answered the needs of the moment so well that even the Roman church was glad to follow his lead.

Presently things became more settled. The laity of Carthage steadily supported him, the bishops of Africa and Italy declared in favour of his policy, and the persecution abated as soon as Decius left Rome for the frontier in the autumn of 250. So a twofold schism began to form, of the extremes on either side —a party of laxity at Carthage, which restored all offenders without distinction, and a party of rigour at Rome, which shut out all without distinction. The head of the opposition at Carthage was Cyprian's old enemy the presbyter Novatus, a man of unsteady and unruly character, whom nothing but the opportune outbreak of the persecution had saved from an investigation which might have led to his deposition from office.[1] Now, with the help of his active deacon Felicissimus, he made his church a centre of open rebellion against the bishop. The leader of the Roman schism was a more serious character—the austere and learned Novatian—

---

[1] This seems as much as can safely be said, for the charges in Cyprian *Ep.* 52 are best disregarded. Yet the facts known of Novatus are not in his favour. One of the charges to be investigated (we need not assume its truth like Cyprian) was that he had given his wife a kick which caused her to miscarry.

perhaps the ablest of the presbyters who ruled the church during the long vacancy which followed Fabian's death. If he had received only clinical baptism in a dangerous illness, his eloquence and orthodoxy justified Fabian in making him an exception to the custom forbidding such converts to be ordained. We know nothing against Novatian—nothing but the ascetic bitterness which has wrecked his fame.[1] He had accepted Cyprian's plan with the rest of the Roman presbyters, but of late he had grown more severe. Presently came the long-delayed election of a new bishop (*cir.* Mar. 5, 251).[2] As usual, Rome passed over her ablest man ; and this time with good reason, for the choice of Novatian would have committed her to a policy of rigour. The election fell on Cornelius, a Roman of high family, perhaps a kinsman of the future empress Salonina, who had quietly risen from one church office to another, filling them all with dignity and making no mistakes. But he was essentially a second-rate man, neither a statesman like Cyprian, nor a scholar like Novatian.

Meanwhile Cyprian had returned to Carthage, and was holding a council. They had recognized Cornelius and condemned Felicissimus, when startling news was brought from Rome. Novatus had gone there and promptly joined Novatian![3] and the confessors (they were out of prison by this time) had been won over to elect Novatian bishop of Rome. His envoys were turned out of the council, and the question of the

---

[1] Cornelius *ap.* Eus. vi. 42 seems even more unfair to Novatian than Cyprian is to Novatus.

[2] Benson *Cyprian* 127.

[3] There is but one explanation of this sudden change of party. Novatus cared nothing about the renegades, only how to check the growing power of the bishop. So Benson *Cyprian* 137.

renegades was taken up. By this time there was a general feeling that the rule of penance till the hour of death was too severe for any but the worst offenders. It was neither charity nor policy to be so hard on men who had sinned from weakness, and might again soon need all the help the church could give them. So it was agreed that only those who had sacrificed should not be restored till the hour of death. In other cases extenuating circumstances were to be taken into account, but there was always to be a long penance, and even then the bishop was not to restore them without a public application. As for such as refused to accept their penance, they were not to be restored even in the hour of death.

This will not seem a lenient decision, if we remember the severity of penance. Yet in three different directions it marks a clear advance on older ideas. First, it rules against the rigorists that even apostasy (and still more any other sin) is within the power of the church to pardon. Then it recognizes degrees of guilt in the sin. Lastly it takes the matter entirely out of the hands of individual confessors or presbyters, and commits it to the bishop as the one constitutional head of the community. But it will be noticed that no change is made in the character of penance, or in the rule that a cleric who has once done penance must remain for the rest of his life a layman.

Meanwhile events at Rome were finally establishing the rule contended for by Ignatius, that all the Christians in a city must be subject to a single bishop. The breach of this shocked Cyprian more than anything else in the election of Novatian. It is more the breach of order than the twofold breach

of charity in the fact and the motives of the schism
which stirs his utmost horror.   To the Roman confessors he tells his " intense and almost crushing
grief to hear that against God's ordinance, against
the law of the Gospel, against the unity of the
catholic foundation, they have consented to the
setting-up of another bishop—that is (a thing which
neither divine nor human law allows) to found
another church, to tear in pieces Christ's members,
to rend the Lord's flock to the dividing of the soul and
body with their factiousness." [1]   On this ground—that
there can be but one bishop, and this proved to be
Cornelius—the confessors returned to his communion,
and were received with open arms.   On one ground
or another, Christian opinion was declaring itself
against Novatian.   It is better represented by the
grave pleadings of Dionysius of Alexandria than by
the reckless tirades of such an evil-minded partizan
as Cornelius.   In answer to Novatian's excuse that
he had accepted the bishopric unwillingly,—"This,
says he, you will prove by retiring willingly.
Suffering in order to prevent division is not less
glorious (in my opinion it is more so) than suffering
for refusing to worship idols.   If you can make the
brethren come back to unity, your good work will
be greater than your failure ; and while your failure
will be forgotten, your good work shall have praise.
But if you cannot overcome their disobedience, at
least deliver your own soul." [2]   In this letter he is
only saying that the division is a plain breach of
charity : but writing a few years later (when the
issues were clearer) to the presbyter Dionysius, who
was one day himself to be bishop of Rome, he sums

[1] Cyprian *Ep.* 46.   [2] *ap*. Eus. vi.45.

up the doctrinal dispute in words which link on the
Novatianist question to the controversy on rebaptism.
"We hate Novatian with good reason, in that he
divided the church and led some of the brethren
into impieties and blasphemies, and brought in a
most unholy doctrine concerning God, and slanders
our most compassionate Lord Jesus Christ as merciless.
In addition to all this he rejects the holy washing,
and overthrows the faith and confession which goes
before it, and utterly banishes from them the Holy
Spirit, even if there were any hope at all that he
would remain with them or return to them." [1] The
last sentence would seem a condemnation of the
Novatianist refusal to recognize orthodox baptism.
If so, the judgment of Dionysius is the judgment of
history on Novatian.

To return to Carthage. Though the council had
softened the punishment of offenders, it was still
cruelly severe. All cases were condemned to a long
period of misery; and to the sacrificers no hope was
given till the hour of death. In their case no
distinctions were made. The weakness which yielded
only to repeated tortures was dealt with like the
impudence which gloried in apostasy, if only the
outward act it ended in was sacrifice. Though this
was better than Novatianism, it almost equally
"slandered our most compassionate Lord Jesus
Christ as merciless." It drove many to desperation,
and created a mass of greater misery than men could
bear to see. They were not heartless, only entangled
in a false theory, and the suffering of their fallen
brethren was a real sorrow to them. If Cyprian
could not rise above the misconception of the church

[1] *Ibid.* vii. 8.

which caused and alone made possible these inhuman penances, he was not unmindful of the bishop's duty to bind up the broken, bring again the outcasts and seek the lost. Was it right to expose them unprotected to the danger of another persecution? So when the tumults in the time of Gallus seemed to bring that danger near, a new council (May 252) issued a general amnesty to all who had continued steadfast until now in penance, "that they might be armed for the impending conflict."[1] Thus Lucian's aim was vindicated in the end, though to the utter condemnation of his action. Lucian raised the question by his lawless offer of impunity; Cyprian settled it by the regular issue of a lawful pardon.

The last phrase, "that they may be armed for the impending conflict," goes to the bottom of the matter. Neither the Lord's teaching nor St. Paul's example warrants the use of excommunication as pure and simple punishment. The defiant sinner shuts himself out: but if he makes a serious and apparently sincere request for restoration, we have no right to delay it further than may be needed to make reasonably sure of his sincerity. If any grace at all is given in the ordinance, the repentant sinner is the man who most sorely needs it, "to arm him against impending temptations." He is not only a fit person for the Lord's Table, but the only fit person, for we do not ourselves presume to come there except so far as we too are repentant sinners.[2]

[1] Cyprian *Ep.* 57.

[2] St. Paul's direction "not even to eat" with open sinners who are Christians, refers to the impenitent only, for he tells the Corinthians to restore at once a very gross offender, if they are satisfied of his repentance. There is no reason for taking this as an exceptional indulgence.

If it be answered that the churches generally have used excommunication as simple punishment, the reply is easy. Every practice of every church

Felicissimus felt the blow, and tried a counterblow. A junta of five tainted bishops (among them Repostus of Tuburnuc) made Fortunatus bishop of Carthage in opposition to Cyprian. The scandal was too great; and the party collapsed at once. Crowds went over to Cyprian, and we hear no more of Felicissimus.

Novatian fared better, One important bishop, Fabius of Antioch, was inclined to favour him, and Dionysius and others had much ado to hold him back for the short remainder of his life. His successor accepted the position of Cyprian and Cornelius (March 252). But Novatianism was not thereby suppressed. The ideal holiness it strove to realize in the visible church has a charm for every age of stirring life. If it falls in with human pride, and is near akin to the spirit of persecution, it is also near akin to those final facts of Christian certainty which it goes far to undo by want of charity. It may be the weakness of the most prosaic natures, or it may do duty for the thing austere and high which quick and vivid natures need to give unity to the ever-changing phases of spiritual excitement. And in the throes of a grim and desperate struggle with some over-mastering power of evil, when Calvinism or asceticism is let loose from the depths of human nature according as hope is strong or weak, the spirit of Puritanism is never far off. Hildebrand and Calvin are alike in this, and few great churchmen have quite escaped it. Novatianism was not likely to die out in such an age

depends on an interpretation of Scripture—that either there is not anything to the contrary in Scripture, or that if there is, we are at liberty to disregard it. And if the churches have undeniably gone wrong generally on points of criticism, there is no reason why they should not also go wrong generally on points of interpretation.

as the third century. If it never greatly flourished in Rome, it found more genial quarters among the Gauls of Asia, and remained strong in Africa till it was absorbed by its more rigid and fanatical successor, Donatism.

If Cyprian had guided Rome in the contest with the confessors, and worked in union with Rome against the rigorists of Novatian, it was not long before questions arose which divided Rome and Carthage, and plainly shewed how little the churches admitted any Roman jurisdiction. Lucius of Rome died in May 254, and his successor Stephen was involved in a series of disputes with Cyprian. The first of these is sufficiently significant. Two Spanish bishops, Basilides of Leon and Martialis of Merida, had accepted *libelli* in the persecution, and been guilty of further heathen sin : so they were deposed from their office, and others were duly elected in their place. Presently they went to Rome, and Stephen recognised them as the lawful bishops of Leon and Merida—their apostasy notwithstanding. Thereupon the aggrieved churches appealed to Cyprian ; and their appeal was accepted without hesitation. An African council summarily reversed the Roman decision, on the ground that " our colleague Stephen was deceived, being a long way off and ignorant of the facts and of the truth." [1] It does not even occur to them that Stephen has any authority that needs to be reckoned with.

The next dispute (in 255) was over Marcian of Arles, who not only excluded all the *lapsi* even in the hour of death, but (like the Donatists of the next

[1] Cyprian *Ep.* 67. 5.

century) renounced communion with the churches
which restored them.   Faustinus of Lyons wrote to
Stephen, and also to Cyprian ; and when Stephen
did nothing, he wrote again to Cyprian, who took up
the matter and pressed it on Stephen.   " It is our
duty," says he, " as governors of the church to consider the matter and find a remedy." [1]   So he instructs
Stephen to write first " a very full letter " to the
Gaulish bishops, that they should stop the insolence
of Marcian as the insolence of Novatian had been
stopped—by excommunication, which would at once
vacate the see.   Stephen was also to write to the
laity of Arles, to remind them of their duty to elect
a new bishop in Marcian's place ; and in due time
he was to inform Cyprian who was chosen.   The
only primacy here allowed to Rome is that of near
ness to Gaul.   It was not Stephen's duty but that
of the Gaulish churches to remedy the grievance ;
and it was no more Stephen's duty than that of
Cyprian or any other bishop to remind them of it,
except that he was the nearest great bishop to Gaul,
and therefore the most convenient person to do it.

The third dispute was on the rebaptism of heretics ;
and this raised important questions.   If an act of
baptism were performed by a person outside the
church, it had to be completed by the laying-on of
hands—so far all parties were agreed—but was it
therefore null ?   On this there was no general agreement in Cyprian's time.   In Africa heretical baptism
seems to have been first condemned about 213,[2]
at a council held by Agrippinus of Carthage.   The

---

[1] *Ibid.* 68.
[2] Benson *Cyprian* 335-348 for this date and the next.

practice of rebaptism may have been brought to
Rome in the time of Callistus; but we cannot
suppose it to have been more than an occasional
abuse, in the face of Stephen's distinct declaration
that it had never been allowed in the Roman church.
Even in Africa the decision of the council seems to
have been forgotten; though it was still observed
in Numidia. In the East the principle seems to
have settled, that "all baptism must be rejected,
which is outside the church."[1] Councils at Iconium
and Synnada (*cir.* 230) rejected it in the full belief
that they were only continuing old customs, and
Dionysius of Alexandria tells us[2] that similar decisions
were made in many districts by other councils of the
same period. Upon the whole then there was a
custom of rebaptizing in Asia within Mount Taurus,
and a custom of not rebaptizing at Rome; while
Dionysius (as we shall see) held a mediating position,
and Africa was divided.

But Africa was not for long divided. The
Novatianists made the question urgent by rebaptizing converts from the church. If the Novatianists
treated the baptism of the church as null, might not
the church reply by declaring Novatianist baptism
null? No, replied Stephen. The man who tolerated
lapsed bishops in Spain and an ultra-Novatianist
bishop in Gaul was not likely to reverse the old
custom of his church by annulling Novatianist
baptism. Instead of this, he was ready to admit
even that of Marcion, and "the rest of the heretical
pests." This aroused Cyprian. His mind was clear.
If there is no grace outside the church, no baptism
outside the church can confer grace. If Marcion is

---

[1] Firmilian *ap.* Cypr. *Ep.* 75. 19.   [2] *ap.* Eus. vii.

a particularly pestilent heretic, Novatian cannot plead his orthodoxy, for the fact remains that he is out of the church, and therefore has no grace to give. He may " ape the church," but his baptism is only "lying water." [1] As for the heretics who do not rebaptize—a nice model truly for Stephen to hold up to us ! " But if any one reply that Novatian holds the same law as the church, uses the same creed in baptism, and recognizes the same Father, Son and Holy Spirit, let him know that we have neither the same use of the creed nor the same questioning as schismatics ; for when they ask, Dost thou believe in the forgiveness of sins and life eternal through the holy church, they lie, because they have no church. Then again with their own voice they confess that no forgiveness of sins is given but through the holy church : and as they have not this they make it plain that with them no sins can be forgiven." [2]

The controversy ran a fairly simple course. Cyprian is questioned on the matter first by a layman named Magnus, whom he answers himself ; then by eighteen Numidian bishops, who are answered by the majority of a council of thirty-three African bishops—for all did not agree. A third question came from Quintus, a Mauritanian bishop, who was also answered by Cyprian. Next year a council of seventy-one African and Numidian bishops decided that " those who are washed outside the church, and defiled among heretics and schismatics with the stain of profane water must be baptized when they come to us and to the church, which is one." They prove the incapacity of those outside the church by the

---

[1] Jer. xv. 18 as quoted by Cyprian *Ep.* 73. 6 *aqua mendax non habens fidem.*   [2] Cyprian *Ep.* 69, 7 (condensed).

command (Lev. xxi. 21), No man that hath a blemish shall come near to offer gifts to God, and other like passages. Howbeit "we compel no man and lay down no law, since every bishop has freedom to govern his church according to his own judgment, whereof he shall give account to the Lord."[1] Once more the question was asked of Cyprian by the Mauritanian bishop Jubaianus, whom he answered in an elaborate letter[2] which gives his final views. This letter he laid before a third council which met Sept. 1, 256, of eighty-seven bishops from Africa, Numidia and Mauritania, with presbyters and deacons, and a great number present of the laity. Then, "It remains for us each to state what he thinks, judging no man, and removing no man from his right of communion if he thinks otherwise. For none of us makes himself a bishop of bishops, or obliges his colleagues by a tyrannous terror to any necessity of obedience."[3] Then the bishops gave their opinions in order—the whole number of them unanimous for rebaptism. The variety of argument and temper is remarkable ; but in the conclusion they are all agreed.[4]

[1] *Ibid.* 72.   [2] *Ibid.* 73.   [3] Cyprian *Sentt. Epp.*

[4] A few specimens may be given :

12. If the blind lead the blind, etc. : quoted again by 82.

24. Are heretics Christians or not ? If so, why are they not in the church ? If not, let them become Christians.

37. We know that heretics are worse than heathens.

60. Christ instituted the church, the devil heresy.

62. "God heareth not a sinner." How can a heretic, who is a sinner, be heard in baptism ?

70. A heretic cannot give what he has not : much more has a schismatic lost what he had.

Benson *Cyprian* 424 for the most characteristic utterance of his whole work, explaining the error of the Council—"uncharitable, anti-Scriptural, un-catholic, and unanimous"—by the silence of the laity, among whom broader principles were at work. I am afraid this is too favourable to the laity.

If Cyprian was far from conciliatory, Stephen was thoroughly insolent, " quarrelling at one time with the Easterns, at another with the Africans. A deputation of bishops from Carthage he received with patience enough and gentleness, for he refused even common conversation with them, and was moreover so mindful of love and charity that he forbade the brotherhood to receive them in their houses. This was the way he kept the unity of the spirit in the bond of peace." [1] The speaker here is Firmilian of Caesarea in Cappadocia ; and his sarcasm was well deserved. Firmilian ranked with Dionysius of Alexandria and Gregory of Neocaesarea—two other disciples of Origen—among the great leaders of the Eastern church. Of this man Stephen wrote to Dionysius, as well as " about Helenus of Tarsus, and all the nations of Cilicia and Cappadocia and Galatia and those next bordering on them, threatening to break off communion with them also for the same reason, that (says he) they rebaptize heretics." [2] Much Firmilian cares for that threat. His arguments are mostly borrowed from Cyprian ; but he confirms the custom of Africa by that of Asia, and tells a story of a woman some two-and-twenty years ago, after Alexander's time," who was in ecstasy, gave herself out for a prophetess, and deceived many. Would Stephen say that baptism is valid if administered by such a demoniac as that ? At Roman "custom" he scoffs. Christ called himself truth, not custom. [3]

[1] *ap.* Cyprian *Ep.* 75, 25.

[2] Dionysius *ap.* Eus. vii. 5 ὡς οὐδὲ ἐκείνοις κοινωνήσων viz., as he had already threatened the Africans.

[3] The argument comes through Cyprian from Tertullian *de virg. vel.* 1. In exactly the same way it is quoted by Gregory VII. to Wimund of Aversa (Jaffé *Mon Gregoriana* 576).

Rome has made many changes since the apostles' time, and there are many diversities of custom; yet they have never caused any such breach of peace and unity as Stephen is now making. I am rightly angry at Stephen's manifest folly, that one who boasts the rank of his bishopric, and maintains that he holds Peter's chair by right succession should bring in many other rocks and set up new buildings of many churches. In excommunicating all these churches, he has only excommunicated himself.[1]

Firmilian denounces Roman insolence with un-measured scorn; Dionysius of Alexandria meets it with grave entreaty—all the graver for the fact that in practice he agreed with Stephen. Clement had spoken of heretical baptism as "strange water,"[2] but Dionysius did not rebaptize "those who had made profession in baptism, *whether in pretence or in truth*, of" the Trinity.[3] When an old convert of times dating back perhaps to Demetrius found out that his own heretical baptism had been quite unlike the orthodox, Dionysius refused to rebaptize him, telling him that a communion of many years was sufficient, and that he would not venture to unsettle him by a regular baptism. So it was not to Stephen's practice that Dionysius objected, but to his want of charity in forcing it on the Easterns. It was a serious thing to disturb the Pentecostal peace and harmony that had been restored to the churches. Rebaptism was no new custom in Africa, nor (so it proved) in Asia either. It was enjoined by many councils and practised in many populous churches;

---

[1] Cyprian *Ep.* 75 is a translation of Firmilian's letter.
[2] Clem. Al. *Strom.* i. 19 ὕδωρ ἀλλότριον τὸ βάπτισμα τὸ αἱρετικόν.
[3] Dion. Al. *ap.* Eus. vii. 5-9 (fragments of several letters).

and "I cannot endure to unsettle their opinions and
stir up strife and contention, for says he, Thou shalt
not remove thy neighbour's landmark."[1]

Stephen died in peace (Aug. 2, 257) and his
successor Xystus dropped the quarrel. Perhaps it
was forgotten in the outbreak of Valerian's persecution ; but every church seems to have kept its own
custom. At Arles in 314 the Roman view (that
of Dionysius of Alexandria) prevailed, that even
heretical baptism is valid if given in the name of the
Trinity ; but its nullity was a settled question in the
East and Africa [2]—as witness the *one baptism* of
Eastern creeds, and the Nicene command to rebaptize the Paulianists (followers of Paul of
Samosata), who certainly used the name of the
Trinity.[3] When the question settled down, the
baptism of schismatics (if with water and in the
name of the Trinity) was recognized, while that of
heretics was rejected in the East, and theoretically
accepted in the West, for Rome rebaptizes only on
the theory that heretics are sure to be careless. The
church of England has deliberately (since 1604)
withdrawn the former sanction for baptism by others
than its own ministers, but nowhere pronounces such
baptism invalid.

----

[1] Thus *Can. Apost.* 46, 47. Athanasius *Or. c. Ar.* ii. 42, 43 (Arians,
Manichees, Montanists). Cyril *Procatech.* 7. Basil *Ep.* 188 (but Novatians
only schismatics, so left to local custom) *Ep.* 199. 47 (Encratites etc., reading
οὐ τῷ αὐτῷ : Marcionites). Didymus *de Trin.* ii. 15 (Eunomians, Montanists).
Optatus i. 12. Also *Can.* 7 C.P. (381) which though spurious is not a century
later (Eunomians, Montanists, Sabellians, and all others except Arians,
Macedonians, Sabbatians, Novatians, Quartodecimans and Apollinarians).

[2] Dion. Al. to Xystus of Rome—newly discovered fragment translated
from the Armenian by F. C. Conybeare, *Engl. Historical Review*, January
1910, p. 115.

[3] *Can.* 19. The Roman gloss—"Paulianists ; therefore not others"—
is not what the Council meant.

The question really at issue was of the unworthiness of the minister, whether it hinders the effect of the sacraments. The stricter sects have always inclined to answer Yes, in the most general way. Cyprian replied that separation from the church is the only hindrance, while the church of Rome rightly held that even that is no hindrance.

CHAPTER XXV

THE long peace (260-303) which followed the edict of Gallienus is almost as obscure as the subapostolic age. We really know more of the seventh century, which is the obscurest part of the middle ages. No great character properly belongs to the period, and its records are of the scantiest. We have a few chapters about Dionysius of Alexandria and Paul of Samosata, notices of Manes and of Anatolius of Laodicea, accounts more or less legendary of Gregory the Wonderworker and of Gregory the Illuminator, lists of bishops, a few fragments of Pierius and Theognostus, and some inscriptions. This is nearly all. Fortunately the period is not a very long one, and we can form some idea of the changes going on by comparing the times of Origen and Cyprian before it with the Nicene age after it.

The story of the Empire will not detain us long, for none of the emperors between Gallienus and Diocletian (268-284) is known to have had any direct dealings with the Christians, Aurelian excepted. They are not likely to have been friendly rulers. Claudius, Aurelian, Probus,[1] and Carus were

---

[1] To the time of Probus we may refer Trophimus the martyr (of the Pisidian Antioch), who suffered at Synnada. Inscription discussed by

great soldiers, Tacitus was an old senator, Carinus
a vicious tyrant : there remains only the cultured
Numerian, of whom very little is known.   But the
most hostile of rulers could not refuse to see that
the barbarians and the mutinies were a much more
pressing danger than the Christians.   Even Marcus
in his worst distresses had no such tremendous task
as that which now confronted Claudius.   The state
of things was bad enough in Valerian's time ; but
it was much worse now.   For nearly twenty years
(249-268) the sword and the famine and the noisome
beast [1] and the pestilence had been doing their worst.
The Empire must have lost half its population, and
perhaps quite as much of its scanty fixed capital.
The Euphrates and the Rhine were guarded for the
moment by Zenobia and Victorina, though neither
the Queen of the East nor the Gaulish legions could
be trusted.   Zenobia had her ambitions, and a
Gaulish Caesar was bound to march on Rome when
he could do it.   But the danger on the Danube was
greater than ever.   The Goths were overflowing all
the Balkan region, and Claudius cannot have had
very much more than the resources of Italy at his
disposal.   But the result was decisive.   The Goths
were completely routed near Naissus, and "the
provinces were filled with barbarian slaves and
Gothic serfs."   The conversion of prisoners into
serfs was the settled policy of the emperors, and
must have given the provinces a large infusion of
Teutonic blood.

Ramsay in *Expositor* Seventh Ser. vol. ix. 481 (June 1910).   The general
peace would not prevent occasional executions, especially of soldiers.

[1] The noisome beast must be taken literally.   We find some of the
richest parts of Gaul (the Médoc and the Côte d'Or) abandoned to the
beasts in the time of Diocletian.

Here then was the first great blow struck for the restoration of the Empire. But Claudius did not even live to finish the Gothic war, so that the main part of the work had to be done by his successor. That successor was one of the greatest soldiers in the entire history of Rome. Lucius Domitius Aurelianus reigned but five years (270-275) yet by the end of those five years he had recovered both East and West, and was obeyed from Palmyra to Carlisle. His proud title of *Restitutor Orbis* does him no more than justice. In his career of conquest he was like Severus; like Severus also in his excessive cruelty, but unlike Severus in being little more than a great soldier. Some terrible examples may have been needed to keep in hand that brutal soldiery; but in Diocletian's judgment Aurelian was too cruel for an emperor, and ought never to have been more than a general.

However, he began with a work of peace. By giving up Trajan's Dacia to the Goths, he secured an alliance which covered the lower Danube for a century. Two short wars excepted, there was no more trouble with the Goths till 376. Then he turned upon Zenobia, who had taken the opportunity of the Gothic war for the conquest of Egypt. In fact, it was time to suppress her, for she was more Syrian than Roman. A battle near Emesa enabled him to besiege Palmyra and capture Zenobia in her attempt to escape. Leaving Probus to complete his work by the conquest of Egypt, Aurelian returned to the West. The Gaulish Caesarship was most unstable. A mutinous army had set up and slaughtered a whole series of emperors; and though Victorina was "Mother of the Camp"—now a common title for empresses—through several reigns, she had been put to death by Tetricus, who now ruled in daily terror of his mutinous soldiery. He was only too glad to be conquered or delivered by Aurelian, who made him a *Corrector* in Italy. Then Aurelian shewed his want of statesmanship. Instead of giving the Empire the rest it so sorely needed, he marched against the Persians. But by this time his cruelty had made him intolerable, and he was assassinated as he was nearing Byzantium (March 275).

Aurelian was a devoted worshipper of the Sun, to whom he built a splendid temple in Rome, so that he was not likely to look kindly on the Christians. The one saying about them recorded of him does not sound friendly—when he rebukes the Senate for their delay in consulting the Sibylline books, "as if they were debating in a Christian church, not in a temple of all the gods." Still in the main he does not seem to have molested them. He decided for them, as we shall see, the question of the bishopric of Antioch. At the end of his reign however there were at any rate rumours of his intention to renew the persecution. Whether the edict was actually issued is not clear; but in any case its operation was cut short by Aurelian's death.

Three times the council of officers had chosen great soldiers—Valerian, Claudius, Aurelian—but now they turned to the civilians. The Senate was still in theory the giver of the purple; and its credit must have risen as that of the emperor declined in the anarchy: and it had done good work of late in the defence of Italy against Maximin, and in the recent Marcomannic inroad, which had nearly

defeated Aurelian himself at Placentia. So it seemed
a hopeful plan when the council of officers invited
the Senate to name an emperor and assume the
supreme direction; and they agreed to do so when
they were satisfied that the officers were in earnest.
Clearly the right policy for them was to choose the
ablest and most vigorous man they could find in
the *Curia*. But this is precisely what such an
assembly never does. Rank and age come first;
and they chose their worthy old *princeps* Tacitus.
The mistake was fatal. Tacitus was loyally accepted
by the army, and was not wanting in activity:
but he soon sank under the fatigues of the camp.
This time the army chose for itself, and chose
Probus the general of the East, one of the best of
Aurelian's lieutenants. The Senate might have
preferred Florianus the brother of Tacitus; but
Probus was respectful to them, and allowed the
new government to continue. But when he too
perished in a mutiny (282) his successor Carus put
an end to it. Carus marched against Persia with his
younger son Numerian, leaving Carinus the elder to
govern in Rome. In the midst of a thunderstorm
near Ctesiphon (so runs the story) it was announced
that Carus was dead, and young Numerian led back
the army under the guidance of his father-in-law,
the Praetorian Praefect Arrius Aper. Presently
Numerian was found dead in his litter, and the
officers chose the *Comes domesticorum* Diocletian,
who at once slew Aper with his own hand as the
murderer of Numerian (Sept. 17, 284). It only
remained to decide between Diocletian and Carinus.
The armies met near Margus (285) and the Western
legions were fast winning the day when Carinus was

311

killed by an officer whose wife he had violated. Diocletian remained, to be even more than Aurelian the restorer of the Empire.

Our knowledge of church history during the Long Peace is almost limited to the East; and in the East the disciples and followers of Origen take the lead. To its early years belong Dionysius of Alexandria, Firmilian of Caesarea Mazaca, and Gregory of Neocaesarea; a little later the succession of the Alexandrian school is carried on by Theognostus and Pierius, while Pamphilus of the Palestinian Caesarea brings us to the edge of the Nicene age, and his friend Eusebius was a friend of Constantine, and overlived him.

Though Dionysius of Alexandria (*cir.* 197-265) belongs rather to the time of Decius and Valerian, he may be taken here as the greatest of church leaders in the first years of the Peace. He seems to have been a man of some rank, which he lost when his habit of reading books of all sorts led him to Christianity. In after years he tells Philemon the Roman elder how "one of the brethren the elders" warned him against reading heretical books, and told him they would do him harm (and he was quite right, too) but "there came a vision sent from God which strengthened me, and a word of command came to me, expressly saying, Read all the books that come into your hands, for you are well able to correct and try each statement; and this was also the original cause of your conversion. I accepted the vision as being in agreement with the apostolic utterance which says to the stronger brethren, Shew yourselves tried money-changers." [1]

---

[1] The narrower sort of Christians always thought it wrong to read heretical

When bishop Demetrius died in 232, Dionysius succeeded Heraclas as head of the catechetical school, and afterwards as bishop in 247. He soon found himself in the thick of persecution. Outrages began even in Philip's time, and must have been connived at by the Praefect. They ceased on Philip's death, but then came the edict of Decius. Without an hour's delay the Praefect Sabinus sent an officer to arrest Dionysius. The man hunted everywhere for four days, never dreaming that the bishop would stay quietly in his own house. Then "at God's command," he left with his children [1] and others, but was captured by the soldiers and brought to Taposiris, some fifteen miles from Alexandria, where he was rescued by a wedding party of rustics. He remained in hiding for the rest of the persecution, and the authorities appear to have searched no further for him.[2] On his return he was much troubled with the pestilence and with the tumults, which made it "easier to pass from the East to the West than from one quarter of the city to another." When the persecution was resumed by Valerian in 257, Dionysius and some of his clergy were brought before the Praefect Aemilianus. Dionysius gives the whole story from the official records. Aemilianus begins by promising them full security (such is the clemency of the emperors) if they will only "do the natural thing" by worshipping the gods who preserve the

---

or heathen books. Serapion of Antioch has to explain that he only borrowed them for a purpose ; Origen and Dionysius have to defend themselves for doing it, and the Syriac *Didaskalia* (c. 2) expressly forbids heathen literature.

[1] οἱ παῖδες may be pupils : hardly servants, for Dionysius dedicates his Περὶ φύσεως to one of them (Eus. vii. 26).

[2] Here we see some reasons for the failure of the Decian persecution. The authorities were remiss, and the rustics sympathized with prisoners generally —for there is no reason to think it was a wedding party of Christians.

Empire and "forgetting the unnatural gods." Dionysius replies that all men do not worship all gods, but
each those he thinks fit. We worship the one God,
and pray to him for the emperors. "Well, who
hinders you from worshipping him, if he is a god,
along with the natural gods?" "We worship no
other." Aemilianus replies by exiling them to
Cephro in Libya, "where neither you nor others
will be allowed to hold meetings, or to enter the so-
called cemeteries." With that, he ordered them to
go to the place at once, not allowing Dionysius a
day's delay for sickness. But Dionysius not only
held meetings at Cephro, and converted many of the
heathen, but kept up the meetings at Alexandria.
So Aemilianus divided the party, quartering them in
villages of the Mareotis—which enabled their friends
at Alexandria to pay them frequent visits.

Dionysius was released from exile by the edict of
Gallienus, and spent the last five years of his life in
such peace as was allowed him by the pestilence and
the continued civil strife at Alexandria. In 265 he
excused himself from attending the council to be
held at Antioch against Paul of Samosata. His
excuse of old age and sickness was only too true : he
died before the council's work was done.

In his own time no man spoke with greater
weight in Eastern Christendom than Dionysius : He
was more than a man of learning and a master of
clear and simple writing. His discussion of the
authorship of the Apocalypse is of itself enough to
place him among the best and soundest critics of
ancient times. But the noblest thing in Dionysius
is his moderation and soberness. We have seen it
already in his accounts of his own sufferings, and in

his dealings with Novatian and with Stephen of Rome, and it is equally conspicuous elsewhere. He has no word of railing for Aemilianus, and is not scurrilous even against Macrianus, whom he regards as the instigator of Valerian to evil. But nowhere does he shew himself better than in his plea for gentleness with penitents. We, says he, reverse the Saviour's action. He sought out the sheep that was lost: we give it a kick when it returns. But such severity is bad even for ourselves. For even as we do good or evil to others we fill our own hearts with divine virtues or with wild passions. In the one case we shall have peace and be companions of good angels both here and hereafter: in the other we shall lose God's peace and our own, and be with the tormenting demons both here and after death. Let us therefore not reject penitents but receive them gladly, and count them with those that never strayed, and so fill up that which is lacking.[1] To Dionysius everywhere the sin of sins is that of the man who "slanders Christ as merciless."

We have seen Firmilian of Caesarea Mazaca in alliance with Cyprian against Stephen of Rome, and we shall meet him again when we come to the councils against Paul of Samosata : but Gregory (Thaumaturgus) of Neocaesarea needs mention here. Gregory was a native of Neocaesarea, and a heathen. But when he went to study law at Berytus, he fell under the influence of Origen, and remained five years with him. To his parting speech we owe our best information on Origen's methods of teaching, and on his own life so far. On his return he was chosen quite young for the bishopric of Neocaesarea :

---

[1] *Letter* vii. (Feltoe p. 63).

and after that he is almost lost in a cloud of legend. The chief purveyor of legend is Gregory of Nyssa, who wrote a Life of him more than a century later from the information of his grandmother Macrina ; and the old lady had a taste for the marvellous. However, it is clear that our Gregory was a great bishop more or less in the style of Dionysius. Like Dionysius, he hid himself in the Decian persecution, and strove to calm the troubles left behind by that of Valerian. If he was less hindered by civil strife than Dionysius, he had to face the horrors of Gothic inroads, most safely dated after the fall of Trebizond in 256. Great numbers of captives were carried off ; but they spread some knowledge of Christianity among the Goths. The time however was not quite come for a Gothic mission : Gregory's fame in history is as the chief organizer of the churches in Pontus. Though we need not believe that he found only seventeen Christians in Neocaesarea, and left only seventeen heathens, we cannot doubt that his work made an enormous change even in his own time. In the next age it is indirectly represented by the conversion of Armenia and the rise of the new Nicene party which gathered round the three great Cappadocians.

Christian schools and Christian learning grew in the later years of the Long Peace. There were Dorotheus and Lucian at Antioch, Pierius and Theognostus at Alexandria, Hieracas in Egypt ; but the typical scholar of the time is Pamphilus of Caesarea. Like Dionysius, he gave up good worldly prospects to become a Christian student. He learned of Pierius at Alexandria, and on his return became an elder of the church of Caesarea.

There he devoted his life to austere study, and to the collection of a library, chiefly of manuscripts of Scripture and commentaries thereupon. Some of these were copied by Pamphilus himself, others by the band of students he gathered round him. A copy of Origen's commentary on the Twelve Prophets in five-and-twenty volumes came down to Jerome in the autograph of Pamphilus. The inspiration came from Origen, for Pamphilus was his devoted follower. For years Pamphilus and the historian Eusebius worked together; and when they were arrested in the last great persecution, Pamphilus devoted his two years of imprisonment to writing a Defence of Origen. Five books were completed when Pamphilus became a martyr (309). Eusebius added a sixth, and thenceforth called himself Pamphili—the friend of Pamphilus.

Even as Catholicism and Protestantism both rightly claim Augustine for their spiritual father, so Athanasius and Eusebius, Arius and Paul of Samosata only developed principles which lay side by side unreconciled in the works of Origen. The dilemma of the Person of Christ was growing sharper in the third century. If he is God, we have two gods; and if he is not God, we worship a creature. Origen cleared one side of the difficulty by his theory of the eternal generation, and essayed to clear another by his doctrine of the human soul of Christ; but the dilemma was more than he could resolve. All that he could do was to insist at once on the deity of Christ and on his subordination to the Father. It might for awhile seem possible to reconcile these positions by counting Christ a secondary God, and this was a common tendency at the opening of the Nicene age, as with Eusebius. But sooner or later there was no escape from the conclusion that a secondary God is unthinkable, and would in any case be a second god. The use of such a desperate expedient was enough to shew that the problem was nearly ready for its solution at Nicaea.

Meanwhile, if the two sides of Origen's teaching could not be held on equal terms, one or the other must be dominant. Given the current conception of the divine as transcendent and simple, the deity of Christ led straight to Sabellianism. If he was God, he must be some form, appearance or modification of the Father. On the other hand, Arianism in the next age gave a final demonstration that he could not be subordinated to the Father without reducing him to a creature. Sabellius himself, though he lived quite early in the third century, belongs rather to the Nicene age, for he developed a Patripassion theory of the Person of Christ into a full system of the Trinity. His own doctrine is not easy to ascertain; but he seems to have stood on third-century ground in making the Father the one God. This God appears in the Old Testament as the Father, and expands himself (πλατύνεται) in the New as the Son, and in the Church as the Holy Spirit. Thus the Trinity he reaches is only a Trinity of temporary appearances without any eternal background. It has three faces to the world, and that is all.

As Paul of Samosata is known to us only from the accounts of his enemies, we must use them with some reserve. But the public facts of the case cannot be outrageously falsified in an official document like the letter of deposition, even if the glosses put on them are prejudiced. Paul then was bishop of Antioch from *cir.* 260, and soon became notorious. A council was called in 265, which Dionysius of Alexandria was prevented from attending by an illness which proved fatal. But Firmilian of Cappadocia came this time and to a second council. We hear that Paul got off both times by sophistical excuses and promises of amendment. A third council was held *cir.* 267, after Firmilian's death; and now Paul's sophistics were unmasked by the presbyter Malchion. So he was deposed; but it was a startling stretch of authority when the council appointed Domnus in his place. Paul must have been well supported by his flock when he refused to recognize the sentence; and he was also a *procurator ducenarius,* a high official in great favour with Zenobia, so that he could not be dispossessed of the church property till after her fall in 272. Then the bishops appealed to Aurelian, and he gave " a very reasonable decision," that the lawful bishop of Antioch was the one in communion with the bishops of Rome and Italy. This was Domnus; and Paul was ejected.

Aurelian might be reasonable enough; but the process marks two momentous facts in the growth of the church. The first is that the council did what no council seems ever to have done before. They not only renounced Paul's communion but deposed him, and not only deposed him but appointed a successor, apparently without regard to the rights of the church of Antioch. The second fact which came out was that questions of property can only be decided by the state; and the state could not decide them without laying down its own definition

of orthodoxy. Constantine replaced Aurelian's definition by requiring subscription to the Nicene Creed:
but Theodosius added to this the demand that the
bishop must be in communion with certain chief
bishops of the East—which is in principle Aurelian's
decision again. In all cases the emperor necessarily
decided what the state recognized as orthodoxy.

But to return to the letter of deposition addressed
by Helenus of Tarsus and the rest to Dionysius
of Rome, Maximus of Alexandria, and the whole
catholic church under heaven. They tell us that
Paul was more *ducenarius* than bishop, that he
grew rich by oppression, and that he was a great
lover of worldly pomp and luxury. He appeared in
public with a guard, and had a tribunal and private
room like a magistrate. In church he behaved like
a sophist, and put a stop to the hymns to Christ
as recent innovations. Instead of them he had
hymns to himself on Easter Day, to which he listened
with much delight. He would not admit that the
Son of God came down from heaven, but said, "Jesus
Christ is from beneath," whereas his flatterers averred
that he was himself an angel from heaven. He
connived at the *subintroductae* of the clergy, even
when the scandal was proved. In fact he carries
about with him two beautiful women, whose relation
to him is most suspicious. Had he been sound in
the faith, we should have called him to account for
these things; but his heresy is good reason for
deposing him without investigating his further misdeeds. So we have appointed Domnus in his place,
with whom you may exchange commendatory letters.
As for Paul, he may write to Artemas.[1]

[1] Eus. vii. 30, apparently Artemon.

Though the story of the hymns to himself in church on Easter Day seems quite incredible, and some of the other stories may be groundless or exaggerated, we can hardly doubt that Paul was thoroughly worldly and unscrupulous. But what was his heresy ? The bishops only glance at it, though they say that it made other grounds of deposition superfluous. Paul seems to have held firmly the unity of God and the manhood of Christ, and to have made the Logos the connecting link. But the Logos of Paul was not a divine Person—only the Reason and Wisdom of God which were the principles of his working in the world, and therefore called the Son. This impersonal Logos from above dwelt in Christ from below, not personally (οὐσιωδῶς) but as a quality (κατὰ ποιότητα). As this made no union of God and man in Christ, Paul adopted Origen's conception of a human soul joined with God in unwavering love and unity of will, and through the working of the Logos he made it become divine.

This theory was a general failure. It admitted neither a personal Logos nor an eternal Son, nor a true union of God and man in Christ. There was a point in the sarcastic reference to Artemas, who made Christ nothing more than a man. Paul thoroughly roused the antagonism of the churches, and his name was a name of horror for the next century. One of the more lasting results of the controversy was the condemnation of the word ὁμοούσιον by one of the councils held against him—for this proved inconvenient when the same word was proposed as a test of orthodoxy at Nicaea. It is not clear how the condemnation came about. Athanasius tells us that Paul objected to it as materialist, and the council accepted his objection. But Athanasius wrote in exile, and without his books : Hilary and Epiphanius report that Paul accepted it in a Sabellian sense, and therefore the council rejected it. Athanasius [1] refuses to set one council against the other as the greater or the older, but endeavours to shew that while the bishops at Antioch condemned it in one sense, the Fathers of Nicaea enforced it in another.

Paul of Samosata was the last of the great heretics before the rise of Arianism. Heresies must have arisen in the obscure thirty years which followed, but the traces they have left in history are faint. After that, schisms rather than heresies were the monsters that came up from the stormy sea of persecution. We hear more of separatists like Donatists and Meletians than of such heterodox thinkers—if heterodox they were—as Hieracas and Lucian of Antioch.

Here then on the edge of the last great persecution let us once more sum up the progress of the Gospel. In the course of the third century it had reached every corner of the Empire. We can trace churches to Britain and the Pillars westward, and again to Pontus and Armenia, and far beyond the Persian frontier. Eighty-six bishops in Cyprian's Council bear witness to its spread in Africa; and in the next generation Marcellus of Tingis answers for the far West of Mauritania. In Spain we find bishops at Merida, and at Leon below the Asturian mountains as early as the time of Decius; and the nineteen bishops at Elvira (*cir.* 306) represent the whole country from Saragossa to the Algarves. Christians were fewer in Atlantic

[1] Ath. *de Syn.* 45.

Gaul; yet we get a fair sprinkling at Arles in 314. With them come three British bishops, from London, York and possibly Lincoln, for the name is corrupt. The Christians in " Germany " mentioned by Irenaeus now appear as organized churches, with bishops at Köln and Trier. In Northern Italy the ground is covered : sixty bishops meet Cornelius to discuss the Novatian question. We may presume that there were churches in the strongly Roman province of Noricum, for we meet with bishops and martyrs in the valley of the Save at Siscia and Sirmium, and at Petavio on the Drave. There is no trace of Christians on the lower Danube, though they were fully settled in Macedonia and Thrace, and had found their way— at least as captives—to the Goths of the Crimea. The coast of Pontus had been reached by the end of the first century. Though the Gospel made slow progress eastward till the time of Gregory of Neocaesarea (*cir.* 245-270), it had gained a footing in Armenia in the time of Dionysius of Alexandria, but the chief work was done by Gregory the Illuminator after the restoration of Tiridates in 287, and the decisive victory was won before the Empire yielded. We have already seen Christian communities in Persia; and the churches found in India by Theophilus of Diu date back long before his visit *cir.* 356. Christians were numerous in Syria, and even the province of Arabia had bishops enough to hold councils. We have a Christian inscription of this period at Cyrene, and a translation of the Gospels was needed before this in the Thebaid, which moreover furnished martyrs in abundance for Maximin Daza.[1]

[1] I think this account will be found well within historical bounds ; though it might be much extended if doubtful *Acta* were used.

Of course this vast expanse of country was by no means uniformly overspread. Any attempt to estimate the number of the Christians or the proportion it bore to the heathens in the Empire would be lost labour. Some things however may safely be laid down. The first is that the Christians were a minority. In parts they were numerous, and in a few places the bulk of the people may have been Christian, though the only case we know is the Phrygian city of Eumenea; but upon the whole they must have been far outnumbered by the heathens. Again, they were more numerous in the East; less so in the West, except in Africa. The 1500 widows and needy persons in Rome in Cyprian's time [1] imply a Christian population of perhaps 50,000. Their numbers were greater now; but they cannot even yet have been more than a small minority in Rome. Christianity always tended to flourish wherever culture flourished. Thus the cities seem always to have been more Christian than the country. A century later, when heathenism was dying out of the cities, the villagers were still *pagani*.[2]

But if the Christians were a minority in every province, that minority carried weight far beyond its numbers. In this we may compare the Protestants in France to-day. The Gospel attracted the best elements of society, both industrial and moral. Its converts came most freely from the artisans, the retailers and the owners of small property who were not

---

[1] Cornelius *ap.* Eus. vi. 41. This reckons them at 3 per cent. May not this be too low a ratio? If so, 50,000 will be too high a figure. See Lightfoot *Hist. Essays* 77.

[2] *Paganus* was a civilian as opposed to an official, who was in theory a soldier (*militavit in palatio*: of the *viri inlustres*, only the P.U. wore the toga). The word was used of heathens from the second half of the fourth century.

above healthy labour—the very classes on which the
economic soundness of a state depends. The slaves
were hindered by the difficulties of their position, the
upper classes by social prejudice. All classes indeed
found their way into the churches—we have seen
Revocatus and Felicitas from one end of the scale,
Cornelius and the empress Salonina from the other—
but all our evidence goes to shew that the vast
majority of the Christians were neither rich nor needy.
Again, the churches drew in from all classes the best
moral elements of society. True, the years of peace
were filling them with waverers and unworthy members. But weaklings of this kind count for nothing
in the day of trial. They make scandals ; they can
do no more. The effective strength of the churches
was in their nucleus of sound and resolute Christians.
If anywhere in the Empire a man was willing to
renounce pride as well as vice, and give himself
without reserve to truth and mercy, such a man was
likely to bear the seal of Christ, and such a man
was not likely to quail before the fires of persecution.

Such then was the Church of Christ when the
Empire challenged it to final battle. The old question,
Christ or Caesar ? was now to be decided once for all.
Yet even from the standpoint of those from whom the
secret of Christian life is hidden, the issue was hardly
doubtful. Strong as the Empire seemed, its moral
strength had mostly gone over to the Christians. Its
power radiated from a single centre, whereas the
Christians had a centre of life in every city. And
the best of that life (its lower forms do not count in
such a crisis) was far above the highest heathen level.
Decius and Valerian had fought in vain against the
churches, and the prudence of Diocletian shrank for

twenty years from the growing difficulty of resisting them. Would a Galerius be able to crush them out in bloodshed?

BOOKS

Feltoe *Dionysius of Alexandria* ; Radford *Two Teachers of Alexandria* (Theognostus and Pierius) ; Harnack *Ausbreitung.*

CHAPTER XXVI

THE GREAT PERSECUTION

WE must not picture the elections of emperors by the army as so many scenes of clamour and disorder. They were more commonly held by councils of officers —serious men who often combined civil with military experience, and strove to do the best they could for the army and the Empire. They had one clear policy when they set aside Aemilianus and Gallienus, choosing brilliant soldiers in Valerian, Claudius and Aurelian; another when they tried the experiment of asking the Senate to govern. In 284 they took a third plan. Diocletian was not chosen for his military skill, real as it was,[1] but for general wisdom and ability. As he said himself, soldiership like Aurelian's was not then the greatest need of the Empire. Only a statesman could put an end to the mutinies; and behind the mutinies lay the dilemma which finally wrecked the Empire, and civilization with it.

The Roman army was never equal to its gigantic task of guarding some six thousand miles of frontier, from the Euphrates to Carlisle and back again. True,

---

[1] The charge of military incompetence made by Lactantius *de Mort. Pers.* 7 —against a *comes domesticorum* trained in the school of Aurelian—is absurd. As well make it against Napoleon's marshals. Carus too was not a Caracalla : and Diocletian was not a Macrinus.

no enemy could meet it in the shock of battle.   If
the Germans broke through the cordon of the Rhine,
they soon had their answer on the Neckar or the
Elbe; and if Parthia snatched a victory from the
army of the Euphrates, she was always overborne by
the legions of the Danube.   But while one frontier
was victoriously defended, another lay unguarded.
Hadrian's thirty legions no longer sufficed.   Yet how
could the army be increased without a further impulse
to the spirit of mutiny which had cut off at least
fourteen emperors in sixty years, and claimants
without number?   Diocletian solved that problem;
but there was a harder one behind it.   The increased
army and the vast civil service with which he
balanced it were at best a heavy burden; and bad
taxation made it crushing.   In the last period of the
Empire all policy was shaped by dire financial need.
Taxpayers could not be spared : so society was more
and more fixed in castes, the army more and more
filled with barbarians who were not taxpayers.   They
were good fighters, less mutinous than their predecessors, and generally willing to serve the Empire.
But here came in the Roman's old contempt of the
barbarian.   Even Theodosius could hardly keep the
peace between them—the massacre of Thessalonica
was not unprovoked—and the great *Roman* mutiny
at Pavia in 408 which overthrew Stilicho was decisive.
When the Empire of the West refused to be defended
by barbarians, it had to pass away.

Diocletian's reign is upon the whole obscure.
The *Historia Augusta* comes to an end with his
accession, and the lost part of Zosimus covers nearly
the whole of his reign, so that we have to put
together what we can from the codes, the inscriptions,

the panegyrists, the "epitomators," and the Christians. Of the latter, Eusebius and Lactantius lived under him, and are so far very competent witnesses: but their interest is ecclesiastical, and their temper is naturally embittered by the persecution. Eusebius indeed is no lover of scandal. After denouncing once for all "unspeakable hypocrisy and dissimulation, pushed to the extreme of wickedness,"[1] he gives fair warning that he means to tell no stories of Christian divisions and apostasies. He does not even go out of his way to blacken Diocletian. Upon the whole, he is a good witness. We can allow for indignation, and we find no trace of malice or untruth. But Lactantius[2] is a partizan pamphleteer. His text is God's promise to "cause the evil beasts to cease out of the land,"[3] the evil beasts being Diocletian and his colleagues. Yet there is no sign of untruth even in Lactantius. He only devours every scandal greedily, puts the worst meaning on all Diocletian's acts, and

[1] Eus. viii. 1. 7. The account may be over-coloured as regards the favour of Diocletian, the prosperity of the churches, and the bitterness of their dissensions. But its substantial truth is beyond question, and its transparent sincerity ought to have disarmed criticism.

So too in the next chapters he gives us fair notice that he means to tell us of the martyrs, and not of the renegades, so that he cannot fairly be charged with suppressing the scandals. As for the bitter language in which he speaks of the persecutors, it is not unnatural. When will our pedants learn to allow something for the oppression that maketh a wise man mad?

[2] The pamphlet *de Mortibus Persecutorum* (written end of 314 or not later than middle of 315) seems a genuine work of Lact. The objections of Brandt, *Über d. Entstehungsverhaltnisse d. Prosaschriften d. Lact.* 1891 are not convincing. As Bury points out in his edition of Gibbon i. 482-4 (1909), the one serious difficulty is the statement that Lactantius returned to Gaul in 308 as tutor to Crispus Caesar. So Jerome: but though the title may be proleptic, for Crispus was not Caesar till 317, there are still the difficulties that Constantine would not have chosen a Christian tutor for his son before 312, and that Crispus was hardly out of the nursery in 308.

[3] Ezek. xxxiv. 25. More precisely, the evil beasts are Diocletian, Maximian, Galerius and Maximin Daza. Maxentius is not of the number, nor of course Constantius and Licinius.

makes him out a tyrant, a coward, and a madman, without stopping to consider that the great emperor cannot have been fool as well as knave.

The main changes which the Empire underwent are clear, though we cannot always distinguish Diocletian's part of the work from Constantine's. The first step was to strengthen the supreme power. As we have seen, the Senate aimed at weakening it by placing the highest military and civil authority in different hands : Diocletian strengthened it by making his old comrade Maximian a separate *Augustus* for the West, and further strengthened it in 293 by choosing two subordinate emperors or *Caesars*.[1] Constantius was placed in Gaul, with the task of recovering Britain from Carausius, while Galerius was retained for service in the East generally.   Constantius was an eclectic, a man of some culture, and a gentle ruler, while Galerius was like Maximian, a brutal soldier and a fierce pagan.   All four imitated the pomp of Eastern sultans, all four ignored the Senate and avoided Rome ; and the four together, united as they were by common reverence for Diocletian while he lived, formed a college of emperors which was never seriously shaken by mutinies.   But if the supreme power was strengthened by division, subordinate powers were weakened. The great provinces were cut up into fragments, the great legions were divided, civil authority was separated from military.   Officials generally were set to check each other in a way which tended rather to the emperor's personal security than to the

---

[1] We may *perhaps* see the first sketch of Diocletian's policy in the words ascribed to Macrianus in *Hist. Aug. Trig. Tyr.* 12 *juvenes aliqui sunt quaerendi, nec unus sed duo vel tres fortissimi, qui* ex diversis partibus *orbis humani rem p. restituant.*

efficiency of the public service. Burdensome however as the vast establishment was, and in the end
ruinous, it kept the peace fairly well, and gave
the Empire a century of respite in the West. The
emperor was now as absolute as a Tsar; but like the
Tsar, he gradually lost control of the machine. The
interested resistance of bureaucracy and landowners
foiled every effort at reform. The empire fell at
last, largely because it had convinced its subjects
that the outrages of barbarians could not be more
intolerable than the oppressions of civilized government.

Diocletian's reforms were in themselves rather
favourable than otherwise to the Christians. They
gained as much as their neighbours by the restoration
of order, and suffered only as others suffered from
the bad finance and arbitrary officialism of the new
system. But they had a gain of their own in the
weakening of the old Roman ideals. The Senate
had always been the focus of heathenism; and now
it was practically set aside by a ruler who treated
Italy as a province, and developed out on new lines
the universalism of the Empire which it had in
common with the Church. True, the universal
religion aimed at by Diocletian was only the old
paganism and emperor-worship: but by this time
any one might see that if he failed like others in
making it a living power, nothing remained but
Christianity. The idea of a Christian Caesar was
not now so far from practical politics as it seemed
to Tertullian.

This however was a question for the future
Meanwhile, for nearly twenty years (284-303) the
Christians had no reason to complain. They flourished

as they never had flourished before, and built stately
churches in the cities for the crowds who flocked
together.   They found their way into high civil
offices, and the courtesy of heathenism excused them
heathen ceremonies.   The scruples were more on their
own side.   Thus the Council of Elvira forbids a man
to attend the church during his year of office, in
which he had to judge cases of life and death, and
to overlook the Temples.   In Diocletian's palace they
abounded.   His trusted chamberlains were Christians, and his wife and daughter were more than
rumoured to be Christians, though that daughter
was the wife of Galerius.   But now that the fear of
persecution seemed to have passed away for ever,
the churches gathered numbers of unworthy followers,
and so disgraced themselves with disputes (all but
fightings) and episcopal quarrels and intrigues that
the storm which burst on them seemed a fitting
punishment for their " unspeakable hypocrisy." [1]   The
scandals were much the same before Constantine as
after him.

There are legends as usual of persecution in the
years of peace, like the cruelties of Rictius Varus in
Gaul, or Maximian's butchery of the whole Thebaean
legion in Rhaetia ; to which we may add the execution
of Alban in Britain, and perhaps that of the *Quattuor
coronati* by Diocletian.   But there do seem to have
been some Christians punished in the army, though
rather for insubordination than for their faith.   Thus
Maximilian and the centurion Marcellus had con-
temptuously renounced the service, and Cassianus
had approved such conduct in open court.   These
were under Maximian in 295 ; and if others were of

[1] Eus. *l.c.*

like mind, Galerius had some reason for turning Christians out of the army some years later. He dismissed officers who refused to sacrifice, and civil servants he "treated most disgracefully," even threatening some of them with death.[1] But he certainly did not carry out his threats; and it was quite understood that an officer might any day be required to sacrifice or leave the service. Hostile as Galerius was, his action does not seem to have raised any immediate fear of a more serious persecution.

Diocletian reminds us of Severus in his dealings with the Christians. He let them alone, and may have been really attached to individuals : yet he was not so friendly as he seemed. All accounts of him indicate a man of serious religion—there is no stain on his private life—and one of the last great men of the old Roman type. He was no monotheist like Constantius, but full of the superstitions of the camp; and his superstition, unlike that of Severus, turned to the gods rather than the stars. He began his reign with the prophecy of the "Druidess" at Tongres, took the name of Jovius, counted himself a special minister of the gods, and consulted the old oracle of Apollo at Miletus on the question of the persecution. Such a man was as far as possible from being only "not yet a Christian."[2] If he was driven to a final choice between the Galilean and the gods, he could not hesitate a moment.

---

[1] Eus. viii. *Appendix*.

[2] The "Letter of Theonas to Lucian" the Librarian, from which I take the phrase *nondum Chr. religioni ascriptus*, is a forgery of Jerome Vignier. It was denounced as such in 1886 by Batiffol, *Bulletin critique*, vii. 155. Harnack replied *Th.L.Z.* 1886 col. 319, suggesting an earlier date (say Valerian's time) and a Greek original, but allowing it to be very suspicious. Later study has satisfied him that the court presumed by the Letter is not Diocletian's, but that of Louis XIV. See *Th.L.Z.* 1904 col. 81.

But Diocletian was a wise man, and therefore in
no hurry to deliver an ultimatum to the churches.
In any case he was too busy to do anything till his
hands were freed in 297 by the peace with Persia ;
and even then followed five years more of quiet.   He
might well hesitate.   Some of the ablest of his predecessors had utterly failed to put down the Christians ;
and if the Empire was stronger now than in the days
of Decius and Valerian, so were they.   Their advance
in the last forty years was enormous.   They were not
scattered groups of skulking rebels who might sometimes be overlooked, but a great and strongly organized society which openly defied all Roman principles
of order and religion.   Diocletian may long have
hoped that the monster would not have to be grappled
with in his time : but if the need arose, his Manichaean
Edict of 296 [1] was warning enough that he would do

---

[1] Mason (*Pers. of Diocl.* 279) endeavours to clear Diocletian by shifting the
date to 308, and assuming that Galerius had restored him against his will at
Carnuntum in 307 as a purely nominal partner in the Empire.

In Haenel's text the edict runs *Impp. Maximianus, Diocletianus et
Maximinus nobilissimi A.A.A. Juliano proconsuli Africae. . . . Dat.
pridie Kal. Aprilis, Alexandriae.*

Given this text and looking no further, there is a fair case for explaining
the preference of Maximian to Diocletian (in this law alone out of some 1200)
by referring it to the *younger* Maximian (*i.e.* Galerius) and dating it after
Maximin Daza made himself Augustus in 308.

But (1) the reading is certainly corrupt (Huschke).   The MS. evidence is
confused, but not in its favour ; and Mommsen boldly reads the usual *Impp.
Diocletianus et Maximianus A.A. et Constantius et Maximianus nob. C.C.*
which gives 293-305 as the possible limits of date.

However that may be, (2) the reading is impossible.   Diocletian might
give orders to a proconsul of Africa, but neither Galerius nor Maximin, for
Africa under Alexander and Maxentius was subject to neither of them.   So
Mason proposes an imaginary *Proconsul Armeniae.*   A proconsul of Asia
would at least have had an existence : but the dilemma is hopeless.   Galerius
ruled Asia, but was certainly never at Alexandria after 308.   Maximin might
date from Alexandria, but was not master of Asia till Galerius was dead ;
and of Achaia he was never master at all.

We are thus driven back to Diocletian, and can safely take the date Mar.
31, 296 after the suppression of Archillaeus in Egypt.   Maximian was then

his work with a strong hand. If men were forsaking the old worship of the gods and going astray after novel and disgraceful superstitions, some of them brought in from Persia, such worthless persons must be punished for endeavouring in their blindness to destroy the good gifts which the mercy of the gods has granted to us. So the leaders of the heretics are to be burned, "together with their abominable books." Their followers are to be beheaded, or if they are men of rank, to be sent to the mines: and in all cases their property is to be confiscated.

An excellent way of dealing with the Christians, thought some of Diocletian's counsellors; and indeed the Christians were much more dangerous offenders than the Manichees. Galerius and Maximian hated them, and the court was full of soothsayers and Neoplatonists like Hierocles who clamoured for blood. Philosophy and superstition were made friends together as they drew to final battle with the church of Christ. Still Diocletian refused to give the signal, till some time in the winter of 302-3 he came to the conclusion that the struggle could no longer be avoided. He had spent a good deal of time in the East since 299, and come in direct collision with the Christians. One day the sacrifice was a failure. The gods would give no omens; and after awhile the chief haruspex declared that they were offended by the presence of profane persons. This touched Diocletian closely. He commanded that all persons in the palace should be required to sacrifice; and if they refused, they were to be scourged before they

---

busy in Africa with the Quinquegentiani. This date also suits well the hostile allusions to Persia. It is as well to add that *one* of the two years 295-6 and 296-7 is open for the proconsulship of Julianus in Africa.

were dismissed the service.   At the same time he
sent orders to the provincial governors that the
soldiers (as well as the officers) must sacrifice or leave
the service.[1]   However, he went no further at the
time; and even these orders were not fully carried
out.   Christians still held high office at Nicomedia,
and the army did not cease to furnish martyrs.   It
looks more like an explosion of superstitious terror
than a settled policy.   Diocletian's last hesitation is
said to have been overcome by Galerius after his
return to Nicomedia.   This is likely, for Galerius is
counted the worst of the Evil Beasts; but we may
be sure that it was not overcome by dint of worrying.
Diocletian was not a man to venture on the most
difficult work of his reign without reason shewn,
though he asked final guidance from the oracle at

---

[1] I follow here the clear note of time in Lact. *m.p.* 10 (*Cum ageret in
partibus Orientis*) distinguishing Diocletian's command on one side from the
earlier doings of Galerius, who disgraced the officers without scourging, and
on the other from the edict of Maximin Daza, who would not let them leave
the army.

To this period we may refer the persecution (Eus. *Chron.*) by Veturius a
magister militum (title proleptic) who may be the nameless στρατοπεδάρχης
(not στρατηλάτης) of Eus. viii. 4. 3.   Eus. also viii. 1. 8 confirms Lactantius
by saying that the persecution began with the army—which must be before
the First Edict.

We can name one sufferer with little risk of error.   Eus. *Mart. Pal.* 11
tells of the Cappadocian Seleucus, τῶν ἀπὸ στρατείας τις ὁμολογητής.   He was
in the picked troops (? Jovii) of the Empire, and held high rank in them.
After the scourging "at the beginning of the persecution," he devoted
himself to works of charity, and was one of the last of the martyrs.

Maximin's edict is known only from the recently discovered inscription of
bishop Eugenius of Laodicea (discussed by Calder and Ramsay *Expositor*
Seventh Ser. v. 385-419 Dec. 1908).   Eugenius fared worse than Seleucus.
He was not simply scourged and dismissed, but "endured innumerable
torments" without being allowed to leave.   But he was a man of rank
(married a senator's daughter) and got off at last.   Ramsay's discussion is
masterly: yet we may doubt whether Christian disaffection in the army was
serious enough in 311 to extract the edict of toleration from Galerius.   If the
danger was serious anywhere, it was in Maximin's dominions; and we see
little sign of it there before 313.

Miletus : and when he did venture, his policy was
not that of Galerius, who saw no difficulty in sending straight to the fire every one who refused to
sacrifice.

The signal was given on the morning of the
Terminalia (Feb. 23, 303) by the demolition of the
great church at Nicomedia. Next day the first
Edict of the Persecution was issued. The churches
were to be destroyed, the Scriptures to be burned.
Officials were to lose all civil rights whatever, and
Caesariani to be reduced to slavery.[1] It is policy,
not mercy—we may trust the author of the Mani-
chaean Edict for that—if there is no bloodshed here.
The edict is a careful revision of Valerian's. It

---

[1] Eus. viii. 2, Lact. *de mort. pers.* 13. The chief difficulty is in the last
clause τοὺς δὲ ἐν οἰκετίαις . . ἐλευθερίας στερεῖσθαι, answering to the previous
τοὺς μὲν τιμῆς ἐπειλημμένους, Krüger, *Preuszische Jahrb.* 1889 takes it to
mean that Christian slaves lost the possibility of freedom : but ἐλευθερίας
στερεῖσθαι (not στέρεσθαι) implies free men. Mason *Pers. Diocl.* 343,
followed by Harnack *Th.L.Z.* 1877 p. 169, interprets it of private persons,
and Harnack completes the edict from Rufinus by adding a further clause
depriving slaves of the possibility of freedom. Heinichen and M'Giffert *ad
loc.* reply that τοὺς ἐν οἰκετίαις (*qui in familia sunt*) is too clumsy for private
persons, who did not always belong to a *familia.* They quote *inter alia*
c. 6 of Dorotheus and Gorgonius ἑτέροις ἅμα πλείοσι τῆς βασιλικῆς οἰκετίας,
as shewing that it means the underlings, the *Hofleute*, contrasted with the
great officials (οἱ τιμῆς ἐπειλημμένοι, or οἱ ἐν ἀρχαῖς καὶ ἡγεμονίαις). The
absence of the article shews that the attendants of provincial governors
are also contemplated. They also quote the parallel of the *Caesariani* in
Valerian's edict, and add that it is difficult to explain the omission of the
clergy on any other theory, and that Diocletian was not likely to attempt
so vast a scheme as that of reducing all Christians to slavery, and that in
fact he did not do it. These arguments seem decisive also to v. Schubert
(*KG.* 394).

It may be safer to omit the further statement of Lactantius *m.p.* 13,
that Christians generally *religionis illius homines* were placed outside the
law—all charges admissible against them, all remedies of law refused them.
That would be true for the degraded officials and the *Caesariani* reduced to
slavery ; and the indirect results of the Edict may often have come to something like this for other Christians. But the statement is not confirmed by
the more careful words of Eusebius, and seems quite inconsistent with the
caution of Diocletian and his evident policy of striking only at the civil
service.

substitutes complete outlawry for death as the
punishment of officials, and says nothing of summarily executing the clergy, of confiscating and
exiling the great ladies, or of enslaving *Caesariani*
who had long ceased to be Christians.   On the other
hand, it enforces Valerian's prohibition of Christian
worship by destroying the churches, and introduces
a new policy [1] of burning the Scriptures, which had
important results on their text and on the Canon.
But there is nothing in it against private Christians,
or even against the clergy, and nothing that could
make martyrs, unless they refused to give up the
sacred books.   The policy is Valerian's, though there
is no sign of panic yet.   The Christians might be
put down without bloodshed if they were deprived
of their books, debarred their public meetings, and
thoroughly rooted out of the bureaucracy.

But the Christians were not more willing to be
put down than the Protestants of Mary's time.
Though they generally obeyed within the limits of
conscience and submitted beyond them, deep resent-
ment was universal, intemperate language common,
fierce defiance not rare.   No sooner was the edict
posted up at Nicomedia than some Christian tore it
down with bitter irony.   "More victories forsooth,
over Goths and Sarmatians."   The offender was
burned according to law for treason.   The next
thing was a fire in the palace, and another a fort-
night later—both of course set down to the Christians.
A panic followed.   Galerius took himself off in a
hurry, lest the miscreants should burn him alive.
Diocletian was wild with rage and suspicion, used

[1] New as against the Christians.   Hadrian had burned the copies of the
Law, and Diocletian himself those of the Manichaean books.

torture daily, put to death his favourite Christian chamberlains, and burned whole families in one fire ; but the cause was never found out.[1] Presently came news of commotions in Melitene and Syria, of course ascribed to the Christians, and even of a rival emperor set up for a moment at Antioch. Strong measures were needed against preachers of sedition ; and a second edict ordered the imprisonment of all Christian clergy.

Still there was to be no bloodshed for religion : and the emperor's moderation was rewarded by the sight of numbers returning to a better mind. Things quieted down before the autumn, so that when he went to Rome for the great festival of his Vicennalia (Nov. 21) he thought it safe to do an act of grace— for grace it was from his point of view. A third edict allowed the imprisoned clergy to go free on condition of sacrificing ; but it also allowed the use of all tortures to compel them. So the overcrowded prisons emptied fast. Some sacrificed, some got off in various honourable and dishonourable ways without sacrificing, and the rest remained, in some cases

---

[1] Accident or lightning may have kindled one fire, but a second is less likely. Supposing it designed, Christians may have hoped to frighten Diocletian from persecution, Galerius to frighten him into persecution. Schiller leans to the first theory ; but the second is the more likely of the two, for the servants of Galerius were not examined. After all, accident is not impossible. The late spring, I am told, is the time for thunderstorms in Asia.

Lactantius at Nicomedia was an eyewitness of the horrible cruelty of the panic ; and the worst feature of all, the wholesale burnings (*m.p.* 15 *gregatim circumdato igni ambiebantur*) is confirmed by Eusebius viii. 6, by his account *c.* 9 of similar doings in Phrygia, and by Ramsay's discovery (*Cities and Bprics. of Phrygia* ii. 505) of the great massacre at Eumenea. It is poor criticism to doubt such things merely because they are horrible. Exaggerated as they have been thought, I fear they must be set down for sober truth. They may however belong rather to the panic than to the more deliberate stages of the persecution.

till the edict of Galerius in 311.   Donatus was tortured nine times in the interval.[1]

Rome and Diocletian disagreed.   No love was lost between the grave statesman and the licentious mob, for even his triumph compared badly with the "jolly times" of Carinus.   So (Dec. 20) he left hastily, without even waiting to enter on his consulship on the Kalends of January.   Then came fourteen months of illness; and when he appeared again in public (Mar. 1, 305) he could hardly be recognized.   Meanwhile Maximian at Rome was presiding over the *ludi saeculares*, and took advantage of the cries of, Down with the Christians, and the ready approval of the Senate to issue a fourth edict, by which "it was ordered that all persons without exception in their respective cities should offer sacrifice and make libations to the gods."[2]

This was new.   Diocletian had avoided bloodshed for religion : Maximian liked nothing better. Diocletian aimed skilful blows at the churches, the books and the clergy : Maximian's only idea was to

[1] Lactantius *m.p.* 16.   Eusebius *Mart. Pal.* 2 tells us how Romanus saw Christians sacrificing σωρηδόν at Caesarea, and that he was the only person left in prison at Antioch at the amnesty.   The rest escaped ; and the case of Eusebius himself shews that they sometimes escaped honourably.   The methods of Roman prisons were lax ; and the stories in Eus. viii. 3 shew the lengths to which the officials went (sometimes, perhaps, in a sort of rude mercy) to get the jails emptied.

[2] Eus. *Mart. Pal.* 3.

I follow Mason (*Pers. Diocl.* 212) with some hesitation in accepting the historical data of the *Passio S. Savini*.   The edict is vouched for by Eusebius, the *ludi saeculares* in 304 by Zosimus ii. 7 ; and if we allow three days for them as in 248, and make them clear days before the birthday of Rome Apr. 21, when Philip held them, we come to the date Apr. 18.

But Mason has overlooked the difficulty that Eugenius Hermogenianus was not then P.U.—the usual president of the Senate and the natural intermediary between the emperor and the mob.   Another reading makes him Pf.P., which is a very unlikely office for a great Roman noble.   But a mistake in his title does not disprove an otherwise likely story.

force on every private Christian the choice between apostasy and death. But it was not all Maximian's doing. Diocletian may not have been quite laid aside by illness till later in the year; and if so, Maximian's edict would not have been carried out in Palestine if Diocletian had not been at least willing to try the experiment. The persecution had been very successful so far — persecutions usually do succeed at first—and he may well have thought it time to give up tactics and venture a frontal attack like that of Decius. Be that as it may, the new policy was hopeless from the first, because it could not be thoroughly carried out. It was wrecked on the conscience and humanity of heathenism. Only some of the officials had any liking for such dirty work, and even the mob was not very zealous. It was all very well to have some sport with the beasts every now and then; but when brutal torture of decent neighbours became an every-day affair, they voted it "vulgar, and grossly overdone."[1] Within two years this very mob of Rome had swung so completely round that Maxentius could win favour with them by stopping the persecution in Italy; and before it ended in the East, heathens at Alexandria were hiding the fugitives in their own houses. Heathenism produced some bad miscreants, and did hideous things by fits and starts; but Galerius and Daza were at worst no worse than Carlo Borromeo and Pius V, and they were never canonized.

Diocletian had long contemplated retirement, if we may judge by the splendour of his buildings at Salona, but his abdication (May 1, 305) was a surprise to the world. It was a surprise also, or at

---

[1] Eus. *Mart. Pal.* 3. 3.

least a disappointment, to his colleague Maximian,
who had to abdicate the same day at Milan.
Constantius and Galerius now became *Augusti*. But
first, who were to be the new Caesars? Diocletian
and Galerius had daughters only; Maximian and
Constantius had each a grown-up son. Maxentius
the son of Maximian had most of his father's vices
with few of his merits, so that his exclusion surprised
nobody. But Constantine the son of Constantius
was an officer of tried merit, and Diocletian seemed
reserving for him a place in the succession. He had
kept him at the court, betrothed him to Fausta the
daughter of Maximian, and must have given some
public intimation of his intention, for coins were
struck about this time at Alexandria with the legend
Constantinus Caesar.[1] But when the time came, the
Caesars announced were both connexions of Galerius
—his old comrade Severus, and his nephew Maximin
Daia or Daza. They were not incapables. Severus
was a good officer; and if Daza was as brutal as his
uncle and more malicious, he had also more shrewd-
ness. His last attack on the churches was as ably
planned as Diocletian's own. Severus replaced
Maximian in Italy, Africa and Spain, but Daza did
not replace Diocletian in the East. He received
Egypt and Syria, while Asia inside Taurus increased
the position of Galerius.

Constantius was now the first *Augustus*; but his
health was declining, and Galerius might fairly hope

---

[1] Count de Westphalen *Rev. Numism.* 1887, 20-39 : discussed by Schiller
Röm. Kaiserzeit ii. 167.   This confirms Lactantius *m.p.* 19, who tells us
how all expected to hear Constantine announced as Caesar.

Diocletian must have changed his plan at the last moment.   If we suppose
that he was reserving Constantine to succeed his father, the actual choice of
Caesars can be explained without ascribing any undue influence to Galerius.

soon to complete his control of the Empire by setting up some nominee of his own in Gaul and Britain. Two unexpected events defeated his plans. First, Constantine escaped to his father, and on the death of Constantius at York (July 25, 306) was hailed emperor by the army of Britain, headed by Crocus the Alemannic king — the first imperial election guided by barbarians. After his first fury, Galerius acknowledged him, but only as *Caesar*, giving the title of *Augustus* to Severus. It mattered little. Constantine had the power, and the title came a little later.

Three months later (Oct. 28, 306) the discontent of Rome was exploded by an attempt of Galerius to impose on the city the full taxation of the provinces. Praetorians and Senate set up Maxentius for Caesar, and invited his father to resume the purple. Maximian wanted nothing better, and his military skill enabled him to repel Severus and force him to surrender on honourable terms. But Maxentius [1] "made siccar" by putting him to death when Galerius himself invaded Italy. Galerius also was driven out of the country, narrowly escaping capture. In his distress, he turned for counsel to Diocletian, and held a meeting with him at Carnuntum (Nov. 307). Thither also came Maximian, who by this time had quarrelled with his son, and been obliged to leave Italy. Diocletian could not help much; but he removed one difficulty by forcing Maximian to abdicate again. The old man betook himself to Gaul with his daughter Fausta, whom he gave in marriage to Constantine. Severus was replaced as

---

[1] As Schiller points out, Maximian could not have appeared at Carnuntum if the execution of Severus had been his work.

Augustus by Licinius, another old comrade of Galerius, who gave up to him the Illyrian provinces. So for the next four years we have an uneasy tetrarchy of four emperors—Galerius, Daza, Constantine and Licinius; besides Maxentius, whom none of them recognized, and Alexander, who revolted from him for a couple of years (308-310) in Africa. Maximian was put out of the way when he seized the purple a third time, and tried to displace Constantine.

We can now trace the history of the persecution. In Gaul and Britain it was not serious. Constantius pulled down a few churches, but did nothing more. Even the books were not given up; and he abandoned all pretence of persecution as soon as his hands were free. In the rest of the Empire the edicts were at first vigorously carried out. The work was done in Italy by Maximian himself, and under his orders by Dacianus in Spain and Anulinus in Africa. After his abdication it slackened, and it was definitely stopped by Maxentius, who even restored the confiscated church property when he recovered Africa in 310. Worthless as he was, he is not counted among the Evil Beasts.

The East was less fortunate; and the difference was made by the character of its rulers, not by any greater "fanaticism of the Christians."[1] Syria was

---

[1] Schiller *Röm. Kaiserzeit* ii. 160. Like Gibbon, he makes too much of Christian "fanaticism." It is misleading to tell us p. 155 that "Christianity denied the heathen state . . . in the second and third century forbade the faithful all share in a heathen administration, and counted military service pure and simple sin." Christians only "denied the state" as English nonconformists deny it now, by refusing it all authority in religion. Speratus the Scillitan martyr, who said, "I allow not this world's rule," went on, "but I pay my taxes, because God is a king of kings." The other two points were private opinions then, as they are private opinions now. The Christians generally were not more eccentric then than they are now.

hardly more " fanatic " than Africa, and the Egyptian martyrs could not be more defiant than the Spanish. Even in the East however, Licinius was never an active persecutor, and Galerius himself presently tired of the work of blood. He had not done well as senior *Augustus*, and withdrew to the more useful occupation of cutting down trees and draining swamps in the regions of the Danube, so that the persecution was relaxed in Asia. Its full fury fell on Maximin Daza's provinces of Egypt and Syria; and there too it was kept up longer than elsewhere. Shortly, the persecution lasted in Gaul and Britain till Constantius became *Augustus* in 305, in Italy and Africa till the revolt of Maxentius in 306; in Asia it was finally stopped by the edict of Galerius in April 311, in Egypt and Syria not till after Maximin's defeat at the end of April 313.

Of the character and methods of the persecution, there is little that needs to be said. Horrible as the accounts are, they seem to be substantially true. It is likely enough that Eusebius has exaggerated the number of the victims in a few of his rhetorical passages, though one of the worst of his tales, the burning of a whole community in a Phrygian village, is confirmed not only by Lactantius,[1] but by recent discoveries at Eumenea; but there is no reason to doubt that the tortures he mentions were actually inflicted. Such had always been the treatment of slaves in Roman law courts, and the Empire steadily extended it to the higher classes. It was sharpened in that age by the blind violence of a weak Executive, which was less and less able to make sure of catching offenders, and therefore more and more in the habit

---

[1] Lact. *Div. Inst.* v. 11.

of making terrible examples of those it did catch :
and it was further sharpened against the Christians
by the savage hatred of some of the officials, and by
their growing consciousness of failure.   And if the
cruelty was often moderated, it was not uncommonly
increased, by loose methods of administration.[1]   Nor
need we mistrust the general impression we get, that
the persecution shocked the better sort of heathens
not only by its inhumanity, but by the number of its
victims.   No doubt a vast mass of legend grew up
in ages which cultivated an unhealthy taste for the
physical facts of martyrdom ; but the authentic
narratives imply an enormous amount of suffering
not directly recorded.   It is uncritical to take for
granted, as some writers seem to do, that there were
no executions but those Eusebius by name records,[2]
and no sufferers from persecution but those actually
brought into court.

After all, the worst mischief of persecution, like
that of slavery, is not the suffering of the few, but
the demoralization of the many.   The heroic scenes
in court must not be allowed to obscure the growth
of spiritual pride and quarrelling and general confusion in the churches.   Persecution always brings to
the front the men who manufacture scruples, make
divisions, and are hard on the weak and fallen.   In
this case, the new scruple concerned the burning of
the books.   All parties were agreed that the canonical
books must be defended at every hazard, and stigma-

---

[1] For samples.   On one side the significant words of the officers to Felix
of Aptunga, " Books, books ; have you no useless books to spare ? " and the
refusal of Anulinus to listen to information that Mensurius of Carthage had
not given up all the books.   On the other, the illegal scourgings of the
woman at Caesarea by an underling Eus. *Mart. Pal.* 9.

[2] Especially when *Mart. Pal.* 8 he distinctly tells us that there were many
others.

tized as *traditores* those who gave them up. But was it right to give up other books? The question became acute in Africa, where Mensurius of Carthage gave orders to remove canonical books from the churches, and leave the officers to seize those that were read only for edification—which often satisfied them. Out of this arose the Donatist controversy, which figures so largely in the history of the next century. Extreme men first made it an offence to give up books of any sort. Then they disputed the election of Caecilian, the successor of Mensurius, because he had been consecrated by Felix of Aptunga, who had given up books, though not canonical books —that is to say, they advanced to the position that the unworthiness of such a *traditor* made all his ministerial acts invalid. Then when it was decided against them that Felix was not a *traditor*, they separated from the church. And as they did not simply separate like the Novatians on the ground that the church was acting *ultra vires*, but denounced its action as apostasy pure and simple, they took up the further position that a church which allows the ministrations of such *traditores* is no longer a church at all. The Donatist controversy was therefore much more bitter than the Novatian.

Things were not so bad elsewhere, but there must have been much confusion. With churches destroyed, books burned, and clergy in prison, it was impossible to keep things orderly. Eusebius expressly tells us[1] that he passes over " the greed of power on the part of many, the hasty and unlawful ordinations, the divisions among the confessors themselves, and all the schemes which the lovers of novelty and faction

[1] *Mart. Pal.* 12.

so zealously devised against the remnants of the churches, inventing one new device after another, and forcing it on without sparing, in the midst of the calamities of the persecution." Even Rome did not escape. When bishop Marcellus (307-9) endeavoured to restore order after the persecution, a strong rigoristic party refused its consent to the restoration of penitents, and in the time of his successor Eusebius formed a schism under one Heraclius. Maxentius exiled both bishops, apparently as disturbers of the peace. The schism was, healed, no doubt by the defeat of the rigorists, in the time of the next bishop, Miltiades or Melchiades.

In Egypt, where the persecution was fiercer and continued longer, Peter of Alexandria held a moderate position. He condemned fanaticism, advised flight when possible, and was willing to restore penitents without waiting for the end of the persecution. But when he went into hiding like Cyprian, Meletius of Lycopolis took upon himself the government of the churches, entirely disregarding Peter's commissaries, encouraging fanaticism and making irregular appointments in all the churches. As these views agreed better than Peter's with the temper of the native Copts, a serious division arose in Egypt when peace was restored. The Nicene Council healed the actual schism; but the bitterness resulting from it lasted far into the long reign of Athanasius at Alexandria.

Our best picture of the persecution is given by Eusebius on the Martyrs of Palestine, a small work commonly inserted between the eighth and ninth books of his History. It is the evidence of an eye-witness, and differs from the History generally in its excellent arrangement. It refers only to Palestine, though we know that similar scenes were going on all over the Empire except in Gaul and Britain. As the first edict did not reach Palestine till April 303, it must have been somehow delayed. The first victim (June 7) was Procopius, a reader of the church at Caesarea. It is not clear whether his case arose under the first edict or the second; but either way it was quite irregular. Neither the one nor the other authorized a demand of sacrifice to the gods or libation to the emperors, and after all, he was not beheaded for his refusal, but for quoting Homer's οὐκ ἀγαθὸν πολυκοιρανίη—a dangerous text in Diocletian's time, and doubly dangerous now that the authorities wanted to make up a charge of treason. Then came the arrest of the clergy under the second edict and the tortures inflicted under the third, to make them sacrifice. Some yielded, some got off in the usual ways, for the authorities were anxious to empty the jails, and in the end only two were beheaded, for the treason of declaring that they had no king but Christ. With the fourth edict a dreadful time began. Neither youths nor women were spared. But it is a shame even to speak of those years of horror.

By 308 it was becoming evident that the persecution was a failure. It had long ceased in the West, and was not very active even where Galerius ruled. At last Maximin came to the conclusion that it was prudent to avoid public burnings. So a fifth edict commanded that the Christians should have the left foot disabled and the right eye cut out and its socket seared, and then be sent to slavery in the mines, where further cruelty could be used without attracting too much sympathy. Once thirty-nine of them were put to death in one day. But public executions did not cease even then ; and a reissue of the fourth edict brought forth fresh victims. But no efforts could keep up for long the full horror of the persecution. The last of the Palestinian martyrs was given to the beasts Mar. 3, 310.

The deliverance began in the next year. The Evil Beast was passing to his account. Galerius was stricken with a mortal sickness (in which the Christians read the wrath of heaven) and issued an edict of toleration (Apr. 311) a few days before his death. Its purport is :—[1]

Galerius, Constantine and Licinius to their subjects, greeting. Amongst our other efforts for the public good, we formerly desired so to reform the state in accordance with the old laws and public discipline of the Romans that the Christians also, who had given up the manner of life [2] laid down by their own ancestors, might return to a better mind. For these Christians had reasoned so strangely, and become so possessed with self-will and folly, that they were not following those institutes of the ancients which perhaps their own ancestors had first established,[3] but were making laws for themselves after their own good-will and pleasure, and by divers means collecting assemblies of divers peoples.[4] When therefore we issued our command that they should betake themselves to the institutes of the ancients,[5]

---

[1] The Latin (simply as *Edictum Galerii*) in Lact. *m.p.* 34 : translated κατὰ τὸ δυνατόν in Eus. *H.E.* viii. 17. He renders *disciplinam* ἐπιστήμην, and adds after *deturbati sunt* the excellent gloss παντοίους θανάτους ὑπέφερον.

I have shortened a few sentences in my own translation.

[2] *Parentum suorum sectam.* *Secta* is not here αἵρεσις religious persuasion (Eus.) but general manner of life, as freq.

[3] *Illa veterum instituta, quae forsitan primum parentes eorundem constituerant.* *Forsitan* with *parentes*, not with *constituerant* (*Ind.* : not *Subj.*).

[4] *Per diversa varios populos congregarent* i.e. it was not a national worship.

[5] *Multi periculo subiugati* (and yielded), *multi etiam deturbati sunt.*

many of them were overcome by the danger and many were utterly ruined; and when further [1] a great number of them held to their persuasion, and we saw that they neither gave due reverence to our gods nor worshipped their own god, we thought fit to extend to them our accustomed clemency, that it may be lawful for Christians to exist again [2] and to hold their assemblies, provided they do nothing contrary to the discipline. In another letter we will give particular instructions to our officials. In accordance then with this our indulgence it will be the duty of the Christians to make prayer to their god for our welfare, for the welfare of the state, and for their own.

There is no repentance here. The persecution was well meant; but there was a serious oversight. The thought is so intensely heathen that we shall need some care to trace it. Galerius seems to say, "We never quarrelled with the Christians for worshipping their own god, but for not worshipping our gods also: and it was right and good that we should try to bring them back to a truly Roman way of life. But we forgot one thing. In compelling the Christians to worship our gods we made it impossible for them to worship their own god; and this was not our intention. We never meant to deprive him of his proper worship—only to see that our own gods were not deprived of theirs. He is also a god who has lately shewn a good deal of power, so that he may be able to help us now in our extremity, if we set right the wrong we are doing him. We still regret the self-willed and undutiful action of the Christians;

---

[1] *atque* (not *etsi*) reciting a third and still more serious evil.

[2] *Ut denuo sint Christiani.* The opposite would be *Non licet esse vos.*

but even so, we are satisfied that it is better to let them worship their god in their own way than to continue doing what prevents him from being worshipped at all; and for this our clemency we hope they will be duly grateful to us."

Thus understood, the edict gives a dignified and fairly true account of the persecution from the official heathen point of view. Galerius is not making inconsistent and absurd excuses for it,[1] but confessing a serious oversight, and frankly asking the Christians for their intercession with their god. The long contest of nearly 250 years is at last decided. Nero took up the sword of persecution, and now Galerius lays it down. The victory is not yet complete, for Maximin's action remains to be seen : and there may have been another limitation. Galerius is not now unfriendly, but grants on his own heathen principles that the Christians must be treated as a nation,[2] and therefore allowed to worship their god in their own way. So far the toleration is ungrudging, and the letter of instructions to the officials is not likely to

---

[1] I really cannot follow Keim and others, who make Galerius say that the Christians had broken out into sects, and the persecution was only meant to bring them back to primitive Christianity, *ut denuo sint Christiani* —to make them genuine Christians again.

Could Galerius possibly mean anything but the good old customs of heathen Rome in such phrases as *iuxta leges veteres et publicam disciplinam Romanorum—parentum suorum sectam—ad bonas mentes redirent—illa veterum instituta, quae forsitan primum parentes eorundem constituerant?* Again, as to many Christians, there was a fair doubt (*forsitan*) whether their barbarian ancestors first set up Roman heathenism ; but there could be no doubt at all that the ancestors of the Christians first set up Christianity.

Galerius was a brute, and therefore a short-sighted statesman ; but when we can get a perfectly clear and consistent sense without straining his words, we need not take another meaning which makes him a public liar or an absolute fool—or both. Even weaker is von Schubert's theory (*KG.* 298) that the edict is designedly ambiguous.

[2] So they are expressly called in the instructions of Sabinus, and again in Maximin's Edict of Toleration.

have contained " many hard conditions." [1]   But Galerius holds to the old theory, that every nation has its god, and every god is entitled to the worship of his own nation.   But unlike Licinius, he gives no hint that this toleration extends beyond those who were Catholic Christians ; and on his principle, we should rather expect that it would not.   However, the advance was very great.   Had Galerius only repeated the action of Gallienus, the change of circumstances would have made an enormous difference.   The Peace of Vervins in 1598 simply repeated the conditions of Cateau Cambresis in 1559 ; but between them lay the great failure of Philip II. So here, between Gallienus and Galerius lay the failure of Diocletian ; and Maximin and Julian were not likely to succeed in a task which had been too hard for Diocletian, and grown harder since.   But while Gallienus only undid the persecution, Galerius gave legal toleration.   For the first time Christianity was recognized as a *religio licita*, with all the rights therein implied.

We shall have noticed that the edict does not bear Maximin's name.   As the Empire was not divided— only the imperial power—it is unlikely that Galerius and Licinius omitted to insert it.   Rather it was erased after his fall.   The edict was most distasteful to him, and yet he could not disregard it ; so he published it, not as an edict, or even as a rescript, but simply as an instruction issued by his *Praefectus Praetorio* Sabinus to the *praesides* of the provinces. And in this it appears with serious changes.   It similarly justifies the persecution, but the reason for

---

[1] The Letter of Licinius, as we shall see, is not referring in this phrase to the edict of Galerius, but to Maximin's later doings.

stopping it is simply that Maximin does not wish to
bring the Christians into so great danger, since they
cannot be reclaimed from their obstinacy. The
conclusion is not *ut denuo sint Christiani*, but that
directions are to be given to the curators and praetors
of the cities and the overseers of the villages, that
they are not bound to give further attention to the
matter. This is not the toleration of Galerius : it is
a mere respite which gives no sort of security that
the persecution will not be resumed at the next
convenient time. However, it was enough. The
officials were not sorry to release the confessors from
the prisons and the mines, and—for the moment—
there was general rejoicing, not unshared by the
heathens themselves.

The edict of Galerius was published at Nicomedia
Apr. 30, 311, and the emperor died a few days later
After a sharp quarrel between Licinius and Maximin,
they divided his dominions, Maximin taking the
Asiatic provinces. In less than six months he began
a fresh persecution, though not quite on the old lines.
Craft was needed, now that brute slaughter was
impossible : and to do Maximin justice, his policy
was even abler than Diocletian's. His first step
indeed, forbidding meetings at the tombs of the
martyrs, was a bit of petty malice reminding us of his
endeavour two or three years before to starve out the
Christians by ordering all food sold in the market to
be first defiled with idols. Nor did he go beyond the
older Maximin (235-238) in striking at the Christian
leaders. So far as we know, his victims were men
of mark—Anthimus of Nicomedia, Silvanus of Emesa,
Peter of Alexandria, and the learned elder Lucian of
Antioch.

It is in other measures that we trace the three
lines of skilful policy distinctive of Maximin's last
persecution. The first is the plan of systematically
stirring up, not mobs to lynch the Christians, but
the municipal authorities to repress them. His chief
agent was Theotecnus, an active persecutor in
past years, and now a great charlatan at Antioch.
Petitions came in, from Antioch first, either instigated
by Maximin himself or presented in reliance on his
known wishes. Some objected to the building of a
church within the walls, others asked permission to
expel the Christians entirely from the city and its
territory. Such piety was heartily welcomed, and the
gracious answers of the Lord Augustus were inscribed
on pillars by his loyal citizens *in perpetuam rei
memoriam*.[1]

The next step was to bring the chaos of heathenism
into better order. The priests of the official gods
had never formed a clergy like those of the Eastern
worships and the Christians. The priests of Rome
and Augustus were magnates, and first and chiefly
magnates. A few of the gods had priests at Rome
and elsewhere, but the old royal houses were extinct
in most of the cities, and left no regular successors.
In many cases, any one who knew the ritual, or said
he did, or had been commissioned in a dream to
restore it, would come forward and act as priest.
After all, the priests were in no greater confusion
than the gods themselves. Could not a hint be
taken from the strong organization of the Christians,
with their bishops and clergy, and regular arrange-

[1] Eusebius x. 7 gives in full the inscription set up at Tyre. It has quite
a modern ring. "Now that Christianity is altogether exploded etc. etc."
The gods are a paraphrase for Science.

ments for worship? Could they not be confronted
with a great catholic church of heathenism? So,
says Lactantius,[1] he appointed a high priest for each
city from among its magnates. His duty was to
offer sacrifices daily to all the gods, and with the
help of the old priests to hinder the Christians from
building churches or holding public or private
meetings; and he had authority to arrest them and
compel them to offer sacrifice and to bring them
before the courts. Moreover, he established in each
province a man of higher rank as Superintendent. It
was a clever imitation—if there had been any life in
it. One feature of the scheme was of itself enough
to make it a failure. Maximin has not got over the
old aristocratic spirit of heathenism, which ruled that
priests must not be *probati seniores*, but magnates.

After this, education had to be put on a sound
heathen footing. Some *Acts of Pilate* were found
useful. They were not a very skilful composition,
for they dated the Crucifixion before Pilate became
procurator of Judaea. But they were full of slanders
on Christ; and that was enough. So they were set
up everywhere by authority for public edification,
much as the Bible was set up by Henry VIII: and
it was further ordered that they should be studied
and diligently learned in all the schools. Maximin
had discovered the merits of "definite teaching" in
religion. If a child is trained up from his tenderest
years in hatred and disgust for some very pestilent
error (in this case Christianity) he is very likely to
give up all serious belief in religion; but he will
seldom fall into the more deadly sin of going astray
after that particular heresy.

[1] Lact. *m.p.* 36.

Given his twenty years of resolute government, Maximin might have done wonders; but he did not get as many months to carry out his policy.

There were now four emperors — Constantine, Maxentius, Licinius, Maximin—corresponding to the four great praefectures of the Gauls, Italy, Illyricum and the East in later time, except that Maxentius, held Spain, and Licinius Thrace. Their relations to each other were naturally determined by their geographical position, for Constantine stretched across Italy to Licinius, and Maximin across Illyricum to Maxentius. So also Constantine was more and more a monotheist and well disposed to the Christians, and Licinius had never been an active persecutor; whereas Maximin was their chief enemy, and Maxentius was not friendly. He had stopped the persecution only because the public opinion of heathenism was disgusted by it. Standing as he did for Rome, the Senate, and everything reactionary, he could not but be in principle hostile to them.

The personal contrast of the Western rulers was very great. Constantine was blameless in private life, careful of his subjects, and active in the work of government, though even the heathens blamed him [1] when he gave Frankish kings to the beasts, along with their followers by thousands. Maxentius was oppressive and slothful, and seemed to value his imperial dignity only as an opportunity for unlimited adultery. Yet he had his ambition, and gathered forces to crush Constantine, while Maximin was to deal with Licinius.

Constantine did not wait to be attacked by over-

[1] The applause of the Panegyrists vi. 4, vii. 12 is too laboured to be genuine.

whelming numbers. Breaking up his camp at
Colmar, he pushed rapidly across the Alps with a
seasoned army, though a small one, for he would not
leave the Rhine unguarded. First he stormed Susa :
then came a cavalry fight near Turin, in which the
Gauls overcame the formidable *cataphracti*—horse
and rider clad in mail [1]—of Maxentius. After a few
days of needed rest at Milan, he made straight for
Verona ; and there he found in Ruricius Pompeianus
a foeman worthy of his steel. Right well did
Pompeianus hold Verona for his unworthy master,
and he escaped from the siege only to gather an
army for its relief. Then another great battle was
fought. Pompeianus was killed, Verona surrendered,
and Constantine marched at once on Rome. He could
not have besieged the city with far inferior forces ;
but at the last moment Maxentius came out (Oct.
27, 312) a few miles to Saxa Rubra, and offered
battle with the Tiber behind him and the Mulvian
bridge for his retreat. [2] Once again the Numidians
gave way before the Gaulish cavalry, the Praetorian
guard fell fighting where it stood, and the rest of the
army was driven headlong down the steep banks into
the river. Maxentius perished in the waters, and
Constantine was hailed by Rome as her deliverer
from his " pestiferous tyranny."

Though the war was not a war of religion,
Constantine's cause was the cause of the Christians
and their hopes must have risen higher at each
successive step of this wonderful career of victory.
Had not God raised up a Cyrus from the West ? and

---

[1] Description in Ammianus, xvi. 10. 8.

[2] Yet v. Moltke is said to have approved his strategy. Napoleon did the
same thing at Leipsic ; and with disastrous consequences, when the bridge of
the Elster blew up.

would he not subdue the nations before him? It
was a crisis too for Constantine himself. Somewhere
between Colmar and Saxa Rubra came the vision of
the Shining Cross. Shortly after noonday he saw in
the sky a cross of light, with the words *Hoc vince*,
and the army saw it too; and in a dream that night
Christ bade him take it for his standard. So
Constantine himself told Eusebius, and confirmed it
with an oath, and so Eusebius recorded it in 338;[1]
and there is no need to charge either of them with
deceit. Lactantius[2] has the story as early as 315;
but he puts the cross in the night vision. That
something of the sort happened seems clear from the
heathen Nazarius[3] in 321. Yet neither need we
take it like Eusebius, as a miracle. The cross in the
sky may very well have been some halo, like the
three crosses for his three lost companions, which
Whymper saw as he came down after the accident
on the Matterhorn in 1865: the rest would be
Constantine's interpretation of it. But here it must
be noted that the cross was not a distinctively Christian
symbol, but one of the ambiguities so characteristic
of Constantine. He was beyond all doubt a clear
monotheist, but he does not seem himself to have
been quite certain (at least till 323) whether his one
God was the God of the Christians or *Sol invictus*.
The Gauls had fought of old beneath the Sun-god's

---

[1] Eus. *V.C.* i. 28, 29. He does not mention it in his *H.E.* : but we do
not know when Constantine told him.

[2] Lact. *m.p.* 44. His evidence need not be discredited by the similar
vision he gives (c. 46) to the old heathen Licinius. If Constantine had one
vision, why should not Licinius take the hint, and claim another? It might
be a good stroke of policy.

[3] *Pan.* x. 14. Schiller (*Röm. Kais.* ii. 204) is reckless. He ignores
Lactantius, charges Eusebius with falsehood (*angeblich* Konstantin selbst)
and gratuitously discredits Nazarius as *christianisierende*. This is special
pleading.

cross of light; so while the Christians would see in
the Labarum the cross of Christ, the heathen soldiers
would simply be receiving back an ancient standard.

Maximin soon received from Constantine the news
of Saxa Rubra. As his connexion with Maxentius
was known, the letter is not likely to have been
friendly: but the fact he had to reckon with was
that he had lost his ally, and must do something to
keep the Christians quiet while he made his attack
on Licinius. So before the end of 312 he issued a
rescript to Sabinus. It is a strange document, and
Mason's summary of it is not too severe. "First he
justifies bloody persecution, then plumes himself on
having stopped it, next apologizes for having set it
again on foot, then denies that it was going on, and
lastly orders it to cease."[1] He actually tells us that
no Christian was exiled or insulted "after he first
came into the East" in 305. Neither Christian nor
heathen could find any meaning in such a mass of
inconsistencies, except that Maximin was a prodigious
liar. With all his cleverness, he never stopped to
consider that a malicious and crafty persecutor like
himself could not hope to conciliate the Christians
without the plainest and fullest assurances, and the
most resolute action on them. Even then they would
have been slow to trust him: to issue such a mysti-
fication as this was only playing the buffoon.

Constantine remained two months in Rome,
abolishing the Praetorian Guard, introducing the
Galerian taxation, and preparing for his meeting
with Licinius at Milan in Jan. 313. Its public
occasion was the marriage of Licinius to his sister
Constantia; but the two rulers especially discussed

---

[1] *Pers. Diocl.* 334. I see no escape from his conclusion.

the subject of religion, in view of Maximin's persistent evasion of the Galerian edict. Their own edict (the Edict of Milan) is lost; but Licinius recites[1] the substance of it a few months later. They had long ago given complete liberty in religion to all men, and particularly to the Christians : but the rescript issued in pursuance of this edict had encumbered it with so many detailed conditions that the Christians were deterred from availing themselves of it. So on the auspicious occasion of their meeting at Milan, they thought fit especially to treat of religion, and to grant full power to Christians as well as others to follow whatever religion they please to think best suited to them; that so, whatever divinity there is in heaven[2] may be able to look with favour on the emperors and their subjects. And these decisions would seem to have been embodied in an edict now lost.[3]

The wedding festivities were rudely interrupted

[1] I am taking it that the passage *Cum felicitur . . . benevolentiamque praestare* in the *Litterae Licinii* (Lact. *m.p.* 48) is a preamble reciting their decisions at Milan, so that the Letter properly begins at *Quare scire Dicationem tuam convenit.*

Eusebius x. 5 has it in Greek, with variations generally for the worse. But he calls it ἀντίγραφον βασιλικῶν (Κωνστ. καὶ Λικ.) διατάξεων, and prefixes to the preamble of Lactantius another. "Considering long ago that freedom of worship ought not to be denied, but that authority should be given to every one by his own understanding and will to attend to things divine as he purposes himself, we had commanded all men, and the Christians in particular, each to preserve the faith of his own sect. But since in the rescript (ἀντιγραφή) in which such liberty was granted them, many various conditions (αἱρέσεις) appeared to be set forth in detail (σαφῶς), some perhaps of them were after a short time deterred from such observance."

"Our command" will therefore be the edict of Galerius, the rescript that of Maximin.

[2] No English can do justice to the magnificent vagueness of ὅ τι ποτέ ἐστι θειότητος καὶ οὐρανίου πράγματος, as Eus. translates it.

[3] The issue of an edict from Milan seems proved by the heading in Eus. x. 5 ἀντίγραφον (copy) βασιλικῶν διατάξεων (edict) where the context shews that βασ. refers to Constantine as well as Licinius. But what he actually

by the news that Maximin was on the move. A
sudden attack in the depth of winter might repeat
the success of Constantine. So Byzantium fell, and
Heraclea. Presently Licinius met him near Hadria-
nople with so inferior an army that he tried to
negotiate. But the battle (Apr. 30, 313) was
decisive. By sundown the next day Maximin was
a fugitive at Nicomedia across the Bosphorus, 160
miles away. He could not even defend Asia, but
was thrown back on Taurus. As he could not hope
to maintain himself in Egypt and Syria without
conciliating the Christians, he made up his mind to
do it effectually. This time he issued no rescript to
Sabinus, but an edict to all his subjects. Its purport
is—Our constant care for our subjects and their
welfare is well known to all. When therefore it
became plain to our knowledge, that under pretence
of the command of Diocletian and Maximian abolishing the meetings of the Christians, many oppressions
and spoliations were perpetrated by the officials, and
that these abuses, so painful to all good rulers, were
growing worse in course of time, we sent letters last
year (the rescript to Sabinus) to the governors of the
provinces, in which we decreed that if any one wished
to follow such a nation [1] or to observe the same
worship, he might do so without hindrance. But
even now we cannot help seeing that some of our
judges have mistaken our commands and caused our
subjects to doubt our meaning and hesitate to use the

---

gives in Greek is the *Litterae Licinii* of Lact.—the ἀντιγραφή (*rescriptum*) in
which Licinius recites it and gives orders to carry it out.

The substitution is natural. Maximin of course did not publish the edict
in the East, where Lact. and Eus. lived ; and very likely neither did Licinius
trouble to publish it afresh. If so, it would be represented to them by the
rescript of Licinius which they give.   [1] ἔθνει.

freedom we had granted them. In order then to remove all suspicion of doubt or fear, we have commanded this decree to be published, that it may be plain to all, that such as wish to follow this sect and worship are by this grant of ours at liberty to do so —namely, to adopt and to practise this religion. They are also allowed to build Lord's Houses. We also decree that if any houses or lands belonged of right to the Christians, and have been confiscated either to our treasury or by the cities—that these are to be restored to belong by right again to the Christians.

If Maximin does not speak so truly as Galerius had done, he speaks with as much dignity, and is quite straightforward this time. He might be trusted now that he had no choice. It mattered little. The edict cannot have been published beyond Egypt and Syria, which still remained to Maximin. On his death about June 313, Licinius of course ignored it, and published his own rescript instead. This rescript was posted at Nicomedia June 313. It begins, as we have seen, by reciting the conclusions reached at Milan. Then it goes on—

Wherefore you must know our pleasure that all the conditions contained in letters formerly sent to your office concerning the Christians shall be utterly annulled, and that every one of those who are agreed in desiring to observe the Christian religion shall observe the same without any trouble or annoyance. The same liberty of confession and of worship is extended to other religions, so that every one shall have freedom in the worship he has chosen, for we will have no distinction made against any rank or religion. This also we have determined concerning the Christians—that if the places where they formerly assembled (concerning which special orders were given in the former letter) have been sold by our treasury or by any others, they shall be restored freely, without delay or equivocation, to the Christians. Present owners shall give them up at once, and shall obtain relief from our bounty by petition to the *Vicarius praefectorum.* All these shall be restored at once and without delay by your mediation to the corporation of the Christians. So also of all other possessions which belonged of right to the Christians. You will publish these commands and diligently perform them.

A similar rescript of Constantine to Anulinus the proconsul of Africa commands the restoration of church property, but to the catholic church only, not to heretics. The limitation is deliberate : Constantine repeats it in another letter to Anulinus, granting exemption from political offices to the clergy " of the catholic church, over which Caecilianus presides." [1]

Comparing together the edicts of Galerius, of Maximin, and of Constantine and Licinius, they are all agreed in frank allowance of Christian worship : but Galerius allows it on the old heathen principle that every god is entitled to the worship of his own people, Maximin allows it of his imperial clemency without stating any principle at all, but Constantine and Licinius lay down the new principle, that every man is entitled to choose his religion and to practise it in his own way. A very Christian principle no

---

[1] Eus. x. 5, 7. Anulinus was no longer proconsul in Oct. 313 ; so the letters must be earlier.

ἡ καθ. ἐκκλ. cannot be taken for the Christians in general. This is not its usual sense ; and Constantine had had trouble enough with the Donatists to impress the difference on him.

doubt; but there is no sign that they came to it from any Christian ideas of the supremacy of conscience. For Licinius it was manifest policy to tolerate the Christians, and for Constantine it may also have been something more; but they overshot their mark when they laid down a principle which implied toleration of heretics. They did not understand what they were doing. Before long Constantine persecuted heretics, and Licinius did not even hold to the toleration of Christians. Still the principle was declared, the omnipotent state recognized a domain of conscience beyond its jurisdiction, and there was a good deal of toleration in the fourth century. True, heathenism—every nation its god, and every god his nation—was soon restored, with the one modification that the catholic church is the only nation which has any right to exist. Nevertheless, the Edict of Milan, like the decision of Nicaea, marks an epoch of thought political as well as religious, though the world has been slow to realize either the one or the other.

"Let God arise, and let his enemies be scattered." The great deliverance had fallen like the fire of heaven, the tyrants had vanished away, the scenes of shame and horror were for ever ended. Well might the old rhetorician burst out in savage triumph over the fall of the Pharaohs of heathenism. "The Lord hath heard our prayers. The men that strove with God lie low; the men who overthrew his churches have themselves fallen with a mightier overthrow; the men who slew the righteous with torments have perished under the blows of heaven in torments well deserved though long delayed—yet delayed only

that posterity might learn the full terrors of God's
vengeance on his enemies."[1]   The old man's words
are impressive ; yet a higher and a more Christian
note is struck by the young deacon Athanasius.   His
de Incarnatione is the noble preface of a heroic life.
He too had seen the horrors of the persecution, and
the slaughter of his early teachers was an abiding
memory : but his eyes are fixed on the eternal Word,
and he never for a moment lowers them to revenge
on men of yesterday.   " The powers of sin are overthrown.   The old fear of death is gone.   Our children
tread it underfoot, our women mock at it.   Even the
barbarians have laid aside their fightings and their
murders, and learned in Christ a new life of peace
and purity.   Heathenism is fallen, the wisdom of
the world is turned to folly, the oracles are dumb,
the demons are confounded.   The works of Christ
are more in number than the sea, his victories are
countless as the waves, his presence is brighter than
the sunlight."[2]   No enthusiasm of modern times,
not even when

> Bliss was it in that dawn to be alive,
> But to be young was very heaven,

can surpass the tremulous excitement and exulting
hope of those first years of world-wide victory, when
the kingdoms of the world seemed already to have
become the kingdom of our God.

The fair vision soon clouded over ; but the Edict
of Milan marks a great scene ended on the stage
of history.   The victory was even greater than it
seemed, for heathenism scarcely looked like a beaten
enemy.   It was still strong in the imposing memories

[1] Lactantius *m.p.* 1.
[2] Athanasius *de Inc.* ad fin.

of past ages. Greek philosophy and literature, Roman law and education, Oriental mysteries and magic, were all its own, and the spirit of the old society was heathen to the last. A formidable rearguard covered the slow retreat of heathenism; and in the time of the great catastrophe, when men saw the everlasting Empire breaking up around them, none but the boldest of the Christians could shake off misgivings, that there might still be power in the wrath of the immortal gods. Yet for all this, the old order of the world was doomed. The weary Empire seemed to feel a touch of new life on the day of the great Council's meeting. New life indeed it was; and therefore it was more than that age of waverers and half-believers would receive; and therefore it could only give the Roman world another hundred years of respite before the bursting of the northern deluge.

For in another and a deeper sense, the victory seemed greater than it was. It was not the end of toil, but the opening of a still mightier conflict. The reward of works well done is greater works than these to do. If Caesar was conquered, the natural man remained. Even as the Christians had saved a people from the world, so now they were called to the greater work of saving the world itself. For sixteen centuries the church of God has toiled, and not in vain; and the mighty task looms up year by year before us vaster and more complex than ever. But the Shining Cross of Constantine is more than a legend of the past and a parable of the future. It stands for the conquest of the Empire: and the conquest of the Empire is a visible and enduring earnest of our sure and certain hope that sooner or

later, in one way or another as our own good Lord
shall please, the empires of the world which are
passing away shall give up their place and office to
the everlasting Empire of the love of Christ which
passeth not away.

TABLE OF EMPERORS

B.C.   27. Augustus.

A.D.   14. Tiberius.

37. Caius (Caligula).

41. Claudius.

54. Nero.

68. Galba.

69. Otho.

Vitellius.

Vespasian.

79. Titus.

81. Domitian.

96. Nerva.

98. Trajan.

117. Hadrian.

138. Titus Antoninus (Pius).

161. Marcus Aurelius Antoninus (and Lucius Verus till 169).

180. Commodus.

193. Pertinax.

Didius Julianus.

Septimius Severus.

211. Caracalla (and Geta for a few months).

217. Macrinus.

218. El Gabal (Heliogabalus).

222. Severus Alexander.

235. Maximin.

238. Gordian I., Gordian II. (for a few days in Africa.)

Pupienus and Balbinus.

Gordian III.

A.D. 244. Philip.

249. Decius.

251. Gallus.

253. Aemilianus.

Valerian.

258. Gallienus.

268. Claudius.

270. Aurelian.

275. Tacitus.

276. Probus.

282. Carus, Carinus and Numerian.

284–305. Diocletian.

285–305. Maximian (in the West).

293–306. Constantius (in Gaul and Britain).

293–311. Galerius (in Illyricum, and from 305 in Asia).

305–307. Severus (in Illyricum).

305–313. Maximin Daza (in Syria and Egypt, and from 311 in Asia).

306–337. Constantine (in Gaul and Britain, from 312 in the West, from 315 in Illyricum, from 323 sole emperor).

306–312. Maxentius (in Italy).

308–323. Licinius (in Illyricum, from 311 in Thrace, from 313 in Asia; loses Illyricum in 315).

INDEX

Entries without number of volume belong to Volume 1.

Abgar bar Manu (king of Edessa 179-
216) 172, ii. 47 ; seized by Cara-
calla, 142
Abgar Uchama, correspondence with
Christ, 171, ii. 47
Achamoth, ii. 40
Acta S. Savini, ii. 339
Acte, freedwoman of Nero, 222
Acts of Pilate, ii. 355
Adventus, Oclatinius, *Pf. P.*, ii. 144
Aemilianus (emperor 253) ii. 265
Aemilianus, Præf. of Egypt, ii. 312
Aequitas, 24
Africanus, Sextus Julius (chrono-
grapher) ii. 197
Agathonice, martyr, 117 *n.*
Agricola (Roman general) 223
Akiba, rabbi, 136
Albinus (D. Septimus Clodius, emperor
in Gaul 193-197) ii. 116
Alcibiades the vegetarian, 157-160
Alcibiades the quack, ii. 12
Alexander the Great, 21
Alexander, bp. of Baccanae, martyr,
ii. 130
Alexander (emperor in Africa 308-310)
ii. 343
Alexander, martyr at Lyons, 157-162
Alexander, bp. of Jerusalem, ii. 191 ;
martyr, 254
Alexander Severus, see *Severus,
Alexander*
Alexander of Abonoteichos (quack) ii.
46
Alexandria, Jews at, 39 ; origin of
church obscure, 61, ii. 156 ; account
of the city, 154-156 ; School of,
ch. xix. *passim* ; Orthodoxasts of,
167
Alexis Michaelovitch (Tsar 1645-1678)
268
Allegorism, samples from Irenaeus,

196-199 ; use of, ii. 100-102 ;
Porphyry on, 200
Almsgiving, Jewish and Christian, 247
Alogi, 112 *n.*, ii. 185
Alonim of Carthage, ii. 234
Ambrosius, friend of Origen, ii. 150 ;
presses him to write, 194
Ammonius Saccas, philosopher, ii.
155, 199
Andrew (apostle) in Asia, 61, 100
Andronicus and Junias, apostles, 65
Angels (Jewish doctrine) ii. 27, 172
Angels, of the seven churches, 71, 72
Anicetus, bp. of Rome, meeting with
Polycarp, 147, 264, ii. 109, 220
Anteros, bp. of Rome, ii. 224
Anthimus, bp. of Nicomedia, martyr,
ii. 353
Anthusa (mother of Chrysostom) 252
Antichrist, Nero as, 90 ; doctrine of
Irenaeus and Hippolytus, ii. 119,
260 ; of Commodianus, 258-261
Antinous, 207, ii. 162
Antoninus Pius (Titus Aurelius
Antoninus, emperor 138-161) 140,
141 ; Christians under, 144
Antoninus, Arrius, proconsul of Asia,
ii. 131
Apelles (Marcionite) ii. 66, 67
Apocalypse, angels of, 71, 72 ; perse-
cution in, 81, 82 *n.*; contrast with
Gospel, 109 ; ascribed to Cerinthus,
ii. 35
Apocalypse of Enoch, 48
Apocryphal writings, 100, 282, ii. 23
Apollinaris, Claudius, bp. of Hierapolis,
264
Apollonius, martyr, 168, 169
Apollonius (heresy-hunter) ii. 88
Apollonius of Tyana, ii. 133, 136 ; *Life*
of, 142, 143
Apostles, dispersion of, 60 ; authority

of, 63 65 ; the Two at Rome, 81, 82 ; name discredited, 97 ; in *Teaching*, 104

Apuleius of Madaura, *Golden Ass*, 9 ; 176, 214 ; ii. 235, 236

Ardabau, birthplace of Montanus, ii. 73

Aristides, Apologist, 141, 176, ii. 16

Aristion, 109

Aristotle, 21

Arles, Council of, on rebaptism, ii. 304

Arnobius (Apologist 305-308) 177 ; on argument from miracle 194 ; ignorance of Scripture, 195 ; 201 ; conversion of, 226

Artemon (-as) ii. 185, 187, 319

Asceticism in early times, 240-248

Asclepiades, confessor, ii. 123

Asia, advance of (B.C. 327-A.D. 1683) 21

Asinarii tantum sumus, 207

Asper, a governor, ii. 132

Athanasius, *Festal Letters* of, 267, 303 ; on councils, 307 ; ii. 180 ; on Person of Christ, ii. 189 ; on condemnation of ὁμοούσιον, 320

Atheism, charge of, 122, 188

Athenagoras, Apologist, 176 ; on digamists, 244 ; ii. 162

Athens, empire of, 19 ; state in Ap. age, 34 ; emperors as archons, 92 ; persecution at, 144

Attalus, martyr at Lyons, 158, 160, 162

Atticus, consular, 131

Attis, ii. 74

Aurelian (L. Domitius Aurelianus, emperor 270-275) decision on Paul of Samosata, ii. 307, 318 ; sun-worshipper, 141, 309 ; reign of, 308, 309

Authority, heathen, 216 *sq.*; Christian, 231 *sq.*

Avircius at Rome, ii. 219

ἄθεοι of Christians, 122

ἀπάθεια, ii. 175-177

Babylas (bp. of Antioch) and Philip, ii. 153 ; martyr, 255

Baptism, in *Teaching*, 102 ; account of, 248-258, in Justin, 250, of infants, 250, 254, clinical, 252 (Novatian), ii. 290 ; and creeds, i. 282 ; in book of Elchasai, ii. 12 ; Perpetua's vision, 125

See also *Infant Baptism, Rebaptism*

Barbarians, Roman hatred of, 19, ii. 327

Bar-Cochab (false Messiah *cir.* 133) 54, 136

Bardaisan of Edessa, 172, ii. 42 ; account of, 46-48 ; 196

Barnabas, 56, 57, 58

Barnabas, Epistle of, 98, 101, 105, 246, ii. 15

Basilides, martyr, ii. 124, 125

Basilides (Gnostic) ii. 21 ; system of, 51-56 ; 68

Basilides and Martialis (Spanish bishops) case of, 306

Beasts, evil, in Gaul, ii. 307 *n.* (the emperors) 328

Benedicta (a Christian ?) 153 *n.*

Berbers, ii. 233

Berenice (Agrippa's sister) 40, 90

Beryllus (bp. of Bostra) 305, ii. 194, 206

Bethar, capture of, 137

Bible in the Church, 280-284

Biblias, martyr at Lyons, 159

Bishops, in Ap. age, 66, 69-72 ; in *Teaching*, 103 ; origin of, 287-298 ; and penance, ii. 84 ; in early third century, 274, 275 ; on Cyprianic Theory, 276-282

Blandina (slave girl), martyr, 159-163, 234

Blastus, Quartodeciman, ii. 109, 223

Britain, Roman conquest, 34, Christians in (Tert.) 173, (C. Arles) ii. 321

Bruttius, chronicler, ii. 105, 197

Buddhism, ii. 2

Bunyan, John, 235

Burial, refusal of at Lyons, 163 ; clubs, ii. 120, 121 ; 269

Byzantium, Christians at (in 196), 172, ii. 116, 117

Caecilian (bp. of Carthage) ii. 346

Caecilian, presbyter, ii. 284

Caesariani (Valerian) ii. 269, (Diocletian) 336

Cainites, immoral, 187

Caius (*Caligula*, emperor 37-41) 47

Caius of Rome quoted, 81

Callistus (bp. of Rome 217-222) 170, 233, ii. 188 ; account of, 224-231

Canon of N.T., formation of, 280-284 ; Marcion's, ii. 63 ; limits in second century, 99

Capella, Caecilius, at Byzantium, ii. 116

Caracalla (M. Aurelius Severus Antoninus, emperor 211-217) ii. 47, 122 ; reign of, 130-132 ; Persian war, 143, 144 ; 192

Carpocrates (Gnostic) ii. 59

Carpophorus, owner of Callistus, ii. 227, 229

Carthage, Roman colony, 32 ; account of, ii. 232-236

Carus, Carinus, Numerian (emperors 282-284) ii. 310

"Cat" School (India) 268

Cataphracti, ii. 357

Catechumens, 248, 257 ; Marcionite, ii. 64, 247 ; Manichaean, 71 ; persecuted by Severus, i. 248, ii. 122 ; 202

Catholic Church, conception of the, 299 ; first mentions, 300

Cato (the younger) 23

Celerinus, confessor, ii. 255 ; illiterate, 258 ; 286

Celsus, heathen writer, 174 ; date and character, 183-186 ; appeal to Christians, 190

Centurions, at Capernaum, 32, 310 ; others, 223 ; ii. 244

Cerdo, heretic, ii. 60, 219

Cerinthus, and St. John, 112 ; system of, ii. 34

Cestius Gallus, defeat by Jews, 88

Charity, Christian, 228

Children, position (heathen) 217, (Christian) 233

Chiliasm, ii. 79 ; and Montanism, 91-93 ; of Irenaeus, 112 ; decay of, 181

Chorepiscopi, 70, 309

"Chrestus," ii. 216

Christian Life, argument from, 200, 211 ; general account of, 212 *sq.*

Christian Ministry, see *Church Government*

Christian Worship, 255-277 ; originality of, 268-286 ; Tertullian's account of, ii. 120

Christianos ad leonem, 189, 209

Christmas Day, not early, 267

Church Government, in Ap. age, 64-72, 260 ; later, 286-302 ; in earlier third century, ii. 274-275 ; Cyprianic Theory, 275-283

Churches (buildings) modelled on basilicas, 259 ; first traces of, 261, ii. 122

Circumcision forbidden, ii. 122

Class feeling, heathen, 215

Claudian (poet, *cir.* 400) on work of Rome, 52

Claudius (emperor 41-54) expels Jews from Rome, 40, 61

Claudius Gothicus (emperor 268-270) ii. 273 ; reign of, 308

Claudius Apollinaris, bp. of Hierapolis, account of, ii. 105

Clement of Alexandria, quotes *Teaching*, 101, story of St. John, 112 ; 176 ; view of heathenism 177 *sq.* ; analysis of *Protrepticus*, 202-206, 242 ; Christianity and the mysteries, 274 ; in persecution of Severus, ii. 123 ; 157 ; account of, 163-179 ; 181, 191 ; and Tertullian, 238 ; not sacerdotal, 277

Clement of Rome, 98, 106-108, 246, 277 ; on episcopacy, 292 ; ii. 107 ; on Roman Church, 216 ; not sacerdotal, 276

Second Epistle, 106, 257 ; quoted, ii. 184

Clementines, 8, 249 ; account of, ii. 13-15 ; 30

Colossians, Epistle to, ii. 158

Commodianus, 236 ; account of, ii. 258-261

Commodus (Marcus Aurelius Commodus, emperor 180-192) his reign, 165-171, ii. 114 ; devoted to Serapis, 135

Conference, Apostolic, at Jerusalem, 57

Conserva, 218 *n.*, ii. 125

Constantine (Flavius Valerius Constantinus, emperor 306-337) 122, 217, 306, 308, ii. 141 ; passed over by Diocletian, 341 ; succeeds in Gaul, 342 ; reign of, 356-364 ; the Shining Cross, 358

Constantius (emperor 293-306) death of, ii. 342 ; no persecutor, 343

Conversion, different ways of, 226

Corinth, Roman colony, 32 ; no bishop in Clement's time, 292

Cornelius, bp. of Rome, ii. 255 ; exiled 265 ; election of, 291

Councils, growth of, 306-308 ; on Montanism, ii. 90 ; Cyprian's view of, 300

Creeds, origin of, 284-286 ; difference from rules of faith, ii. 204, 207 ; use by Novatian, 299

Crispina, Bruttia, wife of Commodus, 168, 170

Crocus, Alemannic king, ii. 342

Cross, use of symbol, 275 ; of Constantine, ii. 358

Cybele, 223, ii. 73, 74 ; "missions," 89

Cyprian (bp. of Carthage 247-258) 177 ; conversion of, 226 ; *ad Fidum*, 250 ; theory of councils, 306, 309 ; compared with Clement, ii. 164 ; in Decian persecution, 255 ; exile and death, 268-271 ; account of, chap. xxiv. *passim*

Mentioned, i. 247, 270

Damasus (bp. of Rome 366-385) ii. 225

Damis, disciple of Apollonius, ii. 143
De mysteriis Aegyptiorum, ii. 138
Deacons, in Ap. age, 66-68
Dead, commemoration of the, 300 ;
    worship of the, ii. 161
Deadly Sins, the Seven, ii. 86
Decius (C. Messius Quintus Trajanus,
    emperor 249-251) reign of, ii. 253-
    262 ; *lapsi* under, 285 *sq.* ; 312
Demetrius, bp. of Alexandria, ii. 190-
    193
Demiurge (Gnostic) ii. 27, ch. xv.
    passim
Demons, belief in (Christian) 177
Didache, see *Teaching*
Digamists, 243 *sq.* ; tolerated by
    Callistus, ii. 228
Dinocrates, ii. 126
Diocletian (C. Aurelius Valerius
    Diocletianus, emperor 284-305),
    Manichaean edict 116, 119, ii. 70 ;
    judgment of Aurelian, 308, 326 ;
    election of, 310 ; reign of, 326-341 ;
    at Carnuntum, 342
Diognetus, writer to, 176 ; account
    of Christian life, 212
Dionysius (bp. of Alexandria, 247-265)
    on authorship of Apocalypse, 9, ii.
    313 ; conversion of, i. 226 ; Philip a
    Christian, ii. 151 ; 193 *n.*; in
    Decian persecution, 255, 312 ; on
    Novatian, 294, 314 ; on rebaptism,
    299, 302 ; account of, 311-314 ;
    318
Dionysius (bp. of Corinth *cir.* 170)
    81 ; on penance, 230 ; letters of, 304,
    ii. 106, 220
Dionysius the Areopagite, 274
Dionysius (bp. of Rome 259-269) ii.
    293-319
Disciplina arcani, 272-274, ii. 21
Discipline, 230, 257 ; Marcionite want
    of, ii. 247 ; ch. xxiv. *passim*
    See *Penance*
Disloyalty, charge of, 79, 119, 120 ;
    discussed, 189-191
Dispersion (of the Jews) 17
Divorce, 217
Docetism, ii. 11, ch. xv. *passim*, ii.
    206
Domitian (emperor 81-96) 20 ; reign
    of, 93-95
Domitilla (Domitian's niece) a
    Christian, 95
Domnus, bp. of Antioch, appointed by
    Council, 303, ii. 318
Donatists, ii. 346
Donatus (bp. of Carthage †248) ii.
    284

Druids, 115 ; "druidess" at Tongres,
    ii. 332
Δαναΐδες καὶ Δίρκαι, 80 *n.*

Easter question, 263-267, ii. 222
Eastern worships, 25, 26, ii. 137-142
Ebionism, Pharisaic and Essene, ii. 9-
    15 ; and Cerinthus, 34
Eclecticism, ii. 136, 139 ; of Severus
    Alexander, 147, 252
Edessa, Christianity at, 171, ii. 47 ;
    seized by Caracalla, 143
Education, and Origen's method, ii.
    198-204 ; Tertullian on, 242
El Gabal or Heliogabalus (M. Aurelius
    Antoninus, emperor 218-222) 20,
    223, ii. 48 *n.*; reign of, 144-146 ;
    234 ; 252
Elchasai, Book of, ii. 12
Elders, in Ap. age, 66-69
Elegeia, disaster at, 152, ii. 114
Eleutherus, bp. of Rome, 160, ii. 89,
    90, 187, 188, 219 ; and Montanism,
    222
Elvira, Council of, forbids images,
    188 ; on *immolatio*, 191 *n.*; forbids
    marriage of clergy, 245 ; 249 ; on
    Christian officials, ii. 331
Encratites, 242, ii. 65
Epictetus, 23
Epicureans, 22, 35 ; "tares," ii. 169
Epiphanes (son of Carpocrates) ii. 59
Epiphanius (bp. of Salamis †403)
    account of Gnostics, ii. 24 *n.* ; letter
    of Ptolemaeus to Flora, 43
Epiphany, 267
Episcopacy, not in N.T., 69-72 ; origin
    of, 287-298
Eucharist, see *Lord's Supper*
Euelpistus, martyr, 234
Eugenius, bp. of Laodicea, confessor,
    ii. 335 *n.*
Eulalia, martyr, 116
Eumenea, city of, 155 ; Christians in,
    ii. 323 ; massacre of, 338 *n.*
Eusebius (bp. of Caesarea *c.* 270-339)
    general accuracy, 8 ; as Apologist,
    177 ; impatience of Papias, ii. 104 ;
    Philip not a Christian, 152 ; 180 ;
    191 ; ignorance about Hippolytus,
    223, 225 ; connexion with Pamphilus,
    311, 317 ; on Diocletian, 328 *n.*
    331 ; on confusion during persecu-
    tion, 346 ; *Martyrs of Palestine*,
    347
Evil, problem of, ii. 4 ; Gnostic solu-
    tion, 25, 67
Exorcism, 253
Extra ecclesiam nulla salus, ii. 288

Fabian, bp. of Rome, 252, ii. 225 ; martyr, 255, 285 ; ordains Novatian, 291
Fabius, bp. of Antioch, leans to Novatian, ii. 296
Fanaticism, Christian, discouraged, 116, 117 ; of Quintus, 147
Fasting, in *Teaching*, 102 ; in N.T. and early times, 263 ; of Montanists, ii. 79, 81 ; 241
Fausta, daughter of Maximian, ii. 341 ; marries Constantine, 342
Faustinianus, father of Clement, ii. 14
Faustinus, bp. of Lyons, ii. 298
Felicissimus, deacon of Carthage, ii. 290, 296
Felicitas, martyr, 234, ii. 125-128
Felix, procurator of Judaea, 31, 34
Felix, bp. of Aptunga, not a *traditor*, ii. 346, 347
Festus, procurator of Judaea, 31, 85
Firmilian, bp. of Caesarea (Cappadocia), on Stephen of Rome, ii. 302, 303 ; 314
Flamininus, T. Quinctius, deified in Greece, ii. 162
Flavius Clemens (consul 95) a Christian, 95, 106, 175
Flora, letter of Ptolemaeus to, ii. 43
Florinus, letter of Irenaeus to, 145 *n.*, ii. 108 *n.*, 219
Formatae, 303 *n.*
Fortunatus made bishop of Carthage, ii. 296
Fourth Gospel, authorship, 110 *n.*, ii. 35
Fox, George, 235
Freedmen, position of, 219 ; marriage with, ii. 230
Fronto of Cirta, 139, 154, 181, 183, 187, ii. 236 ; archaic taste of, 237
Fuscianus, P.U., ii. 227

Galerius (emperor 293-311) ii. 325 ; cleanses the army, 332, 335 ; at Carnuntum, 342 ; tires of persecution, 344 ; edict of toleration, 349-352 ; death, 353
Galerius Maximus, proconsul of Africa, ii. 270
Gallienus (emperor 260-268) 138 ; reign of, ii. 271-273, 352
Gallus (Trebonianus, emperor 251-253) reign of, ii. 262-265
Gentiles, training of, 18-27 ; preaching to, 55-59
"Germany," Christians in, 173, ii. 322
Geta (emperor 211) ii. 130

Glabrio, Acilius (*cir.* 95) perhaps Christian, 95 *n.*
Glabrio, Acilius (*cir.* 193) perhaps Christian, 169 *n.*
Gloria in excelsis and Polycarp, 149, 256 ; 275
"Gnostic," The True, ii. 175-177
Gnosticism, influence on Ebionism, ii. 11; ch. xv. *passim* ; and Montanism, ii. 77, 78 ; a centre at Alexandria, 155 ; and history, 173
Gordian, I. and II. (emperors 238) ii. 151 ; description of, ii. 236 *n.*
Gordian III. (emperor 238-244) ii. 151, 152
"Gospel," in Cyprian, ii. 287 *n.*
Goths, in Commodianus, ii. 259 ; defeat Decius, 262 ; defeated by Claudius and Aurelian, 307, 308
Greece, condition in Ap. age, 34-37
Greek Language, spread of, 33 ; crumbling of, ii. 159 ; early use in Roman Church, 214
Greek Mythology, decay of, 18, ii. 159
Greek and Latin Christianity, ii. 213
Gregory of Nazianzus, advises delay of Baptism, 252
Gregory (Thaumaturgus, bp. of Neocaesarea) 224 ; account of Origen's teaching, ii. 203 ; 255 ; account of, 314
Gregory, bp. of Tours (*cir.* 594) class feeling, 216 ; rustic style, 236
γνῶσις, ii. 21, 22

Hadrian (P. Aelius Hadrianus, emperor 117-138) account of, 135-140 ; rescript to Minucius Fundanus, 142 ; ii. 117, 272
Harnack, Dr. Adolf, on letter of Irenaeus to Florinus, 145 *n.*; on Clement, ii. 169 *n.*
Hatch, E., on Christian ministry, 68 *n.*
Hebrew, ignorance of, 195 *n.* ; Origen's study of, ii. 194, 195, 199
Hebrews, Epistle to the, authorship unknown, 62 ; argument of, 87 ; not sacerdotal, ii. 276
Hegesippus, on murder of James, 86 *n.*; on St. John in Asia, 112 ; account of, ii. 105
Helena (Tyre) ii. 29
Helenus, bp. of Tarsus, ii. 302
Heliogabalus, see *El Gabal*
Hellenism, influence on Christianity, ii. 6
Helvidius Priscus, 93
Heraclas (bp. of Alexandria 232-247) ii. 191, 193 *n.*, 197, 312

Heracleon (Valentinian) ii. 42;
Commentary of, 45, 68
Herais, martyr, ii. 124
Heretics, classification by Irenaeus,
199; by Origen, ii. 206, 207; hatred
of, ii. 190; furnished by philo-
sophers, 245
Hermas, on penance, 230; 236; on
double standard, 246; 282 *n.*; 293;
date of, ii. 218 *n.*; on Roman church,
218, 219; imitation of, 241
Herminianus, Claudius Lucius, per-
secutor, 118, 167, ii. 131
Herod the Great, 29, 44
Herod Agrippa, 40, 87, 89, 92
Hesterni sumus, 208
Hieracas, ascetic, 245
Hierocles, heathen, ii. 142 *n.*, 334
Hilary (bp. of Poitiers, *cir.* 353-368),
96
Hippolytus, 70 *n.*, 233; on digamists,
244; 267; *Syntagma*, ii. 24 *n.*, 224;
30; account of Basilides, 51-54; *de
Antichristo*, account of, 119; stories
of enthusiasm, 129, 130; to Severina,
148; 150; account of, 223-231;
whether sacerdotal, 277
Hɪstoɪ iɑs Jɪ ɑyɪɑsɑɑ, ɔ , Lɪcɑɑcɪ oɪ Ɪɪɑɑcɪ ɪɪɑɪ
to Servianus, 138 *n.*; credibility of,
ii. 253 *n.*
Holy Spirit, feminine (Gnostics) ii. 12,
49, 57
Hort, F. J. A., on Christian ministry,
68 *n.*
Hyacinthus, Roman Presbyter, 170
Hymn of the Soul, ii. 48
Hymns, Christian, 256; Bardesanist,
ii. 48
Hymns to Christ, 129, ii. 320
Hystaspes, a prophet, 195

Ialdabaoth, ii. 57
Ignatius, bp. of Antioch, 99; general
account of, 131-134; 146, 160 *n.*;
246; and Empire, 289; on episcopacy, 293-295; catholic church, 300;
on Roman church, 293, ii. 218;
274; not sacerdotal, 276; 292
Images Jews had none, 42; Christians
had none, 188
Immanence, Stoic doctrine of, ii. 171
India, Christianity in, 60 *n.*, ii. 322;
"cat" and "monkey" schools, i.
268; Pantaenus in, ii. 163
Infant Baptism, 249, 250; objected to,
251, ii. 86
Irenaeus, bp. of Lyons (*c.* 130-200),
general accuracy, 8; mistake on Ap.
age, 99; and Fourth Gospel, 112 *n.*;

letter to Florinus, 145 *n.*; 158;
bears letter to Eleutherus, 160, ii.
89; on *Dem. of Apost. Preaching*,
i. 196-199; on Easter Question,
265; on Four Gospels, 282;
mistakes Elders of Ephesus, 291 *n.*;
travels, 303; on Simon Magus, ii.
28, 31; account of Saturninus, 35;
of Valentinus, 39; of Basilides, 51-
54; of Carpocrates and Epiphanes,
59; 92, ch. xvii. *passim*; on Roman
primacy, 221; not sacerdotal, 277
Isis, 25, 115 *n.*, 156, 223; "missions,"
ii. 89, 134; women votaries of, 139
Islam, 22, ii. 233
Issus, battle of (194) ii. 116
Izates (king of Adiabene) 42
ΙΧΘΥΣ, symbol, 275

James, the Lord's brother, 71, 72;
murder of, 85, 86; in Clementines,
ii. 15
Jerusalem, destruction by Titus, 88
Jewish Christians, 85-87
Jews, training of the, 16-18; in
Roman Empire, 37-50; Roman
war (Titus) 83-90; Roman war
(Tɪɑɪɑ ɪɪɑɪ) 160, ɪɑɪɑɑɪoɪɪɑ ɑɑ
Christians, 148, ii. 15-18
Johanan ben Zaccai (pres. of Sanhedrin)
136
John (the elder) 109, 111 *n.*
John of Gischala (Jewish chief, 66-
70) 54
John Philoponus, ii. 155
Jubaianus (Mauritanian bishop) ii. 301
Judaism, influence on Christianity, ii. 3,
8-18; connexions with Gnosticism,
11, 27
Judas Maccabaeus, treaty with Rome,
29
Judas the commentator, ii. 129
Jude, the Lord's brother, grandsons of,
before Domitian, 94
Julia Domna !(wife of Sept. Severus)
217, ii. 118; government of, 132,
133; 142; death of, 144
Julia Maesa, ii. 132; at Emesa, 144
Julia Mamaea (mother of Severus Al.)
217, ii. 132, 144, 146-149, 194
Julia Soaemias (mother of El Gabal) ii.
132, 144, 145
Julian (emperor 361-363) 5, 118;
compared with Marcus, 151; 270
Julianus Didius (emperor 193) ii. 115
Juno Caelestis, ii. 146
Jus gentium, 24
Justin Martyr, execution of, 155, date
of, 176, view of heathenism, 177 *sq.*;

and argument from miracle, 193; conversion of, 226; account of Baptism, 249, 250; 256; no "reserve" in, 274; travels, 303; *Dialogue* with Trypho, ii. 16-18; on Simon Magus, 29; and Tatian, 65; 105, 107; not sacerdotal, 276

Karma (Buddhist) ii. 209
Kyrie eleison, ii. 214

Lactantius (Apologist *cir*. 303-315) 177; on the Evil Beasts, ii. 328; *de mortibus*, i. 276 (genuineness) ii. 328 *n*.
Laity in church government, 229, 305; right to preach, ii. 192
Lapsi, ii. 256, 257, 286 *sq*.
Latin language, spread of, 34
Learning, Christian view of, ch. xi. *passim*; 235; ii. 167
Lent, development of, ii. 81
Leonides, father of Origen, ii. 123, 189
Leontopolis, Temple of, 39, 89
Lessing's *dictum*, 10
Letters, Commendatory, etc., 303, 304; *Festal* (Ath.) 267, 304; to churches, 304; of confessors, ii. 286; abolished, 291
Leucius Charinus (*discipulus diaboli*) 8, ii. 23
Libelli-atici, ii. 256, 257; treatment by Cyprian, 285-295; case of Spanish bishops, 297
Liberian List, ii. 224
Licinius (emperor 307-323) appointed, ii. 343; marriage with Constantia, 359; defeat of Maximin, 361; 363
Logos (Word) in Philo, 44; doctrine generally, ii. 172
Lord's Day, see *Sunday*
Lord's Supper, in *Teaching*, 102, 103, 257; solvent of class feeling, 225; exclusion from, 230, not to be made a punishment, ii. 295; account of, i. 257-260; doctrine of Irenaeus, ii. 111; *stationes* no excuse for absence, 241; revolutionized by sacerdotalism, 278
Lucian (confessor 250) reckless amnesty, ii. 286, 295
Lucian (of Antioch, martyr, 313) ii. 353
Lucilla, sister of Commodus, 166, 170
"Lucina," ii. 121
Lucius, bp. of Rome, ii. 265, 267, 297
Lusius Quietus (Trajan's general), 139, ii. 233
"Lying water," ii. 300
Lyons, battle of (197) ii. 116

Lyons and Vienne, martyrs of, 157-164; account possibly by Irenaeus, ii. 112; on penance, i. 230; Letter to Eleutherus, 160, ii. 89

Macrianus, general of Valerian, ii. 267, 273, 314
Macrina, grandmother of Gregory of Nyssa, ii. 315
Macrinus, M. Opellius (emperor 217-218) ii. 144
Magicians, skill of, 192
Malchion, presbyter, 305; unmasks Paul of Samosata, ii. 318
Mamaea (Mammaea), see *Julia M.*
Manichaeism, ii. 2; account of, 69-72; edict of Diocletian, 333
Mappalicus, martyr, ii. 286
Marcellina (Gnostic) ii. 58, 219
Marcellus (bp. of Rome 307-309) ii. 347
Marcellus, bp. of Ancyra, 285
Marcellus, of Tingis, martyr, ii. 331
Marcia, concubine of Commodus, 170, 171, ii. 227
Marcian, bp. of Arles (ultra-Novatianist) ii. 297
Marcion, 8; meeting with Polycarp, 147, ii. 61; account of, 60-65, 68; in Irenaeus (Bk. IV.) 111; 245; criticizes with a pen-knife, 247; indiscipline, 247
Marcus Aurelius Antoninus (emperor 161-180) 23, 116 *n*.; 126; reign of, 150-164; ii. 148
Marcus (Valentinian quack) ii. 42, 46
Marriage, Christian view of, 232; denounced by Marcion and Tatian, 242, ii. 26; Tertullian on, i. 243 *sq*., ii. 82; Roman law of, ii. 230; mixed, inconveniences of, i.,232,238; second, 243; forbidden by Montanists, ii. 79, 82; of slaves, i. 232, ii. 230; after ordination, i. 243, 245, permitted by Callistus, ii. 228; unequal, ii. 230
Marseille (Massilia), 33, 157
Mart. Polycarpi, 147 *n*.
Masada, siege of, 74, 89
Matthias, apostle, 65; apocryphal Gospel of, ii. 23, 38 *n*.
Mattidia, mother of Clement, ii. 13
Maturus, martyr at Lyons, 159, 161
Mavilus of Hadrumetum, martyr, ii. 131
Maxentius (emperor 306-312) ii. 340, 341; made emperor, 342; exiles rival bishops of Rome, 347; policy of, 356; defeat by Constantine, 357

Maximian (emperor 285-305) ii. 334 ;
  issues Fourth Edict, 339 ; at Car-
  nuntum, 342 ; put to death, 343
Maximilla, prophetess, ii. 74
Maximin (C. Julius Verus Maximinus,
  emperor 235-238) reign of, ii. 149-
  151 ; 194 ; 353
Maximin (Daza, emperor 305-313)
  accession, ii. 341 ; persecution by,
  344, 348, 352-364
Maximus of Madaura (heathen writer)
  168 n.
Meletius, bp. of Lycopolis, forms
  schism, ii. 347
Melito, bp. of Sardis, Church and
  Empire twins, 116 n. ; 266 ; account
  of, ii. 106 ; 119
Memra (Jewish) ii. 171
Menander (Gnostic) ii. 31
Mensurius, bp. of Carthage, ii. 346
Messianic hope, in Philo, 44 ; Jewish, 48
Milan, Edict of (313) 5, 124 ; ii. 360-
  364
Militia dei vivi, 233, 236, 310
Minim (Christians) ii. 9, 15
Minucius Felix (Apologist 222-235 ?)
  177 ; outline of *Octavius*, 181 *sq.*
Miracles, Pseudonymy, ascription of
  Hadrian to, 142
Miracle, Argument from, in Apologists,
  192-194
Mithra, 25, 156 ; communion of, 177 ;
  267 ; ii. 134 ; account of Mithraism,
  139-142
" Monkey " School (India) 268
Monnica (mother of Augustine) 252
Montanism, 117 ; letter of Lyons and
  Vienne confessors, 160 ; ch. xvi.
  passim ; tendency of Hermas, ii.
  219 ; at Rome, 221, 222 ; of
  Tertullian, 239
Muratori, Fragment of, 61, 112, 293,
  ii. 106 ; on date of Hermas, 218 n.
Mystery, and Christianity, 273-275

Naissus, battle of, ii. 307
Namphamo of Madaura, martyr, 168,
  ii. 235 n., 237
Narcissus, bp. of Jerusalem, 70 n., 246,
  264
Natalitia of martyrs, 268
Natalius, confessor, ii. 123, 186
Nazarenes, ii. 10
Nero (emperor 54-68) persecution by,
  73-83 ; as Antichrist, 90 (Barnabas)
  104 (Commodianus), ii. 259 ; buried
  by Acte, i. 222
Nerva M. Cocceius (emperor 96-98),
  127

Nicaea, Council of, rejects celibacy
  of clergy, 245 ; 305, 307 ; and
  Meletians,310; rebaptizes Paulianists,
  ii. 304
Niger (Pescennius, emperor in Syria,
  193-194) ii. 116
Noetus of Smyrna, ii. 187
Noricum, Christians in, ii. 322
Novatian (presb. of Rome) and
  Novatianists, 252 ; ii. 84 ; 290-
  297, 346
Novatus (presb. of Carthage) 245, ii.
  290 ; joins Novatian, 291
Number of the Beast, in Irenaeus, ii.
  112 ; in Hippolytus, 119

Oaths, by Caesar's *Genius*, 123, 208 ;
  unlawful (Basilides) ii. 124 (Tert.)
  244
Oberlin, ii. 121
Offertory, 258 ; in Irenaeus, ii. 113
Ophites, account of, ii. 56-59
Optatus in Perpetua's vision, ii. 126
Orientalism, ii. 2 ; influence on
  Christianity, 4-6 ; ch. xv. *passim*
Origen (185-254) *c. Celsum*, 176 ; on
  argument from miracle, 193 ; from
  spread of Christianity, 201 ; 250 ;
  on infant Baptism, 251 ; travels,
  303 ; in persecution of Severus, ii.
  123 ; 150, 152 ; and Mamaea, 148,
  194 ; account of, ch. xx. *passim* ;
  condemnation at Rome, 224 ; in
  Decian persecution, 255 ; not really
  sacerdotal, 277 ; defence by
  Pamphilus, 316 ; development of
  his theology, 316 *sq.*
(Origen),*c. Celsum*,183-186; *Philocalia*,
  ii. 195 ; *de Principiis*, ii. 204-207
Orthodoxasts of Alexandria, ii. 167 ;
  similar narrowness, 311 n.
Orthodoxy, imperial definitions of, ii.
  318, 319
ὁμοούσιον condemned at Antioch, ii.
  320

Pamphilus, scholar of Caesarea, ii.
  311 ; account of, 315, 316
Pantaenus of Alexandria, ii. 157,
  account of, 163
Papias (bp. of Hierapolis)110 n., 111 n.,
  282 ; account of, ii. 103-105 ; 109,
  112
Papinian, Roman lawyer, ii. 117, 133,
  Patria potestas, 217
Patripassianism, ii. 187 ; supported by
  Callistus, 227
Paul of Antioch (heretic *cir.* 202) ii.
  123, 190

Paul of Samosata, bp. of Antioch, 303 305, 307, ii. 187 ; account of, ii. 317 *sq.*

Paulianists, ii. 304

Paul of Thebes, 246

Paul (Roman lawyer) ii. 117, 133

Pella, retreat to, 88

Pelops, bones of, at Olympia, 8

Penance, in second century, 230 ; in Montanist times, ii. 82 ; of Callistus, 228

Perennis (*Pf.P.* 180-185), 166 ; and Apollonius, 169

Pericopa adulterae, Q. from Papias ? ii. 105

Perpetua, martyr, 234 ; baptism of, 252 ; mosaic of, 276 ; account of, ii. 125-128

Persecution, by Nero, 73-83 ; by Domitian, 94-96 ; general account of, 115-126 ; by Trajan, 124 *n.*; of Jews, by Hadrian, 136 ; by Marcus, 154-164 ; under Commodus, 166-169 ; under Severus and Caracalla, ii. 122-132 ; by Maximin, 151 ; in Philip's time, 155, 251 ; by Decius, 254-257 ; 286 *sq.*, 312 ; by Valerian, 267-273, 312 ; by Aurelian, 309 ; by Diocletian, 331-341 ; by Maximin Daza, 344, 353

Persians defeat Severus Alexander, ii. 147 ; defeat Gordian, 152 ; 252 ; capture Valerian, 271 ; repulsed by Odenathus, 272 ; peace with (Diocletian) 333

Person of Christ 54 ; history of the doctrine, ii. 181-188 ; human soul (Origen) 209 ; Commodianus, 258-261

Pertinax, Helvius (emperor 193) ii. 115

Pestilence under Marcus, 152, under Gallus, ii. 263

Peter, bp. of Alexandria, 82 *n.*; in persecution, ii. 347 ; martyr, 353

Pfaffian Fragments of Irenaeus, ii. 112

Pharisees, 45, 84

Philip (M. Julius Philippus, emperor, 244-249), reign of, ii. 152, 153 ; 194 ; riots under, 251

Philip (apostle) at Hierapolis, 61, 109, 265

Philip (of the Seven) 67

Philip (Asiarch in *Mart. Pol.*) 148

Philip (Bardesanist) ii. 47

Philip of Side, ii. 163

Philippi, Roman colony, 32 ; church at, 66 ; no bishop at, 293

Philo, 44, 48, ii. 172

Philosophy, solvent of old religion, 20-24 ; in Ap. age, 35 ; reply of Apologists, 202 ; dominance of, ii. 159 ; Clement's view of, 168 *sq.* ; Tertullian on, 245

Philostratus, sophist, ii. 133 ; *Life* of Apollonius, 142

Phoenician language in Africa, 34 ; spoken by Severus, ii. 117 ; survival of, 233

Phrygia, Montanism in, ii. 73, 75, 89

Pinytus, bp. of Cnossus, 304

Pius, bp, of Rome, ii. 214, 218

Plato, 21, ii. 169, 171, 172, 174 ; "medicinal" lie, 176 ; 198

Platianus, *Pf.P.*, favourite of Severus, ii. 133

Pliny (the younger) correspondence with Trajan, 124 *n.*, 128-131

Plotinus, ii. 198

Plutarch of Chaeronea, ii. 137

Polycarp (bp. of Smyrna) 112 *n.*, 116, 133 ; account of, 145-149 ; baptized in infancy, 250 ; *Gloria in excelsis*, 149 ; 256 ; and Anicetus, 264 ; 266, ii. 109, 214, 220 ; i. 282, 297 ; and Marcion, ii. 61, 63 ; 98 ; and Irenaeus, 108 ; not sacerdotal, 276

Polycrates (bp. of Ephesus) 113 *n.*, 155, 235 ; letter to Victor, 265 ; ii. 277

Pompeianus, Claudius (son-in-law of emperor Marcus), 165, 169 *n.*

Pompeianus, Ruricius, defends Verona, ii. 357

Pomponia Graecina, *cir.* 57 ; a Christian, 76, 175 ; account of, ii. 216

Pontianus, bp. of Rome, ii. 150, 224

Ponticus, martyr at Lyons, 162

"Pope" of Carthage, ii. 284, 285, 287

Poppaea (Nero's wife) 31, 40, 42

Porphyry on Origen, ii. 199, 200

Postumus, Gaulish Caesar, ii. 272

Potamiaena, martyr, ii. 124

Pothinus (bp. of Lyons) martyr, 159 ; ii. 108

Praxeas, confessor, ii. 187, 222

Prayer, Tertullian on, ii. 240-242, see also *Christian Worship*

Prepon, ii. 46, 66

Presbyters, see *Elders*

Priesthood, Christian and Cyprianic, 270, ii. 276-278

Priscilla, Montanist prophetess, ii. 74 *sq.*

Priscus, rebel, ii. 262

Probus (emperor 276-282) ii. 308, 310

Procopius, martyr at Caesarea, ii. 348

Procopius, historian, 51 *n.*

Procurators of Judaea, 47, 84

Prophecy, argument from, 194-200 ; ecstatic, ii. 80 n.
Prophet, (N.T.) 66 ; in *Teaching*, 103 ; 287, ii. 94 ; (Montanist) ii. 74-95
Proselytes, 42, 43
Prunikos, ii. 57
Ptolemaeus, martyr, 144
Ptolemaeus (Valentinian) ii. 42 ; letter to Flora 43
Pudens, a governor, ii. 132
Pupienus and Balbinus (emperors 238) ii. 151
Περιστερὰ in *Mart. Pol.*, 147

Quadratus, Apologist, 141, 176 ; on our Lord's miracles, 193
Quadratus, and Ammia, 287
Quartodecimans, 264-268, ii. 223
Quattuor Coronati, martyrs, ii. 331
Quintus (Phrygian fanatic) 147
Quintus (Mauritanian bishop) ii. 300

Rebaptism, ii. 228, 231 ; Controversy, 298-305
Redemption, Gnostic idea of, ii. 21 ; Origen's doctrine of, ii. 210, 211
Religion of Rome, unspiritual character, 19
Relics of Polycarp, 149 ; at Lyons, 163 ; 188
Repostus, apostate bp. of Tuburnuc, ii. 257 n., 296
Reservation of elements, in Justin, 260
"Reserve," 274 ; ascribed to our Lord, ii. 23
Revocatus, martyr, ii. 125-128
Rhodon, ii. 66, 67
Roman Church, origin obscure, 61 ; notorious in Nero's time, 76 ; in Clement's letter, 106, ii. 217 ; was Clement bishop, i. 293 ; 302 ; ch. xxi. *passim* ; Ignatius on, 293, ii. 218 ; Hermas on, 219 ; Irenaeus on, 221
Roman Emperor, worship of, 27 ; 30, ii. 161-162
Roman Empire, 27 ; description, 28-54 ; in false position, 121 ; in second century, 126
Roman Law, solvent of old religion, 24, 25
Roman Legions, 31 ; *legio fulminea*, 156 ; distribution under Commodus, ii. 116
Rome and Israel, 46-50, 83-90
Rule of faith (Origen) ii. 204-207, (Tert.) 245

Rusticus, Junius, 141 ; condemns Justin, 155

Sabellianism, ii. 183, 188, 226 ; described, 317
Sabinus, Praefect of Egypt, ii. 312
Sacerdotalism, first clear in Cyprian, ii. 276-278
Sagaris, bp. of Laodicea, martyr, 155, 266, ii. 107
St. John, 59 ; at Ephesus, 109-113, 265 ; intercourse with Polycarp, 145 n.; and episcopacy, 294, 298 ; whether teacher of Papias, ii. 104
St. Paul, work of, 57-59 ; at Rome, 61 ; little understood in Early Church, 97, 98 ; 110 ; historical insight, 179 ; on slavery, 233
St. Peter (apostle) at Antioch, 58 ; at Rome, 60, 82 n.
Sanctus, martyr at Lyons, 159, 161
Sardica, Council of, 307
Satisfactio (Tert.) 247
Saturninus (or Satornilus) Gnostic, system of, ii. 35
Saturninus Vigellius (proc. of Africa 180) 167, ii. 131, 236
Saturus, martyr, ii. 125-128
Saxa Rubra, battle of, ii. 357
Scandals against the Christians, 76, 186 ; Tertullian's answer, 207
Scapula proconsul, 176, 276, ii. 131
Scillitan martyrs, *Acts* of, 167 ; ii. 237
Secundulus, martyr, ii. 125-128
Semen est sanguis Christianorum, 210
Semo Sancus, ii. 29
Serapion, bp. of Antioch, ii. 312 n.
Serapis, worship of, ii. 135
Sermon on the Mount, not centre of the Gospel, 54
Seven, The (Acts vi.) 67
Severa, Otacilia, empress, ii. 152, 194
Severus, Alexander (emperor 222-235) 261 ; ii. 144 ; reign of, 146-149
Severus L. Septimius (emperor, 193-211) 261 ; ii. 48 n.; reign of, 116-123, 130 ; Aurelian compared to, 308
Severus (emperor 305-307) ii. 341, 342
Severus, Cincius, a governor, ii. 132
Shema, Shemoneh Esreh, 41
Simon Magus, ii. 13 ; system of, 28-30
Slaves, position (heathen) 217-223 ; (Israel) 220 ; (Christian) Blandina, 159-163 ; 230, 233-235 ; under heathen masters, 238 ; case of Felicitas, ii. 125, 128 ; marriage with, ii. 230
Sobieski, John (King of Poland 1674-1696) 21

Society, account of, 213 *sq.*

Soter, bp. of Rome, 170 ; ii. 215 ; account of, 220

Spain, Christians in, 114, 173, ii. 297, 321

Speratus, Scillitan martyr, 167

Spread of Christianity, in Ap. age, 62 ; at end of first century, 113 ; at end of second, 171 ; at end of third, ii. 321

Stationes, 261, ii. 81, 241

Stephen (Acts) 55

Stephen (bp. of Rome 253-257) 301 ; and Spanish bishops, ii. 297 ; and Marcian of Arles, 297 ; and re-baptism, 298-304

Stoicism, strength and weakness, 22-24; in Ap. age, 35 ; of the emperor Marcus, 151 ; in Tertullian, 254 ; in Clement, ii. 171, 175-177

Subintroducta, scandal of, and Cyprian, ii. 285-286 ; connived at by Paul of Samosata, 319

Succession, apostolic, first pressed by Cyprian, ii. 280

Sulla, L. Cornelius, *Felix*, ii. 162

Sunday, in *Teaching*, 103 ; 255 ; observance of, 262-263

Superstition, Christians not specially given to, 235

Susanna, History of, criticism of Julius Africanus, ii. 197

Symbols of devotion, 275

Symeon, son of Clopas, martyr, 131

Synagogue Service, 40-42, 255, 256

Syneros, ii. 66

Syrian churches, ii. 46

Tacitus, 8, 20, 76 ; account of Neronian persecution, 78 *sq.* ; 187, 214

Tacitus (emperor 275-6) ii. 310

Tatian the Assyrian, 172, 176 ; as Apologist, 180 ; conversion of, 226 ; denounces marriage ; 242, *Diatessaron*, 282, ii. 46 ; account of, 65

Taurobolium, ii. 140, 142 *n.*

Teaching of the Apostles, 101-106 ; on charity, 228 ; on double standard, 245 ; on Baptism, 252 ; on Jews, ii. 15 ; not sacerdotal, 277

Tecusa, sister of Celerinus, ii. 286

Telesphorus, bp. of Rome, martyr, 143, ii. 214, 218

Tertullian (*cir.* 150-225) picture of civilisation, 52 ; 116 *n.*, 123, 155 ; contrast with Clement, 178, 203 ; 214 ; conversion of, 226 ; objects to Infant Baptism, 251 ; account of Baptism, 252 ; travels, 303 ; on

Valentinus, ii. 37 ; on marriage, 82 ; on penance, 84 ; against infant baptism, 86 ; on Empire, 119 ; account of Christian worship, 120 ; *pro mora finis*, 181 ; on Praxeas 187 ; 189 ; account of, 237-250 ; not really sacerdotal, 277 ; 284 ; 289 ; *Apology*, i. 176 ; on scandals, 187 ; analysis of, 206-210 ; ii. 118 ; *de Corona*, i. 176, ii. 130 ; *ad Scapulam*, i. 176, 276, ii. 130 ; *de Spectaculis*, i. 276 ; *Testimonium animae*, i. 200 ; *Acts* of Perpetua (?) ii. 126 ; *de Praescr.* sophisms of, ii. 168 ; account of, 244-250 ; *de Oratione*, ii. 240-242 ; *de Idololatria*, ii. 242-244

Testimonium animae, argument from, 200

Theodotus (ὁ σκυτεύς) ii. 185, 228

Theodotus (Valentinian) ii. 42, 46

Theonas to Lucian, a forged letter, ii. 332 *n.*

Theophilus (bp. of Antioch *cir.* 180) 171, 176

Theophilus of Diu (India) ii. 322

Theotecnus (*cir.* 311) revives the scandals, 187, ii. 354

Thomas (Apostle) in India, 60 *n.*

Thraseas, bp. of Eumenea, martyr, 155, 266

Thundering Legion, story of, 156, ii. 106

Tiberianus, not P.U., ii. 253 *n.*

Timothy and Titus, not bishops, 71

Titus (emperor 79-81) destroyer of Jerusalem, 40, 88 ; 93

Toleration, Edict of Galerius, ii. 349-352 ; of Milan, 360-364 ; of Maximin, 361

Trades, which lawful, 230, 236 ; Tertullian on, ii. 242-244

Traditio (redditio) Symboli, 253

Tradition, 280-284, 301 ; outworn, ii. 99 ; as used by Papias, 104 ; argument of Irenaeus, 110 ; argument of Tertullian, 246

Traditores, ii. 346

Trajan (M. Ulpius Trajanus, emperor 98-117) 127-134

Transmigration of souls, Origen not Pythagorean, ii. 209

Travel in early times, 302

Trypho the Jew, ii, 16-18

Turbo, Marcius (*Pf.P.*), 141

θεός, indefiniteness of, ii. 161

Ulpian, Roman lawyer, ii. 133, 147

Urbanus, bp. of Rome, ii. 224

Urbicus, Lollius, P.U., 144

Valentinus (Gnostic) and his school, ii. 36-51 ; in Gaul, 109 ; 245
Valerian (P. Licinius Valerianus, emperor 253-260) ii. 151 ; Censor, 254 ; reign of, 265-271 ; 312 ; edict imitated by Diocletian, 336, 337
Varus, Rictius, ii. 331
Verus, Lucius (emperor 161-167) 150
Vespasian (emperor 70-79) 88, 89, 91 *sq.*, 135
Vettius, Epagathus at Lyons, 158
Veturius, *mag. mil.* persecutor, ii. 335 *n.*
Vice sacra, used of bishops, 311
Vicisti Galilaee, 5
Victi victores, 5
Victor (bp. of Rome 189-199) and Marcia, 170 ; on Easter question, 264-266, 301, ii. 109 ; excommunicates Theodotus, 186 ; account of, 222, 223, 227
Victorina (*mater castrorum cir.* 265), 217, ii. 307, 308

Victorinus, bp. of Pettau, ii. 24 *n.*; account of Valentinus, 37

Women, as missionaries, 62 ; position (heathen) 216 ; position (Christian) 231 ; pertness of heretics, ii. 247 ; Montanist prophetesses, ch. xvi. *passim*
Word, see *Logos*

Xenophanes, ii. 160
Xystus, bp. of Rome, martyr, ii. 269, 270 ; 304

Zealots, 46, 49, 84 ; hold Masada, 89
Zenobia (*regina orientis cir.* 270), 217, ii. 272, 307 ; defeat of, 308 ; supports Paul of Samosata, 318
Zephyrinus (bp. of Rome 199-217) 24 *n.*, ii. 186, 224, 227, 229

THE END

Printed by R. & R. Clark, Limited, *Edinburgh.*

By Professor H. M. GWATKIN

SELECTIONS FROM EARLY WRITERS

ILLUSTRATIVE OF CHURCH HISTORY TO THE
TIME OF CONSTANTINE

Crown 8vo.   4s. 6d. net.

CHURCH QUARTERLY REVIEW.—"The students of our theological colleges ought to be grateful to Professor Gwatkin for bringing together in a handy form so many valuable passages.   To speak only of a few of the selections, viz. Pliny's Letter to Trajan, Justin's Account of the Sunday Service, the Martyrdom of Lyons and Vienne, the Extracts from Eusebius upon the Canon, and the Muratorian Fragment, it will be a real gain if students will read these in the original. . . . This collection of extracts will be an excellent companion volume to Westcott's *History of the Canon*, and will be read with advantage by those who are studying the Church history of the first three centuries."

EXPOSITOR.—"It is superfluous to recommend what comes from the hands of such an authority as Professor Gwatkin ; and it need only be said that as an introduction to the use of the sources of Church history, or as a handy book of reference to the passages one is always needing to use, nothing could be better than this volume."

ATHENÆUM.—"The selection is judicious and calculated to be most useful."

SPECTATOR.—"Few students of theology are wholly ignorant of the work of the early Christian Apologists and Fathers ; but their knowledge is almost universally second-hand.   Not one in a hundred has ever read a word of either of the Clements, of Hippolytus, or Origen, or Tertullian, in the original.   This is what Mr. Gwatkin's little volume will now enable them to do.   It is certainly a happy instance of the way in which knowledge is now being opened up to the many."

CAMBRIDGE REVIEW.—"It needs scarcely be said that the extracts are carefully selected and include most of the chief authorities for the first three centuries of Church History. . . . The book will serve as a most useful companion to early Church Histories, and will, we may hope, serve also as an introduction to the study of the early Christian writers from whose writings the extracts are selected."

MACMILLAN AND CO., LTD., LONDON.

A HISTORY OF
THE ENGLISH CHURCH

EDITED BY THE LATE

VERY REV. W. R. W. STEPHENS, D.D.

DEAN OF WINCHESTER.

AND

THE REV. WILLIAM HUNT, D.LITT.

A Continuous History, based upon a careful Study of Original Authorities, and of the best Ancient and Modern Writers.

In Nine Volumes, uniform binding, Crown 8vo. With Maps.

Each Volume is sold separately, and has its own Index.

Vol. I. **The English Church from its Foundation to the Norman Conquest** (597–1066). By the Rev. WILLIAM HUNT, D.Litt. 7s. 6d.

Vol. II. **The English Church from the Norman Conquest to the Accession of Edward I.** (1066–1272). By DEAN STEPHENS. 7s. 6d.

Vol. III. **The English Church in the Fourteenth and Fifteenth Centuries** (1272–1486). By the Rev. Canon CAPES, late Fellow of Queen's College, Oxford. 7s. 6d.

Vol. IV. **The English Church in the Sixteenth Century, from the Accession of Henry VIII. to the Death of Mary** (1509–1558). By JAMES GAIRDNER, C.B., LL.D. 7s. 6d.

Vol. V. **The English Church in the Reigns of Elizabeth and James I.** (1558-1625). By the Rev. W. H. FRERE. 7s. 6d.

Vol. VI. **The English Church from the Accession of Charles I. to the Death of Anne** (1625–1714). By the Rev. W. H. HUTTON, B.D., Fellow of St. John's College, Oxford. 7s. 6d.

Vol. VII. **The English Church from the Accession of George I. to the End of the Eighteenth Century** (1714–1800). By the late Rev. Canon J. H. OVERTON, D.D., and the Rev. F. RELTON, A.K.C. 7s. 6d.

Vol. VIII. (In Two Parts). **The English Church in the Nineteenth Century.** By F. WARRE CORNISH, M.A., Vice-Provost of Eton College. 7s. 6d. each.

MACMILLAN AND CO., LTD., LONDON.